BASEBALL:

THE EARLY YEARS

BASEBALL:

BASEBALL

THE EARLY YEARS by HAROLD SEYMOUR

OXFORD UNIVERSITY PRESS
NEW YORK   OXFORD

Oxford University Press

Oxford   New York   Toronto
Delhi   Bombay   Calcutta   Madras   Karachi
Petaling Jaya   Singapore   Hong Kong   Tokyo
Nairobi   Dar es Salaam   Cape Town
Melbourne   Auckland

and associated companies in
Berlin   Ibadan

First published in 1960 by Oxford University Press, Inc.,
200 Madison Avenue, New York, New York 10016

First issued as an Oxford University Press paperback, 1989

Oxford is a registered trademark of Oxford University Press

Library of Congress Cataloging-in-Publication Data

Seymour, Harold, 1910–
     Baseball / Harold Seymour.
     p.   cm.
     "First published in 1960[–1971] by Oxford University Press"—
V. 1–2, t.p. verso.
     Includes bibliographies and indexes.
     Contents: [1] The early years—[2] The golden age.
     1. Baseball—United States—History.   I. Title.
   GV863.A1S48   1989
   796.357'0973–dc20   89-3406
                                                                               CIP

ISBN 0-19-500100-1
ISBN 0-19-505912-3 (Pbk.)

10 9 8 7 6 5 4 3 2
Printed in the United States of America

Since this book was first published in 1960, much has happened in the field of baseball history. Yet on re-reading it for the purpose of making any necessary alterations, I was struck with how little needed to be done and how valid the content remains.

This book, like many of the events described in it, was a pioneer. It was based in part on my Ph.D. dissertation for Cornell University, which was the first doctoral dissertation on baseball accepted by a history department. The book was the first scholarly history of baseball's early years by a professional historian. Today, sports history is recognized as part of history, but when I first presented my plan for investigating baseball history to the members of my graduate history committee at Cornell in 1941, some were dubious of my choice of subject, and I had to convince them that baseball history is part of American history and was a legitimate subject for scholarly study.

Courses on the history of sport are now offered in colleges and universities, but when I suggested such a course to the faculty of the college where I was teaching in 1947 I was unanimously voted down. I entered business in 1950, so it was not until I was teaching again, in New York in 1957, that I was able to include baseball history in an American history course.

Since those pioneer days of baseball history a number of scholars have entered the field, investigating various aspects of baseball and other sports; however, some stigma remains. As recently as the mid-1970s one doctoral candidate who wanted to write his dissertation on an aspect of baseball history fecklessly kept quiet about it because, as he said later, baseball was not normally the stuff of a successful career in history. He chose a more conventional topic and came out of hiding only after being safely nestled in a teaching position. And that was many years after I had completed the first doctoral dissertation ever written on baseball history.

This book has been well received by readers, reviewers, journalists, and baseball scholars. If imitation is the highest form of praise, then my work has indeed been complimented by those who have used it without crediting their source. To those who have recognized the quality of my work and have credited it in their own publications, I express appreciation.

When the hardcover version of this volume sold out, many prospective readers—including those who had enjoyed my subsequent volume, *Baseball: The Golden Age* (1971)—wrote to ask how they could get a copy, so Oxford University Press has decided to reprint it, this time in paperback. I am pleased that the book is available once more.

Keene, N.H.   H.S.
October 1988

SOME time ago a newly appointed United Nations delegate from a foreign country wanted to learn something about America. The usual sight-seeing tours were suggested, but he passed them up and asked to see a baseball game instead. His choice is significant. It reveals how closely baseball has become associated with America in the eyes of the rest of the world.

Baseball has become a symbol of America in much the same way that the Olympic Games are associated with Greece or cricket with England. By any measure—whether it be space devoted to it in newspapers and magazines, time on radio and television, economic interest direct and indirect, or simply barbershop conversation—baseball enjoys a prominent place in our American society. No President would omit the ritual of throwing out the first ball at the opening game of the season, and during the World Series most Americans, even those who do not follow baseball regularly, pause to discuss the contest. As Jacques Barzun once said, "Whoever wants to know the heart and mind of America had better learn baseball."

This book is a history of baseball which describes the growth of the game in the perspective of American history. It traces baseball from its real origins through its evolution from a simple, boyish pastime to a polite amateur sport for young gentlemen, and then into a highly organized business monopoly in the hands of professional promoters and players, with an inevitable loss of its character as a sport. This volume carries the story down to 1903, a year of natural demarcation which ended baseball's formative era—a period of experimentation and change, in which the professional organization of the game groped its way to stability. A second volume now in preparation will cover the history of baseball in the twentieth century.

The history of baseball's development is the story of nineteenth-century America in microcosm. While America was changing from a simple, predominantly rural society into a nation of large cities and giant industries, baseball was developing from a children's game played in open lots and pastures into a highly skilled game of professionals performed for the entertainment of paying urban spectators. Baseball's transition into a commercialized amusement was characterized by trade wars between rival leagues, conflict between owners and players, and the introduction of monopolistic practices. In this it was only following the pattern of cutthroat competition, bitter industrial warfare between owners and workingmen, and the drive toward monopoly of American business in general. Baseball's history also reflected other significant aspects of American society, such as the changing status of women, attitudes toward the Negro, public morality and ethics, new styles of journalism, and the gradual increase in leisure time.

Baseball not only reflected American life, it left an indelible mark upon it. This book shows how it added a new dimension to our economy, contributed color and flavor to our language, provided a theme for song, story, and stage, and supplied many names to the galaxy of American folk heroes.

While the book gives attention to outstanding players and teams, playing records, and pennant winners, it subordinates these to the economic and social aspects of baseball and its development as a part of Americana. It punctures numerous myths that have become an accepted part of baseball, and reveals that much which has been considered new or recent in baseball history is older than people realize. Necessarily, the account builds up to the establishment and growth of the major leagues, since they have dominated baseball. The minor leagues, and such offshoots as college and amateur baseball, are brought in only as they relate to the main theme. They are a full story in themselves.

Baseball, like some other aspects of our popular culture, has been badly served by history. Heretofore, no scholarly account of it has been written. The most substantial work that has appeared is Lee Allen's *100 Years of Baseball*. From time to time, books about baseball are published which purport to be authoritative histories, but they are not. They are put together after only the most cursory kind of research. While they have their place, they repeat the same tired legends and misinformation about baseball handed down, and copied uncritically, from one writer to another. They concentrate on the exploits of teams and players and pay little or no attention to the workings of the baseball business and its deeper significance as an American institution.

Baseball deserves better. So do the millions of people who are interested in it, either as fans or as those who want to know more about baseball as a colorful part of American life. Baseball warrants the same level of treatment which the professional historian has applied to other areas of America's past. This book presents a fresh approach by showing what really happened in baseball's formative years. It tells the baseball story in much greater detail than ever before, and reveals many aspects of it which have not previously been considered. It does not employ invented conversations or rely on stale anecdotes. It is based on wide research into the sources of baseball history which were examined—many of them for the first time—in libraries and archives in various parts of the country, especially in New York, Cleveland, Cincinnati, Chicago, St. Louis, and Cooperstown. While it is true that many of the early business records have disappeared or been destroyed, perhaps the time will come when officials of Organized Baseball will emulate other industries and make available to scholars what records they do have.

All statements in the book are supported by documentary evidence. Since this is not a work addressed to specialists, I have not attempted formal documentation of every point. Thus, I have included only a general bibliographical note describing the nature and location of the materials used. However, all my notes showing sources of information are available to any readers who wish to consult them.

This book, the research for which, though not constant, has been fairly continuous over a period of more than ten years, was originally prepared as a doctoral dissertation for the Ph.D. degree in history, received from Cornell University. Since then additional research was done, and the dissertation revised, expanded, and completely rewritten. More than that, the book is the product of a lifetime love of baseball that began as a boyhood enthusiasm and developed into the mature interest of the professional historian.

No book of this scope is ever completed without assistance, and I have received much help and co-operation in its preparation. The courteous assistance of many librarians who frequently went beyond the requirements of their routine duty is gratefully acknowledged. Especially do I appreciate the work of Francis Sommer of the Cleveland Public Library. Among other individuals who went out of their way to help me are J. G. Taylor Spink, publisher of *Sporting News,* who on several occasions kindly let me examine the early files of his paper in his St. Louis offices; Dean Fletcher R. Andrews of the Law School at Western Reserve University, who allowed me to use the facilities of the law library; Dr. Charles Upson Clark, of Englewood, New Jersey, who lent me his collection of early scorecards; Lee Allen, presently historian at baseball's Hall of Fame, who gave me what information he had from his notes on some obscure incidents I was trying to clarify; and Joseph M. Overfield, of Buffalo, New York, who made available his manuscript collection on early baseball, and also gave the manuscript of the book a careful reading. Professor Harvey

Wish of Western Reserve University's history department also read the original manuscript.

Valuable suggestions were also made by Professors Paul W. Gates, Frederick G. Marcham, and David B. Davis, members of the graduate faculty in history at Cornell University, who gave my doctoral dissertation the benefit of a critical reading.

I acknowledge the co-operation of the editors of the *Ohio Historical Quarterly*, the *New-York Historical Society Quarterly*, the *Missouri Historical Review*, and the *Cleveland-Marshall Law Review* for granting permission to use material which I previously published in those journals. I also acknowledge permission granted by the Historical and Philosophical Society of Ohio to use material from its manuscript collection on baseball, and by the Library of the National Baseball Hall of Fame and Museum to use material from the correspondence and papers of Abraham G. Mills. I also acknowledge permission to quote from *The Baseball Story* by Frederick G. Lieb, published by G. P. Putnam's Sons and from *The Pocket History of the United States* by Allan Nevins and Henry Steele Commager, published by Pocket Books, Inc. Most of all, I wish to acknowledge the help of my wife, Dorothy Zander Seymour, who contributed her time, knowledge, and patience, in all stages of the work. It is not too much to say that without her, the book would never have been finished.

H. S.

New York City,
15 October 1959

CONTENTS

PART FOUR – MONOPOLY AT ITS APEX

PART ONE

THE AMATEUR ERA

1

HOW BASEBALL REALLY BEGAN

B ASEBALL in America is many things. But, contrary to widespread belief, professional baseball is not a sport. It is a commercialized amusement business. Strictly defined, sport means participation in some physical activity for its own sake—for the sheer pleasure and recreation one gets from it. Sandlot and college baseball may fit this definition, but professional baseball does not. As the famous pitcher Grover Cleveland Alexander once pointed out, players are first of all businessmen. A few, like Bob Feller, have even incorporated themselves. Their primary reason for playing is to collect their pay checks.

Neither does owning a professional ball club make one a sportsman, any more than the Queen of England is a sportswoman because she owns horses and enters them in races. Fans are not sportsmen either—not any more so than theatergoers. Their role is passive, their thrills vicarious. Other than using their lung power, the only exercise they get is on the seat of their pants. Furthermore, the ethic of the professional game is anything but "sporting." It condones taking all one can get under the rules and, if possible, a little bit more. Arguing and brawling with opposing players and umpires are part of the struggle for victory. Theodore Roosevelt knew what he was talking about when he said, "When money comes in at the gate, sport flies out at the window."

The realities of Organized Baseball show that it is not only a business but a monopoly as well. It is a vast conglomeration of 166 professional clubs (at the start of 1959) organized into two eight-club major leagues and some twenty-one minor leagues, comprising a far-flung network which extends throughout the United States and into several foreign countries. Its total annual receipts are in the neighborhood of a hundred million dollars. As recently as 1950, it employed some 10,000 players and an enormous number of other men and women. Over 50 million people attend 30,000 "games" annually. The sale of

3

one of its clubs in 1956, Detroit of the American League, brought more than five million dollars. This combine operates under its own complicated body of "law," which includes a variety of restrictive practices governing its employees and controlling consumer markets.

Old-time clubowners of the nineteenth century freely admitted that they were running a business and trying to operate baseball on a business basis. But modern owners and their spokesmen have tried to disguise the nature of professional baseball. We are told that "baseball is too much of a sport to be a business and too much of a business to be a sport," or that it "belongs to the fans and the youth of America." We are also told that baseball is a sport because Justice Holmes, in the Federal Baseball Case of 1922, said it was—when the fact is that even he, while exempting it from the antitrust laws, still called it a business. Clubowners, when they do concede that they are engaged in a business, plead its smallness. But one of them, forgetting himself in 1951 during their trouble with Baseball Commissioner Happy Chandler, said: "We can't have a commissioner who makes too many mistakes. We have a big investment in this business. Baseball is big business." All this is not to say that professional baseball is without beneficial attributes. To the contrary, a lengthy catalogue in its favor could easily be prepared. Only it should be recognized for what it is and evaluated realistically.

But if professional baseball is a business, it is also a religion. Mohammedans may have their Mecca, but Americans have Cooperstown, New York, where baseball supposedly was invented by Gen. Abner Doubleday in 1839. Every year thousands of Americans make the pilgrimage to the shrine at Cooperstown, site of the Baseball Hall of Fame and Museum. Here they can see pictures and statues of former baseball heroes and look at sacred relics used by players of the past—old bats, balls, mud-stained uniforms, and other artifacts of bygone times. They can also visit Doubleday Field—the "hallowed field" where, it was said, the general devised the game. Words such as "shrine," "pantheon," "sanctuary," "relics," and "pilgrimage" are constantly used in newspaper descriptions of Cooperstown. Outstanding players are chosen each year for "enshrinement," after which they become "immortals." Taking the cue from Cooperstown, some states and cities have established baseball shrines of their own. And at the heart of this religion is the widely accepted myth that Abner Doubleday created baseball.

Actually, baseball stems directly from the English game of rounders, and it was known by that name and played in America before 1839, the year in which Doubleday supposedly invented and christened it. The unquestionable link between baseball and rounders was proved in

1939 by Robert W. Henderson, a librarian. His examination of early game books for children demonstrated that the rules for rounders and baseball were at first identical. Henderson found the rules for rounders printed in *The Boy's Own Book,* a collection of children's games written by William Clarke and published in London in 1829. It was reprinted in America the same year. Five years later a Boston firm copied the rounders rules in a little volume called *The Book of Sports* by Robin Carver, but changed the heading from "Rounders" to "Base, or Goal Ball" because, as Carver said, those were "the names generally adopted in our country." In 1835 a Providence, Rhode Island, firm did the same thing in *The Boys and Girls Book of Sports.* With this minor alteration English rounders became American baseball.

Rounders was played on a field on which were placed four stones or posts from twelve to twenty yards apart in a diamond-shaped pattern. The number of contestants was not specified; those on hand merely divided into two equal groups. The "out" side scattered about the field more or less haphazardly without taking any set positions, except for the "pecker" or "feeder" (pitcher), who gently tossed the ball a short distance to the "striker" (batter) from a fixed position also marked by a stone or post. The striker, if successful in meeting the ball, ran the bases *clockwise* as far as he could go. Outs were registered when the striker either missed three swings (three strike rule), hit the ball behind his position (one foul out), had his batted ball caught, or was struck by a thrown ball while trying to negotiate the bases. The "in" side continued until each of its members had been put out; then the other side had its innings. Running the bases counter-clockwise, long since taken for granted, was written into the rules for the first time in 1839.

Even the name baseball was known to both English and American boys long before Doubleday supposedly hit upon it. As early as 1744 John Newbery published in London *A Little Pretty Pocket-Book,* containing a rhymed description of "base-ball" along with a small picture illustrating the game. The book was extremely popular and widely known in England. It was also republished in several American cities at different times between 1762 and 1787.

Many references to ball games being played in America in the late eighteenth and early nineteenth centuries may be found, especially in diaries and memoirs. Those written at the time are, of course, more reliable than the ones written later from memory. These accounts do not always tell which game of ball was played, but often baseball is mentioned specifically. Possibly the first record of an American baseball game is that recorded in the journal of George Ewing, a Revolutionary soldier, who tells of playing a game of "base," April 7, 1778, at Valley Forge. A diary entry by a Princeton student in 1786 briefly

describes a game of "baste ball" on the campus. Another example is
Thurlow Weed, upstate New York political boss, who writes in his
autobiography that Rochester, New York, had a baseball club of fifty
members, ages eighteen to forty, which played every afternoon during
the ball season in 1825. Weed even lists the best players, among whom
were some of the leading citizens.

BASE-BALL.

This English woodcut appeared in *A Little Pretty Pocket Book* (Worcester,
1787), an American reprint of the 1744 London edition, the earliest
illustration of the game on record.

Besides baseball, other simple ball games were played by these early
settlers. The Dutch of New Netherland played "stool ball," thought to
be the forerunner of cricket. Even in Puritan New England the play
spirit was not as dead as commonly supposed. Ball playing there was
prominent enough to be forbidden by the governor of Plymouth. The
simplest of these early games was barn ball, limited to two players and
requiring the smooth side of a building with some level ground in front
of it. One boy threw the ball vigorously against the wall; the other,
having taken his position about a dozen feet away, struck at the re-
bounding ball with his bat. If he hit it, he tried to run to the wall and
back before his opponent recovered the ball and hit him with it. Naturally, the boys took turns, switching about after the batter was put out,
so that each one had his "innings."

Games of "old-cat" were variations which made it possible for more boys to participate. The most elementary version of "old-cat" was borrowed from the English game of "tip cat," in which a wooden "cat," shaped like a spindle, was placed on the ground, tipped in the air, and struck with a stick. "Old-cat" merely substituted a ball for the spindle. "One-old-cat" had a batter, pitcher, and two bases. The batter hit from one base, ran to the other, and then returned; he was retired when the batted ball was caught either on the fly or on one bounce. The number of lads could be increased by playing "two-, three-, or four-old-cat," which meant simply adding to the number of bases and batsmen. These games were still played in the streets and vacant lots of Brooklyn in the 1920's.

For yet larger numbers of players, games variously called "town-ball," "round-ball," and later the "Massachusetts" or "New England" game—to distinguish it from the "New York" game—were devised. These were the Americanized versions of English rounders, played by large groups ranging anywhere from twelve to twenty or more on a side. Regulations differed, since there were no uniform rules, so each community had its own particular variations—just as present-day sand-lot players generally add their own touches to the official rules. One side might bat until all of its players were put out; then the other had its turn. Or when one player was put out, the side was considered out. On some teams the catcher was on his own; others had one or two players back him up, in case he failed to stop the ball.

By the early nineteenth century, these simple, informal ball games were a common sight on village greens and college campuses, especially in the more settled areas of New York and New England, for it was only when communities became established and enjoyed a certain amount of leisure that ball games could flourish. Ball playing was less known in the South, because the pattern of Southern sport was formed chiefly by the dominant planter group, which tended to favor aristocratic pastimes like fox-hunting. On the frontier the immediate battle to subdue the wilderness was too pressing to permit much leisure for games, so sport tended to be combined with necessary work, like barn-raisings and corn-huskings.

The ball games of the period were admirably suited to a young, essentially rural America. Few people had great wealth or leisure. Playing sites were plentiful and convenient. Only the rudest preparation was necessary—laying "goals" or bases by driving sticks into the ground or placing flat rocks at approximate distances. Equipment was cheap and easy to come by. Any stout stick, wagon tongue, ax or rake handle made a capital bat, and a serviceable ball could be made by winding yarn around a buckshot or chunk of india rubber and then sewing on a leather cover, perhaps cut to size by the local shoemaker, to prevent unwinding. No other paraphernalia were needed. Projecting one's power by swatting and throwing an object hard and far, and experiencing the excitement of the race to reach base ahead of the ball, satisfied elementary human urges. All these factors made for popularity and wide participation.

Baseball being played on Boston Common, 1834.

Relatively few people watched games. Commercialized amusements were still unknown, and the promoter who sold baseball games as entertainment was not to appear until a later day when American society became more urbanized. Meager press coverage further indicated the unorganized character of amusement. Ball playing and recreation were more synonymous than they are in our day of mass spectator sports and vicarious thrills.

If baseball in America evolved from English rounders, the reader may well ask how Abner Doubleday and the Cooperstown shrine came into the picture. The myth about baseball's origin began to take shape in the spring of 1889 at famous Delmonico's in New York City, where some three hundred people, including such celebrities as Mark Twain and Chauncey M. Depew, gathered to lionize a squad of professional ball players. The stars had just returned from a world tour under the leadership of Albert G. Spalding, president of the Chicago Club and by then head of a thriving sporting goods business.

Organized Baseball was approaching the end of a decade of financial success and increasing popularity, and Spalding felt the time opportune for spreading abroad the gospel of "the American National Game," and incidentally, for promoting his sporting goods business. He took his own club and a picked group of all-stars from the rest of the National League on a globe-circling exhibition trip, which included stops at Honolulu, Australia, and the Pyramids, and a game in England with the Prince of Wales among the spectators.

At the Delmonico banquet, one of the speakers, Abraham G. Mills, fourth president of the National League, warming to the occasion, said he wanted it distinctly understood that "patriotism and research" had established that the game of baseball was American in origin. His audience greeted this pronouncement with enthusiastic cries of "No rounders!" According to the New York *Clipper,* this assertion "forever squelched" the English claim that baseball was a descendant of rounders.

This vehement denial of rounders is understandable. After the Civil War, organized teams became important, and baseball developed into a popular show business, enjoying a prestige enhanced by American pride in having a "national game." Its devotees found it increasingly difficult to swallow the idea that their favorite pastime was of foreign origin. Pride and patriotism required that the game be native, unsullied by English ancestry.

Nevertheless, rounders was not to be squelched as predicted. Up to the decade of the 'eighties it had been generally recognized as the ancestor of baseball, and this claim continued to enjoy support. The issue was brought to focus by an article favoring rounders written in 1903 by Henry Chadwick, first great baseball sports writer. Chadwick had always upheld rounders, claiming he had played the game in England as a boy and pointing out its similarities to early American ball games which became the baseball of a later day.

Spalding, champion of the American theory, met Chadwick's challenge by calling for a settlement of the question once and for all. A blue ribbon commission was appointed, consisting of seven men of "high repute and undoubted knowledge of Base Ball" and including two United States Senators. It was a hand-picked group made up of men who were at one time or another prominent in Organized Baseball and therefore not entirely disinterested. While the committee supplied the window-dressing, the chairman, A. G. Mills, did what actual work was done. After three years of collecting testimony, consisting of recollections but no solid documentary evidence, Mills published a

report, dated December 30, 1907, claiming that baseball originated in
the United States, and the first method of playing it was, "according
to the best evidence obtainable to date," devised by Gen. Abner
Doubleday at Cooperstown, New York, in 1839.

The dragooning of Doubleday and Cooperstown was based solely on
the testimony of an elderly man named Abner Graves, a onetime resi-
dent of Cooperstown, recalling what happened sixty-eight years earlier.
Graves said that one day in 1839 during a game of town ball between
Otsego Academy and Green's Select School:

> Doubleday . . . improved Town Ball, to limit the number of players,
> as many were hurt in collisions. From twenty to fifty boys took part in
> the game I have described. He also designed the game to be played by
> definite teams or sides. Doubleday called the game Base Ball, for there
> were four bases in it. Three were places where the runner could rest
> free from being put out, provided he kept his foot on the flat stone
> base. The pitcher stood in a six foot ring. Anyone getting the ball was
> entitled to throw it at a runner between bases, and put him out by
> hitting him with it.*

Doubleday was born in Ballston Spa, New York, and went to school
at Auburn. If he ever attended Green's Select School in Cooperstown, it
was certainly not in 1839. He had matriculated at West Point the previous autumn, so to be in Cooperstown when Graves claimed, Doubleday must have been A.W.O.L. from West Point. If he had any particular connection with the game it is not revealed in local histories or
even in his own writings. Recalling his boyhood, Doubleday omits any
mention of interest in baseball:

> You ask for some information as to how I passed my youth. I was
> brought up in a book store and early imbibed a taste for reading. I
> was fond of poetry and art and much interested in mathematical studies.
> In my outdoor sports I was addicted to topographical work and even
> as a boy amused myself by making maps of the country around my
> father's residence which was in Auburn.

Besides, Abraham G. Mills, chairman of the commission, had known
Doubleday for years, dating from their association as soldiers in the
Civil War; yet he never mentioned anything about Doubleday's alleged
contribution to baseball prior to the publication of the Graves statement. He missed the perfect opportunity to proclaim the General's
supposed role while addressing that glittering company at Delmonico's.
Doubleday may have played ball with Graves and others. He may

---

* The Commission did not even give a faithful rendition of Graves's letter,
inaccurately crediting Doubleday with eliminating soaking as a method of retiring
base runners.

even have shown them how baseball was played in other communities, but he certainly did not invent the game.

The climax in the perpetuation of the Doubleday myth came in 1939 when the major leagues dusted off the Mills Report and made elaborate preparations to commemorate the "centennial" of the game. Impressive ceremonies were held at Cooperstown. The Hall of Fame was dedicated, a pageant portraying the historical highlights of baseball was presented, and an all-star contest between teams composed of the game's all-time great players was played—all accompanied by the usual publicity build-up. Even the United States Government joined in by authorizing a special baseball stamp marking the event. However, it did so not because of Doubleday, whose claims admittedly were "questionable," but because the date was "universally recognized in sport circles as marking the centennial"—a rather nice point. Doubleday's picture was cautiously omitted and a sandlot scene substituted as the central motif, with a house, barn, church, and school in the background, thus associating baseball with these time-honored American symbols.

A legislative committee of the State of New York charged with studying the situation was less fortunate, or perhaps more gullible. This committee held a public hearing at Cooperstown in 1937, at which representatives of the local Chamber of Commerce and of the local committee dealing with the problem appeared. According to the official report of the State legislature, "It was put in evidence that Cooperstown, New York, is the birthplace of baseball," and the State committee recommended that "a centennial be properly celebrated at Cooperstown, New York, on the home site of the first game, the inauguration of baseball being the proud heritage of New York." The committee suggested that the event be "advertised and publicized in the pamphlets of the Conservation Department of the State of New York, and by road signs erected under its supervision." Finally, the State was asked to appropriate ten thousand dollars "to be used in advertising and generally furthering the baseball . . . celebration."

In the midst of preparations for the "centennial," Robert W. Henderson published his unimpeachable evidence that baseball was derived from rounders. Bruce Cartwright, descendant of an early baseball figure, further undermined the Doubleday story by claiming he could prove that his forebear, Alexander Cartwright, was the real founder of baseball. Although embarrassed and chagrined, baseball officials, having already committed themselves—especially financially—to Doubleday, proceeded according to plan. Some sports columnists pointed out the discrepancy; others got around it as gracefully as possible.

So it was that the Doubleday myth was crystallized and given concrete form by Organized Baseball. The average fan continued to think
that an inspired, spontaneous act by Abner Doubleday created the
game. The tale is still printed as fact in books, magazines, newspapers,
and encyclopedias. Some reference books have more recently accepted
the new evidence, while others equivocate on the issue. The Congress
of the United States in its 1952 Celler Report on baseball still held
that baseball "is a game of American origin," and New York State
officially promotes Cooperstown as the place where "Abner Doubleday
devised modern baseball."

Even though the Doubleday myth was thoroughly discredited more
than twenty years ago, the Hall of Fame publicists continue to claim
Cooperstown as the birthplace of baseball. They used to make much
of the so-called "Abner Doubleday baseball," an old ball reputedly
found in a trunk by a descendant of Abner Graves. They asserted that
the ball once belonged to Graves and therefore must have been handled
by Doubleday as well. This mystic laying-on of hands, as it were, was
seriously offered as evidence to support baseball's origin in Cooperstown. Hall of Fame promotion literature also pointed to the findings
of the Mills Commission of 1908, which were "officially sanctioned"
by Organized Baseball, and to the "persistent tradition" in the Cooperstown area as "sturdy links in the chain of evidence." In short, the Commission was used to substantiate the very myth which it created in the
first place. Of course, the fact that Organized Baseball gave "official
sanction" has no historical weight whatever. More recently, Hall of
Fame publicity writers have watered down their claims. They still
foster the Doubleday myth, but they are more circumspect about it.

To be sure, there is no particular harm in establishing a Museum
and Hall of Fame for baseball, and the lovely village of Cooperstown
provides as fine a setting as any. But we can enjoy visiting the Hall
of Fame without deceiving ourselves about the origins of a game which
has become so important in America.

2

THE PIONEER TEAM

EVERYONE knows the old joke about the love of Americans for organizing. Whenever three of them meet casually, they cannot resist electing each other president, vice president, and treasurer of a new organization—and, if time permits, drawing up a constitution. For Americans, a new idea is usually an excuse to organize into some kind of group, and probably no other people are so given to associating privately for common purposes.

This American liking for private association can be traced all the way back to the social clubs of colonial-day taverns, where people congregated not only for drinking but to enjoy tavern sports like billiards, backgammon, dicing, cards, ninepins, shooting matches, dances, and shuffleboard. Group activity was even more pronounced in the first half a century following our independence from Britain. In the 1840's and 1850's a host of organizations of every variety and purpose sprang up. Political action groups increased, and trade unions were formed. Especially prominent were humanitarian organizations working for all kinds of reform, like the American Temperance Society, American Peace Society, American Anti-Slavery Society, and even an association for redeeming "Females who have Deviated from the Paths of Virtue." Secret societies sprang up, and even immigrants formed groups, such as the Ancient Order of Hibernians and B'nai B'rith. The habit of organization became so widespread that foreign visitors were impressed by it, and Americans even noticed it themselves. Matters had come to such a pass that one observer wrote that "a peaceful man can hardly venture to eat or drink, or to go to bed or to get up, to correct his children or to kiss his wife, without obtaining the permission and direction of some . . . society."

People found it easier to get together because these were decades of transition in which America began to change from a rural, agrarian society to an urban, industrial one. Improved transportation, the increase in commerce and traveling, the post office, the steamboat, and the growing number of newspapers and periodicals were helping those in different localities but of the same mind to associate. Soon the canal, railroad, and telegraph added their impetus to the tendency to private organization.

The sports of the period reflected these changes. The agrarian and utilitarian nature of games and amusements was fading under the influence of the new industrialism and the rising city. Rustic pleasures and the early American outdoor pursuits of hunting, fishing, horse racing, field sports, and informal schoolyard games were becoming less available to those taking work in the factories of towns and cities.

In the 1820's and 1830's the only organized sport of interest to most Americans was horse racing, but soon organized teams began to replace informal groups playing casual games. The growth of cities in the pre-Civil War decades brought the need for new forms of recreation, and the rising standard of living and the increase in leisure helped city and town dwellers to develop them. The reader may be surprised to know that the foremost team sport of the period was not baseball but cricket. A manual published in 1858 devoted eighteen and one-half pages to cricket but only four and one-half to baseball, and pointed out that cricket was "the leading game played out of doors... the favorite game of the country village and the country town, as well as of the larger commercial cities."

Naturally, English settlers brought the game with them, and numerous matches were played by cricket teams, especially in the northeastern cities. In 1859 the England-United States cricket match at the Elysian Fields in Hoboken drew a crowd of 24,000, and extra ferries had to be put on to handle the crowds crossing over from Manhattan. The games were regularly reported in the press, and during the 1840's and '50's *Porter's Spirit of the Times,* a top sports journal, gave cricket substantial coverage. Cricket was even known on the frontier.

Devotees of the game held a convention at the Astor House, New York, in 1857 to organize a United States Central Club to act as mentor for the sport in the way the Marylebone Club presided over the game in England. Twelve clubs were officially represented, and delegates from Albany and Philadelphia took leading parts in the proceedings. In 1858 another attempt was made to organize the game on a national basis, but without success. When baseball started to become popular, many clubs played both games interchangeably.

Meanwhile, baseball was growing steadily in popularity, and after the Civil War left cricket far behind—a victory symbolized by Harry Wright, who began as a cricket player with the St. George Club but

deserted the English game to become baseball's first professional manager in 1869. Today cricket can still be seen in many parts of America,
notably in Van Cortlandt Park, Manhattan, and Prospect Park, Brooklyn, where members of the British West Indian colony in New York
enjoy regular league matches. But they are only a vestige of the game's
early popularity.

The first organized baseball team about which anything substantial
is known is the Knickerbocker Base Ball Club of New York.* For
several seasons, beginning in 1842, a group of gentlemen had been
meeting at 27th Street and 4th Avenue, Manhattan, to play baseball.
In 1845 one of the group, Alexander Cartwright, a bank teller and
volunteer fireman, suggested that they form a club. The idea was
accepted, additional members were recruited, and a permanent playing
field was secured at the Elysian Fields in Hoboken, a four- or five-acre
tract fronting on the Hudson River and surrounded by woods—"one
of the most picturesque and delightful places imaginable," and easily
accessible from the New York side via the Barclay Street Ferry. The
field and dressing rooms were rented for seventy-five dollars a year.
For their business sessions they rented a room for two dollars a meeting
at Fijux's Hotel, 42 Murray Street, owned by one of their members,
Charles Knickerbocker Fijux. However, "Madame Fijux" took care to
collect the rent.

The Knickerbockers were not a sandlot or semi-pro team in the way
we think of such outfits today. They were primarily a social club with
a distinctly exclusive flavor—somewhat similar to what country clubs
represented in the 1920's and 1930's, before they became popular with
the middle class in general. The very idea of forming a club and, under
its auspices, playing a boys' game heretofore open to all, introduced a
note of exclusiveness.

To the Knickerbockers a ball game was a vehicle for genteel amateur
recreation and polite social intercourse rather than a hard-fought contest for victory. They were more expert with the knife and fork at
post-game banquets than with bat and ball on the diamond. Their rules
and regulations emphasized proper conduct, and the entire tone of
their organization was more akin to the atmosphere surrounding cricket
—a far cry from the ethic of modern professional baseball. The spirit in
which they played the game is revealed in a verse from one of their
quaint songs lauding various rival clubs:

* The Olympic Town Ball Club of Philadelphia was formed about 1833, but,
aside from its ponderous title, little is known about it, and besides, it was not a
baseball club.

The young clubs, one and all, with a welcome we will greet,
On their field or festive hall, whenever we may meet;
And their praises we will sing at some future time;
But now we'll pledge their health in a glass of rosy wine.

The rather select membership of the Knickerbockers, limited to
forty, was dominated by professional men, merchants, and white collar
workers. Among some fifty-odd names on their roster from 1845 to 1860
were 17 merchants, 12 clerks, 5 brokers, 4 professional men, 2 insurance
men, a bank teller, a "Segar Dealer," one hatter, a cooperage owner,
a stationer, a United States Marshal, and several "gentlemen." Mere
skill in playing was not the only requisite for admission; a certain
standing in the community was necessary as well.

They protected their exclusiveness by a system of blackballing still
used by fraternal groups—a fundamentally undemocratic procedure,
since it makes possible barring a candidate on the strength of only one
or two secret votes cast for reasons of personal dislike or prejudice. A
kind of natural selection also operated, since only privileged young
men of some substance and leisure could afford to devote every Monday and Thursday, the Knickerbocker "Play Days," to baseball, and
also meet the various financial obligations which membership entailed:
dues, fees, purchase of uniforms, and assessments to cover deficits in
the treasury.

The Knickerbockers blazed a path others were to follow. If any
individual or group must be singled out as the founder of modern baseball, the credit has to go to Alexander Cartwright and his friends. Theirs
was the first step in the evolution of an important entertainment business which in a matter of decades became commercialized on a nation-
wide scale.

Even though they were somewhat snobbish toward outsiders, within
their own group the Knickerbockers reflected the belief in democracy
and majority rule so boisterously asserted since Andrew Jackson's day.
Administrative authority of the Club was in the hands of a Board of
Officers composed of the president, vice president, secretary, treasurer,
and three directors. They were elected annually by majority vote for
one-year terms, and met monthly during the playing season. It was
their duty to get suitable grounds, determine when to begin and end
the playing season, select the days and hours of play, see to it that the
necessary equipment was on hand, decide on the style of uniform, and
arrange for dressing-room facilities. The Board also determined what
other clubs to play and not to play, chose players and team captains,
and controlled the conduct of all matches in general.

Disciplinary authority, too, was vested in the Board, which could fine, suspend, or expel members for improper conduct. However, members had the right to appeal within thirty days. They had to show up on time with their uniforms, ready to play, and were not marked "present" unless they actually played or acted as umpire. Sometimes some very lame excuses were given. One truant, explaining eight consecutive absences, said, "I have been too weak to run and to achey to strike a ball," and another claimed, "My Business has required every moment of my time thus far in the season."

Knickerbockers were not permitted to leave the game unless excused by the captain. Annual dues were five dollars and the initiation fee was two dollars. If a member joined another club, he forfeited his membership. Besides the more severe punishments of suspension and dismissal, the Club had a schedule of fines for various minor infractions, and modern ball players who lose money through disciplinary action may find some solace in knowing that fines have been a part of baseball since the first organized club. If a Knickerbocker player refused to obey the captain of his side, he was fined fifty cents. Twenty-five cents was the penalty for disputing the decision of the umpire or even expressing an opinion on a play before his verdict—quite a contrast with the extreme rowdyism and physical attacks on the umpire of the professional era ahead. If a captain left the field beforehand or neglected his duty in any other way, he was charged a dollar.

Profane or "improper" language brought a lighter penalty. In the Knickerbockers' very first outside match, J. W. Davis was given the dubious distinction of paying what was probably baseball's first fine when he was docked six cents for swearing. Presumably the gentlemen of the Knickerbockers were not often guilty of this breach of decorum, but profanity eventually became so common in baseball that in 1899 John T. Brush, owner of the New York Giants, instituted an unsuccessful "purity campaign" to stop it, and the courts recognized that swearing was so much a part of ball playing that a club was unjustified in suspending a player for using opprobrious language, because he was entitled to summon up stronger words than ordinarily used by the average citizen.

When the Knickerbockers assembled on the field, the president of the Club picked two captains to take charge of the game, keeping in mind that every member was entitled to an equal chance at this job. The captains then "made the match," as choosing sides was called, and tossed to see which side batted first. Each player was assigned to a set position—an important innovation introduced by the Knickerbockers. The earlier town ball teams allowed an indefinite number to play, but Knickerbocker rules implied nine men on a side, because if fewer than eighteen showed up, members of outside clubs were allowed to fill in. The Knickerbockers had a "first nine," made up of their best players, for match games with other clubs.

Meanwhile, the players were warming up by batting fungoes to each other—that is, tossing the ball in the air and batting it before it touches the ground, a pre-game practice still used by coaches and pitchers. Now, however, a special fungo bat is used, lighter, longer, and smaller in circumference than the regular bat. It is easier to handle, permits greater leverage, and is particularly effective in driving long, high fly balls to outfielders. Hitting against pitched balls in pre-game batting practice, which has been routine for years among professional clubs, was not introduced until a later day, reputedly by George Wright.

The umpire was selected by the two captains. Besides deciding all disputes, he was supposed to "keep the game in a book" and note all violations of rules and regulations. There was no appeal from his judgment. This practice of upholding the umpire on all decisions of judgment has been characteristic of baseball ever since.

The Knickerbockers' first match game was played against a squad of gentlemen who, for the sake of having a name, called themselves the New York Base Ball Club.* It was played June 19, 1846, at Elysian Fields, but went only four innings, because by that time the New York Club had scored the 21 "aces" (runs) necessary to win under the rules. In fact, the New York nine scored two additional aces for good measure, making the final score 23 to 1. A celebration commemorating this first official game of baseball was held at Hoboken in 1946 and a plaque dedicated to counter the Cooperstown claim.

In these match games the Knickerbockers were dashing figures in their uniforms of blue woolen pantaloons, white flannel shirts, and chip (straw) hats. Standing along the sidelines were their friends, spurring them on with polite, subdued applause. The delicate complexions of the ladies in the audience were protected from the sun by a colored canvas pavilion.

When the Knickerbockers went into action they were playing under their own rules, the first written rules of modern baseball. They had molded the crude material at hand into a structure containing the basic, familiar features of the modern game. They specified a ball to weigh between 6 and 6¼ ounces and to measure from 10 to 10¼ inches in circumference. It had an india rubber center, wound with yarn and covered with leather. In match games the challenging club furnished the ball, which later became the property of the winner as a trophy of victory. The bat was made of wood, round, and not over 2½ inches

---

* It is possible that the New York Club existed even before the Knickerbockers (their one-sided victory indicates they were not novices), but the club was only "half-organized" and lasted not more than a season.

in diameter in the thickest part. It could be any length. No other equipment was used. Knickerbocker players took up their positions on a square field with 90-foot base lines, three bases, and a home plate. The pitcher stood on a plate 45 feet from home. The bases were canvas, but home and the pitcher's plate were flat, circular iron discs. All five stations were painted or enameled white.

Baseball revolves around pitching. Change the pitching rules and you change the entire complexion of the game, so baseball's evolution has been characterized by constant experimentation in this department. This was especially true in the nineteenth century, as the rulemakers constantly juggled pitching distances and ball-and-strike rules in order to get the best balance between offense and defense. The recent controversy over whether or not the spitball should again be made legal shows that the balancing act is still going on and probably will continue to do so as long as the game is played.

To a modern fan the style of a Knickerbocker pitcher would be amusing, if not incredible. He was not allowed to jerk or throw the ball to the batter. Instead, he had to toss it gently underhand as near the plate as possible so that the batter would have the fullest opportunity to hit it! How different from the modern hurler, who uses the full throwing power of his arm and calls on every skill and strategem to keep the hitter from meeting the pitch effectively! Once a Knickerbocker pitcher made a move to deliver the ball, he had to complete it. He could not feint or fake a throw. Neither could he step over his line. These regulations are the dim beginning of the complicated modern balk rule.

If the batter or "striker," as he was called in those days, swung at and missed three pitches he was out, provided the last one was caught either "flying or upon the first bound." Otherwise it was a fair ball and he had to try to "make his run." He was also out if a foul was caught on the fly or first bounce, or if a fair ball was caught on the fly. Most important, the old practice of "soaking" or "plugging"—that is, retiring a runner by hitting him with the ball—was replaced with the new method of putting him out by throwing the ball to the base ahead of him, or touching him with the ball.

Players had to take their turns at bat in regular rotation, just as they do nowadays. The Knickerbockers also decided that the inning was over when the third "hand," or player, was put out. Nine innings of play were not mandatory, however, because the side first to score 21 runs was the winner. Of course, "equal" innings were played, so that each side would have the same number of chances at bat. Baseball's rules have been refined and polished over the years, but the hard Knickerbocker core has remained central. The four-base diamond;

90-foot base paths; three out, all out; batting in rotation; throwing out runners or touching them; nine-man teams, with each player covering a definite position; the location of the pitcher's box in relation to the diamond as a whole °—these are still fundamental in baseball.

The Knickerbockers dominated baseball in the New York area for more than ten years. Their form of organization was adopted by other clubs, and their playing rules became generally accepted as "the New York game." Many of the new clubs deliberately aped the Knicker-bockers. The demand for their by-laws grew so heavy that they had a hundred copies printed for distribution, and even allowed their secretary to list his address in the Sunday *Mercury*. Proof that the Knickerbocker constitution served as a model is unmistakable to any-one who examines other early club constitutions, some of which still survive. The Social Base Ball Club, for example, had comparable in-itiation and membership fees, a system of blackballing, and a rather elaborate set of fines, including a one dollar penalty for being "inebri-ated" at a meeting or on the field. The Independent Club had very similar regulations, and the constitutions of the Excelsiors and Eagles were almost replicas of the Knickerbockers. The Eagles boasted perma-nent club rooms large enough to permit practice in bad weather. A stanza from the team song of the Putnams was both a compliment to the Knickerbockers and a hint to clubs of lesser breeds which might not adhere to their gentlemenly code:

> And should any club by their cunning and trick
> Dishonor the game that it plays;
> Let them take my advice and go to "Old Knick,"
> And there learn to better their ways.

New clubs also adopted the "Knickerbocker look" in uniform fashions. The Eclectics disported themselves in dark blue flannel pants, white shirts trimmed with blue, red belts, and white caps decorated with blue stars. But the leaders in sartorial splendor undoubtedly were the Charter Oaks of Brooklyn, who cavorted in white pants with pink stripes, pink shirts with white facings and stars, white caps with blue peaks, and black belts on which the name Charter Oak was inscribed.

As already suggested, a Knickerbocker ball game was a prelude to the pleasures of the table. In the evening after the game, the members of both clubs and their friends invariably celebrated with a gala dinner, like the one following a victory over the Excelsiors in 1858:

> After the close of this match, the Excelsior Club was escorted to Odd
> Fellows Hall, Hoboken, by the Knickerbocker Club, and entertained in

---

° Actually, the distance between bases is slightly less than 90 feet, since the bags and home plate are set inside the 90-foot square which makes the "diamond."

splendid style, covers being laid for over two-hundred gentlemen. Dodworth's Band was in attendance to liven the scene, and all the arrangements were exceedingly creditable to the taste and liberality of the committee who had charge of the festive occasion.

Other clubs were not outdone in after-game festivities, however. Following a game between the Enterprise Club of Brooklyn and the Poughkeepsie nine, the latter proved themselves excellent hosts. After a "fine supper" they all went for a moonlight drive to Hyde Park. On the way back they stopped at the "beautifully fitted up and tasty establishment of Messrs James Smith & Son . . . to partake of his unequalled ice cream and other refreshments." On another occasion the Putnams and Excelsiors enjoyed an especially convivial evening enlivened by innumerable toasts, speeches, and responses which left everyone "highly pleased with their day's entertainment and with each other."

It was also customary for these clubs to have a social affair during the off-season. The Knickerbocker, Eagle, and Gotham Clubs joined in a memorable annual dinner at Fijux's in 1854, at which "the utmost hilarity prevailed and everything passed off in a happy manner." At the annual ball of the Manhattans in 1859, a large company of ladies and gentlemen enjoyed "the most fashionable dances" in a ballroom decorated with flags and baseball paraphernalia. During the intermission a "splendid supper on the most liberal scale was served up."

Baseball players were praised for holding their dinners "after the fatigues of the day are over" (in contrast with cricketers who "indulge in the middle of the game"), since heavy dinners were considered "injurious to sight and judgment." Both ball players and cricketers were advised to abstain from "spirituous liquors" during hot weather—yet were told that "to allay thirst and relieve exhaustion, lager-beer answers every reasonable purpose"! Occasionally deportment at these baseball social gatherings was criticized in the high moral phraseology of the time:

> We regret to notice that a marked feature of these social entertainments is the indulgence of a prurient taste for indecent anecdotes and songs—a taste only to be gratified at the expense of true dignity and self-respect.

The first important club after the Knickerbockers was the Gothams,* who appeared about 1850. This Club gained an influential place in baseball during the 1850's, especially since it was for a time the only competitor the Knickerbockers had. It was the "excitement" growing out of games between these two clubs that inspired others to form clubs

---

* They were first called the Washington Club.

of their own. By 1854 New York had a well-organized, firmly established quartet of clubs, the Knickerbockers, Gothams, Eagles, and
Empires. They were soon joined by a second foursome from Brooklyn, the Excelsiors, Putnams, Eckfords, and Atlantics—all famous in
their day. Many more quickly followed, so that by the end of the 1850's
a boys' game had entered a new phase and taken on a new dimension.

The times were ripe for the marked expansion which baseball was
undergoing. America's shift from farm to city was well under way.
The foundations of an industrial society were already recognizable,
particularly in the new railroad network being forged. The development of these early clubs was a portent of the tremendous spread baseball was to enjoy, which was to carry the game far beyond anything
the Knickerbockers could have foreseen.

3

THE GAME TAKES HOLD

THE KNICKERBOCKERS wanted to restrict baseball to their own social class. For a while they limited their matches to clubs that used the Elysian Fields, hoping in this way to meet only their social equals. But their attempt to keep the game exclusive failed. Moreover, as the scene changed, the Knickerbockers were increasingly reluctant to participate in the great growth of baseball interest, so the show simply passed them by. The Knickerbocker effort to monopolize baseball has its parallel in other sports. The upper classes tried the same method in tennis, roller skating, and golf, with equal unsuccess. In the 1880's, when lawn tennis was little more than a mild game of pat-ball for ladies and their escorts, *Outing Magazine* assured its feminine readers that the game was "too refined to be attractive to the lower orders of society." New York's social leaders hoped that roller skating could be restricted to the "educated and refined classes," and for a long time golf remained a symbol of social and economic status.

In our own day scarcely a sport is confined to the Social Register. Rising living standards and the automobile have given Americans the means and the mobility to participate in practically all sports. At the same time heavy taxes on top-bracket incomes have dampened the desire for extremes in sporting luxury like J. P. Morgan's famous yacht *Corsair*. Baseball least of all could be kept exclusive, simply because anybody could afford to play it, even in Knickerbocker days. The absence of rigid class lines in America made it doubly difficult for a privileged group to keep the game to themselves. Ironically, when wealthy people try to monopolize a sport they help spread it, because their stamp of approval makes others anxious to copy them. In this way the social elite have unwittingly contributed to the widespread participation of the lower classes in healthy outdoor exercise.

First to thrust aside the Knickerbockers' "horsehide curtain" was a group of young workingmen—shipwrights and mechanics—named the

23

Eckford Club after Henry Eckford, a Scottish immigrant and Brooklyn shipbuilder, whose vessels were known for their strength and speed. As workingmen they were hard put to find time to practice, and thus were greatly worried over what would happen if they took on one of the more experienced, better-drilled teams. But they need not have worried on this score, for it was a year before they were invited to play another team—the Unions, an even newer club. The Eckfords won 22 to 8, to their astonishment as well as that of their friends, many of whom stayed away to avoid seeing their favorites beaten.

As baseball began to spread among people in all walks of life, new clubs began to be formed according to occupation: the Mutuals, firemen of the Mutual Hook and Ladder Company No. 1; the Manhattans, composed of New York policemen; the Phantoms, an association of barkeepers; the Pocahontas, representing a dairy; the Metropolitans, an aggregation of schoolteachers; the Æsculapians, a group of Brooklyn physicians; and a nameless nine made up entirely of clergymen. Naturally, as the number of clubs increased, more games between them were played, generally on a "home-and-home" basis. In the summer of 1856, for example, there were fifty-three games in New York and the metropolitan area. About fifty organized clubs were operating around the city in 1858. Junior teams were also being formed to serve as feeders for senior clubs, and by 1858 there were at least sixty of them in the area. Favorite playing fields were the Capitoline Grounds in Brooklyn; Englewood, New Jersey; Red House, Harlem; grounds near Carroll Park, South Brooklyn; Hamilton Square, New York; "Excelsior's Grounds," corner of Smith and Degraw Streets, South Brooklyn; Wheat Hill, East Brooklyn; and Manor House, Greenpoint, Long Island.

Unquestionably, baseball was spreading rapidly in the New York area. In 1856 *Porter's Spirit of the Times* said that every available green plot within ten miles of the city was being used as a playing field. Brooklyn, already the "city of churches," was fast becoming the "city of baseball clubs," inspiring a New Yorker's blessing, "God speed the churches and ball clubs of our sister city!" In fact, securing grounds was getting increasingly difficult with each passing year. Noting this in 1862, the Brooklyn *Eagle* pointed out that vacant lots were getting scarce as the demands of ball clubs increased and the city grew. On neighboring Long Island the story was the same. Any pleasant afternoon all the vacant fields were put to use by the ball clubs, and across the Hudson, Hoboken, known even then as the "stronghold of lager bier," threatened to become the stronghold of baseball clubs as well.

The increase in the number of teams and games did not show the full measure of baseball's grip. Players and spectators alike showed an intensity of interest which approached zealotry. Workingmen would get up at four or five o'clock in the morning to practice before going to work. Even severe March and November days did not chill their ardor. Some nines were hardier than others. In a late November game between the Excelsiors and Atlantics in weather unfit for baseball, the Excelsiors, who were mostly merchants and clerks, were not as well prepared to stand the severe weather as the Atlantics, whose outdoor jobs made them "weatherproof." Worst off were the several hundred spectators, including a few women, who bravely shivered through the game. At another match played at the foot of Court Street in Brooklyn, the crowd was so large that some perched on neighboring housetops, and others even clung to the masts and spars of the vessels moored at the wharves.

The feverish excitement over baseball which was building up in the 1850's reached a high point with the Fashion Race Course series on Long Island in 1858. All-star teams from Brooklyn and New York were to face each other, as the Giants and Dodgers were to do countless times later. A challenge of the Brooklyn all-stars had been promptly accepted by the baseball leaders of New York, and after lengthy negotiation the Fashion Race Course, with its impressive stone grandstand, was chosen because it would be a neutral field and could take care of the large crowd expected. Fifty cents admission was charged to cover the expense of putting the grounds in shape, making this the first time, as far as we know, that people paid to see a ball game.

Fans responded in droves. From early morning the road was jammed with vehicles of all kinds, including crowded buses and "the dainty buggy with its fast-trotting single nag." Special trains were run on the Flushing Railroad. According to an enthusiastic reporter, the crowd of 1500 included "a galaxy of youth and beauty in female form who, smiling on the scene, nerved the players to their task, and urged them, like true knights of old, to do their devoirs before their 'ladyes fair.'"

New York took the first game 22 to 18; Brooklyn evened matters in the second, 29 to 8; but New York went on to capture the championship, winning the third game, 29 to 18. Thus New York drew first blood in the traditional baseball rivalry between the boroughs. But former Brooklyn fans can take satisfaction in knowing that their borough dominated the game during the next decade. It was not until 1867 that a team from outside Brooklyn, the Unions of Morrisania, Bronx, succeeded in ending Brooklyn's unbroken hold on the mythical championship of the United States. Every year prior to 1867 the Brooklyn Atlantics captured the coveted "whip pennant," except in 1862 and 1863, when the Brooklyn Eckfords won it.

The important point about the Fashion Race Course series at the time, though, was the interest it stirred and the thousands of new converts it made for the game. Although New York remained the capital city of baseball, its popularity was spreading like a brush fire to other parts of the country. In the late 1850's announcements of new clubs being formed appeared constantly in the newspapers, and *Porter's Spirit of the Times* pointed out that baseball, "a delightful athletic sport," was rapidly finding favor all over the United States. It was catching on throughout New York state—in Syracuse, Cazenovia, Canandaigua, Batavia, and Troy. Albany clerks were said to find relief from musty state papers and the monotony of bank routine in "the healthful and pleasant game of base ball." The Buffalo Base Ball Club was playing inter-squad games, with city aldermen acting as captains and choosing sides, the losers to pay for the supper afterwards.

At the same time the New York style of play was gradually moving westward. In 1857 baseball games were a daily spectacle in Cleveland's Public Square. City authorities tried to find an ordinance forbidding it but, to the joy of the crowd, they were unsuccessful. Numerous clubs were springing up around Chicago, and they often played before large crowds. The Franklin Club, which claimed to be the pioneer club of the West, was organized in 1857 in Detroit, and the first game there was played between the Early Risers and the Detroits before a big crowd. In the Minnesota Territory a magnificent level prairie was leased for a game on August 15, 1857.

The first Pacific Coast club was the Eagles, named after the New York Eagles, several of whose members migrated to California and formed the team in 1859. Knickerbocker influence was brought to San Francisco by William and James Shepard, former Knickerbocker players who crossed the plains in 1861. Californians welcomed these men because they came "direct from the center of the base ball universe" (New York), bringing with them the most up-to-date methods of playing ball. Other clubs like the Red Rovers and the Em Quads followed, and a baseball tournament was held in California before the Civil War. Washington also caught the baseball bug. Government clerks formed the Potomac Club there in the summer of 1859, and that November a second team, the Nationals, composed mainly of government clerks, joined them. These teams practiced and played each other in the backyard of the White House.

In New England, too, the New York game eventually triumphed, but in the 1850's the "Massachusetts game" was still in its heyday. It was played with a smaller ball and permitted runners to be put out by "soaking." We learn from the rules of the Takewambait Club of 1858 and other early publications that there were ten to fourteen on a side, and wooden stakes projecting four feet out of the ground were used as bases. By their rules, a hundred runs were needed to win!

The New York Game

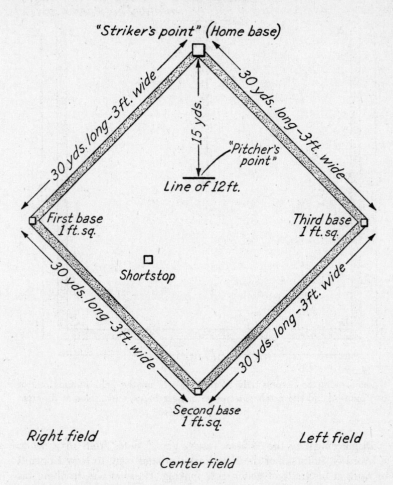

□ Catcher

"Striker's point" (Home base)

30 yds. long - 3 ft. wide

30 yds. long - 3 ft. wide

15 yds.

"Pitcher's point"

Line of 12 ft.

First base
1 ft. sq.

Third base
1 ft. sq.

□ Shortstop

30 yds. long - 3 ft. wide

30 yds. long - 3 ft. wide

Second base
1 ft. sq.

Right field

Left field

Center field

The first regularly organized team in New England was the Boston Olympics of 1854. The Elm Trees followed in 1855 and the Green Mountains two years later. There was also a junior club called the Hancocks. Most Boston business firms closed Saturday afternoons so that clerks could benefit from sports which were supposed to quicken their minds. After-game social gatherings were also popular.

The Massachusetts Game

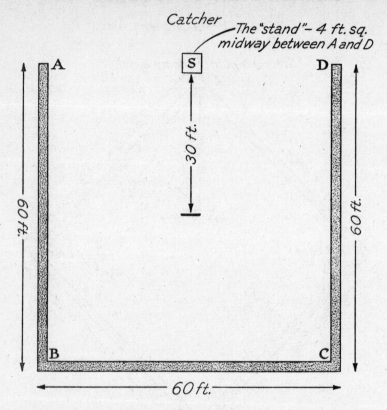

Upon arriving at D, one tally is made. Team on the field stations one or two men behind the catcher, some on or near bases, and others at different points on the field.

Displacement of the "Massachusetts game" dates from 1857, when Edward G. Saltzman of the New York Gothams went to New England to work at his trade of watch case making. He soon was teaching his shopmates how to play ball in the New York manner. Progress was slow at first because of the popularity of the "Massachusetts game." Saltzman's first big success came when the Tri-Mountains, a newly formed Boston club, declared their intention of playing according to the New York style. They stuck to their guns the following May at Dedham during the first baseball convention ever held in Massachusetts. Representatives of ten clubs formed the Massachusetts Association of Base

Ball Players, dedicated to playing the Massachusetts game, but the Tri-Mountains refused to go along with the others and withdrew. Their president, B. F. Guild, had gone to Manhatttan to study the New York game first-hand under the tutelage of the Knickerbockers, and he announced at the convention that his club would abide by the New York rules.

This decision was the opening wedge which gradually widened until the New York game became supreme in New England. In their first year the Tri-Mountains could find no one to play their way, but in 1858 they met the Portland Club of Maine on Boston Common. Other games followed, and soon the New York game outdistanced its rival. By 1860 even the Olympic Town Ball Club of Philadelphia succumbed to the rules of the New York game.

However, as the game started slipping from the polite fingers of teams such as the Knickerbockers into the more lusty embrace of the masses, its complexion began to change perceptibly. Rooting grew more vehement as spectators became noisy partisans. Betting began to creep in. At the Fashion Race Course all-star series, even women were observed exchanging small wagers. Rowdyism and occasional riots also marred the scene. One reporter complained acidly that the crowd seemed to think that games were got up for their special entertainment and that they were conferring a favor on the players by their presence. These new elements heralded baseball's march toward professionalism and commercialism.

The most dramatic example of the changing atmosphere was the final game for the championship of Brooklyn between the Excelsiors and Atlantics in 1860. Tension had built up to the breaking point as a result of the previous two games of the series. The first match was held just after the Excelsiors returned from an upstate tour glorying in an unbroken string of victories, and they trounced the redoubtable Atlantics 23 to 4. The second game, played after the Excelsiors finished the southern part of their trip, was taken by the Atlantics, 15 to 14. So by the time the rubber match was played, all Brooklyn was aroused—schoolboys, clerks, merchants, workmen, and professional people.

The Excelsiors were leading 8 to 6 in the sixth inning when the first mass riot in baseball history broke out. Unruly fans, who probably had bet on the Atlantics, began showering the Excelsiors with personal abuse. A free-for-all on the field followed, and the game was called when the Excelsiors were ordered to withdraw by their captain, J. B. Leggett. Afterwards, Umpire Thorn, in a written statement, defended his decisions and absolved the players, but he made plain his low opinion of the crowd's deportment. A story has come down that Captain Leggett handed the ball, as a token of victory, to Matty O'Brien,

Atlantics' captain, saying, "Here, O'Brien, is the ball. You can keep it."
O'Brien reciprocated this sporting gesture with the reply, "Will you
call it a draw?" "As you please," answered Leggett.

The more brash tone of baseball was also evident at a game in
Irvington, New Jersey, between the home team and the New York
Mutuals. The field was surrounded by a dense crowd of some six or
seven thousand people and hundreds of vehicles of every kind. A
disturbance started by pickpockets broke out in the fifth inning. The
rioters surged onto the infield and, in the absence of police, had to be
driven back by the players with their bats. In the melee Hugh Campbell, outfielder of the Irvingtons, was "sucker-punched" and had to be
replaced.

The new rowdy conduct was not restricted to the New York area.
The Buffalo *Express* complained that the behavior of the Rochester
Live Oaks, in a game against the Olympics of the same city, was "not
exactly proper and creditable." When the umpire called a close play
against them, their captain heaved the ball in the air, and the team
walked off the field.

Some of the principal reasons for the rapidly expanding baseball
interest in these pre-Civil War years were based upon the appeal of the
game itself. First of all, the two opposing sides had an equal chance
to score and the game's movements were independent of time restrictions. Then, it was an open game in which every play was apparent to
the audience. And, finally, it became more exciting to watch as the
long process of rules refinement, which was to make the game increasingly palatable to spectators, got well under way.

The written rules of the Knickerbockers brought greater standardization and helped reduce arguments. The Knickerbockers' decision to lay
out the field in the form of a square set upon one of its points and to
put all the bases 90 feet apart gave the New York game a distinct
advantage over the less-balanced Massachusetts style of play. These
changes were the cardinal factors in turning baseball into a game of
neat mathematical proportions and split-second timing. Throwing out
runners or touching them with the ball made for more fielding, throwing, and catching by individual players, and at the same time it increased opportunities for team play. Putting nine players on a side in
fixed positions fostered the skill which only specialization permits. In
short, baseball was becoming a particularly good combination of individual and team play.

The game also enjoyed the great advantage of having no serious competitor. Cricket, its chief rival for a time, soon lost out. Although baseball was still a slow game compared with what it was later to become,

with further refinement of its rules, alongside cricket it was faster, more action-packed, and better suited to the fast-moving American environment. According to a contemporary writer, it had greater variety and offered more skillful performances than the English game. Besides, during a "time of intense nativism, many Americans experienced an instinctive aversion for cricket just because it was English" and enthusiastically turned to baseball instead. As the Brooklyn *Eagle* remarked in 1862, since cricket "is not an *American* game, but purely an English game, it never will be in much vogue with the Americans." The fact that baseball was already being called the American National Game in the 1850's—much earlier than heretofore believed—reveals the adolescent pride of a young nation:

> Here's a health to our *Base Ball*, and honor and fame,
> For 'tis manly and hearty and free;
> Oh long may it flourish, our *National Game*—
> Here's a health, good old baseball to thee.

Other sports were inconsequential and were to remain so for years to come. Horse racing, first of the popular spectator sports, did not lend itself to mass participation, and the betting associated with it was unsavory to the Puritanism that still pervaded American society. Boxing was illegal and for the most part was conducted surreptitiously by a small coterie of "sports"—"the fancy," as they were called then. When football appeared, it was a game for young men only, and for many years it was stigmatized by excessive brutality and the prevalence of serious injuries. Basketball was not invented until 1892. So, with the possible exception of the bicycle craze, which did not come until the 1890's, baseball had a fairly clear field for sports interest in the nineteenth century.

As has already been said, the fact that the upper classes had given their imprimatur to the game served as a signal for the people at large to rush into it. A contemporary writer was getting at the same point when he remarked that the "great mass, who are in a subordinate capacity," could participate in baseball, while at the same time the "best citizens" were encouraging it everywhere.

Aside from the inexpensiveness of the game and the plenitude of vacant lots, which made it relatively easy for the average person to follow in the footsteps of the elite, baseball also profited from the fact that most adults knew the game because they had played it in their boyhood. Their familiarity with it and their nostalgia for it combined to make them good spectators. This knowledgeable sentimentalism still motivates the American male today and brings him to the ball park to recapture former days and second-guess the home club's strategy.

Finally, in the present day, club owners have come to recognize that the boy of today can be the fan of tomorrow. As recently as a generation ago, boys were about as welcome around a ball park as mosquitoes in a bedroom, but now the gates are thrown open to knothole gangs and boys' clubs of all kinds.

The important part the railroads were to have in advancing baseball was pointed up even then by the first great baseball tour—the dramatic safari of the Excelsior Club in 1860, which in itself did a great deal to arouse enthusiasm for baseball and to inspire the organization of many clubs in the areas visited. In making the trip the Excelsiors were satisfying local communities who wanted to compare their heroes with those from outside. The Club first toured upper New York state, stopping at Albany, Troy, Buffalo, Rochester, and Newburgh, after which they turned south in response to many invitations and invaded Pennsylvania, Maryland, and Delaware. With young Jim Creighton, the pitching star of the day, as their mainstay, they won every game.

A visit by a crack team from New York City was a signal event for the "country clubs," as New Yorkers referred to teams from outside in those days. In Buffalo, for example, the coming of the mighty Excelsiors was heralded well in advance, and news of their conquest of the Albany Champions had a sobering effect on local fans even before they saw the Brooklyn stars in action. The Buffalo Niagaras were the strongest team on the Niagara Frontier, and bettors generally demanded odds on them when they played other teams in the area, like the Auburns. Great pains were taken to put the Niagaras' new grounds in shape for the Brooklyn game. A handsome new flagstaff was set up, along with two platforms, one on each side of the field, on which ladies and gentlemen could be seated.

When the great day arrived, four or five thousand people were on hand, and standing room on the field, as well as roofs and windows overlooking it, was "fully occupied." The Niagaras, "heretofore regarded as invincible," were crushed 50 to 19, the highest number of runs ever scored in a match game up until then—at least among top-level teams. Getting a taste of the "finished skill" of a team like the Excelsiors was good medicine for clubs in the outlying areas, because it had the effect of jarring them out of any complacency they might have had, and at the same time it helped baseball by giving people in these other cities a chance to see the most up-to-date methods of playing.

A more direct boon to baseball than the railroad was newspaper publicity. The interaction between the game and the sporting page was apparent by the 1850's. Baseball news sold newspapers, and newspapers sold baseball. This mutual relationship was to continue on an ever-widening scale. It would be difficult to overestimate the influence of the sports pages and sports writers in promoting baseball and dramatizing it for the American people. And when an occasional player like Ted Williams, the Red Sox star, or Bill Terry, playing manager of the Giants in the 1930's, castigate sports writers and disparage their work, they simply advertise their ignorance of baseball history. If it were not for the sports page, spectator interest would be only a phantom of what it is, and ball players would not receive the fabulous salaries many of them get.

To be sure, sports writers have been critical of baseball at times, but criticism is healthy for the long-term progress of the game. Besides, individual writers have made numerous direct contributions to the organization and administration of professional baseball, and, as we shall see, their advice and counsel have repeatedly been sought by executives and players. Also, some of the best writing in America appears on the sports pages of our newspapers. It is crisp, concise, and colorful. And top-flight sports writers like Grantland Rice, Ring Lardner, Heywood Broun, John Kieran, and Paul Gallico have been good enough to win reputations for themselves in other fields of writing.

At first newspapers carried only short squibs about the game. A few dry, perfunctory remarks and a crude, fragmentary box score were all they printed. Soon full-column descriptions appeared, and by 1860 inning-by-inning accounts of both match games and intra-squad games could be read. Occasionally one of the early reporters attempted a breezy, humorous style:

> Gelsten, catcher of the Eagles, seemed to have donned those stretchable unmentionables again, as his extraordinary movements seemed to indicate; and Yates, who is ever the life of his club, was unusually jocular and good natured on this occasion. Place knew his place, and played it remarkably well, making several masterly catches.

With the number of games increasing, reporters, "not being endowed with ubiquity," as one of them expressed it at the time, could no longer cover all of them personally, but had to rely on referees and club secretaries for results and comments. Newspapers also began printing letters from fans. One wrote the editor of Porter's Spirit of the Times in 1857 pointing out that the "ball-playing mania" of the past few years made it desirable to have a book on how to play ball. Another fan sent in a long letter giving the details of how to form a ball club.

Some clubs made provision for sports writers and some did not, although at best facilities were a far cry from the modern press box and press room enjoyed by reporters in big league parks such as Yankee Stadium and Lakefront Stadium in Cleveland. The Atlantic Club was one which made "proper and judicious arrangements," but there were other cases where the reporters complained that the lack of facilities kept them from giving a detailed account of the game. Achieving recognition and status was to be a long struggle for baseball writers.

Finally, baseball's growth was aided by mere chance. Accidents of history have often been of major importance in determining the affairs of men. What if Stonewall Jackson had not been accidentally shot by one of his own men two months before Gettysburg? And what if the editor of the influential *Porter's Spirit of the Times* had not switched his allegiance from cricket to baseball? Doubtless baseball would have prospered anyway in the pre-Civil War era, but its development might have been much slower than it was. However, history is concerned with what actually happened, not with might-have-beens, interesting as these may be to speculate upon. And the fact is that by the Civil War baseball had taken solid hold on America. It had established numerous outposts in many parts of the country from New England to far-off California. Nevertheless, its main base continued to be New York and the metropolitan area. Not only would New York remain the hub of baseball activity for some time to come, but it would also be the scene of more formal organization of the game to meet the needs and aspirations of the multiplicity of clubs dotting the area.

4

THE AMATEUR ASSOCIATION

As THE CLUBS began to increase rapidly, there was need for them to meet to exchange ideas for improving baseball. It was expected that the Knickerbockers, as the senior club, would take the lead in calling a meeting. But the old club was not anxious to do it. It had become complacent, satisfied to continue along in its customary way. Besides, it feared that if the other clubs organized, its own position and influence would be greatly reduced.

However, it finally succumbed to the pressure and invited the clubs of New York City and vicinity to send three representatives each to a meeting in January 1857. The plan was immediately supported by *Porter's Spirit of the Times,* because it felt there should be "one game peculiar to the citizens of the United States," pointing out that, after all, the German Turnvereins and other importations had been "naturalized," and it was about time that we had a game that could be called "a Native American Sport." Over a dozen clubs sent delegates to Smith's Hotel on Broome Street. They elected Dr. D. L. Adams of the Knickerbockers president, and set up a committee on playing rules. But when the 1857 season was slow to begin, the New York *Clipper* blamed the "old fogies" at the convention for ignoring the young clubs, and causing them to lose interest.

The next year the presidents of the four oldest clubs—Knickerbockers, Gothams, Empires, and Eagles—called another convention of all regularly organized clubs in the metropolitan area, to meet at 298 Bowery, headquarters of the Gothams, on March 10, 1858. This time twenty-two clubs were represented. They formed themselves into a permanent body, the National Association of Base Ball Players, and appointed a committee to draft a constitution and by-laws. Annual editions of these documents can still be found on dusty library shelves. The first officers of the Association were: president, William H. Van Cott, Gothams; first vice president, L. B. Jones, Excelsiors; second vice president, Thomas S. Dakin, Putnams; recording secretary, J. Ross Postley, Metropolitans; corresponding secretary, Theodore F. Jackson, Putnams; treasurer, E. H. Brown, Metropolitans. The absence of a Knickerbocker name among them shows the declining influence of the club. These men were listed as the first officers of the Association by Spalding in his *American National Game,* and copied by others ever since—rightly so, if the formal convention of 1858 is considered the first. But baseball's first real convention was in 1857, and so the honor of being the first president belongs to Dr. Adams of the Knickerbockers.

Of course, the Association was not yet really a national body. It neglected to invite clubs from the rest of New York state and other sections of the country to join. The New York *Clipper* sharply criticized it for this, charging that "a few dictators" were trying to "mold" the group into an exclusive organization like the New York Yacht Club. The editorial urged it to make the game truly national by opening the meetings and competition to ball players everywhere. In succeeding years the Association did extend its membership to clubs from all over the country, until it had a more truly national representation. Soon there were so many ball clubs that state associations were organized, and these sent representatives to the National Association conventions. In its evolution from a local body to a national one, the Association was simply following the pattern of the political parties and the budding labor unions of the time, which first established themselves locally and then on a state, regional, and national basis.

To join the Association a club needed a minimum of eighteen members and was required to submit its application thirty days before the annual convention so its character and standing could be investigated in time to be voted on. A two-thirds vote was required for admission. If a club was not organized until after the convention, it could get probationary status until formally accepted at the next annual meeting. Each member club was allowed two delegates and two votes. Dues were at first five dollars, but over the years were gradually reduced to fifty cents.

The Association regulated players, too. To play in match games, a man had to be a member of his club for thirty days beforehand. If he left one club to join another, he must show a clean financial slate before making the change. No one was eligible to play who received compensation at any time, and no player, umpire, or scorer was permitted to be interested "directly or indirectly" in a bet on the game. This rule was made progressively more stern and explicit, because the inroads of professionalism and betting soon compelled it. To handle disputes and violations the Association set up a nine-man Judiciary Committee. Charges against a player or club were to be submitted to the Secretary of the Association in writing. He turned them over to the Committee, which had to hand down its decision within ten days. However, its rulings were subject to review and reversal by a two-thirds vote of the convention delegates at the end of the year. This later proved to be a fatal weakness.

State and regional associations were pocket editions of the national body. Admission requirements were essentially the same. A player or club that conspired to throw a game was barred from membership, and, furthermore, member clubs were forbidden to play a team harboring any such player. State judiciary committees were armed with authority to summon members and their books and papers, and to suspend and expel. But they, too, could be overruled.

The National Association governed baseball for thirteen years. Its formation was a pivotal event, marking the close of one baseball era and the beginning of another, in which the players and their representatives would meet annually in convention to revise rules, settle disputes, and conduct their own game. The Association determined the eligibility of players and clubs. Especially important, it devised the first centralized administrative and enforcement agencies in the history of baseball government. Although feeble and ineffectual, it nevertheless inaugurated a long process of trial and error culminating in the establishment of a commissioner of baseball with the appointment of Judge Kenesaw Mountain Landis in 1920.

The day of the autonomous club was ending, and with it the Knickerbocker spirit of well-bred play followed by well-laden banquet tables. The Association's ban on refreshments in 1859 set the pattern for the years to come. It realized that a once-friendly custom had degenerated into petty rivalry between clubs to outdo each other in lavish entertainment.

It was time that the clubs settled on common playing rules. While the Knickerbocker code was generally accepted, other ways of playing did not die out suddenly. The reader will recall that the Massachusetts game was still going strong in New England, highlighted by the Dedham Convention. Even town ball could be seen in many communities and it hung on for years to come. Under these circumstances it was sometimes difficult to arrange games and to avoid disputes during them.

What the Association agreed upon in 1857 was essentially the Knickerbocker code, with some immediate changes, notably a provision for seven-inning games, quickly amended to nine, which ended the old 21-aces rule of the Knickerbockers. Fielders were also forbidden to stop the ball with their hats or caps. The importance of the nine-inning rule in both stabilizing and speeding up the game can be further appreciated when compared with some of the long contests played under

the Massachusetts rules or the sudden-death affairs of the Knickerbockers. One game for the "championship" of Massachusetts in 1859
lasted a day and a half. It took the winners 101 innings to score the
necessary 100 runs over the losers, who made only 71!

If a modern fan could somehow be transported to a match a hundred
years ago around New York, he would see a crude exhibition, but he
would recognize it as baseball. His pleasure at not having to buy a
ticket would be reduced somewhat when he found that, unless he had
come by carriage, he would have to stand along the sidelines to watch,
for there were no grandstands. If he had a lady with him, he might
avoid being bleached in the sun by joining her under the tent or
pavilion provided for women. He would see a playing field entirely
covered with grass, except for the worn spots around the bases and
the pitching alley only a rough resemblance to the carefully groomed
diamonds of today. He would be surprised to see the members of the
side at bat standing or sprawling around along the base lines in their
flashy uniforms with long pants and spiked shoes. Some of them would
be stroking their beards or twirling their mustaches; others would be
selecting a bat—possibly a 44-inch mahogany model, more like a
wagon tongue than a bat—from among the collection strewn about on
the ground, for there was no players' bench, dugout, or bat rack. All
the while, as one reporter would have it, the diamond gladiators on
both sides would be conscious of the keen scrutiny of the ladies, who
were sizing them up as possible husband material.

Our visiting modern fan would be highly amused to see each baseman literally playing on his base, and the catcher standing about
thirty feet back of the batter, without the "tools of ignorance," as
catching equipment is now called. Outfielders shifting their positions
for the various hitters would be familiar to him. Occasionally he would
see a base stealer hit the dirt to avoid the tag, because sliding was
introduced at least as early as 1857. On the other hand, our fan would
be puzzled and probably bored watching the pitcher deliver the ball
from a distance of forty-five feet with an underhand motion like a
bowler, while the batter waited "a good while" until he got a pitch
exactly to his liking before deigning to swing.

Our transported friend would prick up his ears at hearing admiring
spectators remark that fielders were developing quickness and showing
considerable nerve and determination in fielding balls—barehanded, of
course. He would wonder at the excitement and applause whenever a
fielding star of the day caught a fly ball without letting it bounce first.
If he watched carefully, he would notice different styles of batting.
There were those who are now called slap-hitters, who gripped the bat

some distance from the handle (choked up on it) and tried to "poke" or "punch" the ball safely, and there were long-ball hitters, who held the bat on the very end (swung from the handle) and tried to drive the ball as far as possible. Another type held the bat with one hand on the handle and slid the other hand down from the large end as they swung. Our visitor would see that the power-hitters found it difficult to hit grounders, and instead lofted fly balls—"very pretty to look at," as an observing fan remarked, but a "losing game" when there were three experienced outfielders.

Perhaps our visitor would be most intrigued of all by the umpiring. Keeping score at a desk or table on the third base side of the field were two "umpires" who were not really umpires at all, but official advocates representing each team, like lawyers representing clients. The real arbiter of the game was seated, "solitary and alone," on the first base side, imposing in top hat, frock coat, side-burns, and cane. On a close play members of each team appealed to their respective advocates, one of whom would yell "Not out!" while the other shouted just as vehemently "Out!" It was then up to the figure in the top hat and side-burns to decide. The uselessness of the two advocates was obvious by 1858, and the Association discarded them in favor of the one-umpire system, which was continued until its shortcomings in turn brought changes.

If our modern fan forgot himself so far as to boo and shout over this disputed play, his outburst would cause lifted eyebrows and provoke polite murmurings of reproof from the ladies and gentlemen in his vicinity. The game at last over, our modern fan, greatly perplexed at what he beheld and doubtless feeling the need for refreshment and enlightenment, could repair to the Toots Shor's of the day, Richardson & McLeod's English Restaurant, 106 Maiden Lane at the corner of Pearl Street. While waiting for a table he could look over a book in which the records of all the season's games were kept, or browse through a file of the leading sports journals of England and America, which the host made available for the sporting crowd which frequented the place. However, he could not get the final sports edition for an account of the game he had seen, but would have to wait until the next day for a short summary; if he wanted a more complete account he could get it later in one of the sporting weeklies.

The deepening interest in baseball was well reflected by the National Association itself. We learn from its old records that its 1858 membership of twenty-two jumped to almost fifty clubs at its annual convention in 1859. Only clubs from New York and Brooklyn came to the conventions of 1857 and 1858. In 1859 there were five clubs from upstate New York and four from New Jersey. Beginning in 1860 clubs from Pennsyl-

vania and other states were represented.* The season of 1860, the
last before the Civil War, was the "most brilliant in the brief annals of
the game." Clearly baseball had cast off its swaddling clothes when
Fort Sumter intervened.

There are two commonly accepted beliefs about the effect of the
Civil War on baseball's history, both of which are incorrect, or at least
only partly true. One is that baseball's growth was halted by the Civil
War. The other is that Southern troops learned the game from Northern
prisoners, took it home in their knapsacks, and introduced it to the
South. Baseball's spread was not stopped by the war; it was only
temporarily slowed. To be sure, twenty-seven of the clubs enrolled in
the National Association failed to send delegates to the 1860 convention
because of the "peculiar state of the times," but their absence was
more than offset by additional delegates representing new clubs from
nineteen cities, bringing the total number of clubs represented to fifty-
three, the highest yet. The full impact of the war was not felt until the
1861 convention, where only thirty-four clubs appeared. Representation continued to fall off slightly at the next two conventions, but picked
up again in 1864, before the war was even over.

True, during the war individual clubs ran into difficulty. Team
personnel was depleted, so many outfits disbanded or had to rely on
youngsters to fill the gaps. Fewer games were played. Attendance at
Knickerbocker games was poor, and sometimes they could not get
enough men to play. In a game with the Excelsiors they had to borrow
two men from their opponents to make up a team. In New England,
enthusiasm for the game cooled off considerably.

As for Northern prisoners bringing the game South, it is true, of
course, that they played in the prison camps. But baseball was nothing
new in the South. Southerners were acquainted with it and played it
much before a Yankee soldier ever set foot below the Mason-Dixon
line. New Orleans had long been a baseball center, where numerous
teams engaged in hot rivalry for the local championship before large
crowds. As one might expect, Southern ball games were played in a
distinctly aristocratic setting. A report on one game in 1859 told of
"commodious tents for the ladies spread under the umbrageous
branches of the fine old live oaks," where refreshments were served by
the "polite stewards of the clubs." Going back much earlier, we know
that students at Moses Waddel's famous school in South Carolina found
relaxation from the stern classical curriculum by playing town ball.

* Sources vary and sometimes contradict themselves as to the number of clubs
attending amateur conventions. Figures used are those which seemed the best
choices.

Before the war Southerners were subscribing to the New York *Clipper*, which featured baseball news, and were writing letters to the editor about the game. And when the war started, the *Clipper* boasted that even though South Carolina had seceded, its readers had no intention of giving up their subscriptions. Red-hot fans were certainly not limited to the northeastern section of the country.

Baseball was played by Confederate soldiers as well as Union men during the Civil War. Whenever leisure and weather permitted, the common soldier of the Confederate Army seized the opportunity to play ball. Captain James Hall of the 24th Alabama revealed that his men played baseball "just like schoolboys" at Dalton, Georgia, while waiting to see what Sherman was going to do. Bell I. Wiley tells us in *The Life of Johnny Reb* that the same could be said of almost any other regiment of the Southern army. The game might be the modern version with four bases, or just two-base town ball. The bat might be a board, a section of some farmer's rail fence, or a slightly trimmed hickory limb. They might have nothing better for a ball than a walnut wrapped with yarn. But still their enthusiasm made up for everything, and the camps reverberated with the cheers and taunts of both players and spectators.

In the Union Army the regiments from New York were naturally the most active ball players, because they came from the game's capital. One company would play another, or if particularly confident of its skill, would challenge a picked team from the rest of the regiment. To make it more interesting, the squads often played for a small side bet. In 1861 the 71st New York Guards, later decimated at Bull Run, played the Washington Nationals behind the White House, and on the way home from Appomattox, the 133rd New York Volunteers also took time out to play the Washingtons. The New-York Historical Society has a beautiful lithograph drawn "from nature" by Acting Major Otto Boetticher in 1862, showing Union prisoners playing ball at Salisbury, North Carolina. But ball playing in the army was certainly not new. Even in the Mexican War soldiers enjoyed it, and, as mentioned previously, the first ball game recorded in America was played at Valley Forge during the Revolution.

Baseball really came into its own in the decades following the Civil War. With peace restored, it continued to advance in growth and popularity, but at a greatly accelerated pace. It became the foremost pastime in America, and was universally regarded as the National Game. Record attendance and a tenfold multiplication of clubs made the season of 1866 the most successful yet, and the New York *Clipper* announced that "nearly every trade and occupation has its votaries in the game of base ball." Each succeeding season was better than the one before. In 1868 around 200,000 people saw the leading games, with some games drawing up to 10,000 in the big cities. The New York *Times* estimated that there were over 1000 clubs active in 1869. It was claimed that 40,000 people poured out to see the Brooklyn Atlantics play the Philadelphia Athletics in 1866. Business houses closed; bosses and clerks bet on the game; men, women, and children rushed to the scene, crowding windows, housetops, and trees. Unfortunately, they swarmed over the playing field as well, forcing the clubs to call the game.

People "had baseball on the brain to an extent hitherto unequaled." All classes were succumbing to the baseball "furore," as it was called, and young men from the masses were taking up the game—fellows like Albert G. Spalding and Albert J. Reach, soon to be baseball leaders. But baseball's democratic trend did not include the Negro. It is generally known that professional baseball had an unwritten rule against colored players for many decades. What has not been revealed before this is that as far back as 1867 there was a written ban against them. The faded official records of the National Association's 1867 convention prove that Negro players and clubs were barred from membership. Here is the verbatim report of the Association's Nominating Committee:

> It is not presumed by your Committee that any club who have applied are composed of persons of color, or any portion of them; and the recommendations of your Committee in this report are based upon this view, and they unanimously report against the admission of any club which may be composed of one or more colored persons.

The reason given for this discrimination was an ingenius bit of casuistry and evasion:

> If colored clubs were admitted there would be in all probability some division of feeling, whereas, by excluding them no injury could result to anybody, and the possibility of any rupture being created on political grounds would be avoided.

Although New York continued to boast the strongest teams, its relative importance decreased. Philadelphia had five times as many clubs. The mania spread "from the icy climate of Canada to the sunny fields of Louisiana." Nearly eighty different teams played in Buffalo in the late 1860's. Midwestern teams were organized before 1860, of course, but baseball's big expansion there came after the Civil War. Cincinnati's first regular baseball organization was the Live Oak Club, formed immediately after the war. In July 1866 the Cincinnati Baseball Club, complete with constitution and by-laws, was organized by several prominent citizens in the law offices of Tilden, Sherman & Moulton. Baseball enthusiasm in Cincinnati and surrounding areas can be gauged by "The Great Baseball Tournament" of September 1867, in which twenty-four local and outside teams played before "immense" crowds, including many women. That year ball clubs throughout the state formed the Ohio Federation and affiliated with the National Association.

The first regular ball game in St. Louis was played July 9, 1860, and interest in the sport stayed alive during the war. At the end of hostilities baseball took a firm hold. Frequent matches were arranged and accounts of them appeared in the local newspapers. The typical amateur flavor of St. Louis baseball is shown by functions such as the Baltic Club's Second Annual Basket Picnic in July 1866. Midwestern clubs became increasingly important in the baseball world, the river towns of Cincinnati and St. Louis especially.

Farther west in Des Moines, Iowa, there were nine clubs by 1867. The Marshalltown, Iowa, club had a young man in its line-up destined for an important role in professional ball—Adrian C. "Cap" Anson. The Iowa State Base Ball Association was formed the same year. For the rest of the decade Iowa teams continued to multiply, and were important enough to get special railroad rates. In Minnesota, the story is similar. Inter-city competition began in 1865, and within two years practically every village and hamlet had a ball club. Minnesota teams held a convention the same year as Iowa and adopted the playing rules of the National Association. In Leavenworth, Kansas, business and professional men sponsored the first team there, the Frontier Base Ball Club. The Midwest also had its own regional organization, the Northwestern Association of Base Ball Players, formed December 6, 1865, at Briggs House, Chicago, by delegates representing sixteen clubs from Iowa, Missouri, Wisconsin, Illinois, Michigan, Indiana, Ohio, and Minnesota. They drew up a constitution and by-laws patterned after the National Association and sent delegates to its convention in 1866.

In Washington the Nationals managed to survive the war years. During an inter-city tournament in 1865, they took on the Brooklyn Atlantics and the Philadelphia Athletics before some 6000 fans. Government clerks were excused early to attend, and Andrew Johnson himself was on hand—the first president of the United States to see an inter-city match. The Nationals' great tour of the Midwest in 1867 did much to arouse baseball interest. This three-week trip, which made the 1860 junket of the Brooklyn Excelsiors seem Liliputian by comparison, took them to Columbus, Cincinnati, Louisville, Indianapolis, St. Louis, Rockford (Illinois), and Chicago. They beat all comers with the exception of Rockford, which scored an upset behind the pitching of 17-year-old Albert Spalding. All gate receipts were turned down, and the entire expense of the trip, about $3000, was covered by the backers of the club. The Nationals' 53-10 victory over the Cincinnati Reds was significant, because it had much to do with the reorganization of the Reds into America's first outright professional team.

Col. Frank Jones, president of the Nationals, was highly praised for the manner in which he handled the club on the tour. All entertainment by host clubs was refused, except for "a slight lunch" served in the club rooms after the game. Passing up these expensive suppers with their "temptations to dissipation" made the difference between victory and defeat in several games, said sports writer Henry Chadwick, who made the tour with the Nationals.

Others emulated the Excelsiors and the Nationals, and road tours became part of the season for many clubs, like the Unions of Morrisania, who took a week's tour through western New York in July 1867, winding up the trip with a 25-19 win over the noted Niagaras of Buffalo. But the Unions' success—the only "country club" to beat them was Lansingburgh—was attributed to having their own umpire along with them and refusing to permit any other. The Buffalo *Express* recommended that the next time the Unions traveled through the state they "secure the services of an intelligent blind man."

In the Far West baseball activity quickened. The number of clubs in California increased, particularly in the San Francisco area. Progress was handicapped by the distance from the baseball centers of the East, which made representation at National Association conventions impracticable. But a state convention was held in 1866 and by the following year there were about a hundred organized clubs in California. Even in the reconstructing South the game was prospering. By 1870 New Orleans had at least thirty clubs, and baseball was "fast becoming the popular pastime in the southern portion of the country."

The beginnings of a baseball literature also attest to the game's growing prominence. Each year the National Association published its proceedings in a small booklet. In 1860 *Beadle's Dime Base Ball Player,* the first of numerous baseball guides, was published. It sold about 50,000 copies annually and remained the standard book on the game until 1866 when another manual, *The Ball Player's Book of Reference,* was introduced. About 65,000 copies of this were sold in 1867. A more ambitious work devoting extensive space to baseball was C. A. Peverelly's *Book of American Pastimes,* which sold for $2.50.

Leading weeklies gave increasing attention to baseball. Some, like *The Ball Players' Chronicle* and *The Bat and Ball,* were devoted largely to baseball news. Baseball also worked its way into popular songs, like *The Base Ball Fever, The Live Oak Polka, The Base Ball Quadrille, Home Run Quick Step, The Bat and the Ball, Union Base*

Ball Club March, and *Catch It on the Fly.* The last-mentioned was dedicated to the Chicago Excelsiors and the Forest Citys of Rockford. Its chorus went:

> Come jolly comrade, here's the game that's played in open air
> Where clerks and all the indoor men can profit by a share
> 'Twill make the weak man strong again
> 'Twill brighten every eye
> And all who need such exercise should catch it on the "Fly."

Old-timers were already moaning that "somehow or other, they don't play ball nowadays, as they used to some eight or ten years ago," the same nostalgic lament they have been sounding ever since. Any further doubt of the game's standing should be erased by the blessing of the Rev. C. H. Everett in a sermon delivered in 1865. He called baseball a game "whose regulations are calculated to prevent the ill-feelings engendered by other games, and one, moreover, which serves to attract our young men from places of bad repute, and to supply in place thereof the right kind of recreation and exercise." The good preacher, of course, could not have foreseen the brawls that have punctuated the history of professional ball all the way down to the present.

The game's phenomenal growth in the post-war years was reflected in the National Association, whose membership skyrocketed from a relatively few clubs within a twenty-five-mile radius of New York City to hundreds all over the nation. Ninety-one clubs were represented at the 1865 convention—nearly double the highest pre-war figure. Attendance records were shattered again in 1866 when the membership swelled to a grand total of 202 clubs from seventeen different states and the District of Columbia. Delegates came from all sections of the nation, from Maine to Oregon, and from Vermont to Missouri and Tennessee. New York state topped the representation with seventy-three clubs, Pennsylvania was second with forty-eight, and New Jersey third with twenty-six.

The following year there were so many delegates that the convention was held in the Chestnut Street Theatre in Philadelphia. More than seventy individual clubs and eight state associations answered the roll call. In fact, conventions were getting so unwieldly that the Association amended the constitution, limiting representation to state associations only, except in states with fewer than ten teams, the minimum required to form a state organization. The treasury balance reached $1,021.76 in 1867, and the confidence of the Association was displayed by Arthur P. Gorman, crack player from Maryland and later United States Senator, who called for a sinking fund to be used for spreading baseball abroad.

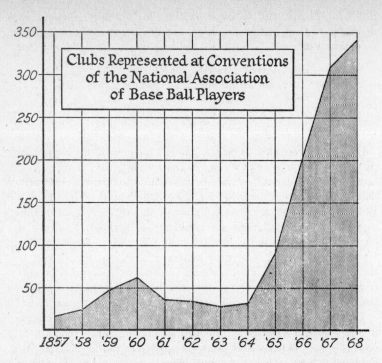

Clubs Represented at Conventions
of the National Association
of Base Ball Players

Dr. J. B. Jones, chairman of the Committee on Rules and Regulations, issued a highly embellished report crediting the Association with bringing health and strength to the sickly and weak. The ball clubs, he wrote, brought into the open air "thousands upon thousands of the sedentary from their death-dealing cloisters, with their pale, wan countenances, emaciated forms, tottering steps, and listless eyes." In addition, Jones claimed that "under the fostering care of the N.A.B.B.P., the seeds sown fructified and brought forth fruit in the home of friends and participants far beyond the expectations of the most sanguine." Translating all this into plain language and discounting the good doctor's grandiloquent phrases, the evidence plainly shows the remarkable stature which baseball had so quickly achieved.

5

THE TWILIGHT ERA

THE VERY SUCCESS of the amateur Association contained the ingredients of its downfall. Baseball was now accessible to the masses. The common people were playing and watching it. When that happened, baseball was bound to change. A game can remain amateur only as long as a privileged minority plays it as an aristocratic diversion. Once those who must also earn a living devote themselves to a game, it ceases to be just a pleasurable pastime, and becomes instead a serious affair.

When players begin considering a game as a livelihood, they have to practice long and hard to succeed, subordinating fun to victory. These few perform while the many watch. As spectators gravitate toward the professionals, their demand for the best players and teams helps to intensify competition. Smart individuals seize the chance to make a dollar from the situation. Promoters convert the game into an amusement business and others attach themselves, legitimately or otherwise, establishing auxiliary enterprises ranging from sporting goods to gambling. The inevitable result of the entire process is professionalism and the sacrifice of true sport.

Baseball was passing through this twilight stage from amateurism to professionalism under the very nose of the amateur Association. Anxious to have topnotch teams, communities were soon searching for the best players they could get. Local players were no longer good enough. Businessmen and team backers began offering various inducements to superior players wherever they could find them. There were complaints that imported players hurt the morale of local performers, and that hand-picked "ringers" were not as good as the home town boys playing together regularly. These protests went unheeded.

Evasion of the Association rule against paying players began at least as early as 1860, when the Brooklyn Excelsiors reputedly paid Jim Creighton under the table, thus making him the first known professional—not Al Reach, of the Brooklyn Eckfords and Philadelphia Athletics in the early 1860's, who is usually said to be the first paid player. The practice was dragged into the open in 1866. The Philadelphia Athletics were accused of paying twenty dollars a week to three players, Pike, Dockney, and McBride. When neither the complainant nor defendants appeared for the Judiciary Committee's hearing, the case was deferred and never reopened. Reach, the star of the club, was undoubtedly getting paid, too, but for some reason he was never indicted.

After the Civil War, so-called gifts were offered to lure players. Some outstanding players were provided with jobs and paid salaries ostensibly for their work but in reality for ball playing—bringing to mind present-day college hypocrisy in providing leaf-raking jobs and "scholarships" for football prospects. In those days businessmen interested in baseball and quick to appreciate the publicity value of a good team were often glad to find openings for ball players. When Al Spalding began to attract attention as a young pitcher for the Forest Citys of Rockford, he was offered forty dollars a week to clerk in a Chicago grocery. He admitted he knew nothing about groceries, but that did not matter, because his real job was to pitch for the Chicago Excelsiors.

Another player who undoubtedly was given an inducement on the side was George Wright, the great shortstop who later was chosen for the Hall of Fame. He would hardly have left the New York Gothams to play with the Washington Nationals in 1867 without a strong inducement, and it is interesting to note that the roster of the club that year gave the government office in which the other players were employed, but George was simply listed as a clerk at 238 Pennsylvania Avenue—which was nothing but a public park!

Amateurism was further breached when prominent New York and Brooklyn clubs began playing for a share of the "gate money" in 1864 at the old Union and Capitoline Grounds, Brooklyn, where admission was generally ten cents. This practice grew out of the experiment of the enterprising William H. Cammeyer. In 1862 he invested considerable capital to enclose the field, grade the diamond, and construct a clubhouse. Then he began charging admission to games.

That early enclosed park was primitive indeed compared with our modern stadia, or even the ball parks of a couple of decades later, but in those days it was considered an "ornament" to Brooklyn. The nearest thing to a grandstand was a long wooden shed, supplied with benches for the ladies. Additional benches interspersed about the grounds made it possible to seat about 1500 people. Others had to watch from the sidelines, and on days of big crowds police were on hand to keep order. In one corner of the field there was a "commodious" clubhouse large enough for three teams. There were also several other buildings, one a saloon, the others probably used for collecting admissions and storing equipment. The field itself was rolled perfectly level and was well drained. A fence six or seven feet high enclosed the entire grounds. The area covered at least six acres, which meant that outfielders had plenty of room to pull down long drives, since on a field of that size the fences were probably about 500 feet away! The park was dressed up with a number of flag poles, where the American flag and the banners of the clubs using the field were flown. One difficulty was that an embankment outside made it possible for freeloaders on foot or in carriages to look over the fence and see the game without paying. When the grounds were opened on May 15, 1862, a band was on hand to celebrate the event. It began patriotically with *The Star Spangled Banner*, and marked the first time there was music at a ball game.

The famous Brooklyn Atlantics, who had been playing on an open field at the corner of Marcy and Gates Avenues, succeeded in getting permission to play on Cammeyer's enclosed field. As the gate receipts grew, the Atlantics soon demanded a share. At first Cammeyer refused, arguing that he had assumed all the risk and had also furnished a fine field and clubhouse free of charge. However, he was soon persuaded to change his mind.

Before long, games were played primarily for gate receipts. The clubs insisted that charging admission was not professionalism but merely collecting a fair dividend on their investment. The "enclosure movement," as it was called, was also praised for providing a clear field and more order and decorum at games.

Knickerbocker purists clung valiantly to the earlier code. Once the Yale Base Ball Club offered them a $50 guarantee and one-third of the gate if it exceeded fifty dollars. When the Knickerbockers protested, the Yale secretary wrote, "Of course we will not charge gate money if you object." But even the pioneer club eventually compromised to the extent of playing in contests for which admission was charged, although they refused to accept a share. As a result they lost one of their oldest members, James Whyte Davis, who had been with them for twenty-four years. In his letter of resignation from "the dear old Club," Davis said he felt it was mistaken in lending its "good name" to the practice of charging admission, and had "desecrated its time honored principles of playing Base Ball for health and recreation merely."

This was just one small voice, though. People were showing themselves willing to pay to see a ball game—a habit from which they never recovered. In 1868 the seven or eight most prominent clubs shared as much as $100,000 in gate receipts. The Mutuals alone were reputed to have $15,000 in their treasury. A contemporary observer was sharp enough to realize the effect of introducing the cash nexus into baseball:

> From a simple pastime it has become a systematic business with hundreds of persons who, either as players or directors of nines, derive their entire revenue during the summer months from the profits of the games played by their respective clubs.

Newspapers encouraged rivalry and emphasis on victory by offering prizes such as silver or gold balls, usually to the club making the best showing in games for the championship. The New York *Clipper* prize was probably the best known of these. Upstate, a gold baseball won by the Buffalo team in 1860 was displayed in the window of Blodgett's Music Store on Main Street. Or an individual club might put up a prize. The Continentals planned a handsome silver ball inscribed with baseball scenes to be awarded the best club in the amateur association during the season of 1862, but most of their members went to war, so they gave it as a prize for the winner of a series between the Eckfords and Atlantics, with proceeds to go to the U.S. Sanitary Commission to help sick and wounded soldiers.

Teams used to practice once or twice a week and play only occasional match games. Now, in their eagerness for victory and gate receipts, they spent more time practicing and played more games. All this made it difficult for those who wanted to play ball and yet had to earn a living. The increase in team tours compounded their problems. Either they neglected their jobs or gave up playing. Some suffered pay cuts because of their craving for baseball. Even the "cranks"—now called fans—resorted to various subterfuges to escape from their jobs to the ball yard.

Soon there were complaints that too many were slighting everything of importance in life for baseball. Young men sacrificed business interests "to worship at the shrine of baseball vanity—not for exercise, but for the plaudits of the crowd." In a letter to the Brooklyn *Eagle*, baseball was attacked as a "curse," which caused "strong, muscular, lazy boys, whose sole ambition is to be good ball players" to lose their jobs, and permitted men who should have been working to play ball. A popular song of 1857, *The Base Ball Fever*, picked up this theme:

> Our Merchants have to close their stores
> Their clerks away are staying,
> Contractors too, can do no work,
> Their hands are all out playing.

Employers began asking job applicants not their draft status, as they did during World War II, but whether they were members of a ball team. An affirmative answer was fatal to the applicant unless the employer also happened to be a baseball crank. Some employers fired every clerk who was a member of a ball club. *The American Chronicle* criticized such extreme measures, asserting that playing baseball was better than drinking or gambling. Give an employee an afternoon to play ball, the paper advised, and he would probably be at his desk earlier doing double work. Another newspaper suggested that it was less costly for employers to allow a clerk a few hours a week for ball playing than "to drive him into the night dissipations which young men are tempted to indulge in when deprived of afternoon opportunities for relaxation."

Thus baseball entered a twilight zone between amateurism and professionalism, a semi-professional period in which hypocrisy reigned. Competition and the dollar created new difficulties and introduced a number of evils. Clubs figured out ways to use ineligible players and pay amateurs in violation of Association rules: they arranged so-called social games—unofficial matches which were not sanctioned by the Association and did not count in their championship records. Once this camouflage failed. In a game between the Atlantics and Athletics at the Capitoline Grounds before 15,000 people July 5, 1869, the Athletics brought in John Radcliffe, known to be a paid infielder for the Keystone Club. To get around the predicament of having a professional in the lineup, the clubs announced just before game time that the game was to be merely a "social one." Many spectators were disappointed and disgusted at being hoodwinked into paying to see a game that would not count for the championship, and they retaliated by staying away the next time these two clubs met.

Bidding for players led to another evil called "revolving." Players made agreements with clubs and even accepted compensation in advance, only to move elsewhere in response to a better offer. These drifters were called "rounders" or "revolvers." Revolving had occurred occasionally even in the days of purer amateurism. In 1856 the Unions of Morrisania and the Knickerbockers objected to the Gothams' using a Mr. Pinckney in a game while he was still a member of the Unions. Another case was that of a Mr. Hudson, who was accused of playing for the Metropolitans only a few days after appearing with the Young America team. It was episodes like these that caused the Association to adopt the regulation that a player had to be a member of a club for thirty days before he could play on the team.

The rule was ineffectual, though, and revolving spread. A flagrant example was William Fischer. He agreed to play for the Philadelphia

Athletics, who gave him a suit of clothes, paid his board bill, got him a job, and advanced him $115. A few days later he left to sign with the Chicago Club. Another revolver was Thomas Berry, whom the Keystones charged with leaving them for no reason to join the Athletics in violation of the "amenities of honor and confidence."

In a pathetic attempt to deal with the problem, clubs sometimes conducted trials of the offenders. One committee investigated the case and brought charges, and another was assigned to defend the accused. Cincinnati went through the whole rigmarole, charging John Hatfield with "Dishonesty and Ungentlemanly Conduct" in forsaking them to go with the Mutuals. They then published the entire proceedings in April 1869 in a pamphlet bearing the pretentious title, "Case of John V. B. Hatfield before the Cincinnati Base Ball Club: Charges, Specifications and Testimony for the Prosecution and Defense." It was all to no avail. Hatfield stayed with the Mutuals.

The Association again tried to halt the practice by extending the probationary period from thirty to sixty days, but without success. Most of the cases brought before its Judiciary Committee were complaints about using men illegally. Revolving was in full tilt by 1869 and continued to be a serious problem for years to come. Although players were denounced for shamelessly hurting "our noble game," they were not entirely at fault. They were simply taking advantage of a good market and seeking out the highest bids for their services in classic laissez-faire fashion. Teams and individuals who dangled the bait before star players were just as responsible for the broken promises and spurned agreements.

An unsavory instance of this was the attempt of the New York Mutuals, controlled by the notorious "Boss" Tweed, president of the club from 1860 through 1871, to entice second baseman Charlie Sweasy from Cincinnati. The Mutuals urged him to break a written contract in exchange for a fat salary. Players on the Mutuals were all well paid, because Tweed saw to it that they were put on the city payroll, especially in the street-cleaning department. According to the *National Chronicle*, Tweedism in baseball cost New York City $30,000 annually.

More serious than revolving was gambling, which began to fasten itself onto baseball, bringing with it dishonesty and corruption. Both spectators and players started wagering on the results of games. *Spirit of the Times* reported that the large crowds at the Elysian Fields in 1857 were attracted by the chance to bet as much as by the game itself and the fame of the players. In an 1857 match between the Gothams and Atlantics, it was said that seven out of ten of the cognoscenti were ready to "plant their tin" on the Gothams at two and three to one. Worse yet, Mr. Morrow, an umpire, allegedly had a bet on a game in which he was officiating.

Gambling on ball games in California had distinctly Western overtones. Just as a fly ball was about to be caught, every gambler who had a bet on the side at bat would fire off his six-shooter to disconcert the fielder and make him muff the ball. By 1860 betting on the big games was commonplace. Gamblers grew bolder. According to the Brooklyn *Union*, they plied their vocation "more vociferously than an auctioneer on the Bowery." The Brooklyn *Eagle* questioned whether public interest would continue when spectators knew that players were participating not out of love for baseball but to decide bets.

The danger of gambling is that it is often a short step to "the fix." Gamblers are no longer satisfied to gamble. They want a sure thing, so they arrange the outcome of the game in advance by bribing the players. Back in the formative days of baseball, fixing or throwing games was called "hippodroming." An early example of it, and the first baseball scandal to come to light, was the game between the Mutuals and Eckfords, September 28, 1865, which the Eckfords won 28 to 11, to the great surprise of the fans. Later it was revealed that players Ed Duffy, William Wansley, and Thomas Devyr conspired to throw the game. This case, celebrated at the time but since forgotten, was investigated by the Judiciary Committee of the National Association. Wansley and Duffy were accused of offering Devyr money to throw the game. These two were both barred from match games, and charges were brought against Devyr. But the Mutual Club, badly in need of a shortstop, reelected him to membership, concocted a plausible case for the Judiciary Committee, and succeeded in having the charges dismissed. Devyr played through the season of 1869 without objection being raised and with no sign of crooked play. But when the Union Club was beaten in a game with the Mutuals it reopened the case. W. J. Herring, spokesman for the Unions, was also chairman of the Judiciary Committee—accuser and judge both. He asserted that the Mutuals had no right to reinstate Devyr. The Committee voted against the Mutuals, but when the controversy was put before the convention at its annual meeting, it voted 451 to 143 to reverse the decision. Emboldened by this victory, the Mutuals restored Duffy to the lineup, too. The club was expelled by the New York State Association in 1869, only to be reinstated later. To complete the fiasco, Wansley, the third guilty one, secured reinstatement from the National Association in 1870.

One team which was notorious for fixing games was the Haymakers of Troy, New York. This outfit was controlled by New York gamblers, including the Honorable John Morrissey, one time congressman and state senator. Morrissey, an Irish immigrant, had a checkered career.

In 1858 he won the heavyweight boxing crown. Later he became proprietor of gambling houses in New York City and in Saratoga, where he also owned controlling interest in the race track. Small wonder Morrissey applied his gambling methods to the Haymaker team, which he "used like loaded dice and marked cards."

Hippodroming teams took turns losing to each other to create the impression of being closely matched, hoping to arouse crowd interest for future contests. The fraud worked for a while, but soon people caught on to it, and attendance suffered. Concrete evidence was seldom available, but the mere suspicion that something was wrong hurt gate receipts.

Perhaps these shady practices should be expected in the era of Grant's administration in Washington, which made the post-Civil War years memorable for widespread public and private moral collapse and scandal. Baseball was reflecting the generally tainted character of the period. Certainly in the case of the New York Mutuals, where Tweed's sinister figure loomed behind the scenes, the connection between baseball and the environment was plain. On the other hand, the theme of corruption should not be overdrawn. Not all the players, nor even a majority of them, were dishonest. After all, wrongdoers make news, and are publicized much more than prosaic, honest performers.

Newspapers and reporters sometimes jumped to conclusions. The Chicago press was so stunned by the victory of the Washington Nationals over the Chicago Excelsiors, champions of the West, that they decided the Nationals must have lost to Rockford—their previous opponents—on purpose, in order to influence the betting on the Chicago game. Colonel Jones and Arthur Pue Gorman, who led the Nationals' expedition, called on the editors in person to protest in the strongest terms, and the next day retractions were printed.

Genuine evils did exist, however, and demands for reform grew more insistent. But the Association was powerless to cope with the situation. Its eligibility rules and its regulations against betting and paying players were increasingly flouted, and in instances where violations were called to its attention the Judiciary Committee was often ineffective in punishing them. Parties summoned before it did not always appear, and when they did the Committee was often hamstrung by technicalities. The Irvingtons of New Jersey, for example, were denied satisfaction in a complaint against the Actives of New York on the legalistic ground that they had neglected to send a copy of the charges to the accused club. Cases which the Judiciary Committee was able to settle were generally of a minor nature. When they did sink their teeth into something important, like the Devyr case, their decisions were nullified.

These difficulties were really manifestations of a more deep-seated problem—the steady advance of professionalism. That was the real issue. Had there been a common core of opinion either for or against professionalism, problems could have been settled and the Association operated more smoothly. But as long as the Association was torn within itself and undecided on this question, no amount of rules or administrative machinery would work.

Some, like the Albany Knickerbockers, went all-out in urging a return to the pure amateurism of former days. They denounced the growing custom of playing for money because it would destroy baseball's enviable reputation as a sport and create unfriendly rivalry between clubs. But soon even the reformers retreated to new positions. They ceased their frontal attacks on professionalism and directed their fire at the hypocrisy of undercover tactics. They even went so far as to concede that professionalism had advantages—if conducted openly and properly. Others proclaimed that the time had arrived when professionalism was essential to the game's progress, and that there was no reason why the Association should not officially recognize a group of professionals. They made this concession in a kind of backhanded way, saying that while the majority of professionals were not men of moral habits or integrity of character—"easily led into evil habits and degrading associations"—there was a decent minority which should be given "an incentive to honorable conduct" and not made to suffer because of the others.

The New England Base Ballist flatly asserted that no laws against professionalism could be enforced by the Association. It favored recognizing professionals, as a way to stop the use of paid ringers in amateur games. It pointed out that many skillful ball players were so attached to the game that they were unfit for everyday occupations, so in order to play ball and at the same time make a living, they were often forced to be dishonest. If professionalism were made legitimate, evils in the hiring system would disappear. What was being done slyly could be done publicly, and anyone who wanted to make baseball his business could do so honestly and openly—"not as corrupt aldermen and assemblymen receive their bribes." Another argument for professionalism was that it would improve the caliber of play. As the New York *Clipper* explained, the professionals had the time to master the game and play it at its best.

In any case, professionalism gained steadily. The Paterson (New Jersey) *Press* observed in 1867 that the baseball "frenzy" was destroying "all regular business habits," and predicted that the time would come "when every member of the first class nines of the country will be a paid professional player, and hundreds of our young men will aim at such a position as one of the most shining pinnacles that fame can boast." Even the Knickerbockers were paying less attention to the social status of new members and more to their ball-playing ability. They stopped bothering to record the occupations of recruits, and required them to show what they could do in a few games before being accepted.

The opening game of 1868 between picked nines from New York and Brooklyn was a trial balloon to gauge public support of professionalism, because it was well known that the majority of players on both sides were pros. Since a thousand people paid a quarter to see the game, the *American Chronicle* announced that for all practical purposes there were now two distinct classes of players. That winter the Association at last recognized the facts of baseball life. At its annual meeting in 1868 at Washington, President Sands admitted that professional baseball had been "gradually gaining strength and influence" to the point where it seemed necessary for the Association to recognize and govern it. The Committee on Rules then reviewed the Association's futile efforts to liquidate professionalism and concluded that the rule against paying players was a "dead letter." It recommended in its report that the baseball "fraternity" should be organized into "two distinct classes of players." This was done.

Professionalism took another giant step forward in 1869 with the formation of the first admittedly all-professional club in America, the Cincinnati Red Stockings. Stung by the beating the Red Stockings took from the Washington Nationals on their tour in 1867, baseball-minded Cincinnatians were determined to have a winning team, even if it meant paying the players. There was good precedent for doing so, because the Reds had four paid men in the 1868 lineup, and even before that they were charging ten cents for home games and twenty-five cents for "foreign," as road games were called then. Now they turned to Harry Wright to put together an all-professional combination.

Wright had come to Cincinnati as player and instructor for the Union Cricket Club in August 1865 at a salary of $1200. He held this job until hired in November 1867 to play on the baseball club at the same salary. Ignoring local amateurs, Wright went far afield to put together a first-class team. The only local man on the ten-man squad was Charles Gould, the first baseman. The total payroll for the season of 1869, which in those days lasted from March 15 to November 15, was $9300 (less than one-seventieth of the modern New York Yankees' payroll), divided as follows:

Harry Wright (jeweler)	center field	$1200
George Wright (engraver)	shortstop	1400
Asa Brainard (insurance)	pitcher	1100

Fred Waterman (insurance)	third base	$1000
Charles Sweasy (hatter)	second base	800
Charles H. Gould (bookkeeper)	first base	800
Douglas Allison (marble cutter)	catcher	800
Andrew J. Leonard (hatter)	left field	800
Calvin A. McVey (piano maker)	right field	800
Richard Hurley (trade not known)	substitute	600

The team also carried three additional substitutes, Fowler, Bradford, and Taylor, who saw some service in games but about whom nothing else is known.

With Harry Wright and his brother George as the nucleus, this fine ball club won games with ridiculous ease, showing conclusively the superiority of a professional team over amateurs. In 1869, the Reds took on all comers and finished the season without defeat, winning 56 and tying one *—a record unmatched by any other club except the Brooklyn Eckfords, who were undefeated in 1863 although they did not play as many games. The tie was with the Troy Haymakers, who walked off the field in the sixth inning on a pretext so that John Morrissey and other New York gamblers, who had bet heavily on them, could avoid paying off. The Reds traveled throughout the East, and then went all the way to the West Coast, playing before an estimated 200,000 people altogether.

The financial condition of the Cincinnati Club on the eve of their tour is not clear. One newspaper claimed that the club was backed by some of Cincinnati's wealthiest citizens. Another story has it that they set out on their eastern swing in such precarious financial straits that a rabid fan, Will Noble, donated his wife's $300 savings to see them through. According to this version, the gate receipts were barely enough to get the team from one town to the next, until they met the Mutuals, Atlantics, and Athletics. Harry Millar, baseball writer, accompanied the team on the trip and telegraphed results of each game to the Cincinnati *Commercial-Gazette*. The following season, 1870, the Red Stockings continued their string of victories until stopped, 8 to 7, by the Brooklyn Atlantics, in a dramatic 11-inning game. Nine thousand people paid fifty cents each to see this thriller, and Atlantic players received $364 apiece.

After completing one of their triumphant eastern tours, the Red Stockings arrived home in Cincinnati 24 hours before expected, so no formal reception had been arranged in time. Nevertheless, small boys began to gather at the railroad depot and soon "dignified citizens and solid businessmen mingled with the throng." On their arrival the play-

* There is some disagreement on the number of victories. More recently, however, Darryl Brock, in careful research, credits the team with winning 60 games without a loss.

ers rode to the Gibson House through streets filled with cheering people. The officers of the ball club were determined that their heroes should have at least an informal supper, "unfatiguing but sufficient to show that their coming had been anticipated." After the affair, each member of the team received a bouquet of flowers and a small square of blue silk with his name and position neatly printed on it in gold. The *Gazette* called the event "one of the most elegant ever seen in Cincinnati," and the club president, Aaron B. Champion, declared that he would rather be president of the Cincinnati Base Ball Club than President of the United States.

THE COMING OF THE PROFESSIONALS

CINCINNATI'S sensational success as a professional club in 1869 was not lost on other cities, which quickly took steps to follow them. Envious of the fame the Red Stockings had brought Cincinnati, Chicago enthusiasts subscribed $20,000 for a professional club of their own, and advertised for players in newspapers and leading sports journals. Ironically, the Cincinnati Club, leaders of the professional parade, collapsed after the 1870 season. The defeat by the Atlantics and later losses melted enthusiasm and shrank gate receipts. A circular issued by club directors announced that the "enormous" player salaries could no longer be met. Years later, one of the directors revealed that the announcement was a bluff to beat down salaries. If so, it did not work, because the players "jumped" to other teams willing to pay them. The Wright brothers, with Charlie Gould and Cal McVey, went to Boston, where they were instrumental in bringing four championships in a row.

The professionals gained steadily in the National Association, and the amateurs correspondingly lost influence. By 1869 the pros were in virtual control of the convention and were bitterly attacked by last-ditch amateur supporters for "adopting the unscrupulous tactics of the New York politicians." They were also accused of "skulduggery" in reinstating Devyr, Wansley, and Duffy of the Mutuals merely because their team needed them. At the 1870 convention about twenty pro clubs were able to dominate the hundreds of amateurs, who gave way under the pressure and adjourned *sine die.*

The following March, ten pro clubs met at 840 Broadway and formed the National Association of Professional Base Ball Players, electing James N. Kerns, United States Marshal and representative of the Philadelphia Athletics, their first president. Charter members of this first organized league were the Philadelphia Athletics, Washington Olympics, Washington Nationals, New York Mutuals, the Unions of

Troy, Boston Red Stockings, Forest Citys of Rockford, Forest Citys of Cleveland, Chicago White Stockings, and the Kekiongas of Fort Wayne, who dropped out in mid-season and were replaced by the Brooklyn Eckfords. The Professional Association did not draw up a constitution at once. Instead, it adopted that of the amateur association insofar as it did not conflict with professionalism. It is important to mark that this association was still one of ball players, not of clubs. The central position of the ball player was accented by the fact that James Ferguson, a former third baseman of the Brooklyn Atlantics, served as president for two of the Association's five years.

The professionals arranged for match tours of various member clubs with each other, and they introduced new regulations governing the championship. Under the amateurs, the title "Champions of the United States" was nominal only, but the pros established a genuine pennant race among their clubs, any of whom could compete by applying to a championship committee and paying a ten dollar fee. Each championship series was to be the best three out of five games played by every club against every other club. The one winning the greatest number of games during the season would be declared champions by a three-man committee appointed by the chairman of the convention. In case of a tie, the club with the best percentage of games won was to be awarded the flag.

No formal season schedule was drawn up by the Professional Association itself. Clubs entering for the championship made their own arrangements. Eastern teams generally made two Western trips, and the Western clubs usually came east twice. However, some clubs made only one trip to the other section, and some did not go at all. Most of the games were between clubs of the same section. Therefore, the greatest activity took place in the East, where the majority of the clubs were located. The Professional Association was saddled with too many clubs widely scattered and unequal in strength. Many of them were unable to stand the expense of traveling to play even the championship series, which they arranged rather haphazardly among themselves. In any event, the Association was racked by a heavy turnover of clubs. Of the twenty-five or more different teams which at one time or another were members, only three—the Philadelphia Athletics, Boston Red Stockings, and New York Mutuals—competed every year. A fourth charter member, the Chicago White Stockings, missed the seasons of 1872 and 1873 because of the great fire. Eleven teams survived only one season. The first championship was won by the Athletics, but thereafter Boston took four straight.

The imprint of professionalism quickly showed itself on the game. Its premium on winning changed the entire ethic of baseball from one of sport to one of victory by any possible method. It sanctioned if not outright violations of the rules at least taking all one could get within them. Ingenuity, trickery, and all kinds of tactics hitherto considered unsportsmanlike were not only accepted but acclaimed in the new passion for victory. Baseball once more reflected America in that it was results that counted, not how hard you tried or how sportingly you behaved. Hard-driving, aggressive play became the order of the day and stayed a part of baseball. As Ross Youngs, outfielder of the 1920's, said when he smashed into Babe Pinelli with a hard slide, "We're not playing for marbles." Some may abhor such an ethic, but there is much to be said for vigorous competition and emphasis on winning. In any case, professionalism was infusing this spirit into baseball.

The influence of professionalism was demonstrated in numerous other ways. Many of the changes had the effect of attracting more paying customers because they helped to develop baseball into a faster, more exciting show—a development which was to continue through decades of experimental changes. Football and basketball were to go through the same process later on. They, too, were "souped up" to make them better spectacles. For one thing, the stiff competition injected into baseball by professionalism brought better playing. Only the best players could make the grade in the first place, and those who did were becoming specialists in one position and at the same time were learning to work together more smoothly. Players were being classified as infielders, outfielders, or batterymen, and assigned regular or "home" positions, and team leaders were advised to select their men for their special skill. How-to books on baseball, giving the "points" (fine points) of playing each position, began to appear. Players were gaining reputations as experts in particular positions. But they were not called stars in those days. They were known as "artists."

Anyone who searches through the old records and pieces together information on how the game was played in the 'sixties and early 'seventies is bound to be impressed with how much was already known about the fundamentals of the game, playing the various positions, and "inside baseball." He will find that there is a lot less new in baseball than is often thought. Much that we generally consider modern was old hat to the early pros. Research into the old records also punctures many a cherished myth. One of the most tenacious of these is the belief that Charles A. Comiskey, when he was manager and first baseman for the St. Louis Browns during the 1880's, revolutionized first-base play by playing back and away from the base instead of anchoring himself to it, as all supposedly had done before him. This story has been repeated so many times that it has long since become baseball gospel. But the truth of the matter is that this method of play was familiar and commonly used back in the 1860's, at least twenty years before Comiskey is supposed to have introduced it. First basemen not only played back and away from the base, as they do now, but with a runner on base they knew enough to move in and cover the bag, ready to take a throw from the pitcher. It was also understood that, other things being equal, it was advantageous to have a left-hander at first base—since it was easier for him to throw to the other infielders, because he would not have to pivot to make his throw—and two of the leading "artists" at the position, Joe Start of the Atlantics and Al Reach of the Athletics, were left-handed players.

The endless see-saw battle for the advantage between batter and pitcher had already begun. The batter could no longer wait as long as he felt like it for the pitch he wanted, because to speed up the game the umpire was now authorized to call strikes. In those days batters stood erect on a three-foot line and swung without moving their feet. Nevertheless, the 'sixties was an era of free hitting and large scores. Critics blamed this on an "over-elastic" ball, and so the strangely familiar cry that the ball was too lively and should be deadened was already heard, ushering in one of the oldest and most recurrent controversies in baseball. Recognizing the situation, the New York *Clipper* pointed out that no matter how good a team was in the field, unless it excelled in batting it was sure to come off second-best against hard-hitting opponents.

The expression "long ball," which seems so modern to us, was already being used to describe long outfield drives. Outfielders had improved so much that they were expected to pull down these long, high flies, so batters were advised to concentrate on hitting line drives or ground balls. On the other hand, pitchers were accumulating a good-sized bag of tricks to foil the hitters. Jim Creighton and others were soon cheating on the pitching rule, which required that the ball be delivered with a stiff-armed, underhand motion. Creighton inaugurated speed pitching by adding an almost imperceptible wrist snap and arm bend to his delivery. To the unhappy batters of the time his pitches were "swift as they could be sent from a cannon" and "most difficult to strike." Others imitated Creighton's ill-disguised violation, and umpires, like good policemen, chose not to see everything. Newspaper accounts criticized their laxity, but the practice continued.

Although Creighton could intimidate "country hitters," he soon found out, like countless others who came after him, that he could not get by on speed alone against experienced hitters, so he learned to "drop the pace"—or, in modern baseball language, to use a "change of pace"—that is, mix up fast and slow pitches to disrupt the batter's timing. Of all pitching devices this is still one of the most effective.

Among the "dodgy" (crafty) pitchers Harry Wright was considered tops. Harry "threw his head up to the plate," as the saying now goes to describe pitchers who depend upon brains and artistry rather than brawn and speed. His "dew drops" (slow pitches) were a "mystery" to the best batters. One of the most devastating pitches developed in this period was the curve ball. Its inventor may never be known for sure. Arthur "Candy" Cummings, who claimed he got the idea from watching clam shells in flight and then experimenting with a baseball, is traditionally credited, and there is a bust of him in the Cooperstown Hall of Fame and a monument to him in Greenwood Cemetery, Brooklyn. However, in 1898 Fred Goldsmith, an early pitcher, said that Charles Avery, a Yale player and later a Yale professor, invented the curve. But then in 1937 Goldsmith told a veteran sports writer that he himself was the discoverer. He backed up his claim with an 1870 clipping in which Henry Chadwick told of seeing him demonstrate the pitch, and the sports writer accepted this evidence as proof of Goldsmith's priority.

The trouble with this claim, however, was that Chadwick told a different story in 1898. At that time he said that he saw Cummings throw the curve in 1866, "long before Goldsmith was known in the base ball world." Chadwick added that a Rochester pitcher, whose name he could not remember, was using the pitch as early as the 1850's. Whatever the truth of its origin, the curve has plagued batters ever since it first broke across a home plate. Skeptics who probably never tried hitting one have questioned whether a ball can be curved. An experiment made in Cincinnati in 1877 supposedly proved it could be, but the issue has cropped up from time to time ever since. Only a few years ago *Life Magazine* had an illustrated piece showing that a curve ball really does curve, but in a gentle arc, not with a sharp break, and just recently the National Bureau of Standards of the United States Government conducted scientific experiments which proved that a ball could be curved.

It was believed that the pitcher should be the "smartest" man on the team, and that he should be a good fielder. In case of injury and for purposes of strategy, clubs were advised to have two pitchers, preferably with different styles of delivery. Except for one season when a tenth man was tried—a kind of roving shortstop who could be stationed almost anywhere—teams had to get along with the nine men who started the game, because no substitutions were permitted unless someone was obviously injured or ill. So if the starting pitcher was hit hard and had to be relieved, he merely swapped positions with the "change pitcher," who was often one of the outfielders or the shortstop. Managers were advised to keep the faster of the two pitchers in reserve, because it was thought better to change from a slow to a fast pitcher rather than the other way around.

Catching was an even tougher job then than it is now, especially when the catcher had to move up close to the batter to be in better position to throw out runners trying to steal. At first the only protection catchers had was a rubber mouthpiece, but in the 1870's the mask, introduced by Fred Thayer, Harvard captain, came into use. When this new contraption appeared, it was variously referred to as a "muzzle," "rat-trap," or "bird-cage," and one wag remarked, "We shall probably soon behold the spectacle of a player sculling around the bases with stove-funnels on his legs and boiler-iron riveted across his stomach."

Catching was so dangerous that one fan, doubtless more tender-hearted than most in those days, proposed a novel idea for eliminating the catcher's need to move up close behind the batter, a practice he thought "barbarous." He suggested that the catcher stay back and take the pitch on the bounce, and that to offset the advantage this would give the base runner, a system of intermediary bases be used, which the runner would have to go out of his way to touch when he tried to steal. The trend toward specialization was also revealed by the growing custom of teams' carrying a reserve catcher, preferably one who knew the style of the change pitcher.

Already infielders were expected to have strong, accurate throwing arms, and to be "plucky" enough to handle hard-hit balls. It was thought that the third baseman should have the most powerful arm and be the most courageous of the infielders—interesting proof that third base was already recognized as the "hot corner," where "either you do or you don't." It was also understood that the quickest, most agile man should be the shortstop. Fortunately, infielders were getting some help from the skin-tight gloves with the fingertips cut off. This type of glove was reputedly first worn in 1875 by Charles C. Waitt while playing first base for St. Louis, and then gradually players like Al Spalding began to add padding for further protection.

Requirements for outfielders were remarkably modern. Managers looked for fast men who were good judges of fly balls, and good throwers. Even then, professional outfielders knew how to relay throws on long hits, how to move in on ground balls and throw the ball back to the infield quickly. They also knew something about "playing the hitters," that is, shifting their position in accordance with where the batters were most likely to drive the ball.

As for base running, sliding was becoming more common, but, to avoid being tagged, it was thought best to run around the waiting fielder, bend, and touch the base from the rear. Runners knew how to "tag up"—that is, return to the base when the batter hit a fly ball—and then advance after the catch. Base runners were being taught to "take ground" (take a lead off the base), and runners on third were advised to dash about twenty-five feet toward home on every pitch, making it easy for them to "steal in" if the catcher missed the pitch. The method used for tagging runners caught between the bases was being perfected: two fielders ran the trapped runner back and forth between the bases, while two others covered each base in case the runner got by the two fielders who had him in the run-down.

The game was being improved in other ways besides allowing the umpire to call strikes and introducing rudimentary equipment. Replacing the earlier long-trouser uniforms with more functional short, knicker-style pants was also symbolic of the changing mode of the game. Another important innovation should be mentioned—the adoption in 1864 of the fly game—that is, the requirement that for an out, batted balls must be caught on the fly. The reader will remember that, prior to this, outs could be made by catching batted balls on one bounce. Back in 1857 the Knickerbockers had unsuccessfully proposed adoption of the fly game. Some opposed it because they feared injury to their unprotected hands, others merely because it was the English method in cricket. Replying to these objections, a sporting paper boasted, "Surely, what an Englishman can do, an American is as capable of improving upon." For a time, teams played either way, depending on prior agreement. So it took years of debate before the question was settled, but once it was, the less exacting "bound" game was relegated mostly to the "muffins"—the name then used for unskilled or inept players.

As winning became all-important, keen-witted players figured out trick plays and ways of circumventing the rules. Indeed, it is not an exaggeration to say that the baseball rule book is in large measure a product of efforts to counteract these sharp practices. Batters and fielders were becoming more astute and resourceful. Scruples of an earlier day were cast aside. Dicky Pierce, star shortstop of the Atlantics, learned to baffle the defense by artfully tapping or "bunting" the ball gently in front of home plate and scampering to first base before bewildered opponents recovered from their surprise. Fielders dropped fly balls intentionally with runners on base in order to convert an easy out into a double play, eventually necessitating the adoption of the well-known but seldom understood infield fly rule.* The process of changing the rules to keep up with deception has never ended. Only recently the rule book had to be changed to stop the practice of base

* See below, Chapter 23.

runners' letting themselves get hit intentionally by batted balls to prevent a double play from being made.

There was no systematic method for securing players. Highly organized scouting staffs "combing the bushes" for prospects—scouting sandlot and school games—were still far in the future. But it is interesting that the rudiments of the farm system, later perfected by Branch Rickey, were already in evidence by 1867, when the Brooklyn Excelsiors admitted twenty or thirty youngsters, ages fifteen to twenty, gave them regular uniforms, and trained them to replace members of the first nine. Junior clubs were organized even before this and regularly played each other. They even had a National Association of their own, which met annually. But the Excelsior Juniors were sponsored by the parent club and enjoyed a closer relationship to it.

The simplest way for the professionals to get players was to grab the best amateurs. Negotiations and hiring players were done mostly by letter. A man who wanted to play on one of the pro clubs wrote giving his experience and record and requesting a tryout. Such an application by Thomas Mullen McGirr to the Buffalo Club is one of many such letters that could be quoted, grammatical errors and all:

> I write this few lines to you to see if you are in need of any Player at the Present time for if you are i would like if you would give me a chance i have bin Playing for this last two or three years in this City [Philadelphia] i can Play any Place in the feild or Catcher and if you are in need of a Player Please let me know as i would like very much to come to Buffalo to Play. . . .

Sometimes friends of the club or newspaper reporters recommended likely prospects. For example, Alfred H. Wright, reporter for the Philadelphia *Sunday Mercury,* wrote H. S. Sprague, secretary of the Buffalo Club, recommending Dave Eggler, "late of the Chicagos, who would prove a valuable acquisition to your nine in the outfield, and who is besides a thoroughly reliable and honest player."

Sometimes the replies from club officials were equally interesting. Harry Wright showed the qualifications he expected in a letter to John E. Clapp, a catcher who had written for a tryout in 1872. Wright remarked that Clapp seemed very confident of holding his own in any position with the best of them—"the kind of player I want"—but that he wished to ask a few more questions. He wanted to know what kind of pitching Clapp caught the previous year and how fast it was; what other position did he play; did Clapp think he could play third base; was he confident he could "catch a swift pitcher" like Spalding "up to or close behind" the batter; was he able to fill in satisfactorily for any of the infielders who might be injured; could he bat swift pitching with confidence; was he prepared to come at his own risk and show what he could do? Wright added dryly that he was taking it for granted that "you are gentlemanly and temperate at all times."

Another letter written by Wright to a young hopeful who had asked him how to become a player shows the special qualifications and high skill required for baseball, and even though the game has progressed tremendously since the relatively crude game of those days, the basic requirements for playing it remain substantially the same. As Wright said, a good ball player must be a "sure catch; a good thrower, strong and accurate; a reliable batter and good runner; all to be brought out, if in you, by steady and persevering practise." Wright also recommended that to make the grade one should live "regularly," keep good hours, abstain from tobacco and intoxicating drink, and "eat hearty—Roast Beef rare will do."

Player salaries were very low, compared with modern figures. The payroll of the Cincinnati Club of 1869 has already been given. On the Boston Red Stockings a beginner generally got $75 a month for nine months—if he lasted that long. After he established himself, he could expect $800 for a season's work. Outstanding players could make from $1000 to $2500 a season. Salaries were also quoted according to position:

Catchers	$2000
Pitchers	2000
First base	1500
Second base (good general players)	2500
Third base (great demand, few in market)	3000
Short stop (good general players)	2000
Fielders	1500

On co-operative nines, players shared in the gate money instead of getting salaries.

Obviously, the chief source of club income was gate receipts. The Association attempted to establish a fifty-cent admission, visiting clubs to get one-third of the total receipts. Harry Wright was one of the strongest advocates of a fifty-cent tariff:

It is well worth 50 cts to see a good game of base ball, and when the public refuse to pay that, then good bye base ball. They do not object to paying 75 cts to $1.50 to go to the theatre, and numbers prefer base ball to theatricals. We must make the games worth witnessing and there will be no fault found with the price of admission. A good game is worth 50 cts, a poor one is dear at 25 cts.

But the plan was rejected in favor of letting clubs make their own arrangements.

When traveling, Wright usually asked the home club for a $150 guarantee, or 60 per cent of the gate. Once a Canadian team tried to get a game with Wright's Red Stockings by offering other attractions in lieu of coin, but Wright refused to fall for such a plan, replying tactfully:

> As you say, we are 'not much on cognac etc.,' and I can assure you we prefer a good game and big gate receipts to 'Hail, Columbia,' 'Won't go home till morn.,' and 'all that sort of thing you know.'

Wright estimated that having a game with a good pro club cancelled meant a loss of $600 to $800. Clubs were also discovering they could make money by renting their grounds while they were away.

A profit-and-loss statement of the Bostons of 1875 gives an idea of the scale on which the business was operated:

Balance from former account	833.13	
Gate receipts	34,987.74	
Members' tickets	1,946.19	37,767.06
Expenses		
Players' salaries	20,685.00	
Advertising & Printing	1,410.88	
Rent of Grounds	617.50	
Care of Grounds & Wages	888.82	
Repair of Grounds	689.27	
Sundry Expenses	304.00	
Uniforms, bases, bats, etc.	223.94	
Old Accounts	470.33	
Rent of rooms and sundry accounts	1,955.37	
Travelling expenses	6,808.56	
Telegrams, postage, etc.	750.82	34,505.99
Balance on Hand		3,261.07

Note, however, that the figures on expenses were incorrectly added. The correct balance should be only $2,962.57. A few popularized accounts of baseball also give these and other figures, but they either have added them incorrectly and copied each others' mistakes, or fail to indicate any source for them, so that they are unreliable.

All this discussion of the professional influence on baseball should not give the reader the impression that amateurism expired suddenly. The professional ethic and way of doing things did not completely wipe out the old Knickerbocker spirit. Newspapers were still enjoining players to "quietly acquiesce" in the umpire's decision, even when thought wrong. An erring teammate should not be "chided nor growled nor sneered at." Players were advised to ignore the taunts of spectators and cultivate "a gentlemanly demeanor" instead. Exhortations to "honorable and upright play" and praise for "fair and manly skill" appeared in sporting publications in monotonous repetition.

Henry Chadwick in particular castigated "crooked" play and the "roughs" in the crowd. As baseball reporter, author, and editor, he turned out a prodigious amount of material on the game throughout a long life, and his contribution to baseball was a tremendous one. Often, however, he saw only the best in the old and the worst in the new. No matter how justified his criticism, it was not always appreciated. Harry Wright, one of the most upright men in the game at the time, thought that baseball would be better off if Chadwick said less about "suspicious play," "crooked players," etc., because the public got the impression that all games were dishonest. Chadwick, Wright wrote caustically, "also uses words he doesn't understand."

Surviving amateur strength is also shown by the great number of non-professional clubs in existence. New amateur teams continued to form along Knickerbocker lines. The Mohican Club of New York City thought itself so "elegant and aristocratic" that it must reject two possible sites for a home field because they were the hangouts of "rowdies and loafers." These gallant gentlemen also elected ladies to honorary membership and toasted them at their meetings. The old handwritten constitution and by-laws of the "Atheletic" [sic] Base Ball Club of Buffalo were practically the same as those of the Knickerbockers. Something of the flavor of this group is revealed in its worn bills for such items as a half dozen "Cuspadores" for the clubrooms and charges for ribbon, carrying coal to the rooms, and printing posters.

Amateurs were classified according to skill, from the first-line teams used in match games down through second and third teams, with the "muffin nines" at the bottom of the scale. Muffins were said to have an "excellent theoretical knowledge of the game" but were "somewhat weak in the practical part of it." A little book published during the period contained sixteen humorous sketches lampooning them, and the press seldom missed an opportunity to poke fun at their "ludicrous" efforts.

There was other evidence of vigor among the amateurs. Although they were completely outclassed, amateur and college nines played numerous games with Association clubs. The growing disparity in skill was conclusively demonstrated by the Boston Red Stockings, who won all 32 games they played with amateur teams in 1871. In fact, to keep his team "on its mettle" and make the game more interesting, Manager Wright sometimes allowed the amateurs five outs per inning!

College ball in those days was becoming ever more vigorous. Colleges found that ball playing improved the students physically and kept them out of a good deal of mischief. The first intercollegiate game was played in 1859 under the rules of Massachusetts ball between Amherst and Williams, which the former won 73-32 in 26 innings. The great interest of some collegians in baseball was well expressed by Birchard Hayes in a letter written in 1873 to his father, Rutherford B. Hayes, then Governor of Ohio and later President of the United States:

> You see I am not yet weaned from base-ball. The love of other boys for smoking, chewing, drinking, skating, and swimming, in my case is all concentrated on ball-playing. And I am inclined to think that one reason for my dread of life after leaving College is because I will be unable to play ball.

Even the professionals could not discard amateur trappings all at once. After the Cincinnati Red Stockings switched to professionalism they continued to ride out to the field in their decorated carriages, singing their club song. In 1871 amateurs even tried to revive their old Association in a vain attempt to check the rising tide of professionalism and to recapture the pristine purity of earlier days—when baseball was a sport played for recreation, and when, they told themselves, employers willingly excused their clerks and sometimes even joined the games themselves, when all classes and ages played, and women attended games. However, the old Association was too far gone. After calling two meetings and failing to get a quorum at either, an eighteen-club remnant tried to make a fresh start by forming a new organization, the National Association of Amateur Base Ball Players. But the professional virus had so infected them that they could not even agree among themselves about gate receipts. Some clubs threatened to resign if gate money was allowed. Others warned they would quit if it were not. They had to put off making the decision, but it was tacitly understood that gate receipts could be accepted by clubs when on tour or by those who owned enclosed grounds and needed to defray expenses of upkeep. However, players were not to be compensated in any case.

In those days confidence was expressed that national, state, and regional amateur associations as well as a professional association could all thrive side by side. Those who believed this thought the country was too large and diverse for any one association to rule baseball. They were soon proved wrong. The best players gravitated to the larger cities capable of supporting professional ball. Stimulated by newspapers and telegraph reports, small-town people tended to focus their interest on the exploits of distant diamond heroes. The newly organized National Association of Amateur Base Ball Players soon declined and died. The ambition, power, and organizing ability of the professional entrepreneurs made themselves felt, and before long the professional clubs, combined in a system called Organized Baseball, would dominate the game, fix its pattern, and point its direction throughout the United States and even abroad. Although more people participate and more equipment is purchased and used by far in amateur and college circles, the professional tail steers the baseball kite and receives a correspondingly disproportionate amount of attention.

This whole hybrid period of amateur-professionalism was personified by Harry Wright, the foremost baseball man of the 'sixties and early 'seventies. Wright was a link between the old and the new. His father was a celebrated cricket player, and Harry was brought to this country as a baby from Sheffield, England. He began his athletic career with the St. George Cricket Club in Staten Island, New York, and then turned to baseball, joining the Knickerbockers in 1858, with whom he starred before going to Cincinnati. Wright was a fine outfielder, although he did not have a strong throwing arm. He also took his turn as "change pitcher," and he was probably the first to use a change of pace. As a batter he was not outstanding, although he had a reputation for coming through with hits in tight situations when they counted most—in modern baseball language, he was a good clutch hitter.

A contemporary described him as a "tall, good-looking man ... dresses very neatly and is somewhat clerical in appearance." A well-built, graceful 160-pounder, Wright did indeed present a striking figure on the field with his sideburns, long mustache, and tuft of beard. Only one other manager in baseball history, Casey Stengel, has equaled Wright's record of winning six pennants in seven seasons, and he was the first manager to win four straight. Wright was a "quiet, persuasive" leader who inspired his men with confidence. His formula for success was getting the players to work together "like a nicely adjusted machine" and to give their best throughout nine innings regardless of the score. It may not be too much to say that he was the first field leader to introduce teamwork, and he is credited with being the first to use hand signals in coaching. It was under his leadership as manager of the Cincinnati Red Stockings of 1869 that knickers first replaced the old-style long pants in the baseball uniform. He set another precedent with those same Red Stockings by having them travel by Pullman on their famous tour. Later in his career he became the first Chief of Umpires in the major leagues.

As the manager of the first professional team, he was quick to envision the possibilities of baseball as a paying profession, but at the same time he never relinquished the ideals of his early sporting experience. His insistence on sobriety and good physical condition was a bright exception in a period of laxity and drunkenness among players. Once, when a player wrote him requesting permission to report two or three days late for spring training, Wright refused in a simple statement which expressed his attitude toward the infant profession and showed that even in that early day he frankly accepted it for what it was: "Professional ball playing is a business, and as such, I trust you will regard it while the season lasts." Wright's recognition of baseball as a business in which young men might engage without apology was also made clear in 1871 when the Philadelphia Athletics saw fit to display their championship pennant in a local saloon. After deploring what the Athletics had done, Wright said that the proper place to exhibit the pennant was in their own clubhouse, because:

> To elevate the National Game we must earn the respect of all; and now the Athletics are Champions—first legal and recognized Champion of the United States—they will be looked up to as the exponents of what is right and wrong in base ball, and will have it in their power, in a great measure, to make the game a success—financially and otherwise. . . .

Wright's baseball eminence was well known and recognized by everyone during his time. In the early 'seventies he was already being called "Father of the Game," but objected to the title because he said it made him feel old. The Cincinnati *Enquirer* termed him a "base-ball Edison. He eats base-ball, breathes base-ball, thinks base-ball, dreams base-ball, and incorporates base-ball in his prayers." When Wright retired from active duty in 1894, his contribution to baseball was admirably expressed by *Sporting Life:*

> Every magnate in the country is indebted to this man for the establishment of base ball as a business, and every patron for furnishing him with a systematic recreation. Every player is indebted to him for inaugurating an occupation by which he gains a livelihood, and the country at large for adding one more industry (for industry it is in one respect) to furnish employment.

Truly, Wright was the father of professional baseball, and when he died major league owners recognized his worth by holding a Harry Wright Day to raise funds for a monument, and digging into National League coffers when bad weather kept receipts low. But in 1939, when it came to selecting the foremost Builders of Baseball from among nineteenth-century luminaries for "enshrinement" in the Cooperstown Hall of Fame, the chief executives of modern baseball did not include Wright, and it was not until September 28, 1953, that they belatedly corrected the oversight.

PART TWO

BASEBALL BECOMES A BUSINESS

7

LAUNCHING A NEW BUSINESS

Baseball entered still another period in 1876. The time was opportune for change. The National Association of Professional Baseball Players was reeling. Its weak organization could not cope successfully with the cancerous evils of gambling, revolving, and hippodroming. As these became more flagrant, spectators began to stay away, and the clamor for reform grew louder.

While it is true that the Association made some effort to correct the situation by fining some players and reportedly pressuring others to resign, results were negligible. Critics insisted that unless crooked players were expelled, they were not really being punished at all, and the press continued to fire questions at the Association: What are you going to do about it? Do you really intend to act? How can the public have faith?

The heavy mortality among Association clubs has already been mentioned. Some clubs caused their own downfall by assuming heavier salary obligations than their resources warranted—like the Forest Citys of Cleveland, who upped salaries in 1872 to hold their players, only to go into receivership in mid-season after losing 15 out of 21 games. Rich clubs raided weaker rivals for players, thus adding to the number of club casualties. This short-sighted policy was detrimental to those who indulged in it as well, because as a result clubs often had trouble finding teams strong enough to give them a battle and bring in the fans.

Gravitation of the best players toward one team meant one-sided competition. For example, the Boston Red Sox, four-time pennant winners, won 71 and lost only 8 games in 1875. Their closest rivals, the Athletics, might just as well have been in another league for all the threat they offered, because they won only 53 and lost 20. The Atlantics, who finished last, were hopelessly outclassed, losing 42 games out of 44. The gap between winner and also-rans was even greater in other years. This disparity in playing strength cooled spectator interest, with the result that even the winners could lose money, as the Red Sox did in 1872.* As long as these uncertain and unstable conditions obtained, it was highly unlikely that backers would risk money in baseball ventures.

At the same time these weaknesses of the Association were becoming acute, profound economic and social changes were taking place in America, changes which created an environment congenial to the new direction in which baseball was to move. In just the brief span of time from the close of the war to 1878, America's modest railroad system became the finest in the world. Her industrial investment practically doubled, and except for periodic depressions, each decade saw the pace accelerated so furiously that "a new vocabulary and almost a new arithmetic" were required to describe it. The transformation of America from a rural to an urban society was accomplished as native and immigrant alike crowded into the urban industrial centers, particularly in the Northeast. The twin forces of industrialism and urbanism were, as one scholar said, "more fundamentally responsible for the changes and developments in sport during the next generation than any other."

Long hours of drudgery at factory machines understandably created a craving among the city masses for diversion and excitement. Their traditional pattern of recreation was broken because they necessarily had to forsake the yeoman sports of an earlier period. On the other hand, cities had not yet assumed any responsibility for the leisure-time activities of citizens, and the recreation movement aimed at supplying these needs was still to come. People therefore turned to the cheap, the passive, the commercial, and the sensational. Typical attractions were the saloon, dance hall, and minstrel show. People also turned to the excitement of spectator sports, where they could experience vicariously the thrills and satisfactions heretofore enjoyed at first hand. Sitting in ball parks passively watching others perform was perhaps not the best form of recreation—there is a whole literature criticizing "spectatoritis" —but at least it was much better than some far less wholesome activities that might have been pursued.

It was no accident that professional baseball reached its highest development in the urban centers which offered a permanent stage and an ever-ready audience. There were entrepreneurs quick to capitalize on the situation. In this buoyant era of confidence and opportunity, men with drive, organizing ability, and an eye for the main chance could climb to the top. Oil had its Rockefeller, flour its Pillsbury, meat its Armour and Swift, railroads their Vanderbilt and Gould. Some historians have been telling us men like these were "business states-

* On the other hand, the champion Athletics of 1871 wiped out a $5000 debt.

men" rather than "robber barons," as they used to be called. Maybe
they were, but making them so requires several heavy coats of white-
wash. Baseball, too, was to have its business leaders, although they
performed on a smaller scale. Men like Cammeyer and Wright had
already sensed the possibilities of converting baseball into a paying
entertainment business. Others now emerged with the ability and
vision to benefit by the Association's experience and to organize professional ball on a real business basis.

Foremost among them was William A. Hulbert. He was born in a
small town in Otsego County, New York, not far from Cooperstown,
but grew up in Chicago. After attending Beloit College, he entered
business and was for fifteen years a member of the Chicago Board of
Trade. In 1875 he became an officer of the Chicago Baseball Club.
Hulbert was a strong leader who applied his business experience to
professional baseball. He was one of those convinced that it could be
made a paying business if properly managed. He was largely responsible for bringing about a new regime in baseball, and it was
under his guidance that the present National League survived during
its first crucial years. Unfortunately, Hulbert died prematurely in 1882
before he could realize the full fruits of his efforts. His contemporaries
fully recognized his contribution, for they erected a costly monument
to his memory and published an appropriate eulogy. But modern
baseball men failed to include his name in the Hall of Fame, so William
Hulbert, the man chiefly responsible for founding the National League,
does not have a plaque in Cooperstown.

Hulbert quickly saw the disastrous financial effects of inflated
salaries, caused by the scramble for players, and he understood the
National Association's need for a "new and better rule" to curb this
competition for men. In October 1875, the Chicago *Tribune* printed a
lengthy article analyzing baseball's difficulties under the Association
and offering a set of proposals to remedy them. According to the
Tribune, too many good clubs were losing money playing second-
raters that could not draw well at the gate—"fun for the little fellows"
but "death" for the leading clubs, as it was called. For the Chicago
Club to cover costs, pay good salaries, and maybe realize a "modest"
dividend, it would have to limit its schedule to games with the more
solid teams. The Chicago management was afraid, therefore, that if the
"whole gang be let in" the Association again in 1876, half the clubs
would not make expenses. The *Tribune* called upon the Association to
institute reforms; otherwise it would be the "plain duty" of its leading
clubs to withdraw from the Association and form an organization of
their own—"a closed corporation, too."

Significantly, the reforms advocated by the *Tribune* were among

those soon adopted by Hulbert for the new National League. Because
of this, Lewis Meacham, sports editor of the *Tribune* and writer of the
article, has been credited with originating the organizational plan of
the National League. However, it is more likely that he was acting as
Hulbert's mouthpiece. The wording of the article sounded suspiciously
like Hulbert, who was probably launching a trial balloon to test the
scheme he had in mind. Besides, in a subsequent article in its February
4, 1876 edition, the *Tribune* admitted that the Chicago Club's management, meaning Hulbert, realized that something drastic had to be
done. At that time it still claimed credit for formulating the new plan
for professional baseball, but when Hulbert died, it modified its stand,
taking only a portion of the glory by stating that "Mr. Hulbert, together
with Lewis Meacham . . . matured the plan of the National League."
Furthermore, once the National League was formed, Meacham worked
closely with Hulbert and upon occasion even acted as Hulbert's emis-
sary in the interests of the Chicago Club. Recently, some writers seized
upon Meacham's original *Tribune* article, took it at face value without
bothering to investigate further, and credited Meacham with preparing the plan for the National League.

Hulbert's first overt act was to strengthen his own club by the bald
expedient of raiding the Boston Red Sox, the standout club of the Association. Much as he might deplore the practice in principle, he did not
shrink from pirating players of other clubs when it suited his purpose.
While the season of 1875 was in progress, he approached Al Spalding,
still under contract to the Red Sox, and induced him to join Chicago
for the following season. Then, with Spalding's help, he signed three
more Boston stars, Cal McVey, James "Deacon" White, and Ross
Barnes. He also enticed Adrian C. "Cap" Anson of the Philadelphia
Athletics, destined to be one of the greatest players of the era, and
Ezra B. Sutton, although the latter changed his mind and remained in
Philadelphia.

This buccaneering was, of course, in bold defiance of the Association's rule that, if a player signed with any club other than the one
he was with before the season was over, he was liable to expulsion.
Spalding and his fellow contract-jumpers took the gamble on Hulbert's
assurance that "you boys are bigger than the Association," backed by
his promise to pay their salaries even if they were expelled. The
Hulbert-Spalding deal becomes all the more telling in view of their
later repeated castigations of players who broke their agreements.

Hulbert was now ready for his next move, a mixture of idealism and
materialism. He had already shown his lack of respect for the Association and felt quite sure he could flout it; but what if the Eastern clubs,
angry over his player raids, ganged up and had him expelled? After

all, he must have realized that the Eastern clubs held the balance of power in the Association. Better to anticipate such a reprisal and move first. Another motive may have been Hulbert's wish to retaliate against the Association, which he "never forgave" for awarding a disputed player, Davy Force, to the Philadelphia Athletics instead of his own Chicago club.*

Hulbert's aim was nothing less than the displacement of the Association with a strong new organization, composed of selected clubs only, East and West, with all others arbitrarily excluded. He hoped that such an organization would check the evils that were reducing attendance, and that better gate receipts would come from exploiting intersectional rivalry with a better balance between Eastern and Western clubs. First, he traveled to St. Louis in the fall of 1875 to confer with Charles Fowle, owner of the local Association club, and Campbell Orrick Bishop, an attorney who had played with the St. Louis Unions in the 1860's and then became Vice President of the Association and a member of its Judiciary Committee. Bishop drew up a constitution for a new league based upon a draft submitted to him by Hulbert. Next Hulbert and Fowle met secretly in Louisville on December 17, 1875, with representatives of the Cincinnati and Louisville clubs, strong independent teams. Hulbert's purpose is shown in a letter to Fowle before the meeting:

> You and I can carry the day for everything we want. Then, firmly established with four powerful clubs welded together, we can easily influence such of the remainder that we desire to join us.

At Louisville, Hulbert and Fowle were appointed a committee with full power to act for the four Western clubs and given the job of going east to negotiate with the Eastern teams they wanted to include. Louisville, therefore, was the real birthplace of the National League, not New York City. Four Eastern clubs—Hartford, Boston, New York, and the Philadelphia Athletics, all Association members—were invited to send representatives armed with authority to act for their clubs to a meeting on "matters of interest to the game at large," especially "reforms of existing abuses" and the formation of a "new association." Boston and Philadelphia of course were victims of Hulbert's recent player raids. Nevertheless, he boldly requested that:

> all past troubles and differences be ignored and forgotten and that the conference we propose shall be a calm, friendly and deliberate discussion, looking solely to the general good of the clubs . . . calculated to give character and permanence to the game.

* Hulbert also was said to have got the idea for a new organization while attending the annual convention of the Association in 1875.

The Eastern clubs accepted, and the delegates met February 2, 1876, at the Central Hotel, New York City. Results were massive for baseball history. This small group proceeded to spring a *coup d'état*, by-passing the Association and setting up a new organization vastly different in character. Glorifiers of Hulbert have claimed for him the same tactics which tradition attributes to J. P. Morgan, who supposedly locked fellow financiers in his office during the panic of 1907 until they agreed to what he wanted. Hulbert is supposed to have called the hostile Eastern delegates to his hotel suite, locked the door, pocketed the key, and told them they could not escape until agreement was reached. The story is no doubt apocryphal. More likely, it was Hulbert's forceful personality, coupled with the appeal of his plan, which convinced the others.

The name chosen by the group for the new organization—the National League of Professional Baseball Clubs—was highly significant. Up until then, all baseball organizations, amateur or professional, were player associations. Now the players were relegated to a secondary position. The clubs would be dominant. The specialization increasingly characteristic of American life, and especially of American industry, was becoming ever more noticeable in the baseball business. The managing end of the game was to be separate and distinct from the playing end, thus allowing the players to concentrate on performance and leave business affairs and promotion to the owners. Spalding later put it this way:

> The idea was as old as the hills; but its application to Base Ball had not yet been made. It was, in fact, the irrepressible conflict between Labor and Capital asserting itself under a new guise. . . . Like every other form of business enterprise, Base Ball depends for results on two interdependent divisions, the one to have absolute control and direction of the system, and the other to engage—always under the executive branch—the actual work of production.

The rest of the proceedings at the meeting were faithfully recorded by Harry Wright, secretary *pro tem.* The constitution readied in advance by Hulbert and Bishop was adopted after a session which lasted all day and throughout the evening, except for a recess for supper. The new document listed as its broad objectives a desire to elevate baseball and make ball playing "respectable and honorable" by enacting and enforcing "proper rules" for the conduct of the game. The founders also expressed the desire to protect and promote the "mutual interests" of clubs and players and to establish and regulate the baseball championship of the United States. They were aware of the need for improving the operation of the business, and there is no doubt that in the years to come the National League did much to put the game on a more respectable plane. However, as time passed and the League became more institutionalized, the idealistic objectives of its founders were emphasized and their other motives subordinated or forgotten. Just as the friends of the new American Constitution of 1789 constantly praised the work of the Founding Fathers and blackened the previous period when America was governed under the Articles of Confederation, in order to make the Constitution appear brighter by contrast; so the men of the National League, particularly when under attack by rival organizations or their own dissatisfied players, conveniently forgot their less worthy motives, such as establishing a monopoly and improving their financial position by dropping the weaker clubs. Instead they preferred to recite the lofty objectives voiced in 1876. The constant refrain was, "The National League was organized in 1876 as a necessity, to rescue the game from its slough of corruption and disgrace." As for the League organizers' statement about "the mutual interests" of players and clubs, it should be remembered that before this, the two were essentially one and the same. Now Hulbert and the others first made a distinction between them and then paid their respects to "mutual interests."

The provisions of the constitution concerning regulation of member clubs made plain the monopolistic intent of the League. Like so many tycoons of the time, they gave lip service to competition while working overtime to eliminate it. Restrictive measures controlling consumer markets were introduced immediately. These so-called "territorial rights" have been maintained by the baseball business ever since. Each League club was given exclusive control of its own city and the surrounding area within a radius of five miles. No League club could play an outside team in another League city, even if the local League club consented. The boon of territorial rights was particularly apparent in the case of the Philadelphia Athletics, still smarting under the loss of Anson to Chicago. The A's had been competing with two other clubs in Philadelphia, to the financial detriment of all three. Now they were to have the field to themselves.

Theoretically, other clubs could join the League. Practically, they had little chance of doing so. Since the constitution allowed but one club to a city, and the owners had no intention of having more than eight clubs in the circuit, a member club had to leave before a new one could enter. To ensure gate receipts, a new club must represent a city of not less than 75,000, unless given special exemption by unanimous vote of the incumbent members. Two blackballs were enough to block admission of a new club. Members were required to pay $100 annual dues—ten times those of the Association.

Each club was to play ten games with every other club between March 15 and November 15. Five of the ten games might be played on the club's home grounds. The team finishing with the greatest number of victories was to be proclaimed champion and awarded an appropriate pennant costing not less than $100. In the event of a tie in total number of victories, the club with the smallest number of losses would receive the title. If a club used an ineligible player or failed to put in an appearance (unless unavoidably prevented by accident or traveling conditions) it forfeited the game. Each club was to furnish sufficient police to preserve order, and after each game the complete score and particulars were to be sent to the League secretary.

Another group of restrictive measures was applied to the employees, the players. They were regarded as members of the League, to the extent of being "amenable to the provisions of the constitution and its privileges." Each club had the right to contract with its players and to discipline them, so long as it did nothing contrary to the constitution. Ever since 1879 professional baseball has required all clubs to use a uniform players' contract, but during the first three years—1876 to 1879—no formal wording was necessary. Each club had to inform the League secretary as soon as a player was signed. By making the secretary's office a clearinghouse for registration of all player contracts, the danger of revolving would be greatly reduced.

No club was prevented from engaging a player, even though he was under contract with another League club, provided his services were not to begin until after completion of his first obligation. A player released by one League club was free to contract with another League club after a lapse of twenty days—if he had an "honorable discharge" from his former club. Otherwise, he was presumed to have been expelled.

The League constitution also provided for a favorite weapon of employers in those days—the blacklist. Players who tried to avoid discipline by the simple trick of jumping to another club found their escape choked off, because no other League club was allowed to employ any man guilty of violating the constitution or playing rules of the League, or one who had been discharged, dismissed, or expelled from any League club. A club that did employ such a disqualified player would itself be expelled and boycotted by the League.

The League was to be governed by a five-man board of directors serving one-year terms. One of its members was to be chosen president of the League. The board was the "sole determinant of violations of the Constitution" when differences arose between clubs. Should a board member's own club be involved, however, he could not "sit on trial." The board was also "sole tribunal" for players appealing dismissal, expulsion, or discipline. Its findings were final in squabbles between clubs or pleas by players. The board was obliged to elect as secretary of the League "a gentleman of intelligence, honesty and good repute, versed in Base-Ball but not connected with the press and not a member of any professional club." His job was to look after League records and funds—all for a salary of not less than $300 nor more than $500 per year plus traveling expenses.

Recalcitrant clubs were to be judged by their peers. A two-thirds vote of member clubs could expel a fellow club for: (1) disbanding or failing to appear for games; (2) failing to obey a lawful rule of the board; (3) violating the constitution; and (4) breaking contractual agreements with players (when the latter were not at fault), either by failing to engage them after agreeing to do so or by not paying their salaries. As far as the players were concerned, however, democracy was conspicuously absent in the League constitution. The players had no franchise, no elected representatives, no voice in the conduct of affairs. They could not get justice through trial by their peers but, as in feudal days, must depend for it on the court of their overlords. And, as time passed, their rights and freedoms were further restricted.

The undemocratic character of Organized Baseball's governmental structure, which exists to the present day, contradicts the repeated attempts of the owners and their spokesmen to equate the business with democracy, or at least to make it a symbol of democracy. One of the earliest of such attempts was made by Al Spalding, who asserted that "The genius of our institutions is democratic; Base Ball is a democratic game." During World War I, John K. Tener, president of the National League and former Governor of Pennsylvania, stated:

> This is a war of democracy against bureaucracy. And I tell you that baseball is the very watchword of democracy. There is no other sport or business or anything under heaven which exerts the leveling influence that baseball does. Neither the public school nor the church can approach it. Baseball is unique. England is a democratic country, but it lacks the finishing touch of baseball.

More recently Ford Frick, Commissioner of Baseball, said that baseball exemplified the Bill of Rights, because of its freedom of assembly, religion, speech, and opportunity. There is much to be said for Frick's contention, insofar as it applies to the playing field, to the atmosphere in the ball parks, and to the opportunities for young men to become professionals—especially after baseball abolished the color line, which it had maintained for decades. But Frick did not mention the fact that the government and economic structure of the game is anything but democratic. Its restrictive labor practices and its monopolistic division and control of consumer markets are hardly in keeping with traditional American belief in freedom of individual opportunity, free enterprise, and competition. They do not square with the basic American view that people should be free to work for whom they please, offer their services to the highest bidder, and enter any business they wish. As a newspaper columnist once expressed it, baseball

> is run as a dictatorship ... it is tied neither to John Paul Jones nor Betsy Ross, and George Washington never played it. But you would think that the Declaration of Independence carried a complete set of baseball rules as a postscript.

Perhaps baseball has to remain as it is for the business to operate successfully; but that is another question.

To the end of the League constitution the owners attached a flowery statement, obviously for propaganda purposes, lamenting the abuses which had crept into the National Game, blaming the Association for the unpleasant differences which had arisen among them, announcing their withdrawal from the Association and the formation of the National League, and repeating their purpose to elevate "our national sport" and protect the interests of "our players." But Hulbert and Fowle expressed themselves more forthrightly to the New York correspondent of the Chicago *Tribune*. Too many weak semi-pro teams (they were reported as saying) were placing themselves on a par with the genuinely professional clubs by simply joining the Association. The "instinct of self-preservation" required the seceding clubs to better their financial condition by banding together and shutting out the weak sisters. Their new regime would have the added advantage of making it possible to eliminate dishonest players.

The president and board were selected by a drawing: the names of the clubs were written on identical cards, and the first five drawn received the honors. It was agreed that the presidency would go to the club whose name came up first in the drawing. Hartford's card was the first drawn, so to Morgan G. Bulkeley fell the honor of being the National League's first president. Bulkeley served only one term, then hastened to resume his insurance business and political activities, eventually becoming director of numerous banks and corporations, Governor of Connecticut, and United States Senator. Despite Bulkeley's slight contribution to baseball, he was one of the first selected for the Cooperstown Hall of Fame. After the League's first year, Hulbert, its real leader, was formally named president and served until his death. The first secretary-treasurer of the League was Nicholas E. Young, long connected with the Washington Club and for several years secretary of the old Professional Association.

As Spalding acknowledged, the new National League was "born in rebellion." It proceeded to grow through trial and error. Policies and measures introduced on this basis became sanctified by time and usage; now they are regarded as essential to the successful operation of the business.

The formation of the National League was one of the most important events in the development of baseball. It provided for a new order, ingeniously designed to be nourished on both monopoly and competition. Under its aegis, member clubs were to compete with each other for renown and receipts, but only within the confines of a prescribed pattern. In the years to come, the League would bring to professional baseball both stability and the disruption of bitter trade wars. It would bring both a superior brand of ball playing and trouble with ball players. It would build up public confidence in baseball, yet at times create public disillusionment.

But these developments lay in the future. At the moment the League was only an idea, a blueprint. The immediate question was whether or not it would work. Could Hulbert and his colleagues give practical substance to their new plan for baseball?

THE GRIM YEARS

Back in 1876 even the most sanguine scarcely could have imagined that the new National League would survive its first trying years, much less be going strong in the middle of the twentieth century. News of the League's formation hit the sports pages with great impact. Much of the press supported the founders for their professions of reform, but it criticized the methods they had used to organize the League. The secret meeting at the Grand Hotel was attacked as "star-chamber" and "anti-American." "Plainly," commented the Chicago *Union,* "the whole thing is a monopoly." The Chicago *Tribune* rushed to defend the League, crediting Hulbert with having "planned, engineered, and carried the most important reform in the history of the game." It praised the "primal idea" of allowing only one club to a city. Such a limitation, it argued, was essential to financial success. Because clubs would be evenly matched, there would be more first-class games. Interest would be heightened further by pitting Western against Eastern clubs.

The League faced serious financial problems and heavy club turnover during those first grim years. Most clubs lost money the first year; probably only Chicago showed a profit. The Philadelphia Athletics and the New York Mutuals were summarily expelled for not completing their playing schedules. If anything, 1877 was more wretched. Estimated losses were: St. Louis, $8000; Chicago, $6000; Hartford, $2500; Louisville, $2000; and Boston, $1500. St. Louis, Hartford, and Louisville dropped out before the 1878 season. Cincinnati was taken over by new owners in July and managed to stagger through the year. Its return in 1878 and the entrance of three new clubs—Indianapolis, Milwaukee, and Providence—restored a six-club league.

Further changes took place in 1879. Milwaukee could not pay its bills and was expelled. Indianapolis collapsed, an "utter failure financially." Four new teams—Buffalo, Syracuse, Cleveland, and Troy —then joined, establishing an eight-club circuit for the first time since the inaugural season of 1876. But again it was reported that every club except Chicago finished in the red that season. The heavy casualties continued for several more years. Only Chicago and Boston continued through this period. Providence lasted through 1885; Syracuse failed to finish even one season; Troy quit at the end of 1882, Cleveland at the end of 1884, and Buffalo after 1885. Worcester, accepted in 1880, lasted only three seasons. From 1876 to 1900 no fewer than twenty-one cities were represented in the National League at one time or another.

Things became so bad that Hulbert and another owner were authorized to appoint any outside club in good standing as an emergency replacement any time a member collapsed. And when A. G. Mills took over the presidency of the League, he did not even want to list the names of the clubs on the League letterhead because they changed so often!

On top of financial headaches, the League had to deal with some other tough problems. The old blight of player dishonesty, which had infected the old Association, soon menaced the League. The new organization had the courage to meet this threat head on. It acted swiftly and decisively to get rid of corruption, thereby giving substance to the League's later claim of having "saved baseball." In 1877 the Louisville Club expelled four of its players—James A. Devlin, pitcher; William H. Craver, shortstop; George Hall, outfielder; and Al Nichols, third baseman—for throwing games. Diamond stickpins and rings sported by the culprits aroused suspicion, and intercepted telegrams sent the players by gamblers clinched the evidence against them. Confronted with these, the accused admitted their guilt. The League then confirmed their dismissal "for conduct in contravention of the objects of this League."

Devlin, the ringleader, offered the hackneyed alibi that he sold out because his family was in want and he had to get money. Cut off from his livelihood, he repeatedly petitioned League officials for reinstatement, and more than once begged Harry Wright to intercede for him so he could get back into baseball, if only as a groundkeeper. Pleading for an interview, Devlin outlined his sad predicament in a letter to Wright:

> I Can asure you Harry that I was not Treated right and if Ever I Can
> see you to tell you the Case you will say I am not to Blame I am living
> from hand to mouth all winter I have not got a Stich of Clothing or has
> my wife and Child. . . . the Louisville People have made me what I am
> to day a Begger.

Spalding later described a pathetic scene, with the wretched Devlin moaning that his family was starving and imploring Hulbert to reinstate him, and Hulbert as upholder of principle, yet of kindly heart withal, slipping Devlin fifty dollars and saying,

> Devlin, that is what I think of you personally; but damn you, you have sold a game, you are dishonest, and this National League will not stand for it.

To all exhortations that Devlin be reinstated, the League remained adamant, finally passing a resolution serving notice on the outcasts, "their friends, defenders and apologists" that the penalties would never be rescinded and that no further appeals would be entertained. The League also answered lingering cries of "fraud" by affirming the integrity of its players and promising to expel any other corrupt players forever, if evidence of their guilt could be produced.

The League was equally ready to crack down on wayward clubs. When in 1876 the Athletics and Mutuals were guilty of not fulfilling their schedules, shirking their last Western tours, they were expelled, even though they represented the most populous cities in the League, and the temptation to retain them must have been strong. In a letter to Hulbert, G. W. Thompson, president of the Athletics, pled injuries among his players, heavy debts, and loss of gate receipts because of competition from the Regatta and Fireman's Parade—free spectacles attracting many Philadelphians who might otherwise have paid to see the Athletics. Thompson offered 80 per cent of the gate receipts to Chicago and St. Louis if they would come to Philadelphia instead. Hulbert rejected both offer and excuses. Complaining of the loss of five games from his own club's schedule, including three as far back as 1874, he told Thompson that the least he should have done was to explain the situation before Chicago had made its own Eastern trip. He was less obdurate with the Mutuals. He and Fowle of St. Louis offered Cammeyer a $400 guarantee if the Mutuals would play two games in Chicago and three in St. Louis in the space of a week, but Cammeyer refused, and as a result was expelled. Thompson made a final plea at the League meeting that winter, but Cammeyer realized he was finished—"acknowledged the corn," as the Chicago *Tribune* put it—and did not attend.

In 1877 Cincinnati ran into difficulty because of the poor performance of the team as well as the personal financial reverses of the owner, Si Keck, a prominent local businessman. Keck disbanded the club and released the players from their contracts early in June. Eight other businessmen took over and supplied funds so the team could finish its schedule. At the meeting of the League's board of directors in Cleveland the following December, Cincinnati was nominally expelled for nonpayment of dues the previous June, then promptly reinstated the next day in compliance with a written agreement made with the new owners in July. According to this deal, the new management had agreed to continue the schedule in exchange for reinstatement of the club that winter. However, Cincinnati's games were not to be counted toward the championship. Here was a clever practical solution which upheld League prestige by technically penalizing a violation without interrupting schedules or sacrificing gate receipts.

During the change-over in Cincinnati's management that summer of 1877, League President Hulbert was alert to the interests of his own Chicago Club. As soon as Keck released his players, Hulbert sent Lewis Meacham, known to be his representative, to sign two of the Cincinnati players, Charlie Jones and Joe Hallinan. Jones was a particular favorite of Cincinnati fans. The Cincinnati *Enquirer* told how the *Tribune* editor descended on the city like a "buzzard hovering over a dying cow" and signed Hallinan. Hulbert himself soon followed. He entered Cincinnati secretly, took rooms without registering, and succeeded in snaring Jones.

Hulbert was immediately accused of "prostituting his official position . . . to further the interests of his Club," "preying upon the Cincinnatis in their adversity," and using their failure to pay dues as a "flimsy, shallow excuse" for denying them reinstatement in order to hold on to the two players. Admitting that he was Hulbert's agent sent to hire Hallinan and Jones, Meacham claimed that both the players and Si Keck told him they were free agents, available for duty with any interested club. Meacham also argued that in the interval between Keck's relinquishment of the club and the new owners' acquisition, there was in fact no Cincinnati Club, and that the blame should be placed on Keck's successors' "fatal error" in not binding the players to them while waiting for League acceptance of the club under the new management. Hulbert finally did return Jones, in response to Cincinnati's plea that it would be difficult, if not impossible, to operate without their prize gate attraction. In doing so, Hulbert did not in principle surrender his right to the player.

Another dispute arose over the rule banning managers from the players' bench during games. Boston was convinced that the legislation was directed at Harry Wright. Harry liked to direct the team from the bench, and at times so far forgot his Knickerbocker upbringing as to heckle opposing players. "Riding" the other team has long since become an accepted part of professional baseball, and every club has its "bench jockeys," experts in needling the opposition. But in those less sophisticated days, other managers, who did not direct strategy as managers later did, complained that Wright's tactics gave Boston an "unfair advantage." The Boston Club suspected that Chicago was in back of the rule, never having forgotten Hulbert's player raid on them. As the *Tribune* remarked, every season the Red Sox found some excuse for starting trouble with the White Sox.

For that matter, Hulbert's dual role as president of the National League and the Chicago Club was a ticklish one. Chicago was wide open to charges of having undue influence in League affairs—with "bossing the League." The *Tribune* retorted, "Who should boss the league if not Chicago?" and used the same reasoning since made famous by Charles E. Wilson's defense of General Motors: "What is good for base-ball in Chicago is good for the league as a whole."

Other problems sprang from efforts of the League, like those of business enterprises of the time, to fix prices. At the first annual meeting in Cleveland, League clubs drew up "Special Club Rules for 1877." This business agreement provided for visiting clubs to get fifteen cents for every adult admitted to the park, excepting police, players, and ten others—"deadheads," in the vernacular. Attendance had to be tabulated by self-registering turnstiles. No mention was made of admission prices, but by gentlemen's agreement fifty cents was the standard charge since the League's inception. For ten cents more, one could get a seat on the "bleaching boards." A seat in the grandstand cost twenty-five cents extra. Season tickets and commutation tickets in blocks of twenty could also be had. By 1880 the fifty-cent admission price was formally stipulated in the constitution.

There were plenty of protests, though. The Buffalo Club delayed joining the League because of its objection to charging fifty cents, and Syracuse was turned down twice before agreeing to boost its admission to the required level. After entering the League, these two clubs agitated repeatedly for the right to charge less, but without success. The public and the press were also critical. Some even blamed the fifty-cent charge for the League's financial trouble. The League was reminded that "a nimble sixpence is better than a slow shilling." It was argued that, although "females" at first were admitted free when accompanied by a man, a New York workingman could scarcely afford to take his wife and daughter to a ball game in Brooklyn, for by the time he gave up a half-day's pay ($1.25), paid the various carfares and ferry charges, and bought his own ticket, the expedition would cost him about $2.50.

Pro-League publications upheld the fifty-cent policy. One of the best defenses was given by a semi-official League organ, Spalding's *Guide*, which asserted that the League's price structure was necessary to cover expenses, protect stockholders, and maintain player salaries.

Reducing admissions would mean cutting salaries and hence increasing the temptation for players to accept bribes. The *Guide* also claimed that fans were showing willingness to pay fifty cents to see games "of the high grade of skill offered by League nines." There was something to this last point, judging from the fact that League charges were not out of line with the cost of other entertainment in those days. Popular prices at the theater ranged from a quarter to seventy-five cents, and people could go to the circus or hear lectures by famous orators such as Robert Ingersoll and Henry Ward Beecher for half a dollar.

Syracuse newspapers advocated charging different rates on the basis of class, because a single admission charge would "throw the entire assemblage into promiscuous relations"—something intolerable to the "higher social classes." Reminding their readers of the "drunken rowdies, unwashed loafers, and arrant blacklegs" who went to the ball games, they decried any policy which prevented "the wealthy and respected gentleman" from getting a seat apart from "his social inferior" by paying a higher price. In this way social classes would be seated separately "without injury to any one's feelings," just as it was done in an opera house.

Sunday ball was another controversial issue. In keeping with its avowed purpose of making baseball respectable, the League frowned on Sunday games. Besides, many cities had ordinances against them. At first, such games simply did not count toward the League championship, but in 1878 the League clamped down harder with a rule expelling clubs that violated the Sabbath or failed to get rid of any man who participated in such games either as player, umpire, or scorer.

The Cincinnati Club was the particular target for the League purists, although St. Louis, too, was criticized for its "usual disregard for righteousness." Beer and Sunday amusements became "a popular necessity" in Cincinnati, with its large German population, so the ball club not only rented its grounds to other teams on Sundays but also allowed beer to be sold at all games. Breweries and distilleries were two of the most important industries in the town, which had no fewer than twenty-seven of them in 1879 (one for approximately every 8000 people), representing about a three million dollar investment. The Cincinnati Ball Club averaged about $3000 a season from the beer and refreshment concessions.

However, after overcoming the gambling menace, Hulbert was now said to be aiming at wiping out barrooms in all League parks—something which Justus Thorner, ex-president of the Cincinnati Club, said he could not understand, because the League president loved his whiskey as well as any man. Cincinnati Club directors did stop selling beer in the grandstand in deference to the ladies, making it necessary, as the *Enquirer* observed, for "the boys who get rusty" to "go downstairs to moisten."

The whole question caused a good deal of acrimonious exchange during 1880 in the newspapers of Cincinnati and other League cities, especially Worcester. A widely circulated article in the Worcester *Spy* asserted that there was no good reason for Cincinnati to continue its "questionable custom," particularly when it was shown by other League cities that Sunday games and liquor selling were not necessary. A Cincinnati supporter replied that were it not for the gate receipts in large cities like his, the Worcester Club would fold. "Puritanical Worcester," he sneered, "is not liberal Cincinnati by a jugful." Out here, he boasted, "we drink beer . . . as freely as you used to drink milk." As a parting shot, he warned that "any attempt arbitrarily to cut off these privileges" would mean Cincinnati's exit from the League.

League clubs continued sniping at Cincinnati on one pretext or another, and Cincinnati replied by refusing to accept "Foghorn" Bradley, an umpire brought west by Worcester. Hulbert was further annoyed over Cincinnati's constant financial troubles and the transfer of its franchise from the Reds to the Stars.

League clubs finally united against the culprit, pledging at a special meeting October 4, 1880, to vote for an amendment at their annual meeting in December which would forbid clubs to allow Sunday games or the sale of liquor on their grounds. When Cincinnati failed to sign the pledge, the other clubs on October 6 passed a resolution declaring that "unless they acquiesce in all legislation the League may enact" Cincinnati's membership would be considered at an end. Then at the same meeting the other clubs went ahead to declare Cincinnati's membership "vacated," because it had "failed to respond in a satisfactory manner" concerning its "intentions regarding observance of the rules, agreements and requirements of the League." So Cincinnati was expelled for past acts which the League intended to prohibit in the future. The Constitution of the United States might ban ex post facto laws, but the National League could and did use them with a vengeance.

That winter the League followed through with an amendment to the constitution banning Sunday ball and the sale of liquor. But, like the ministers who condemned Sunday entertainment, the League was out of harmony with the trend of the times. Immigrants flooding into American cities, bringing with them the Continental Sabbath, made the day increasingly one of recreation among working people. The Germans in particular loved picnics, excursions, and beer-garden entertainment, and these accompanied them to Cincinnati and St. Louis and wherever else they settled in large numbers.

The League's expulsion of Cincinnati turned out to be a great mistake. Baseball interest in the Ohio city proved too strong to be suppressed, and Cincinnati soon became the focal point of a new major league, the first to stand up against the National League successfully and force it to share its monopoly of big-league ball.

9

THE FIRST OUTSIDE THREAT

WHILE THEY WERE occupied with internal affairs, League owners had at the same time to decide on a policy toward outsiders. During these first few years there were plenty of clubs outside the League as good or better than those who were members. In 1877, for example, about fifty professional non-League clubs were in action, and they succeeded in beating League teams no fewer than seventy-two times. Many games between clubs outside the League were just as well played as those in it, and League teams were even accused of avoiding the strong independent clubs. It was asserted that there were many young ball players who could "knock the stuffing out of the old leaguers." One newspaper advised League players to "become ticket-snatchers, run slush stands, umpire for fifty cents—anything but don a uniform and have their old bones creak around the bases."

There were players like Davy Force who urged their clubs against joining the League: "I heard that we was going to Join the League I hope & pray not for if we do we are gone financially ... for there is nothing in it," he wrote the Buffalo Club in 1878. Some clubs thought they were better off playing teams in their own vicinity and avoiding the heavy traveling expenses entailed in League membership. In those days the National League was by no means accepted as "the big league," and there was no guarantee that it was going to last, let alone become supreme. It was only by following a consistent policy aimed at dominating the baseball world that the League achieved its objective.

From the beginning its policy of setting itself apart made for hard feelings among those who did not like being left out. The Philadelphias were highly incensed at the "selfish and mercenary motives" of the League in excluding them and admitting the rival Athletics. The New Haven Club published a letter of protest, and their club secretary even traveled to Chicago, Louisville, and Cincinnati to plead their cause, but, as the Chicago *Tribune* said, he might just as well have stayed home and saved the carfare, for all the good it did him. The League was especially criticized for ignoring the unsavory reputation of the New York Mutuals and taking them in solely because of their drawing power.

Even in those first years, many independents wanted to align themselves with the League in order to attract its first-class teams to their own cities. They believed that through League membership they could also count on a certain number of games, avoid paying guarantees to makeshift clubs, and enjoy territorial rights that would protect their local markets. But because League policy and philosophy permitted admission of relatively few clubs, relations with outside clubs continued to be strained. For example, with sixteen teams trying to get into the League's 1879 circuit and another group of candidates seeking admission the next year, it was obvious that many would be disappointed.

The League couched its policy of exclusiveness in diplomatic but unmistakable terms. In a statement to the public at the end of its first season, it explained that to invite outside clubs

> as a class to join . . . under equal obligations with ourselves would be to invite them to bear financial burdens that many of them would be unable and unwilling to assume, while to invite them to join us and at the same time deny them . . . equal participation in our games or in any of the rights and privileges which we enjoy, would be a proposition unworthy of ourselves and disparaging or disrespectful to them.

As a sop, the League condescended to recognize the "existence and merit" of non-League clubs in a constitutional amendment providing for the admission of one club each year under certain strict conditions. The club had to win the greatest number of games from the other outsiders during an entire season played under League rules, and its organization and conduct had to conform with the objectives of the League and its constitution. Indianapolis managed to gain admittance to the League in 1878 under this ruling. But for most outside teams the chances were almost invisible.

Modern spokesmen for the League have found it difficult to explain precisely why the major leagues have been limited to eight clubs. Research into the past would have told them that President Hulbert spoke from the beginning of the "impracticability" of writing a schedule for more than that many clubs. His reasons have a familiar modern ring. He pointed out as early as 1881 that increasing the membership would make the League an "unwieldy body" burdened with too many "tail-enders" to the detriment of the box office. Hulbert also felt that there were not enough first-class players to man more than eight teams.

Earlier still, the Chicago *Tribune* pointed out that having more than eight clubs in the League was "wholly incompatible with success, considered from a financial standpoint." It correctly called League clubs "a firm in which all are partners," and said that to admit more clubs would merely add to traveling expenses without augmenting revenue. The *Tribune* went on to raise the question as to whether allowing all clubs to enter the League was not "rather too communistic even for these liberal days." Modern spokesmen have also cited the failure of the twelve-club circuit, tried in the 1890's, as another reason for limiting the majors to eight clubs. They might also have cited the less-known twelve-club experiment of 1884.

The League's population requirement was another obstacle to clubs ambitious to join. The Tecumseh Club of London, Ontario, was kept out because its 25,000 population fell far short of minimum requirements. The League's popularity was not furthered by its inconsistency in admitting the Syracuse Stars and the Troy, New York, Club, even though neither city had the necessary 75,000 people.

A squabble between Troy and Albany, and eventually Worcester, involving admission prices, population, and territorial rights provides a graphic illustration of the complexity of some of the business problems the League was up against. It also reveals the squirming and twisting it took to solve them in these early, experimental years when the League's situation was so precarious. Troy first applied for admission to the League in December 1878, on condition that they could continue playing their profitable games with their natural rival, Albany, but were refused until they reluctantly agreed to give up this condition. Albany, "always ambitious to be on a level with her neighbor," hastened to ask for admission. But because the League did not want a ninth member, Albany was turned down.

Albany was not too unhappy about this, because it was confident it could continue playing twenty-five cent ball with all League clubs, which had to come to Troy anyway. However, the Trojans objected, on the ground that Albany was only four and three-quarters miles away, and therefore within Troy's five-mile zone, which was protected by the League constitution. Troy proved its point with a sworn statement from the city engineer that the distance between the two cities was less than five miles.* Therefore, out of respect for the League's rule on territorial rights, National League clubs did not play Albany during 1879.

Ironically, Troy, too, was soon stymied, for as a League club it

---

* The two ball parks were eight miles apart, however.

likewise had to cancel its own games with Albany. To "pacify" and "accommodate" the Trojans, the League constitution was changed at the end of the 1879 season, reducing territorial limits from five to four miles. In this way Albany was placed outside Troy's geographical jurisdiction, making it possible for the two rivals to play each other once more during the League season. Of course, now other League teams could also play Albany as well. But still Troy was not content. It now sought to have Albany fill the vacancy in the League created by the loss of Syracuse.

Meanwhile, Worcester was seeking to gain admittance to the League, but it had two stumbling blocks to overcome: admission price and population. Worcester removed the first one by agreeing to charge fifty cents. The second was not so easily surmounted, for Troy served notice that it would vote against Worcester unless Albany was admitted first. This threat was carried out. Since Worcester lacked the requisite 75,000 population, it would take a unanimous vote to get her in. Thus, Troy's one negative ballot would have stopped Worcester. But the League board of directors found a way to circumvent its own rules. It tied the new four-mile territorial regulation to population. The board decided to count not only the people in Worcester proper, but all those within its four-mile radius as well. This stratagem lifted Worcester over the 75,000 figure, obviating the necessity for a unanimous vote, and thereby cutting the ground from under Troy's threats to hold up Worcester's entrance.

Another practice of some League clubs added to the irritation of outsiders. The player contracts of independents were often ignored as League clubs went foraging for men. Like a tiger blaming the sheep's carelessness for letting himself be devoured, Abraham G. Mills blamed the "defective organization or actions" of the non-League clubs for losing their players, but said vaguely that the League intended to do something to protect these clubs.

Al Spalding remembered in his later years that after a game in St. Paul one League club left town with five of the finest Red Cap players in tow, "practically breaking up the team" and causing a great outcry over the "high-handed" raid. He also told of his personal embarrassment when A. G. Mills sent out several hundred circulars, over Spalding's signature, appealing to players to remain loyal to clubs with whom they had signed. That season, whenever Spalding tried to pick up an extra player, he was met with lifted eyebrows, a copy of the circular, and a rebuff. But despite promises and official resolutions, the League did practically nothing to end the abuse until it needed to counteract the bad public relations it was receiving from the practice.

Fortunately for the League in these trying years, no rival organization was formed strong enough to challenge it successfully. There were rumors, however, of plans for competing associations almost as soon as the League was organized. In November 1876, L. C. Waite, secretary of the St. Louis Red Stockings, sent out circulars accusing the League of wanting a monopoly and trying to dictate to outside clubs. He called for non-League clubs to band together, charge their own prices, and boycott League teams. Out of this came plans for a convention of outside clubs to be held at Pittsburgh in February 1877.

The Chicago *Tribune* regarded all this as the machinations of "a certain class" of club managers who wanted to "wipe out" the League in retaliation for being left out of it. The League itself was watching these maneuvers closely, and on the eve of the convention it moved swiftly in an effort to put a crimp in Waite's project and forestall the possible creation of a strong rival. Hulbert, Spalding, and Mills worked out a plan which the New York *Mercury* said was "to protect their interests." They drew up a "sensational circular" offering liaison between the League and outside clubs. The idea was inspired by an article previously published by Mills criticizing the League for pirating players and outlining a program for reform. Hulbert saw the article and, appreciating the need for improvement, invited Mills's counsel.

The League's proposed plan meant junking its earlier resolve against admitting outsiders on a second-class basis. The new deal offered mutual respect for player contracts to clubs which would ally themselves with the League. They were to notify the League secretary as soon as they engaged or terminated the services of a player, and no club was to employ a man under contract with another member. To check revolving—still a problem for non-League clubs—and tighten discipline, clubs which joined had to agree to expel players who violated their contracts or were guilty of "disreputable" conduct. They also had to refrain from playing a club which used such an "ineligible" player. National League playing rules were to govern all games, and all disputes were to be adjudicated by the League's Board of Directors. In short, the League proposed setting up a group of satellite clubs under its hegemony, but without offering them League membership or equal status.

Spalding immediately sent a copy of the plan, with a covering letter explaining its advantages, to certain clubs he thought might "fairly consider" it. Declaring that he had always urged "a liberal and paternal policy" toward non-League clubs, Spalding wrote that the new plan bestowed the benefits of League membership without its burdens. He said it guaranteed all clubs uniform hiring rules, a tribunal for settling disputes, and security against revolving, while leaving the co-operating clubs free to manage their own affairs. Coming on the eve of Waite's contemplated convention, the scheme was a shrewd diplomatic stroke aimed at diluting any possible threat to the League.

Waite reacted angrily. Spalding's "walk-into-my-parlor epistle" and his "heads-I-win-tails-you-lose" plan, he scoffed, were intended to shut out clubs in League cities, else why did he not wait for the forthcoming convention of independent clubs and invite them all to participate? The reason, he charged, was that Spalding "desires to monopolize baseball patronage in this country." Spalding never would have bothered with the non-League clubs, wrote Waite, if a new league was not in the offing. Spalding denied knowing anything about the proposed convention. He had simply forwarded the plan to the officers of three or four clubs who he

> believed to be intelligent, clear-headed, experienced men, working, not for personal notoriety but for the material interest of their clubs and capable of passing impartial judgment upon the merits of the plan. Consequently, I did not send it to Mr. Waite.

This clever mixture of flattery for some and sarcasm for Waite was concluded by Spalding with the statement that the organization of an outside association was "a matter of profoundest indifference to League managers." Nevertheless, the convention instigated by Waite was held in Pittsburgh as planned, where ten delegates representing seventeen clubs formed the International Association of Professional Base Ball Players. Candy Cummings, the old curve-ball pitcher, was chosen president; H. Gorman of the London, Ontario, Tecumsehs, vice president; and Jimmy Williams of the Columbus, Ohio, Buckeyes, secretary-treasurer.

The International was never a serious threat to the National League, however. For one thing, its membership was too diffuse and scattered, not sufficiently well-knit and balanced to make possible a tight, economical playing schedule or to present a strong front against the League. Like the early amateur and professional associations, the International did not limit its membership to any particular number or quality. About all a club had to do to be accepted was pay ten dollars annual dues. Clubs that wanted to compete for the championship simply notified the Secretary by April 1 and paid an extra fee of fifteen dollars. (Both these charges were doubled after the first season.) The International charged only twenty-five cents admission for championship games, and visiting clubs were guaranteed either seventy-five dollars or half the gross receipts, whichever was greater. Thirteen clubs joined at the beginning of the 1877 season and ten others came in during the season.

The International also repeated the mistake the National League made in its first season—allowing its clubs to contract with players while they were still bound to other clubs, provided that the second contract did not begin until the expiration of the one currently in force. Again paralleling the National League, the International in its second year banned contract negotiations prior to October 1. Most important, the International showed by its actions at the very outset that National League magnates had little to fear from it. The much-talked-of boycott of League teams never came to a vote, and International clubs continued to play League nines. The International even fell for the League's "proffer of amity" and agreed to notify the League secretary about all its player contracts so the League could honor its resolution to respect them. What is more, the new association, despite Waite's misgivings, signified its willingness to accept the League's new plan of alliance, provided the League would strike out the provision dealing with adjudication of disputes, because it had its own machinery for that purpose. But then, without even waiting to see if the League would do so, four International clubs went ahead on their own to affiliate themselves with the League plan in 1877, although the International did not officially ally itself with the League as a unit.

As far as can be ascertained, the League succeeded in lining up thirteen clubs under its plan during 1877. After the season it decided to make the relationship more formal by recognizing the clubs under its wing as members of "the League Alliance." Clubs that joined were now required to file an agreement with the League secretary according to a prescribed form and pay a fee of ten dollars to cover postage, correspondence, and printing.

Subsequently, the League Alliance became more exclusive. Not more than one club in any given city could join, and applicants had to be elected by incumbent members. Two adverse votes meant rejection. Markets were protected by extending territorial rights to prohibit games in Alliance cities between League clubs and outside clubs who were not members of the Alliance. At the same time, some degree of representation was granted by allowing each Alliance team to send two delegates to League meetings to discuss matters involving their interests, although they had no vote.

While it was experimenting with the Alliance, the League, always considering its own interests first, decided the time had come to put restrictions on its games with all non-League clubs, Alliance members included. At first there were no limits on these games. In fact, failure to book them was considered poor management. But the League now realized that to enhance the value of its own product, it would have to make its games something special. League men figured that too much of a good thing glutted the fans' appetite, so they cut out all pre-season games. During the season League teams played their own championship games on Tuesdays, Thursdays, and Saturdays. On off days they could still play outsiders, but not on League grounds. The Chicago *Tribune* of December 30, 1877, bluntly explained the reason:

> The truth is, gentlemen of the smaller cities, the League ... finds that it doesn't want you on their grounds. ... The League can make more money off thirty first-class games than they can off sixty ... and they are going to play the thirty with the clubs they think most likely to interest their patrons.

Yet League clubs did not hesitate to play each other in non-League cities when they thought gate receipts would make it worth while. The League also insisted that mixed games on non-League grounds had to be played with a League ball, according to League rules, and under the direction of a League umpire.* Besides, outside clubs always faced the possibility of having a game with a League club called off at the last minute, because a rained-out League game was usually played off the next day. So even if a game with an outside club had been scheduled previously, it had to be canceled in favor of the League playoff. But if a non-League club refused to play a scheduled game for any reason, it had to pay the League team $50. Non-League clubs also had to furnish a $100 guarantee to League teams, or half the gross receipts if they exceeded $200.

Non-League clubs were offended by the League's new legislation on guarantees and by what they considered a one-sided territorial rights policy. On this score, even those outside clubs who became members of the Alliance were in little better position. While membership protected them from games between League clubs and non-Alliance outsiders, Alliance members found their territory was still open to games between two League teams. And of course when an Alliance team played a League team, it had to do so under League regulations, including furnishing the required guarantees.

Non-League clubs deluged each other with letters calling for retaliation. The secretary of the Auburn Club wrote to every club in New York state, calling on them to "stick together and kick together." The Syracuse Stars expressed readiness to "act promptly, and with firmness, against any attempt at monopoly from whencesoever it comes." A boycott of League nines was urged by H. B. Phillips, manager of the Hornell, New York, Club. H. Gorman of the Tecumseh Club said that, instead of boycotting League teams outright, outside clubs should

---

* In 1878 and 1883 League clubs were given the option of waiving these conditions.

offer them only the same terms on which International Association clubs played each other—no more, no less.

The most severe indictment of the League was written by A. B. Rankin, a member of the International's Judiciary Committee. Attacking "the high hand" with which the League was undertaking "to control the baseball fraternity" as "unreasonably absurd," he asked, "Are we to submit to the caprice of a clique, or ring?" Rankin also criticized the League Alliance as an example of the "old 'pitch and toss' game" of " 'heads I win, tails you lose' " whose aim was to destroy the International. The Alliance merely invited clubs to a " 'feast of empty dishes,' " where they had no voice in the legislation that governed them.

The Chicago *Tribune* answered these objections with the argument that large guarantees were necessary to meet the higher payrolls and traveling expenses of the League. Outsiders were reminded that they were being offered the best quality baseball and, in any case, were free to purchase "these goods" or not, as they chose. In a letter to the Buffalo Club, Harry Wright tried to explain the League's point of view. He felt sure that the "feeling of bitterness" was due to "misrepresentation and general misunderstanding" of the League's motives. The purpose of the League's legislation, he said, was to improve the caliber of its games by playing fewer games and being more selective in choosing opponents. Playing only League games on League grounds would tend to make them all equally attractive. This policy worked no injustice on outsiders, because experience had proved that games with them on League grounds were "unremunerative." He defended the League's insistence on guarantees when visiting outside clubs as a means of giving "more dignity and importance" to those games. He had learned that when a team had to give a guarantee, it was much more likely to advertise in advance and to stimulate fan interest further by not playing on the days preceding the big game. The League did make a concession, in response to demands for a more liberal policy, by sanctioning pre-season games with local nines on League grounds.

The belief of A. B. Rankin that non-League clubs throughout the country could build a "grand organization" if they would "only stand firmly by each other" turned out to be a will-of-the-wisp. Despite all the discussion, the International's lack of solidarity was again demonstrated the following season when six of its members entered into a special arrangement with the League that gave them certain advantages in booking games. And from then on, the International gradually disintegrated. After two seasons it no longer had its Canadian members and then, as the National Association, limped through two more years before expiring at the end of 1880.

Other leagues founded during these years were, if anything, even weaker. For example, both the Northwestern League, founded in 1879, and the Eastern Championship Association of 1881 lasted only one season. These ephemeral organizations shared common characteristics. They all played twenty-five cent ball and often had no fixed schedules for their games. Inability to control their players or to stop revolving hastened their collapse. The National League scorned them as "weak efforts" at rivalry by clubs "left out in the cold." And certainly none dared challenge the League in League cities.

In 1883 the League Alliance, having served its purpose and now become a "nuisance," was abolished by the National League. Short-lived though it was, the Alliance expedient chronicles the League's first effort to extend its control beyond its own teams. It foreshadowed the time when the business would be molded into the single, all-encompassing, hierarchical structure called Organized Baseball.

As yet, during these years from 1876 to 1883, the overall baseball situation had an unsettled cast to it. Fly-by-night leagues and a host of independent clubs were operating. Some of these might associate themselves with the League Alliance, and then disband shortly after. Such a situation led to conflicting loyalties and contributed greatly to the fluid state of baseball affairs. And there were even those who still entertained the old dream of one loosely formed association to which all baseball clubs could belong on the same level.

Lastly, there was the National League. By 1882 it had emerged as the dominant, most stable baseball institution. It had dealt successfully with outside clubs and leagues while keeping its own organization intact. And now after a hazardous financial period it was beginning to glimpse a solvent, stable future. It was also, as we shall see, developing a workable labor policy. When the time came, therefore, to meet a serious challenge from another league, it was ready.

10

THE RESERVE CLAUSE

LABOR relations are of prime importance in any business. They are especially significant in baseball, because the business has distinct peculiarities. While it is true that any business can claim unique features, the business of running a baseball club does have some special characteristics. The baseball owners are interested in turning a profit, but they are also motivated, to a greater extent than those in other businesses, by the psychological satisfactions that come with having a winning team. Indeed, spokesmen for Organized Baseball frequently stress the "sporting" interest of the club owners and pay slight attention to their concern with running the clubs as a business investment. But even if this were true it does not necessarily mean, as Professor Simon Rottenberg points out, that they "will be prepared to take a loss on their baseball operations but only that they are prepared to take a smaller return from baseball investment than their capital would earn in some other use." The University of Chicago economist goes on to explain that, with the average baseball property worth five million dollars and some as much as fifteen million, "it seems unlikely that people will subject capital of this magnitude to large risk of loss for the pure joy of association with the game."

In the earlier baseball era, the need for entrepreneurs to establish the business on a paying basis was perhaps more pressing, although even then it was claimed that many of them had sources of income apart from baseball and were involved in it only for their own amusement. Certainly Al Johnson of Cleveland and Henry V. Lucas of St. Louis were men of means before venturing into baseball. On the other hand, Al Spalding of Chicago and Chris Von der Ahe, owner of the old St. Louis Browns, got their money directly and indirectly from baseball.

Whether interested primarily in money or fame, owners still must market their product successfully. To do this their teams must approximate each other in skill. Contests have to be sufficiently interesting and uncertain of outcome to attract fans. People would scarcely pay to see a champion New York Yankees team play a sandlot team. For this reason no single owner can sell the product by himself; he must market it in conjunction with his fellows. Major league owners are not only competitors, therefore, they are at the same time partners who must co-operate with each other to a much greater degree than in more conventional business enterprises.

Employer-employee relations are also unique in baseball. The employees not only help create the product sold; they are part of it. There is also a shortage of skilled men. Probably the only time this was not true was in the two-year period from 1898 to 1900, when the National League cut back from twelve clubs to eight. So while other entrepreneurs can give their support to the law of supply and demand, at least in regard to the legion of industrial workers, baseball owners are in no position to support this classic laissez-faire doctrine. This was especially so in baseball's difficult early days, when professional baseball was just becoming established. As might be expected, the players tried to get all they could for their services, which made the owners complain that the men were using "coercion" to force the clubs into "reckless" competition for them. They grumbled that the players, instead of estimating their worth in relation to the ten dollars a week they would otherwise earn as streetcar conductors, porters, or day laborers, wanted to charge all they could. To meet these special problems in handling their employees, the owners contrived special solutions.

Nevertheless, the broad development of baseball labor policy and philosophy closely parallels American industry at large during the second half of the nineteenth century. Baseball owners, like their contemporaries in American industry, looked upon labor as a commodity to be bought and sold in the market and exploited to the fullest. They often employed stern measures to bend their players to pliant submission and control. Many such measures were necessary to place the business on a firm footing, and some undoubtedly benefited the players as well as the owners. But, still, the players had no voice; the owners decided everything. Even the expulsion of Devlin and the other Louisville culprits, right though it was, represented a one-sided dispensation of justice, and set a precedent for arbitrary action by the owners against their employees.

The League found that the other policies which it instituted in the beginning—separating management from playing, checking revolving, ending corruption, establishing territorial rights, fixing prices, and excluding outside clubs—were not enough to ensure the success of the business. Expenses had to be reduced, and the most obvious way was to cut labor costs. In 1878 the League publicly declared against paying salaries higher than earnings warranted, as judged by the experience of the previous season. Again in 1879 President Hulbert announced that salaries must come down if baseball was "to be conserved in its best state." This theme became an old refrain for League owners and their supporters in the succeeding years. Even John Montgomery Ward, who later became the champion of the players, admitted that "extravagant" salaries were often paid.

The owners felt that they were not obligated to furnish complete financial support for the players, because the men could earn money in the off-season. Nick Young, secretary of the National League, saw no point in paying high wages because the players often squandered their money. The belief that players were being overpaid and would "kill the goose that laid the golden egg" was echoed in the press. The Cleveland *Plain Dealer* of October 10, 1879, exclaimed that players who received $1000 a season were actually earning $12 a game, or $6 an hour!

The owners' desire to cut salaries was understandable, in view of the fact that salaries were a major item of expense, and could represent as much as two-thirds of a club's total outlay, as these figures for the Boston Red Sox prove:

Year	Expenses	Salaries
1876	$30,758.52	$19,331.85
1877	34,443.46	22,420.00
1878	27,783.77	18,814.00
1879	25,620.13	15,759.92

The owners soon realized what was causing high salaries. It was competition among themselves for players. Scrambling for men jacked up payrolls and boosted costs. The owners believed the existence of even the wealthy clubs was threatened, and indeed that of "the whole professional fabric." To meet the problem, League bosses began restricting competition for the services of players. They did this by introducing the famous reserve clause. This device was used not only to stop clubs from bidding up salaries but to reduce the advantage which wealthy clubs had over less prosperous ones in securing skilled players. As Al Spalding acknowledged, the object of the reserve was "to prevent competition for the best players in each of the other clubs, and to keep those clubs together." But this was done at the cost of the players' right to bargain freely in the marketplace.

Clark Griffith, one of the most prominent figures in the business in the twentieth century, has accurately called the reserve "the backbone of baseball." It remains even today the keystone of the organized base-ball structure. Strike it, and the entire edifice trembles. Destroy it, and professional baseball must either collapse completely or be drastically altered. Mark T. Hughes, attorney for the New York Yankees, frankly recognized this in testifying before Justice Julius Miller of the New York State Supreme Court in 1946 that, if the baseball contract were declared illegal, "the great American game as we know it would be destroyed." Still more recently, Baseball Commissioner Ford Frick testified during the second investigation conducted by Representative Emanuel Celler that abolishing the reserve would drastically change professional baseball "to the detriment of players, fans, and club owners."

What precisely is this crucial clause of the baseball contract? It is an ingenious device which gives the club a continuing option on the services of the player and protects its property rights in him. When a player signs his first contract in Organized Baseball, he is in reality signing for the duration of his career, because he not only agrees to perform for the period specified (usually one season), but allows the club to "reserve" him for the subsequent season. Since each suc-ceeding contract which he signs contains the same provision, he cannot escape. The club can terminate the agreement upon thirty days' notice,* or can assign the contract to another club. But the player has no such prerogative. He cannot perform for any other team unless his contract has been assigned or he has been released. By signing with one club, the player surrenders his freedom ever again to bargain with and sell his services to the highest bidder. Once in Organized Base-ball, if a player refuses to sign his contract, or ignores the reserve rule, no other club will employ him. He must either come to terms with his particular club or quit his profession.

Since the baseball contract is a uniform one, all material points in it are the same, and the only subject of negotiation between a club and a player is the question of salary. The player may dicker with his club for more money, or even become a "holdout" by refusing to sign until he gets his price. A few stars like Amos Rusie, Mike Donlin, Dickie Kerr, and Edd Roush have held out for a season or more. Occasionally players like Roush and the famed Ty Cobb did not sign their contracts until the opening of the regular season, in order to escape spring training, which they disliked and thought unnecessary.

To be sure, the player has certain advantages when it comes to arguing for a raise. He knows the owner does not want him to be idle, especially if he is "good box-office." He realizes the owner wants him

---

* At first a player could be released without any notice. From 1887 to 1947 he received ten days' notice.

to sign as early as possible so he can get in playing condition. He also knows the public will support him if he has a good case.* But the owner still holds most of the cards. He knows the player cannot make as much money outside baseball, and he is hurting himself by not getting in shape to play. Most important, the owner knows that, in the final analysis, the player must either come to terms with his particular club or not play pro ball at all.

Like so many of baseball's business practices, the reserve clause grew out of trial and error. The League began by allowing the players to sign at any time with any club for the following year. After only two seasons it modified its original policy. By a constitutional amendment it banned any negotiations between players and clubs during the playing season of 1878. Even this relatively liberal rule was short-lived. At a meeting held in Buffalo, September 29, 1879, the owners introduced the reserve for the first time. They secretly agreed that each of them could keep five of his players off the market. These men would be "reserved" to the owner. The other owners would not "contract with, employ, engage, or negotiate" for the services of those players, and they would not "play any game of ball against any League or non-League club presenting in its nine a player reserved to another League Club." This plan was said to be aimed at the Chicago Club, because it was at first the only money-maker and therefore held the edge in the player market.

As long as only five members of a team were affected by the reserve arrangement, the rest of the players continued to enjoy relative freedom in bargaining, and even the reserved men, if they chose, could ignore the National League's fiat and seek employment with clubs outside its jurisdiction. The opportunity to play elsewhere was more attractive when rival leagues arose and fought trade wars with the National League. But even this escape corridor for players was cut off when the National League either defeated opponents or entered into grudging alliance with them. The first such accommodation came in 1883 with the American Association, which had established itself as a second major league. Such collaboration meant respect for each others' contracts, including reserve rights in players. It is interesting that at first reserved players took pride in being set apart from their teammates, and President Hulbert maintained that there was no feeling against the reserve: ". . . on the contrary, they are all anxious to be reserved, and their only fear is that they won't be."

The advantages of the reserve clause were so great that the owners gradually extended its application. In 1883 both the National League

---

* On the other hand, fans have jeered holdouts when they did appear in the lineup.

and the American Association agreed to let each of their teams reserve eleven men. This was increased to twelve in 1886 and fourteen in 1887, which in those days of small squads meant practically the entire team. The extension of the reserve in 1883 was accompanied by a temporary safeguard for the players—provision for a minimum salary of $1000, which remained in effect for six years.

Before 1887 the reserve clause was not specifically written into the contract. It was included by reference only. Under his contract the player agreed to comply with the constitution of his league as well as the National Agreement—the peace pact among leagues drawn up in 1883—and these two documents upheld the reserve system. This arrangement placed him at some disadvantage, because he was making a blanket commitment to follow rules which might be changed without notice, and it was his responsibility to keep up with them as best he could. Improvement came in 1887, when a players' committee met with representatives of the owners and succeeded in getting the reserve clause expressly incorporated into the contract.

The reserve clause was soon used in a variety of ways not originally contemplated. Their effect was to tighten the traces on the players. A man who stayed out of action for an entire season was still considered the property of his club, and upon his return he remained under its jurisdiction. While he was out, his club simply continued his name on its reserve list, in addition to the regular fourteen active men it was entitled to carry. In effect, this was a further extension of the reserve clause.

Pittsburgh exercised this authority over Jim McCormick. He pitched for the club in 1887 and was reserved for 1888, but refused to sign. Nevertheless, his name appeared on Pittsburgh reserve lists each year thereafter, and he was prevented from playing for another club. Michael Hines, catcher for the Providence Club, was a similar case. He chose to remain idle rather than submit to being reserved, and it was two years before he got back into baseball, because Providence continued to keep him out of action by exercising its right of reserve. The same held true in our own day. Players returning to baseball after serving in the armed forces during World War II remained the property of the same club to which they formerly belonged.

Thomas "Pat" Deasley's experience was a variation on the same theme. He tried to escape the reserve by signing his 1884 contract on condition that he would not be reserved for 1885. When he tried to hold St. Louis to the agreement, in the hope of selling his services elsewhere, the American Association refused to let him, giving the excuse that such an arrangement was an evasion of the reserve clause and "therefore not legal."

Even if a player was released by his club, he was still not a free agent but was at the disposal of his league and had to sign with any other club which within ten days might lay claim to his services. Players of disbanded clubs were technically free to join other clubs in their league immediately, except in 1884 and 1885 when ten days had to elapse before they could do so. However, this right was nullified by keeping active a disbanded club's franchise so it could sell its player contracts before going out of business. The most notorious example of this dodge was Buffalo's sale of the "Big Four" to Detroit in 1885.*

Worse yet, a club could still hang onto a reserved player even though it had not paid his salary. Charles Foley, for example, was ill for most of the 1883 season and received no pay while incapacitated. The following spring he was still unable to play, and the Buffalo Club refused either to sign him to a contract or to release him from its reserve list. Late in the season, when he had recovered somewhat, he offered his services to the club, but they were rejected. Yet Buffalo refused to let him accept minor league offers, and continued to reserve him again that fall, even though they had paid him nothing during the year.

Paradoxically, the reserve clause, originally adopted to enable clubs to retain players, also made it easier for clubs to dispose of them. With property rights in players so secure, it was simpler to sell or assign their contracts to other clubs, either to make money or to strengthen their teams. The "sales system," as it was called, was further encouraged by the rising market value of star players. Selling a player's contract amounts to selling a player. This practice is still an important part of Organized Baseball today. The sports pages repeatedly tell about "deals," "trades," and "swaps" of players, either planned or completed, and few news items are more certain to stimulate fan interest.

In the early days, clubs were accused of using the reserve to retain players for whom they had no possible use, just for the purpose of selling them in "livestock" transactions which players felt were "not at all flattering" to them. Players were all the more resentful when they began to realize that they commanded good prices on the market, yet received no part of the money when they were sold. When Chicago sold its star pitcher, John Clarkson, to Boston in the winter of 1887-88, the club was paid $10,000, more money than Clarkson had received for two and a half years of playing. The way the players saw it, this meant that the White Sox, aided by the reserve clause, had enjoyed Clarkson's services for two and a half years free of charge, with a bonus to boot. The great star Mike "King" Kelly, who had also been sold to

* See below, Chapter 15.

Boston by Chicago for $10,000, benefited at least by getting a sub-
stantial salary increase. On the other hand, when the New York
Metropolitans tried to sell John M. Ward's contract to Washington in
1889, he refused to go—evidence that the practice of selling players,
although greatly facilitated by the reserve, had not yet hardened into
an inflexible mold.

Since Ward's time the reserve clause has become one of the corner-
stones of Organized Baseball, and its pros and cons have been debated
repeatedly. In recent years Congressional investigations of baseball
have brought the controversial reserve into the spotlight once more,
and a great deal of attention has been centered on it in the press and
other media. Some of the arguments offered are not especially new.
They are simply warmed-over versions of those used in past baseball
history. Others have a more modern slant.

The favorite argument of proponents of the reserve is that in an
open players' market the wealthiest clubs would soon corral the best
talent, consequently destroying the necessary balance of playing
strength among teams. Hulbert appreciated this back in the 1880's. He
looked upon the League as a "business coalition," and he defended the
reserve as "a vital necessity" and a "perfectly just and proper stroke of
business."

A corollary to this argument is that the reserve clause, by stabilizing
the business, brings the greatest good to the greatest number. Without
it, inflated salaries would bankrupt not only the less favored clubs,
but by destroying the elements of competition, eventually the wealthy
ones as well, because they would have no one to play. Therefore,
while the individual may at times suffer, ball players in general are
better off. Baseball men and sports writers of the 1880's backed up
this contention by pointing to the heavy casualties among clubs before
the introduction of the reserve, and a modern student of baseball law
has agreed that "conventional solutions of free or 'workable' competition
completely break down . . . [since] Restoration of a free labor market
will return the industry to the chaos which ruled in its early years,"
and Clark Griffith has gone so far as to say that "freedom of contract
would be fatal to baseball."

The reserve clause is even defended as a necessary evil. In 1889
the St. Louis *Globe-Democrat* said, "The reserve rule is, on paper, the
most unfair and degrading measure . . . ever passed in a free country.
Still . . . it is necessary for the safety and preservation of the national
game." An old-time sports writer used the same argument, stating that
baseball's greatest stars may be only "Uncle Toms," but abolish the
reserve and professional ball would become "merely an exhibition of
grand opera." Numerous others have adopted this line, including

Congressman Emanuel Celler, who twice investigated baseball in recent years. The *Sporting News* quoted him as saying, "There's no doubt . . . that it's barbaric to tie a man up for life." But he favored keeping the reserve, on condition that its abuses be "obliterated or amended." Abraham G. Mills, on the other hand, dismissed the alleged injustice of the measure as "purely sentimental," and upheld the reserve on "practical" grounds as "of incalculable benefit to the ball player" and "the salvation of the game."

The reserve is also considered vital to the integrity of baseball—essential to maintaining public confidence in the genuineness of competition:

> Suppose a player, in all honesty, struck out with the bases loaded in a vital game in September, against the ultimate winner of the pennant, and the next season appeared with that winner. How long would the fans stand for that sort of thing?

Another defense, one which applies especially to modern baseball, is that clubs would hardly want to pay large bonuses to young prospects, or to undergo the expense of training them over a period of years, if they were to lose these players to a rival club when they were ready for the majors. Mention is also made of the high salaries paid to major leaguers, in an effort to show that the reserve clause cannot be so bad after all. Former baseball commissioner A. B. "Happy" Chandler justified the reserve on this ground, pointing out that "No major leaguer makes less than $5000 a year * and some make up to $100,000. If you call that peonage, then a lot of us would like to be in on it." Finally, supporters of the reserve cite testimony of the players and polls of player opinion as evidence that the men themselves now overwhelmingly accept the reserve clause.

Critics of the reserve clause, see in it an intolerable restraint upon individual freedom and upon the right to work where one chooses for the best pay one can obtain. News of the reserve scheme had no sooner leaked out when this issue of freedom was raised. The Cincinnati *Enquirer* of August 12, 1880, wanted to know, "What right has the League to say to any player where he shall play next year? The days of slavery are over." An important sports journal also condemned the reserve as "tyrannical" and "unamerican," the creator of a "special class of slaves." This accusation, which is still made, took its most novel form recently in the charge that the reserve was contrary to a provision of the United Nations Charter, which states that each nation must improve labor conditions and adhere to fundamental freedoms. A closely related argument is that the reserve, by making the ball

---

* Increased to $6000 in 1954 and with some exceptions to $7000 in 1957.

player "economically immobile," condemns him to serfdom or peonage. Commissioner Chandler's effort to justify the situation by calling attention to the high salaries paid players was rejected by Judge Jerome Frank in a recent baseball case with the remark that "only the totalitarian-minded will believe that high pay excuses virtual slavery."

The claim that without the reserve the best players would gravitate to the wealthy clubs is also rejected as superficial by those who disapprove of the reserve, because the richer clubs obtain most of the good players and win the pennants anyhow. By paying fat bonuses and setting up elaborate chains of minor league clubs as training grounds, the wealthy clubs can afford to grab the best young talent before the others ever get a chance at them. Other things being equal, rookies are more likely to sign with a rich club, because they can anticipate a greater lifetime return by playing with a club finishing in the money. (Of course, they might balance this advantage against the possibility that with a poorer team there would be more need for good players, and they would have more opportunity to play regularly.) Another argument against the effectiveness of the reserve is that rich clubs have purchased star players from poor clubs. The Yankees were able to denude the Boston Red Sox of stars, including Babe Ruth, in 1919 and 1920 because the Boston owner desperately needed money.

For proof that the wealthy clubs have all the best of it in spite of the reserve, critics offer the record of the wealthy New York Yankees compared with that of the impecunious St. Louis Browns. The Yankees won no fewer than twenty-four pennants in thirty-eight seasons, whereas the lowly Browns captured only one in fifty-three attempts. Moving the franchise to Baltimore in 1954 so far has not been any more productive of pennants.

Opponents of the reserve also claim that it keeps players from making the most of their ability and earning capacity. Players are sometimes condemned to being "bench-warmers," which means they are only able to play occasionally, when they should be developing their skill and earning more money playing regularly for another team. This is especially true of men who have the misfortune to play the same position as a team's star. Well-known examples of this are Ben Paschal and Sammy Byrd, who for years understudied Babe Ruth, and Charlie Silvera, who for years caught mainly in the Yankee bull pen because Yogi Berra was playing every day. In addition, the pro-reserve argument that under free competition, outstanding players would rush to clubs paying higher salaries, simply proves to critics that the men are presently underpaid.

The reserve is also blamed for keeping outstanding stars on perennial tail-end clubs at low salaries, with little chance of becoming members of a winning club and enjoying the higher pay and bonuses that go with it. The classic example in this instance is Walter Johnson, one of the greatest pitchers in baseball history, who for twenty-one years was with the weak Washington Senators, earning only about one-tenth as much as he doubtless would have received with a club like the Yankees. It was not until 1924, in the twilight of his career, that he finally pitched in a World Series. And, finally, the reserve is criticized for keeping players in leagues of lower classification longer than they would otherwise remain if they were working in an open market. For instance, the great pitcher Lefty Grove might have been winning games in the big leagues much sooner if it had not been that the owner of the Baltimore team waited years for the price he demanded before selling Grove to a major league club.

As in so many controversies, there are various shades of opinion as to the need for the reserve clause. Leslie O'Connor, an experienced baseball administrator who was assistant to baseball's first commissioner and later president of the Pacific Coast League, has advocated keeping the reserve, provided abuses are eliminated. Others who have considered the question thoughtfully agree that the reserve should be kept, with various modifications in order to make it more equitable—limiting its application to five or seven years, after which the player would be a free agent; adding safeguards to guarantee that every player could advance as far and as rapidly in his profession as his skill warrants.

More extreme are those who favor doing away with the reserve entirely and restoring free competition. This was the view presented as long ago as 1883 in the St. Louis *Republican* when it maintained that in baseball, as in the theater, competition is the heart of trade, and a player was worth as much as he could get. If small cities went bankrupt, said the *Republican*, let them; if they could not compete, they ought to quit: "as it is, the weak [towns] live off the strong." A modern critic, Attorney Jay Topkis, has also called for "healthy" competition. He thinks the reserve shields weak and incompetent owners, who count upon an irreducible minimum of paid admissions, low salaries, and player sales to keep solvent. He argues that the reserve makes competition fairly cheap for everyone, and under it an owner who does not wish to compete does not have to. In other words, while the wealthy clubs struggle for dominance, the reserve keeps the poor ones in business. He calls this "competition with brakes on." He admits that abandoning the reserve would bring a temporary period of hardship and severe re-adjustment, but he feels it would be worth it to get rid of parasitical clubs which now live off the attendance attracted by the better teams. He also thinks the minor leagues would end up on a more sound basis if the crutch of major league subsidies were taken away, because they would exert greater efforts themselves to retain baseball, and only cities which really wanted a club and could afford one would have one.

The problem here is that, while we know how the reserve works, we cannot be sure of what would happen if it were abolished. Merely citing conditions as they were in the 1870's, before the reserve was introduced, does not prove that eliminating it today would restore those same conditions. Baseball has changed. It is now an established business operated on a nation-wide scale, and changing some of its time-worn practices may not necessarily have the same effect now as it would when it was an infant industry.

The arguments for and against the reserve clause continued down to the present day. But even though the reserve clause has proved to be the main hinge of the baseball owners' labor policy, by no means has it been the only support on which they depended. The owners had more than one idea for controlling the salaries and actions of the players. But the reserve clause was the issue over which baseball men have fought longest and hardest.

11

THE SALARY PROBLEM

ALONG with the reserve clause, player salaries have been a perennial subject of interest and dispute in baseball. But whereas the reserve clause has been an issue periodically, arguments over salaries crop up every year. In fact, the pre-season salary negotiations between star players and owners have become a part of baseball ritual. Before each season, $50-a-week clerks avidly follow the day-by-day, blow-by-blow accounts of salary disputes, eagerly waiting to see whether their favorite stars will hold out for, say, $55,000 or settle for a mere $50,000. The handsome financial rewards enjoyed by leading major league players for hitting and throwing a baseball, like those paid other entertainers, is a singular phenomenon in American society and a striking revelation of contemporary values.

Ball players have not always done as well financially, although even in the decades after the Civil War, because they were highly skilled people, they received relatively higher pay than industrial workers and laborers. Nevertheless, their disagreements with the owners over salaries exemplified the conflict of interest between capital and labor so vividly apparent in those times, for, like their industrial counterparts, the baseball entrepreneurs tried to exploit their employees to the fullest by keeping salaries as low as possible. For their part, the players, like their fellows in industry, suffered the disadvantage of trying to bargain individually with owners who were combined against them. And again like industrial workers, the players tried to compensate for their weakness by forming a union and bringing matters to a head through open war with the owners.

The first effort of the owners to cut salaries by introducing the reserve clause was initially successful. The measure was particularly effective in reducing the salaries of the highest-paid men on the teams. In 1880, for instance, some of the Boston players were given sharp cuts. Tommy Bond, their hard-working pitcher, suffered the most with a slash from $2200 to $1500. On the other hand, a few players on the club enjoyed increases of $100 to $200 a year each. However, in the 1880's big league salaries rose steadily, assisted by the stabilizing effect of the reserve on the industry. Comprehensive figures on salaries paid in those days are non-existent, because some club-owners did not keep formal records. And many of the financial records that were kept have long since vanished. Nevertheless, we can get a good idea of salaries by piecing together fragmentary evidence scattered in various archives. The average salary of the Boston Nationals' ten-man squad was $1730 in 1878, $1430 in 1879, and only $1377.50 in 1880. Providence averaged $1278.51 for sixteen players in 1882 and $1446.66 for fifteen men in 1883.

As the business gradually took hold, salaries got better. An analysis of thirty-two surviving Cincinnati player contracts of the middle 'eighties shows that salaries ranged from $500 to $2000, or an average of $1620. These were agreements for six and seven months, except for one, which covered only five months' service. Cincinnati's complete payroll for a single season during the 'eighties was $28,750, which, divided among sixteen men, averaged $1790—considerably better than the figure based on the thirty-two random contracts examined. The field manager, Gus H. Schmelz, received only $2000 for twelve months' work in 1887, and even that was contingent on the club's finishing third in the final league standings. Otherwise he would get $200 less. (Fortunately for Gus, Cincinnati finished second that year.) Cap Anson did somewhat better as player-manager of the famous Chicago White Sox. Examination of one of his contracts, which is still preserved, shows that for seven months' work in 1884 he received $2500. American Association teams generally paid lower salaries than the older, stronger National League, whose wealthiest clubs, like Chicago and New York, had payrolls in the neighborhood of $40,000. In 1883 newspapers called the New York Nationals "The $40,000 Nine" and "The Gilt-Edged Team."

At the end of the decade, Spalding released a set of salary figures designed to demonstrate the steady increases in pay during the 'eighties. His figures showed a sharp rise from an average of $1243 for sixteen selected players in 1881 to an average of $2670 for a larger selection of sixty-four in 1889. It must be kept in mind that when Spalding gave out these figures, the players were in open revolt, and he was trying to put the National League in the most favorable light for propaganda purposes. He took care to include the salaries received each year by sixteen outstanding players. Less-skilled players received much less money.

Maybe the salary of the old-timer would amount to little more than pocket money to a present-day star, but we have to remember that in those days he was still relatively well off, considering that he could earn three or four times as much as the average industrial worker, whose yearly wages came to only about $440. Andrew Carnegie made 20,000 times as much as a worker in one of his steel mills. And millionaire Jim Fisk was paying workmen on the Erie Railroad $1.62 for a twelve-hour day. Government figures indicate that, depending upon the industry and the state in which they worked, laborers around 1880 might receive anywhere from $1.15 to $1.50 a day, teamsters from $1.20 to $1.65. Skilled workers like machinists, coopers, compositors, and cabinetmakers could make from $1.90 to $2.75 a day. By 1890 these figures were a little higher. The New York *World* reminded the players they were getting considerably more money than the average clerk, laborer, artisan, or even professional man, and for substantially less work. For example, Buck Ewing, who made $10 a week as a teamster before becoming a star catcher, was paid $1000 in 1881 and enjoyed steady increases until he reached $5000 in 1889. Over the nine-year span his baseball earnings totaled $28,000. Cases like these were not lost on the owners, and they were quick to point out that under the reserve system the players were well rewarded, especially compared with what they might have earned at other jobs.

But if salaries were going up during the 'eighties, so were profits, and it is doubtful that salaries kept pace with them. Again, figures on profits for this early period are very fragmentary. Judge Thayer, in a decision involving the Metropolitan Club of the American Association in 1885, stated: "and those Games are, as we well know, the source of very great profits; so much so that the business of this association is becoming a very lucrative business productive of immense sums of money annually to those who engage in it."

What constitutes "great profits" may be a moot question, but some figures can be given to show the scale on which the business was conducted. Scattered information from various sources indicates that a major league club's operating expenses ranged anywhere from $24,000 to $40,000 a year. The Philadelphia Club of 1884 had total receipts of $39,582.84 and total expenditures of $33,554.05, leaving a balance of $6,028.79. The shareholders got three-quarters of this surplus, and the rest went to Manager Harry Wright. In 1885 the club did better than twice as well financially, ending up with $13,106.68, which was divided the same way as the year before. On top of this, the club spent over $2000 on its ball park. The treasurer's report of the Detroit Club in 1881 showed the club opened the season with $5000, had $35,000 in gross receipts, and finished up with a balance of $12,440. Providence, starting with $3,098.19 in 1883, added gross receipts of $48,300.26. After deducting expenses, the club had a profit of $6,649.05 for the year.

The major leagues enjoyed eight successive years of rising attendance and income during the 'eighties. In 1880 only a minority of National League clubs finished with a surplus, but on the threshold of the season of 1881, President Hulbert announced that "at no time since the beginning of the League have the clubs been in so healthy a financial condition at the beginning of the season as this year. There is not a 'weak sister' among them." From then on League finances steadily improved. The season of 1883 was hailed as an "unprecedented success." With the exception of Detroit and Cleveland, who lost an estimated $2500 between them, all National League clubs kept out of the red, ranging from Buffalo, which broke even, to Chicago, with about $20,000 profit, and Boston, with $48,000. The 1885 season, probably the poorest of the decade, was financially more successful than anticipated, while 1886 was marked by "phenomenally large attendance," and "financially, too, it was a very profitable season." The next year was rated the best on record up until then. The season of 1889 was the finest of the decade, and Spalding admitted to a profit of $750,000 for all League clubs in the period from 1885 to 1889, but claimed that $600,000 of this was reinvested in the business.

In spite of the improved profit picture and the help the reserve clause was furnishing them, the owners still complained about the "flood tide of growing salaries" which, in their estimation, was "swelling to unreasonable and ruinous proportions." Much of the blame for this was put on managers, whose enthusiasm outdid their business judgment when it came to signing the players. So in order to bolster the weaker clubs, avoid "universal bankruptcy," and check the "Munchhausen" growth of salaries, League and Association clubowners banded together to put a ceiling on wages. At Saratoga, New York, in August 1885, committees from both leagues drew up a plan which became known as the Limit Agreement. This plan, with minor revisions, was ratified by the two major leagues at a joint meeting in New York City the following October. Under it, all clubs pledged not to pay any player more than $2000 a season. Thus, even before the reserve clause was given full application, the owners were supplementing it with an important restraint of a different kind.

Sporting Life supported the salary lid on the ground that only about a sixth of the players were affected, and that it was necessary to protect the poorer clubs. It invited players who did not like the plan to take up "other lines" if they could make more money there.

Passing this new legislation was one thing; abiding by it was something else. The owners failed to keep their pledge to each other. Unlike the reserve, this rule could be secretly ignored by an owner. The others might suspect he was not living up to it, but it was not easy to prove. It is only now that we have documentary evidence to show how the rule was flagrantly broken. In fact, the ink was hardly dry on the limitation plan before the owners began circumventing it, using under-the-table gratuities or making flimsy pretexts for paying stars more than the limit allowed. Only one week after passage of the rule, all of Chicago's players promptly signed their contracts, even though most of them had received over $2000 the previous season—evidence that either the rule was already a dead letter, or else the management was gifted with superlative persuasive powers. Bid McPhee signed a contract with Cincinnati in February 1887 providing for $2000; but attached to the official, printed document was a further agreement, written in longhand on club stationery:

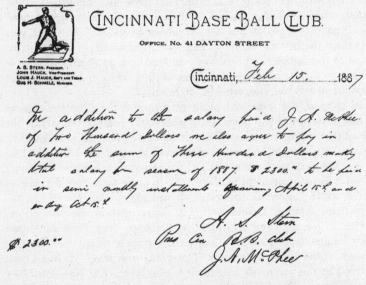

In addition to the salary paid J. A. McPhee of two thousand dollars we also agree to pay...the sum of three hundred dollars making total salary per season of 1887 $2300.00 to be paid in semi monthly installments commencing April 15th and ending October 15th.

Mike Kelly's contract with Boston in 1887 also called for $2000, but the club paid him an additional $3000 for his picture! Check stubs found in old business records conclusively prove other violations. And the salary figures released by Spalding really exposed the practice, because they revealed a number of salaries in excess of the limit.

Some newspapers defended these tactics with muddled logic. They said it was far better to keep a virtually worthless rule than to "silently acquiesce" in existing high salaries by repealing it. The New York *Clipper* openly suggested that the rule could be by-passed by paying bonuses to players for special services or for temperate habits. The players, of course, objected to cuts. Some like Jim Keenan of Cincinnati argued with more stubbornness than polish:

> i played good ball for cincinnatia last year caught well and stood third in the Club in batting i think that pretty good. ... you want me to sign contract fore ... three hundred dollars less than i got last year i don't think that is right ... closing to hear a good answer from this letter as soon as possible don't care if i git release or not.

The Limit Agreement was the boldest move to cut labor costs, but it was not the only method the owners used to accomplish the purpose. They chipped away at salaries by levying various exactions on the players. Beginning in 1877, the National League taxed its men fifty cents a day on road trips to help pay their board. Players had to furnish their own uniforms, keep them clean and repaired, and replace them as necessary. At first, the League simply deducted $30 from salaries for uniforms. Then it began requiring players to provide themselves with "a uniform to be selected and designated" by the club. Both League and Association contracts spelled out in detail each article to be furnished, including a necktie, which professionals sported in those days along with moustaches. However, the O'Rourke boys, John and James "Orator," balked at paying the Boston Nationals for their suits. The "fastidious young men," as the Chicago *Tribune* called them, signed contracts only after some of their friends put up the money for them.

The owners could even save 100 per cent on salary while a player was out with injuries or illness. Under the contract, the player assumed "all risk of accident or injury, in play or otherwise, and of illness from whatever cause," and while on the sidelines he "had no claim for wages." The player was required to take a medical examination or treatment whenever directed, the physician to be selected by the club and paid by the player. But the club reserved the right to decide whether he was fit to play, regardless of the result of the examination. Ross Barnes, Chicago star, was out of action for three months in 1877 because of illness. A thousand of his $2500 salary was deducted, and, when he brought an action against the club to recover it, the court ruled against him, on the grounds that the club need not pay for something it had never received.

A troublesome problem related to salaries was "advance money."

Because they were paid on a six- or seven-month basis, most of the players ran short of money in the winter and were in the habit of asking for an advance on their contracts to tide them over until the next season started. In fact, many of them came to depend upon salary advances. Then, having accepted these handouts, they felt obligated to sign for less money than they might otherwise have done.

Players might draw from $100 to as much as $500 against their future earnings. They even welcomed smaller amounts. Although he thought the practice "most pernicious," A. G. Mills recognized that it was necessary in some cases, otherwise "the poor devil will starve." Others like Gus Schmelz appreciated the financial straits of some of the men. In a letter to the club secretary, he said, "I wish you would send Smith's wife $25 by *express* at once. You can charge the same to my account and I will collect from Smith later on in the season."

Numerous other letters could be cited: "I have Done nothing all winter & My Brother being Sick that I have found use fore all my Money." "necessity compells me..." "I am in Straitend sercum-stances..." "i am in Very Great Nead." "Could you passeable advance me any money on next season salary I know it is against the rule of the Club but I am completely bankrup and if you could advance me something I would feel very grateful to you for I am deeply in need of it." These semi-literate excerpts are from some of the more pathetic appeals. One player, unwilling to trust himself to pay his rent, entered into a formal agreement whereby the club would withhold one-seventh of his monthly wage of $150 and use it for his "landlord's birthday" on the first of each month. Bob Feller and other moderns may think they are taking a completely new line when they advocate that the ball clubs assist players in securing winter employment, but their sug-gestion was anticipated at least eighty years ago. Here are a few lines from Al Bushong's letter to the Buffalo Club dated December 27, 1877: "Now if by any means, You could get a situation for me—why You could advance the fare from here to there—(for which I could give you a note on my salary).... I do not care to mention it to you but any situation would be very acceptable to me, at present, that would pay me some above my board...." Then, with a touch of wry humor, "... I am almost as bad as Devlin after a situation—but not like him in any other respects." Henry Kappel had an original approach. He requested $100 so he could work out during the winter in a Philadelphia gymna-sium, because "they learn you more than the rest of them."

Although the owners were known to charge interest of 6 to 8 per cent, they objected to advance money because it encouraged extrava-gance among the men. They also feared that, having pocketed the advance, a player might "go back on them" and jump to a rival league, as some did during baseball trade wars. Rueful experiences during the 1884 war with the Union Association led the major leagues to legislate the following year against the custom of giving advances. However, this was not the first nor was it the last attempt to abolish it, and the owners were still talking about trying to do so as late as 1891.

Wage policy is always a prime source of friction in labor-management relationships, and the baseball business was no exception. The players were displeased over the preoccupation of the owners with keeping down labor costs. They resented the various devices used to cut their salaries. The bad feeling engendered over this issue was an important factor in the eventual open break between labor and management.

12

THE QUESTION OF DISCIPLINE

IMPORTANT though the reserve clause and salaries were, they were not the only labor-management problems which baseball faced in the era of the 1880's. Here again, the baseball business is unique. While industrial employers have lately become more concerned with the welfare of their employees—in order to keep them happy and so gain more efficient production from them—baseball owners have from the very beginning been vitally concerned with their players' personal habits and conduct. In amateur days, when the players handled everything themselves and winning was less important, physical condition did not need to be stressed so strongly. But when the game became a business and money was invested, the employers became very concerned over the players' ability to give their best performance every day of the season, since the success of the business depended upon it. With this in mind, the owners prepared a series of strict rules for the players' conduct.

The whole question of condition and behavior was of course vitally important to the player as well. For in the long run his salary depended to a large degree on the number of paying customers he could attract, and his drawing power in turn depended at least in part on the skill he could demonstrate. But one of the difficulties was sheer human frailty. Players were not always wise enough, or strong enough in character, to take care of themselves properly in order to play their best and to extend their careers as long as possible. So the owners were hardly to be blamed for taking steps to protect the human property in which they had invested. The rules they passed governing the deportment of their players in the early professional era were often necessary, in view of the rough-and-ready, swashbuckling characters who played professional baseball in those days.

Readers of the sports pages in the 1880's were frequently regaled with accounts of player escapades. They could read how Sam Crane, second baseman of the Metropolitans, was arrested for running away with Hattie Travenfelter, wife of a Scranton fruit dealer, and her husband's $1500; or how seventeen-year-old Zella Coleman had catcher Edwin Bligh arrested on a charge of being the father of her unborn child, she having "yielded to his unholy desires last May." A particularly brazen stunt reported in the Cincinnati *Enquirer*, May 28, 1889, was that of pitcher Leon Viau, who went to the mound drunk—"a head on him the size of a brewery tub"—and blew the ball game.

While many ball players were sober and steady, doubtless fewer looked upon baseball as a serious business career than nowadays. The average modern player is apt to be better educated, more mature, and more intent on taking the best advantage of his relatively short career. Drinking, late hours, and wenching were more common in the early decades of professionalism than they are now—or at least more regularly publicized in the newspapers. One critic asserted that when teams traveled, "the majority [of players] seemed to think . . . that the moment they got on a train or on a steamer, or entered a hotel, then and there commenced their license to indulge in questionable 'skylarking.'" Ball players, of course, had no monopoly on drinking during this period. After the Civil War the consumption of liquor in the United States grew alarmingly. Between 1860 and 1880, investment in the liquor business increased 700 per cent, and saloons multiplied in the cities. Reformers became increasingly concerned with the rising intemperance. But it must also be recognized that professional ball playing was an occupation with inherent opportunities for players to fall into trouble. As A. G. Mills, president of the National League, pointed out,

> The occupation of a ball player is full of life and excitement. Each player is the hero of a certain circle of admirers, and he often finds hero-worship an expensive luxury. Ball players as a rule are generous and companionable. They have friends in all of the many cities they visit, and the frequency of opportunities and temptations to part with their earnings is not common to most other pursuits.

To cope with bad behavior, the League set up a "new system of discipline and penalties" in 1880, presenting it as an "Address to the Players." It announced a crack-down on the wayward, with suspensions "from play, *and from pay*," for "illness, insubordination, or misconduct of any kind." If a club declined to act, the League itself would step in. Suspension might be for an entire season, and even carry over into the next. This disciplinary step, the League explained, "surrounds the player of morally weak tendencies with wholesome restraints," adding that justice to club managers, stockholders, the public, and the game required players, like employees in any business, to be accountable for full performance of their contracts. The way to compel this was to "reach the pocket as well as the pride of a player who deliberately and systematically falls short of the honorable discharge of his obligations toward the club and the patrons of baseball."

These principles were incorporated into the uniform contract, along with strictures against gambling in any form. The problem persisted despite these measures, and the owners continued to be concerned about the deportment of their employees. Drunkenness in particular bedeviled them for years, because it jeopardized "the hundreds of thousands of dollars invested . . . in baseball stock companies." *Spalding's Guide* avowed, probably with some exaggeration, that "every baseball city in the land suffered" from this evil in 1884, and "it undoubtedly bankrupted a third of the clubs which encountered failure that year."

Ironically, Spalding's own club was among the worst offenders. His White Sox got so rambunctious on a road trip that Manager Cap Anson wrote his boss, urging generous distribution of fines. President Spalding backed him completely, because he was "tired of apologizing for the shortcomings of some of our men, and trying to explain away their many misbehaviors." He ordered the players to be in their rooms by eleven o'clock, and if Anson thought they might sneak out for "a night of carousal," he was to hire as many detectives as necessary to keep them in their rooms. Spalding also threatened to fine the players "double what it will be for dissipation" if for any reason he became convinced they were "not playing up to their highest standard, and doing the very best in their power to win games."

As a general rule, team managers did the fining. "Please charge to O'Connor and Smith $10 each which I fined them for being out until 1:20 last night" was typical of countless cases. Of course, players were also docked for stupid plays and for loafing on the field: "Charge Carpenter $5 for not running an infield hit out to first."

The need for discipline and a system of penalties for bad actors is understandable, but the owners overstepped. They began abusing their power. On the matter of fines, for instance, many seem justified; others do not. Providence handed John "Moose" Farrell a $200 penalty for a drunken "shore resort escapade," which took place the night before he made five errors on the field, costing the ball game. Pitcher William "Blondy" Purcell was relieved of $100 for cutting the cover of the ball in order to have a new one brought into play. These and other stiff fines were criticized as "abnormally large," "excessive and outrageous," and "sheer robbery."

A notorious case was the fining of "Yank" Robinson by Chris Von der Ahe, quixotic owner of the St. Louis Browns. The trouble started when

Robinson appeared on the field in dirty pants. Ordered to change them, he sent a boy across the street for clean ones, but for some reason the gatekeeper refused to allow the youngster to re-enter the ball park. Robinson exploded with a stream of curses directed at the gateman, and for his outburst was promptly fined $25 and "roasted" in public from the grandstand by Von der Ahe. Robinson was willing to apologize if the fine were removed, but Von der Ahe remained adamant, threatening the blacklist, expulsion, and forfeiture of salary. The other players supported Robinson, and refused to proceed to Kansas City for the next game. The team, minus Robinson, was finally coaxed into going. The dispute was ended only through the intervention of Manager Charles Comiskey, who insisted that Robinson be reinstated.

The St. Louis *Globe-Democrat* called the incident the "most serious revolt ever known in a ball club," and warned, "The time has come when ball players will, if pressed too far, assert their independence." Charges that the St. Louis players threw the three-game series in Kansas City in retaliation were vehemently denied by Comiskey. Von der Ahe, a colorful German immigrant, concluded the affair with a characteristic statement: "I am still der boss of der club, and I intend to run it in my own way."

There were many other instances of high-handed tactics by the owners. President Arthur H. Soden of the Boston Club fined and suspended Charlie Jones in a dispute over back salary. While the club was on a road trip near the end of the 1880 season, Jones put in a claim for $378, which he said the club owed him. The Boston owner maintained it was customary to defer payment of salaries until the players returned to the home city, and accused Jones of trying to obtain the money ahead of time so he could desert the club in Cleveland and return to his home in Cincinnati. When he was given a $100 fine and suspension, Jones made his way home, whereupon Soden expelled and blacklisted him. Jones argued that since he was already under suspension, the club had no claim over him. Even though the player was upheld by the Common Pleas Court of Cleveland, where he had appealed, the League refused to reinstate him. He remained blacklisted for more than two years, and re-entered baseball only when the American Association allowed him to join one of its teams.

Harry Overbeck fared only a little better. Chris Von der Ahe persuaded him to jump a minor league club and come with his Browns, only to release him after he had played in a few games. Out of a job and unable to return to the Northwestern League, which had expelled him for leaving its Peoria Club, Overbeck sought redress in the courts and succeeded in collecting over $400 from Chris. Overbeck's attorney regarded the successful litigation as proof that players had "well-determined rights" which baseball owners must respect, and a warning that they could not treat players "like slaves or cattle" unless the players put up with it.

Sometimes players scarcely knew why they had been fined, and learned of the penalty only when they opened their pay envelopes. After losing a game to Baltimore, six Louisville players were fined $100 each and threatened with more of the same if they lost the next game. Most of them went on strike. The American Association granted them hearings, and investigation showed that during the season eight men had been fined a total of $1425. Settlement was reached when some of the fines—those for bad playing—were remitted.

Players were even charged for losing equipment. Clarence "Kid" Baldwin, Cincinnati catcher, had to pay $13.50 when he "lost the pad and mask." Instances like these gave credence to the claim that "the unrestricted power of imposing fines is often abused by unscrupulous managers and works great injustice to players."

On the other hand, owners sometimes returned fines and awarded bonuses for meritorious work. The same "Kid" Baldwin was reimbursed $40 "for good behavior and good work." Tony Mullane, famous pitcher, received a bonus of $52.50 for winning five extra games. Once when Jim Keenan went behind the bat though injured, his manager wrote, "He is to have $10 extra if we win the game. Did this because his hands are puffed some and he really ought to have today off." There was even a case in which the National League Board of Directors passed a resolution directing Louisville to pay Charles "Pop" Snyder the balance of his salary for the season, which the club had withheld. And Milwaukee was expelled from the League in 1878 for nonpayment of debts, including back salaries of several players.

An added fillip in the effort to maintain discipline was the hiring of detectives to keep tabs on the men. President Hulbert had early sanctioned the use of Pinkertons to guard against attempts to throw League games, and ever since then, baseball has used detectives to watch out for gamblers and to check on the habits of players off the field. As recently as 1954 Philadelphia shortstop Granny Hamner's protest over finding a detective on his track received widespread publicity.

In 1886 Al Spalding asked National League clubs to employ a detective agency to shadow players and submit weekly reports on their activities. His purpose was to elevate the social standing of the players by extirpating what he regarded as bad habits, especially drinking. Spalding had in mind not just temperance during the playing season; he wanted to enforce total abstinence even in the winter off-season.

He had already ordered his own club to stay away from liquor, having exacted a "bone-dry" pledge from the White Sox—no wine, beer, or whiskey till the end of the season. Cap Anson administered the oath in President Spalding's Chicago sporting goods store. When some of his players slipped from what for them must have been dizzy summits of morality indeed, Spalding engaged a detective to trail them both at home and on the road. After reading the report of his sleuth, the Chicago president called seven of his players on the carpet, suggesting they determine their own punishment. The sheepish culprits decided to fine themselves $25 each—enough to pay the $175 which the detective's services had cost Spalding.

While there is no evidence that the League officially hired detectives, other clubs did use his method. Officials of the Philadelphia and Pittsburgh clubs, for example, hired detectives to watch their players in 1887, when they suspected them of dissipation. The owners were proved right when some of the boys were caught "in the great elbow act."

During the winter of 1888 the magnates tried to solve their two problems of high salaries and misconduct with one piece of legislation, the notorious Classification Plan. They hoped to slay these twin dragons with one fell stroke. This new expedient was particularly odious to the players. The idea, thought up by John T. Brush, then owner of the Indianapolis Club, provided for the classification of all players into five groups, according to their "habits, earnestness, and special qualifications" as displayed during the previous season. Depending upon the category in which they were placed, the players were to be paid as follows:

Class	Salary
A	$2500
B	2250
C	2000
D	1750
E	1500

In other words, personal conduct, as graded by the managers and owners, was to be a determinant of a player's salary.

Actually, the scheme was not new. It had been broached as early as 1882 and again in 1884 as a substitute for the reserve system. It was both praised and condemned, and no action was taken at the time. Now, in the deed, it was denounced as unworkable, because additional salary would be paid surreptitiously. A. G. Mills, who had been lukewarm to the idea when first put forward (as had A. G. Spalding), now stigmatized it as "wrong in principle" and, when added to the reserve, which Mills thought "technically illegal," it amounted to "overloading the business end of the game." In Mills's estimation, a manager who "can't handle salary with the powerful reserve rule at his command ought to have a wetnurse." The legislation was put through nonetheless.

This whole conglomeration of plans, regulations, and penalties was reinforced by the dread blacklist, favorite weapon of industrial employers of that era. It represented a constant threat held over the heads of ball players. The blacklist was only a shade less drastic than outright expulsion. The difference between the two penalties was that a blacklisted player did have a chance of being reinstated. Blacklisting had the same advantage as a milder penalty introduced in 1879—suspension for a relatively short period. Before that year clubs had been reluctant to use the only course open, expulsion, because they did not always care to lose the transgressor's services permanently.

The League formally inaugurated blacklisting in 1881. Players, managers, and umpires could be put on the list for "dissipation" or "general insubordination." This loose terminology could mean almost anything a particular owner wanted it to mean at any particular time. Once listed, the player came up against a solid wall of interclub agreement separating him from his livelihood. Theoretically, he had a right to appeal, but the trouble was that he had to wait until the annual winter meeting of the League before exercising it. Besides, he might not know just how to go about appealing, and he might not have the money to get to the meeting. Meanwhile, his salary was cut off. Even if his appeal were upheld, he would be lucky if he collected his back salary.

The blacklist came in handy when the National League owners were involved in their trade war with the American Association in 1882. In 1884, in an effort to prevent players from going over to the enemy Union Association, the National League threatened to blacklist men who failed to sign contracts within thirty days. The "crowning outrage," as one player expressed it, was the American Association's peacetime attempt to coerce the men into accepting the salaries offered them or be blacklisted. The minutes of the Association's March 1887 meeting record this decision:

> Any player ... who shall hold off and refuse to sign a regular contract ... for the purpose of harassing the club or compelling it to increase his salary, or shall by any means, directly or indirectly endeavor to attempt willful extortion from the club ... shall upon complaint and satisfactory evidence from the club so aggrieved, be placed upon the black list.

Press criticism and public opposition were so strong that this use of the blacklist was not enforced, and the rule was repealed in 1889.

Fragmentary records of blacklisted men show that at one time as many as thirty-four players and one umpire were proscribed. In those days there were no bones made about having a blacklist. Al Spalding, leading figure in the League, praised it highly. "No piece of legislation," he thought, "was so well calculated to give good results since gross acts of intemperance or insubordination were subversive to discipline and good order." He also saw in it protection for "honorable and manly players" who complained of the conduct of others. Shorn of Spalding's polite phraseology, this could be interpreted as encouraging stool-pigeons. Still, John Ward, leader of the players, thought the blacklist had its merit, provided its abuses could be eliminated. In those less sophisticated times, organized baseball did not avoid the use of the term blacklist, and the word appeared without apology in league constitutions. Baseball still has a blacklist, used mainly to enforce its uniform contract and reserve clause, but it is more circumspect about naming it. Documents today euphemistically provide for an "ineligible list," a "restricted list," and a "disqualified list."

Thus the National League—and along with it the American Association, when it came into existence—hammered out a labor policy charted by trial and error and moved by practical considerations. The owners were more interested in what worked than in finely spun theories. Many of their measures, though harsh and arbitrary on paper, were less so in actual application. The Limitation Rule is a good example.

Despite all the bitter disagreements between the owners and the players, however, neither ever resorted to the violence which so often characterized labor-management relations in that era. Perhaps the reason is that the players were too valuable a property, or that they were so much in the public eye that the use of physical force against them would have caused too great an outcry from the fans. As for the players resorting to such methods, even the poorest paid among them was probably too comfortably fixed to accept the violent measures advocated by the minority of extremists like the I.W.W., popularly known as the Wobblies.

Still, disciplinary measures, which at times were carried too far, stirred up player resentment, especially since the players had no effective channels for redressing their grievances. As John M. Ward later attested, major league clubs had for years "been seeking to increase their hold upon the players. They have increased the number to be reserved; they have adopted a maximum salary limit; they have placed the players on Black Lists; have refused to allow them to earn an honest livelihood with other like Clubs while declining to give employment themselves; they have bought and sold them like chattels." These were the thoughts in the players' minds, eventually to be translated into action when the opportunity for revolt arose. But before the open break was precipitated, the National League was menaced from another direction. It was seriously challenged by a group which aspired to enter the business on their own terms and in competition with it. Thus began a series of trade wars which were to rock baseball in the next few years.

PART THREE

ORGANIZED BASEBALL

13

COMPETITION AND TRADE WAR

IT IS IRONIC that the National League itself was partly responsible for the formation of its first successful rival, the American Association. By the early 'eighties the League had solved its most pressing financial problems and was proving that professional baseball could be a successful business operation. With this example before them, it was only natural that others should try to come into the business.

The League also opened the way unintentionally for competition by failing to place teams in several important cities, "all with populations well educated to" baseball, who were "compelled to be content with a few games annually between amateur and co-operative teams." Besides, old animosities toward the League still rankled in some of these communities. Ever since expelling the Athletics and the Mutuals in 1876 the League had stayed out of New York and Philadelphia. There had been trouble when the old St. Louis Browns had resigned from the League in 1877, and their successors remained in bad grace because of their penchant for playing quarter ball on Sundays and for selling beer in the park. Louisville, forced to quit the League in 1877 because of financial difficulty, still was suspect in the eyes of the League. A game booked with Harry Wright's Red Sox in 1881 was cancelled by the Sox after it was learned that Louisville had inadvertently played a team with an expelled National Leaguer in its lineup.

The most recent club to part company with the League, Cincinnati, was also the most bitter toward it. Oliver Perry Caylor, sports editor of the *Enquirer*, had denounced the League's "outrageous proceedings" in expelling Cincinnati, and warned that his favorites would take the lead in forming a rival association. "Anything to beat Boss Hulbert" was the attitude in the city.

League or no League, baseball was very much alive in these localities. In St. Louis the Reds, champions of the League Alliance in 1877, were members of the International Association during 1878. With the organization of the Brown Stockings as a co-operative nine in 1879 from the remnants of the Reds and the old Browns, St. Louis was ready for a new baseball role. An active participant in these developments was Alfred H. Spink, who later recorded, in a book on baseball, how he helped organize the Sportsman's Park and Club Association at the end of the 1880 season to put the Grand Avenue grounds in shape for playing.

Among Spink's associates was Chris Von der Ahe, a picturesque figure who conducted a saloon and boardinghouse adjacent to the Grand Avenue site. Finding the ball fans good customers at his bar, Chris became interested in baseball "as he might have become interested in pretzels, peanuts or any other incitant to thirst and beer drinking," so he secured the refreshment privileges and eventually purchased the ball club.

To stir up interest, Spink wrote O. P. Caylor in Cincinnati, suggesting that he put together a team, label it with the celebrated name of former days, "Cincinnati Reds," and bring it down to St. Louis for a week-end series in 1881. The series turned out to be very successful, and Spink's idea intensified baseball enthusiasm in the city. Spink brought in other clubs, ranging from "prairie" teams like Dubuque and pickup nines from Chicago to the famous Brooklyn Atlantics and the Akron team, regarded the strongest non-League club in the country. Louisville, too, was keen for baseball. A record crowd of 7000 fans turned out the same year for a game with the Akrons.

In the East, the disgrace of the Mutuals forced New Yorkers to be satisfied with a number of undistinguished semi-pro and amateur clubs —especially since League clubs took their pick of both Mutual and Athletic players when those clubs were expelled. But in September 1880, a new outfit, the New York Metropolitans, destined to cut a figure in the baseball world of the decade, was organized and saw action well into the autumn. In 1881 they played 151 games, the greatest number of matches played by one club against professional nines in one season up until then. Included were 60 with regular League clubs, of which the Mets won 18—a good showing. New Yorkers, anxious for good baseball after the many years following the expulsion of the Mutuals, attended the Mets' games in great numbers; estimated gate receipts for the season were over $30,000.

For several years after their Athletics were cast out by the National League, Philadelphia fans followed several clubs who played under the names "Philadelphias" and "Athletics." The 1881 version of the Athletics, managed by Horace B. Phillips, went all the way to St. Louis at an invitation from Spink, where they played a series before excellent crowds. Stop-overs for games were also made at Louisville and Cincinnati.

Heartened by their successful interchange of games, and sharing much in common vis-à-vis the League, these clubs were irresistibly thrown together. They were bound to see the advantages of banding together in a more formal relationship, to establish a regular schedule and safeguard their property rights. The movement in this direction was directly precipitated by Cincinnati's expulsion from the National League in 1880. Hard upon O. P. Caylor's public threats came Cincinnati's attempts to form a new league with a liberal policy, including the right of the member clubs to regulate their own admission prices. Her first two efforts, made during the winter of 1880, were unsuccessful. Hulbert supposedly spiked the second of these by sidetracking the Metropolitans and the Washington Club, two possible members of the new association. He persuaded the Metropolitans to join the League Alliance instead, and even though the Washington Club had been expelled from the Alliance, he arranged for its players to be signed by National League teams.

Undaunted by these setbacks, a Colonel Harris, receiver of the bankrupt Cincinnati Club, continued to work toward the formation of a new league. By June 1881 he succeeded in persuading a coterie of Cincinnati baseball men to pledge money to see Cincinnati either restored to the League or primed as bellwether for a new association. Among them was Justus Thorner, ex-president of the Cincinnati Club, who was also connected with J. G. Sohn & Company, a brewing concern.

These maneuvers were accompanied by jeers from the pro-League press. "By all means form an anti-League Association, with Cincinnati, St. Louis, and a few other villages as members," scoffed the Chicago *Tribune.* "The League would be glad to get rid of some dead wood." Another League defender asserted that despite "faults in its management," Hulbert's organization was the only one capable of controlling professional players and compelling "honest work." It was therefore "nonsense" to think of forming new leagues and "useless to compete further" with the National League "in the race for the control of the professional class of ball players." Convinced that a new league would never materialize, pro-League newspapers disparged its prospective members as "paper clubs."

Such criticism did not stop the new movement, though. Records differ in minor detail, but the evidence points to Horace B. Phillips, manager of the Philadelphias, as the man responsible for instigating the meeting at Pittsburgh, October 10, 1881, which led to the formation of the American Association. After consulting with Justus Thorner, Phillips sent postcards calling a meeting of likely clubs, but then forgot about the whole matter. He was reportedly having some trouble with his players, who decided he was making too much money and deposed him as manager; whereupon he quit baseball in disgust.

The only people to heed Phillips's summons were the Cincinnati promoters, still ready and willing to make another attempt at a new league. Finding themselves alone in Pittsburgh, Thorner, Caylor, and Frank Wright of the *Enquirer,* whom they had brought with them, met Al Pratt, a bartender and baseball "crank," while they were walking about the town. Pratt put them in touch with Harmer Denny McKnight, local businessman and baseball enthusiast. McKnight was a college graduate who had been a bookkeeper in a Pittsburgh bank before he established his own iron manufacturing business. He had also been head of the Allegheny Club during its tenure with the old International Association. These few men then shrewdly turned the unsuccessful Pittsburgh meeting to good advantage by sending telegrams to prominent non-League clubs. The messages were worded in such a way as to give the impression that each absentee was the only one missing from the meeting! The ruse worked. Favorable replies came in, and a second meeting was arranged for November 2 in Cincinnati, where the American Association was actually created. St. Louis, Cincinnati, Louisville, the Brooklyn Atlantics, and the Alleghenys of Pittsburgh were admitted at once as charter members of the Association. Denny McKnight was chosen president, and J. H. Pank, who was also secretary and treasurer of the Kentucky Malting Company—"a mammoth institution in Louisville"—was the vice president. Jimmy Williams, former executive of the old International Association, became secretary and treasurer.

At first the new Association was not completely successful in gaining a foothold in Philadelphia and New York, the important Eastern cities vacated by the National League. Philadelphia was represented at the meeting by two clubs, who refused to consolidate, but the Athletics were finally accepted because they had had the foresight to secure playing grounds. Jim Mutrie, manager of the New York Metropolitans, was also on hand at Cincinnati, but he stayed away from the meeting. "Truthful James" moved cautiously, because he wanted to discover something about the new organization's policy before committing himself. He depended heavily upon games with League clubs and could not afford to join an organization which might be hostile toward the League. Right after the meeting Mutrie set out for Chicago, where he had a long talk with Hulbert, after which he announced his intention to stay out of the Association. Nevertheless, Mutrie continued his flirtation with the Association, showing up again at its meeting the following spring.

At that session, held in Philadelphia March 13, 1882, Billie Barnie withdrew his Brooklyn Atlantics, pleading lack of funds. The gap was filled by Baltimore, owned by Harry Vonderhorst, another brewer interested in peddling beer to the patrons of the ball parks. So a six-club circuit was maintained.

The constitution of the Association was patterned after that of the National League. Territorial rights were established, one club to a city. Each club paid $50 dues,* and the home team had to guarantee visiting teams $65 for each championship game. However, on Decoration Day, the Fourth of July, or a state holiday, the proceeds were to be divided equally. As in the League, clubs could be expelled for a variety of reasons: failure to finish the schedule or to appear for a game, unless detained by accident; neglecting to give a visiting team its share of the gate receipts, or to pay Association dues; using disqualified players, or playing another team doing so; disobeying orders of the Board of Directors, whose decisions were final and "forever binding"; and violating the constitution or playing rules. The Association also matched the League's insistence on honest play. On pain of expulsion, clubs were forbidden to allow pool-selling and betting on their grounds or in buildings which they owned or occupied. Association doors were closed to players or managers expelled from the National League for "crooked or dishonest playing or drunkenness."

In other respects, the Association constitution was more liberal than the League's. Its clubs could play outside teams and exhibition games with each other on off days. Players released without prejudice were given two weeks' salary and could sign immediately with any other Association club that wanted them. But the most important policies which set the Association apart from the League were Sunday ball, twenty-five cent admissions, and liquor selling on the grounds—the last hardly surprising in view of the brewery money behind several of the clubs. Finally, the American Association introduced two innovations. The team with the highest percentage of games won, rather than the most victories, was to be acclaimed champion. And the Association used a permanent staff of umpires.

The formation of the American Association brought on the first of numerous trade wars which have characterized baseball history. These wars reflected the American economic scene, where entrepreneurs in many fields of business repeatedly battled each other for control of raw materials and markets. In the process, business has steadily moved in the direction of consolidation and concentration of economic power. The history of baseball reveals the same pattern. Baseball operators, too, waged trade wars for similar objectives—control of ball players (raw materials) and exclusive control of territories (markets). If any-

* Raised to $100 the following year.

thing, baseball has outdone conventional businesses in establishing monolithic power and engaging in monopolistic practices.

The conflict between the League and the Association was not precipitated abruptly. The two rivals even played twenty spring exhibition games with each other, which proved both financially profitable and highly successful in stimulating fan interest. After all, the League had watched other short-lived associations come and go, so it was not unduly alarmed at this latest organization, especially since the Association did not, at first, invade League territory. Nevertheless, the League took prompt steps to make the League Alliance more attractive,* no doubt as a precaution against possible inroads by the Association. Yet they hardly meant "war to the knife," as the Cincinnati *Enquirer,* with its flair for the dramatic, called them.

Still, it was not long before the knives were unsheathed. The Troy-Wise incident opened the quarrel. Samuel Washington Wise and John "Dasher" Troy, two infielders, no sooner had signed with the Association's Cincinnati and Philadelphia clubs, respectively, than they were persuaded to jump their contracts and join League clubs. Wise went to Boston and Troy to Detroit. Both men had played a few games with the Detroit Nationals the previous season, so the League probably regarded them as its own property. Hulbert added insult to injury with a haughty statement given out in an interview:

> The League does not recognize the existence of any Association of ball clubs excepting itself and the League Alliance. . . . I don't care to go into the question of the League's attitude toward the so-called American Association further than to say that it is not likely the League will be awake nights bothering its head about how to protect a body in which it has no earthly interest, and which voluntarily assumed a position of hostility toward the League.

Hulbert evidently chose to interpret the Association's determination to pursue an independent course as "hostility" toward the League, for there is no evidence that the Association had made any attack on the League up to the time of his statement.

The Association reacted angrily. Denny McKnight said that the only conclusion to be drawn was that the League was anxious to break up the American Association, for fear it would become a dangerous rival. Manager Lew Simmons bluntly asked Detroit if it sanctioned stealing players, while O. P. Caylor tried unsuccessfully to coax Wise back to Cincinnati with a letter "in which taffy, entreaty, and bull-dozing were very beautifully blended." Detroit took the same high and mighty attitude as Hulbert. In a reply to Simmons, it admitted signing Troy,

* See above, page 100.

denied knowledge of the Association's existence, and invited the Athletics to expel the player and seek redress in the courts. Troy himself sanctimoniously announced he did not think it "proper or right to play ball on the Sabbath," and he claimed he did not realize when he signed with the Athletics that he would have to play on Sundays. But the New York *Clipper* chided League officials for condoning acts which it thought could only lead to the crookedness the League had hitherto punished so severely.

The Association retaliated against the League at its spring meeting in 1882. McKnight had previously charged that the League had committed the "Troy outrage" to provoke the Association into hiring the League's blacklisted and expelled players, in order to turn the press and public against the Association, and he had stated flatly that his organization would "do nothing of the kind." Now, however, the Association decided to allow expelled, suspended, or blacklisted National Leaguers to appeal to its Board of Directors, which could admit them to full Association privileges if it decided injustice had been done. The Association also set up its own satellite system by providing for an Alliance which lesser clubs could join. In a third war measure, the Association agreed to start legal action to recover players lost to the League, taking up one case at a time, and if successful proceeding to the next, expenses to be borne by the entire Association.

Cincinnati made good the threat by appealing to a Massachusetts court for an injunction restraining Wise from playing with Boston and compelling him to return to the Reds, on the plea that his loss was irreparable and could not be calculated financially. This action marks the first time professional baseball went into the courts to settle a dispute. The arguments of the plaintiff and defendant are unavailable, because the bill containing them was taken from the clerk's office by H. B. Abbott, attorney for Cincinnati, and never returned; but the court record shows that the judge refused to grant the restraining order, and Wise remained with Boston. Cincinnati expelled him, and the Athletics had to be content with giving Troy the same treatment.

The Association also changed its mind about playing League clubs. In May 1882 it decided on a policy of "non-intercourse" with League teams, but did not incorporate the rule into the constitution until the following winter. So Cincinnati, winners of the Association pennant, arranged a post-season series with the Chicago White Sox, National League champions, showing that the temptation of lucrative gate receipts was stronger than the need for maintaining the quarantine against the League. Two games had already been played when Denny McKnight stepped in. His threat to expel Cincinnati terminated what would have been the first World Series. The Association Board of Directors actually entertained charges against Cincinnati, but "after a few hours' friendly chat" they were dropped.

In the summer of 1882 the Association began to strike even harder at League playing talent. Even though it had failed to hold on to Wise and Troy, by then it had managed to sign at least thirteen other National Leaguers. Now it attempted to get a pre-emption on the enemy's men for the 1883 season. It signed them to "optional" agreements, which committed the men to signing regular Association contracts for 1883 after the current season was over. The Association took the attitude that since it was not recognized by the League it need exercise no compunction about signing whatever League players it could.

However, the scheme backfired. Catcher Charlie Bennett of the Detroit League Club had signed one of these optional agreements with the Allegheny Club of the Association in August 1882. For a consideration of $100 he bound himself to execute a regular contract in October to play for the Alleghenys in 1883 at a salary of $1700. When the time came, Bennett refused to sign the regular contract and was about to sign with Detroit instead. Allegheny went to court to compel Bennett to stick to his original agreement and to restrain him from serving his old club.

Allegheny pled that it was engaged in the business of playing baseball for profit, had spent much time and money in preparing to exhibit games, and expected large sums in return. The plaintiff further argued that Bennett's defection had also influenced Ed Williamson and James Galvin, two other stars, to renege on similar agreements. The season was too far advanced to replace these with men of equal skill, and Allegheny therefore would be seriously damaged to the extent of not less than $1000.

The court upheld the defendant, though, on the grounds that the optional agreement was merely a preliminary arrangement, not a final one. Specific performance would not be compelled by the court when it was not clear that the minds of the parties had met, or that the agreement was "mutual," its terms "certain," its enforcement "practicable," and the complainant without adequate legal redress. Even if a valid contract were involved, the court went on, the plaintiff's bill would not stand up. It was presented prematurely, because no injury could be suffered until the commencement of the 1883 season. So again the Association had to be content with the empty gesture of blacklisting the players involved.

Nevertheless, the competition for players was unabated. The League threatened to blacklist any who signed with the Association, and Denny McKnight promised to step up the attack in 1883 if the League used "dishonorable" methods to prevent the Association from signing League players. Next, League strategists reinstated ten blacklisted players who had been disqualified in September 1881. This stroke not only cleared the way for the return of blacklisted men who had joined the Association in 1882, but also reduced the Association's chances of signing the rest of them for 1883.

The war soon became a struggle over territorial rights as well as for players. Cities left open by the League were in danger of being occupied by its aggressive rival. Besides, the League was encumbered with cities like Providence, Worcester, and Troy, which had been wobbly even before the advent of the Association. In 1882, Troy and Worcester had to be rescued by funds from other League clubs to keep them from quitting before the schedule was finished. Providence managed to finish the season only because its "stockholders were bled anew" for necessary funds. When the Association entered New York and Columbus, thus lining up a strong eight-club circuit for 1883, the League knew it had to close ranks to meet the new danger. So it gave two of the weaklings, Troy and Worcester, "a polite bounce out of the membership" and moved into Philadelphia and New York instead, thus forecasting a struggle at close quarters in these two key territories for the season of 1883.

But as the two rivals girded themselves to continue the fight, it was becoming increasingly apparent that the National League would have no easy job in overcoming the Association. For the first time a non-League combination had completed its schedule, and in the doing had enjoyed unprecedented financial success. Association treasuries were "full of money." Leading beneficiaries of the golden flow were Lew Simmons, Bill Sharsig, and Charlie Mason, known as the Philadelphia triumvirate. They reportedly cleared between two hundred and three hundred thousand dollars.

The foundation of Association strength was the fact that the population of its six cities outnumbered the National's League's eight by approximately half a million. And the popular combination of twenty-five-cent ball, Sunday games, and liquor-selling on the grounds served admirably to tap this source. The Cleveland *Leader* reported that five of the six Association clubs drew larger crowds than the National League's top gate attraction, Chicago, whose attendance was three times larger than that of any other city in its circuit.

Also, the Association developed many outstanding and colorful players, many of them former amateur stars, who thrilled the fans. Among them were Charles Comiskey, Pete Browning, Bid McPhee, and Cub Stricker. The substantial sprinkling of former National Leaguers balanced Association ranks, and its rich treasuries put it in a position to bid still higher for more of them.

League spokesmen might invent curious explanations for the success of the Association, but they had to acknowledge it. *Spalding's Guide for 1883*, for instance, discovered that the success of the Association was due to "the revival of the public confidence induced by the gradual establishment of honest professional play under the auspices of the National League." But W. G. Thompson, owner of the Detroit Club, was realistic enough to realize that the League could not afford to "sneer" at the Association. With the "Beer and Whiskey Circuit" (as its detractors mockingly called the Association) so firmly entrenched, the prospect for 1883 was for more wild bidding for players, higher operating costs, and ruinous competition. But at this juncture a third party intervened.

Delegates from eight Midwestern towns were meeting at Fort Wayne, Indiana, to revive the Northwestern League, a minor circuit which had collapsed in 1879 after only one season. Anxious to ensure protection of their player contracts before launching their new venture, they wired the League, which was meeting in Providence the same day, requesting co-operation and reciprocity. The League responded instantly by appointing a three-man committee headed by A. G. Mills to confer with the Northwestern League and—obviously with the American Association in mind—"with any other association of base-ball clubs."

Mills had recently taken over the presidency of the League following Hulbert's death and Soden's brief interregnum, and he was particularly interested in reaching a settlement, because he thought affairs were "drifting in the direction which nearly ruined baseball many years ago, when contracts were disregarded and players employed . . . without regard to the odium their past conduct had brought upon the game. . . . I take it," said Mills, "these associations are run by full-grown men," and "whatever and wherever the fault of the past," it was "possible and proper" to meet "on the basis of the 'status quo'" and arrange to honor each others' contracts while retaining the "good opinion of the public."

Mills accompanied these statesmanlike pronouncements with a vision of things to come. He wanted to see "a large number of associations and clubs dotted all over this continent," all in agreement on "some general plan of enforcing contracts and barring dishonorable or disreputable players." Each of these associations would be "independent to conduct its internal affairs." Mills had thought that the League Alliance system would accomplish these ends, but he now realized that it was "natural that clubs should prefer to unite in competing for a championship of their own . . ." and that they would rather be "perfectly independent so far as management of their affairs is concerned." Mills's idea of linking together all professional baseball into one great network was the rough outline of Organized Baseball as it was to be—a galaxy of closely associated leagues and clubs operating under its own set of laws for the control of players and the protection of territories.

This willingness to begin peace talks was received coolly by the Association at first, because it felt the League had never treated it with "due courtesy" and had "stolen away its players." When he learned of this reluctance, Mills wrote Elias Matter, president of the Northwestern, suggesting that if the American Association would not "unite in a scheme for the common good," the National and Northwestern might work out an understanding between themselves. He pointed out, however, that without the co-operation of the Association it would be more difficult to enforce contracts.

Prospects for peace improved when the Association finally agreed to name a committee to meet with the League only. With this to work on, Mills skillfully maneuvered to bring about a joint meeting of the three parties. He wrote Jimmy Williams, Association secretary, urging a united conference as the most effective means of serving "the material interests of all the clubs." Then, to exert additional pressure on the Association, Mills asked Matter to write to Denny McKnight and say that the Northwestern had originally planned to meet with the League, but when it found out the Association was also ready to get together with the League, the Northwestern arranged to meet with both organizations. Mills was confident that McKnight could not refuse a joint conference if Matter would write him along these lines.

After considerable correspondence to work out details, Mills finally got agreement on a three-way meeting to be held February 17 at the Hotel Victoria, New York. A last-minute hitch developed over J. H. Pank's refusal to leave Louisville. Mills solved this by suggesting a proxy, so O. P. Caylor substituted for him. Mills prepared the groundwork for the conference by drafting an agreement as a basis of discussion, after consulting with influential baseball men like Al Spalding, Nick Young, Harry Wright, and Al Reach. He took care to send advance copies to the other members of the National League committee, John B. Day, New York owner, and Arthur B. Soden of the Red Sox. As it turned out, Mills's text was adopted almost verbatim, and it became known first as the Tripartite Pact and then, to allow for additional members, the National Agreement.

At the "Harmony Conference," as it was called, the National League men were joined by Association delegates Lew Simmons, O. P. Caylor, and Billie Barnie, who had returned to Baltimore, bringing his Atlantics with him. Elias Matter was the lone delegate for the Northwestern. With his usual careful planning, Mills had an expert stenographer available so that any document drawn up could be "put in shape, and multiplied."

The conference went smoothly, especially since "no delegate introduced any matter which could cause estrangement." First on the agenda was how to dispose of the players. Those currently under contract were considered to be in good standing, and were to stay put. Eighteen disputed players, most of whom had signed two or more contracts, were arbitrarily assigned to specific clubs by mutual agreement. Each association promised to recognize the player contracts of the others.

The reserve was extended to cover eleven players on each club, and each association agreed to respect the reserve lists of the others. League and Association reserved men were guaranteed a minimum salary of $1000; those in the Northwestern or in any Alliance club would get at least $750. All contracts were to be for seven months, and no club was to negotiate with players for the following season until October 10. Clubs were not supposed to bargain with released players until after a twenty-day waiting period. The three associations also pledged to uphold each others' suspensions and expulsions by refusing to employ or play against any man not in good standing. An important contribution to the evolution of Organized Baseball's administrative machinery was the creation of an Arbitration Committee composed of three representatives of each League. Its function was to interpret the Tripartite Pact and to settle all disputes and complaints growing out of it.

The National League and the Northwestern accepted the Tripartite Pact at once, but the American Association did not agree to it until after animated discussion at its March 12 meeting. Some Association men were reported "strongly opposed" to the eleven-man reserve provision, because they feared it would give "great advantages" to clubs which already had the best players. They finally withdrew their objections, but for some time thereafter the Association remained doubtful of the efficacy of the reserve. Every so often, its owners talked about revamping the reserve or dropping it entirely, much to the dismay of the National League.

For its acceptance of the Tripartite Pact, the Association was denounced in one newspaper for eating both "crow" and "humble pie." It was told that it had allowed itself to become "nothing more nor less than the League Alliance." But an Eastern journal praised the peace treaty as the beginning of a new epoch in baseball's history. This opinion was valid.

The Tripartite Pact, or National Agreement, marked the beginning of Organized Baseball. It was the first formula for regulating competition among leagues for players and territories. It was also the first official baseball document to include the reserve provision. Not only did it bring the reserve into the open, but by enlarging its scope it tightened its effect. By placing nearly all men on reserve, the National

Agreement, for all practical purposes, ended bidding for players between clubs and between leagues. As one commentator put it, the clubs
of one league would be saved from "the rapacity" of those in the others.

By staking out and safeguarding territorial rights, the National Agreement contributed immeasurably to the permanency and value of the
club franchises. No longer need a club worry for fear that being prosperous would merely call forth rivals eager to muscle in on its territory.
As the National Agreement proved its worth, new leagues would seek
its protection. With each additional combination in the fold, it would
become increasingly difficult for the remaining ones to stay out of
Organized Baseball. A. G. Mills once declared that without agreements
professional baseball would be a "wildcat affair." Maybe so. Certainly
without agreements the industry would have developed along radically
different lines, if at all. With them it was wild enough, as we shall see.

14

ORGANIZED BASEBALL'S FIRST CHALLENGE

THE ALLIANCE between the National League and the American Association under the National Agreement endured until the end of the decade, when it became a casualty of the great upheaval of 1890. While not a love match, it was at least a marriage of convenience holding the two major leagues together despite stresses and strains which at times threatened to wreck the union. During these years of baseball prosperity, the National Agreement—the Blackstone of baseball law, as a contemporary writer called it—became more and more pervasive, as new minor leagues were organized and placed themselves under its rule.

The first to challenge this system was the Union Association. The Unions were organized in Pittsburgh, September 12, 1883, but their main impulse came from St. Louis. In the beginning they expressed the intention of honoring the player contracts of other leagues, and disavowed any wish to war against them. However, a copy of the Union Association Constitution in the Cleveland Public Library plainly reveals that it was a threat to Organized Baseball's territorial rights and monopsony control over its players. This rare document, almost an exact replica of League and Association constitutions in other respects, not only shows that the Unions were planning to place clubs in six major league cities,* but it flatly states that the Union Association "does not favor the arbitrary reserve rule, which makes the player almost the slave of the club." The Unions reinforced this stand with a resolution, adopted at the Pittsburgh meeting, saying that "while we recognize the validity of all contracts made by the League and American Association, we cannot recognize any agreement whereby any number of ball players may be reserved by any club for any time beyond the terms of his contract with said club."

The Unions seemed to have ample funds to start their venture. The

---

* Baltimore, Boston, Philadelphia, Chicago, Cincinnati, and St. Louis. The two non-major league cities were Washington and Altoona.

secretary-treasurer, William Warren White of Washington, reported they had $100,000 in cash, and would have no difficulty in securing more if needed. As A. G. Mills acknowledged, the Unions had "a good many moneyed men" behind them. Chief backer and soon to be president of the Unions was Henry V. Lucas,* scion of a wealthy old St. Louis family and possessor of a considerable fortune stemming from his grandfather, one of the early settlers of St. Louis, who had purchased large tracts of real estate in and around the city. Lucas was also president of the Mound City Transportation Company. He had deep roots in St. Louis baseball. A brother, John B. C. Lucas, was president of the St. Louis Base Ball Association in the 1870's and of the National League club there in 1877. Henry himself was an amateur player who laid out a field at "Normandy," his country seat, where he delighted to invite his friends to play ball and enjoy an "elegant spread" afterwards. Lucas had in mind placing a club in one of the major leagues, but the American Association, of course, was already represented in St. Louis by the Browns. As for the League—assuming he could get in—its fifty-cent admission rule and ban on Sunday games would make competition with Von der Ahe's team difficult.

Besides, his "frequent chats" with numerous major league players had convinced Lucas that they were being imposed upon by the reserve rule. To him it was "the most arbitrary and unjust rule ever suggested"—one that "ought to be broken"—and he felt it was only a question of time until baseball players revolted against this regulation "which they despise, and will no more submit to than to have rings put in their noses and be led by them." When the chance came, Lucas turned to the Union Association, establishing a ball park at the corner of Cass Avenue and West 25th Street, conveniently reached by two streetcar lines.

Another substantial Union backer was A. H. Henderson, a Baltimore mattress manufacturer who financed the Unions' Baltimore and Chicago clubs. Ellis Wainwright and Adolphus Busch, St. Louis brewers and two of the wealthiest men in the area, had also invested. Wainwright was president of the Wainwright Brewery Company, third largest in St. Louis, and Busch was head of Anheuser-Busch, which returned to baseball in 1953 through "Gussie" Busch's purchase of the St. Louis Cardinals. Lucas also claimed that Pennsylvania Railroad officials were behind the Unions' Altoona Club. George Wright lent prestige as head of the Boston Unions, and the new association officially adopted the baseball manufactured by the Wright and Ditson Company, in which the former great shortstop was a partner. But Lucas was the chief

* Henry B. Bennett preceded him briefly as president.

source of funds, supplying capital for other Union clubs as well as his own team.

Ignoring these supporters of substance and reputation, the Boston *Globe* said, "We search the list . . . for the name of one person of means or responsibility, or whose business and social standing is such as to inspire confidence." To which the Philadelphia *Times* retorted that the Unions' personnel was "fully equal to that of the League and Association in brains, intellect, and financial strength."

A. G. Mills disparaged the Unions as a refuge for "dead-beats" and "played-out bummers," and the opposition press joined in the chorus against the "Onions," lambasting them as a haven for crooked players and "lushers" who "cannot find employment in respectable clubs." O. P. Caylor reserved one of his choice designations for the St. Louis Unions, calling them "The Lucas-Wainwright Lunatic Asylum." There was just enough truth in these slurs to give the anti-Unions a talking point. Outfielder Frank Gardner joined the Pittsburgh Unions after he was "bounced" from the Association for drunkenness. It was not long before he returned to his old ways, teaming up with Charlie Sweeney, a former National Leaguer who had gone to the St. Louis Unions, on a drunken escapade, for which both of them were fined. It was also true that at least one Union player was expelled for drunkenness. Dry pledges were extracted from a few others. Yet, as it turned out, about thirty Union players without previous major league experience were good enough to win places on League and Association clubs either the following year or eventually.

A. G. Mills also spoke scornfully of the "beer money" floating Union clubs, and to discredit them, a story was widely circulated that they were being run in the interests of brewers. This charge was a sore point with the new league. Frederick F. Espenschied, brother-in-law of Lucas and vice president of the St. Louis Unions, labeled the story "contemptible." While acknowledging that some brewers had invested in the Unions, he was quick to call attention to the prominent role of brewers in American Association clubs. The New York *Clipper* tried hard to counter the charge but could find only four Union clubs free of the influence of beer.

When Union supporters took the offense, they concentrated on the reserve clause. To them it was an "iniquitous practice of dictating to a player" and a "most noxious edict." The St. Louis *Republican* declared, "Any St. Louis merchant or manufacturer who would try to dictate to his employees where and for what price they should work, and would attempt to deprive them from working altogether unless they accepted his terms, would be hissed off the 'Change' floor." In a letter to a newspaper editor, a Union fan maintained that to be against the Unions meant upholding the reserve clause, but this was something which was beyond the understanding of some sports writers, who had "as much gift for reasoning as a giraffe would have to play a flute in the dark." What a far cry was all this invective from the polite, restrained amateur days of the Knickerbockers!

The Tripartite partners moved swiftly to protect their territorial rights by officially banning from admission to the National Agreement any new association that had clubs in cities already occupied by Organized Baseball. The Association passed a measure expelling any member club which played against one from an association that had invaded a National Agreement city. Mills tightened the ring by pledging League support of the boycott and suggesting a circular letter be sent to all National Agreement clubs, reminding them they would forfeit their rights under the Agreement if they played a Union team.

However, for reasons of strategy an exception was made. The Eastern League, a minor circuit, was admitted to the National Agreement, although it had been turned down the previous year, and its Monumental Club was allowed to share the American Association's Baltimore territory. The change of heart was spurred by fear that the Eastern and Union Associations might join forces. After the Union challenge passed, the Baltimore Monumentals were unceremoniously dispossessed, although the Eastern League itself was permitted to continue its membership in the National Agreement.

The Unions struck back as best they could against Organized Baseball's boycott. In "spirited retaliation" they ordered their clubs not to play League, Association, or Northwestern teams. They also took steps to admit small-town clubs to quasi-membership by adding an "alliance clause" to their constitution—another testimony to the durability of the National League's alliance concept.

The Union War inspired the formation of "reserve teams." These were auxiliaries of the major league clubs made up of youngsters recruited from semi-professional and amateur ranks. They were paid salaries and played regularly scheduled games with each other, charging twenty-five cents admission. The purpose of these scrub teams was to keep as many players as possible out of Union control and at the same time to siphon away customers from Union parks. Of course, there was always the possibility, as Chris Von der Ahe explained, that these teams might be a means of developing new talent for the parent club, and even supply replacements in emergencies. The reserve teams were also used to keep the regulars on their mettle. The St. Louis Browns were well aware of this, having grown tired of hearing, "If you don't play well you will be dropped to the reserve crowd." The Unions made some effort to counter with reserve teams of their own, but without success.

A number of their "Preserves," as they were jokingly called, melted away as the season advanced. Temporary expedients of war though they were, the reserve teams bore the closest resemblance to modern baseball's farm system yet discernible.

The League was ever alert to other ways of eating into Union attendance. Mills urged Harry Wright to improvise a game of some kind in Philadelphia on the Fourth of July to cut Union patronage on the holiday. He also suggested to Spalding the feasibility of forming another team in Chicago, ostensibly independent but really under Spalding's control. He foresaw that sooner or later there would be a second ball club in Chicago, and saw no reason why Spalding should not run both of them. In the meantime, Spalding would be confronting the Chicago Unions with a double dose of competition. Nothing came of the suggestion just yet. Mills was premature, but his prediction was correct. Spalding gave technical permission to the Association in 1885 for placing a club in Chicago, but with the brief exception of the Chicago Brotherhood Club in 1890, the National League had no competitor in that city until the American League moved in permanently at the turn of the century.

However, these maneuvers were subordinate to the main fight, which was centered on the players. Each side's object was to keep hold of its own players and to obtain as many of the other side's as it could. Main inducements for the players were higher salaries, advance money, and two- and three-year contracts. Even before the 1884 season started, Mills learned that "emmisaries [sic] of the wreckers" were making strong efforts "to debauch our reserved players." He complained that they were offering high salaries and "certainly giving us a good deal of trouble." Organized Baseball must prepare itself for "a battle with that gang," which he predicted must come sooner or later, and the sooner the better, he believed, for it would be a great misfortune to baseball if the Unions should live through the season.

To thwart the Unions, John B. Day, New York owner, introduced a resolution at the November meeting of the League to blacklist any reserved player who jumped his contract. The purpose was not only to discourage a player from going over to the Unions, but to lessen the temptation to lure him back with a higher salary, which would amount to rewarding instead of punishing him for leaving. More important, it meant extending the reserve far beyond its original intent by converting it into a weapon for fending off outside competition. For the time being, the League took no action on the Day resolution, contenting itself with having Mills circularize all club presidents in the three allied leagues for full information about Union tampering with their players. However, the Association did not postpone action, even though, only a month before, Denny McKnight had publicly announced that the Unions were "not causing this association any alarm," and that reports of players deserting were only rumors. In December the Association went ahead to adopt the Day resolution and at the same time reinstate some of its blacklisted players, in order to keep them out of the hands of the enemy. This placed the Association in the anomalous position of imposing the blacklist on some players while they were simultaneously lifting it from others.

The League soon followed suit. At its December meeting it put the pressure on wavering players by threatening to blacklist all who did not sign contracts within thirty days of receiving them. Then it too adopted the Day resolution in March 1884. But before doing so, Mills privately urged clubowners to try to recover reserved players from the Unions. However, he was opposed to making a public statement to this effect. In January he used his influence with George W. Howe, vice president of the Cleveland Club, in an effort to recover second-baseman Fred Dunlap, a reserved player who had signed with Lucas's St. Louis Unions. If Lucas sued, said Mills, Howe could answer that the Union contract was obtained under false pretenses and the transaction was therefore "fraudulent."

Dunlap himself was still willing to talk business with the League, and he let it be known that he was ready to go to the New York Club if they would pay him $4000 and could get Cleveland to waive its rights to him. Pressure was put on Cleveland to let Dunlap return to the National Agreement fold with some other club, if they could not get him back for themselves. Mills, however, thought such a deal was "out of the question," but urged Cleveland to "sound out Dunlap about going back to your club." He evidently feared the Association might pick up Dunlap in the shuffle. After the Day resolution was passed and Dunlap was duly blacklisted, rumors persisted that Cleveland was still quietly trying to get him back.

However, Mills made clear his determination to uphold the Day resolution once it had become official League policy. To all the talk that the "secessionists" could return to Organized Baseball whenever they liked, Mills replied that "he was never more earnest in his life than when he said that these players should never play with any club connected with the National Agreement." He reinforced his statement by going before the Arbitration Committee on April 19 and proposing a supplementary resolution to support the Day edict. Clubs were reminded by this "Order in Relation to Ineligible Reserved Players" that they were prohibited from employing any players who had violated the reserve, and it directed that any club which employed such a player, or played a team which used one, would forfeit all rights under the National

Agreement. The order was accepted unanimously. After the Union War, this directive became a source of serious disagreement and very nearly disrupted the alliance between the League and Association.

In the course of the war, the Unions won over about thirty National Agreement men. Outstanding among them were Jack Glasscock, Hugh "One-armed" Daly, George Schaffer, Emil Gross, Fred Dunlap, Charlie Briody, Jim McCormick, Charlie Sweeney, Larry Corcoran, and Tommy Bond from the National League. The Association lost Jack Gleason, Davy Rowe, William Taylor, George Bradley, Sam Crane, and Tony Mullane. Some of these stars were recovered, among them Bond, Corcoran, Mullane, and Taylor, and the major leagues added a few Union players to their own ranks for good measure. On top of this, the allies refused to recognize Union contracts, and went ahead to sign some players that had already been hired by the Unions. Their justification of this policy was that the Unions had disregarded the reserve clause. Critics reproached the League and Association for their lack of principle in committing acts against outside clubs which they condemned as "dishonorable" when it happened to them.

The Unions, naturally, were incensed at what they regarded as a "systematic movement" to break up their organization by "approaching, bribing, and coercing" players who had signed "legal and valid" Union contracts and by offering money to those who committed "treachery." Secretary White threatened Union players who broke their contracts with expulsion and legal proceedings. In reply, a pro-League reporter used the argument of social Darwinism. After all, he said, the Unions started out to show the older leagues that their system was "wrong and weak," and if the Unions got the worst of it in the struggle "for survival of the fittest," they should accept the verdict without "whining" about "unfair treatment."

Mills answered White by refusing "to dignify that gang by seriously considering any of their nonsense." However, if they should start legal action, Mills advised attacking their contract in the court. Privately, he wrote that the League and Association decided to have each of their clubs fight any injunction separately. He advised paying the salaries of players who might be enjoined and also finding jobs outside baseball for them in order to cut payrolls.

The Unions made good their threat of legal action by going to court over pitcher Tony Mullane. "The Count of Macaroni," as he was sometimes called because of his dandified appearance, was one of the first to violate the reserve clause. In November, he spurned the St. Louis Browns' offer of $1900, jumped the reserve, and signed with the St. Louis Unions for a reported $2500 salary, part of which was paid in advance. But before ever throwing a ball for the Unions, Mullane broke his contract and signed with Toledo of the Association for the same pay.

Mullane admitted that he made an about-face because he was afraid of being expelled and blacklisted under the Day resolution. How he had happened to join the Association's Toledo Club instead of returning to St. Louis, where he belonged, is a story of behind-the-scenes tactics employed during the war. Von der Ahe knew that if he could not get his star pitcher back again at the salary he was willing to pay, the next best thing was to get him away from the Browns' competitors, the St. Louis Unions. At the same time he wanted to make sure that Mullane went to a weak Association club, so he would not hurt the Browns' chances for a pennant by strengthening another contender. The Association's newly admitted Toledo Club met these requirements. The first problem was how to keep other Association owners from bidding for Mullane. Mills showed them how to do it. He suggested to the Browns, who evidently had asked his advice, that they could arrange for the owners to sign a paper pledging themselves not to bid for Mullane. No obstacle to the transaction was raised, so Mullane must have been transferred to Toledo by the gentleman's agreement proposed by Mills, or a similar understanding.

This supposition is strengthened by the fact that both Spalding and Mills urged the owners to persuade catcher Emil Gross to desert the Unions and return to some League club. It was of secondary importance to them whether he rejoined the Philadelphia Club, to which he originally belonged. In the case of Mullane, there was also the problem of how Toledo would meet the $2500 salary he was reported to be receiving from the Unions. Jimmy Williams, secretary of the Browns, categorically denied it, but there was widespread talk that the other Association owners contributed to a pool for this purpose.

When Mullane made his St. Louis debut in a Toledo uniform against the Browns in early May, his reception was unseasonably warm. As he came to bat he was hissed and jeered. He responded by raising his cap to the crowd and making "a chilly, derisive bow." These formalities out of the way, he proceeded to strike out. The next day attorneys for Lucas succeeded in obtaining a court order restraining the colorful Tony from playing in St. Louis.

Flushed with this victory, Newton Crane, one of Lucas's lawyers, followed the Toledo Club to Cincinnati, where he obtained another injunction against Mullane from the Common Pleas Court. The case was appealed to United States Circuit Court, where Judge Baxter heard the arguments in his private chambers and, without waiting for affidavits to be forwarded from St. Louis, dissolved the injunction. To him, the controversy was too trivial to take the time of the court, because baseball was not a business but a sport—a point on which the *Enquirer* quickly set the judge straight, remarking that he was "laboring under a delusion." Nevertheless, Baxter refused to modify his decision at a rehearing soon after. The St. Louis injunction, however, remained in force until 1887, when it was set aside by request of the St. Louis Athletic Association.

Finding himself stymied in court, Lucas announced that he was going to ask the Unions to "go into the contract-breaking business" too. Asked if he thought the Unions would go along with his proposal, he replied, "I am the Union Association. Whatever I do is all right . . . the Association will be with me." This was too good an opportunity for the opposition press, which promptly dubbed him "I-am-the-Union-Association Lucas." Lucas gauged his colleagues correctly. Heretofore committed to respecting contracts, although not the reserve, the Unions now decided to cast aside these scruples. Some supporters of Lucas and the Unions regretted the decision. But the Cincinnati *Enquirer* mocked newspapers friendly to Organized Baseball for remaining "silent as the grave" while League and Association clubs were convincing players to break contracts and then "howling" when the Unions were "forced" to retaliate for self-preservation. Lucas frankly said that "everything is fair in baseball as in war and I want my share of the fun while it is going on."

He soon had his wish. Within a month the Unions made their prize catch of the war, snaring catcher Charles Briody, shortstop Jack Glasscock, and pitcher Jim McCormick from the Cleveland squad. These men went to the Cincinnati Unions in "the base-ball sensation of the season." Each was paid $1000 at once. Glasscock and Briody were to receive $1500 each and McCormick $2500 for the rest of the season's work. All were guaranteed employment for 1885. Lucas was delighted. While he did not "take any pride in contract-breaking as a regular business," he expressed his pleasure at going into the enemy's camp, capturing his guns, and using them on his own side. Justus Thorner, who had the distinction of being president of the Cincinnati Club in the League, the Association, and now the Unions, seconded Lucas. "The League has stolen our players at will, has libeled us, and now we propose to take what players we can get." Briody then went to the root of the matter: "It is a matter of dollars and cents."

Loss of these stars dealt Cleveland a "death blow." In fact, the club had been tottering since the last part of July, and at that time several other National Agreement teams had begun dickering for its players, including the three stars. The Unions simply moved faster than the others. Now C. H. Bulkley, Cleveland president, figured it would cost him $5000 to finish the season, and he was "disinclined" to carry on without help from the League. Mills feared that if Cleveland fell apart, or if the idea that they were about to collapse became known, the rest of the players would fall to the Unions.

To keep the faltering club in the field, Mills called for an indirect subsidy, asking the other League clubs to pay Cleveland half the gate receipts instead of the regular three-tenths when the club visited them, but to accept only three-tenths when they went to Cleveland. As a further aid in holding the players for the League, Mills asked Cleveland's vice president, George Howe, to let League authorities know confidentially "if your club must disband," and, if it must, to reserve all the players beforehand and then release them to other League clubs for a "consideration." Mills acknowledged that such a stratagem was "somewhat irregular," but admitted it was "constantly done."

Cleveland also managed to pick up some players from the disbanding Grand Rapids Club, because the other League clubs agreed to waive the rule which required a ten-day waiting period before a club could negotiate with a released player. In spite of all these assists, Cleveland disappeared from the League that winter, its players going to the Brooklyn Association Club. But by then the Union threat had just about passed.

The League nearly had another casualty in its Providence Club, which wavered momentarily early in the season when it lost its star pitcher, Charlie Sweeney, to the Unions. Again Mills showed his leadership. He wrote the management that he was confident they would hold on. "Disbandment," said the League president, would confer a "crowning triumph" on the "scoundrels" who had "corrupted" the players.

Providence made a remarkable about-face, however. Led by Charles "Old Hoss" Radbourne, they not only won the pennant but also defeated the New York Metropolitans, Association champions, in three straight games on successive days in a post-season series. Radbourne had more than filled Sweeney's shoes. With a remarkable exhibition of stamina and skill, he pitched practically every day, working a record total of 672 innings, and then went on to pitch the three straight victories over the Mets in what was supposed to be a best-three-out-of-five series. In fact, Providence went so well during the season that in August its owner, Henry Root, even proposed "freezing out" the smaller clubs of the League and reorganizing with large cities only. Mills opposed his scheme, although he, Spalding, Day, and Soden actually held a "very secret and confidential" meeting at which the idea was probably discussed—and quashed, for nothing came of it.

The American Association also had its troubles. It had expanded into a twelve-club league, adding Brooklyn, Washington, Toledo, and Indianapolis. This extension enabled it to engross more players and to present a challenge to the Unions in Washington. The experiment proved an unhappy one, however. Three of the new clubs turned out to be poor money-makers, and, worst of all, Washington had to be replaced with the Virginia Club of Richmond six weeks before the end of the campaign. So 1884 was less remunerative for the Association as a whole than the previous year.

The Northwestern, third member of the original National Agreement trio, was the weakest. For one thing, it lost many of its best players to the Unions. It was not helped by the dubious activities of its secretary, Samuel G. Morton. He was accused of supplying players to the Unions through a private employment agency which he ran, using his position with the Northwestern to gather the necessary data about players available throughout the country. When his dealings were questioned, he denied exploiting his office for this purpose, inferring that his information was garnered from newspapers, and he said he was willing to omit his official title from his agency's newspaper advertisements. Mills brusquely rejected his compromise and demanded that Morton have no dealings whatever with the Unions. Otherwise, he expected the Northwestern to find a secretary "who will not allow himself . . . to be made use of by the common enemy for a consideration."

A. G. Spalding himself almost certainly was implicated. Morton was his "right-hand man" and a sales clerk in his Chicago store. Morton's baseball records were kept there, and he evidently used the store as an office for the agency. Mills was not afraid to take on Spalding, who, he had "no doubt," was "the company" or at least "the responsible head" of it, and promised to give Spalding "a piece of my mind somewhat more emphatic than I have sent to Morton." He added angrily, "The trouble I have with the rank and file of our army leaves me little room for patience with its 'sutlers,' and you may be sure that I will either put a stop to this kind of business, or go out of baseball." More amazing, Spalding's answer indicated he was involved, but he gave Mills his word that the agency would not be used in any way helpful to the Unions. On the other hand, Morton evidently played no favorites in his business operations. He could also benefit the League, as shown by a letter, which he doubtless sent at Spalding's bidding, to Joseph J. Ellick, then under Union contract, inviting him to take charge of the Chicago reserve team and requesting him to "Please keep this a confidential matter." Morton was soon reported to be giving up the agency "in disgust." He may have done so temporarily, but the agency was again operating successfully after the Union War.

A third drag on the Northwestern was intrigue aimed at removing it from the protecting shield of the National Agreement. W. G. Thompson, owner of the Detroit League Club, had strenuously opposed admitting the Northwestern to the National Agreement in the first place. Later on, the Association wanted to expel the Northwestern for alleged failure of some of its clubs to pay players and for "other faults." However, A. G. Mills insisted it not only be kept together, but bolstered, because if it were destroyed its players would fall into Union hands.

But the "financial embarrassment" which beset the Northwestern was too much for it. The circuit encompassed several states, and the small towns in it did not have enough fans to pay the cost of all the traveling required. By August its club began to drop out. Near the end of the season only Milwaukee and St. Paul were left. When these two went over to the Unions, the Northwestern ceased to exist.

In spite of these weaknesses and difficulties in the National Agreement camp, the Union Association lost the war. It suffered its first casualty after only six weeks of operation in 1884, when Altoona withdrew. Thereafter, Henry V. Lucas resembled a person with his arms full of packages trying to retrieve them as they fall. Each time he reached for one, he dropped one or two more, and so never quite succeeded in recovering them all. Lucas spent the summer industriously trying to patch up his circuit by finding replacements for clubs as they expired.

Kansas City substituted for Altoona and finished the season. The Chicago franchise was transferred to Pittsburgh in August, where it remained until mid-September, when St. Paul filled in for the balance of the season. The Keystones of Philadelphia also disbanded early in August. Wilmington was brought in from the minor Eastern League to fill the gap, but, even though aided by some special financial concessions, it survived only a month, after which Milwaukee, of the fading Northwestern circuit, was enlisted. All told, only five of the original eight Union clubs—Cincinnati, St. Louis, Baltimore, Washington, and Boston—carried on to the end.

The total of thirteen Union clubs, together with the Association's thirteen and the National League's eight, made thirty-four clubs operating in 1884, a figure unsurpassed in major league history. Out of all, six clubs were concentrated in Pennsylvania, five in Ohio, and four in New York state. All three leagues competed in Philadelphia. Eight other cities contained two competing clubs. Gate receipts naturally dwindled, and, as their large club mortality shows, the Unions were hardest hit.

This constant shifting of clubs disrupted playing schedules and detracted from interest. Public confidence in the Unions was also undermined by the fact that they were newcomers in baseball and had to depend on many new players. But perhaps the Unions' most serious drawback was the lack of balance in playing strength among its clubs.

Lucas's St. Louis team not only outclassed other Union clubs, but was one of the strongest in the country. There was never any doubt that it would win the championship. It finished the season with 91 victories against only 16 losses, for a phenomenal winning percentage of .850. Cincinnati, next-best among clubs playing a complete schedule, won only 68 and lost 35, which left them 21 games behind. And Cincinnati did this well only because of a winning streak due largely to the acquisition of Briody, Glasscock, and McCormick. Most of the other Union clubs were ludicrously far behind.

With the pennant decided early, fan interest slackened. Financial losses were heavy, estimates varying all the way from $50,000 to a quarter of a million. Lucas's personal stake was substantial. He admitted to having lost $17,000. It was claimed later that Lucas had "dissipated" his fortune in the Union War, but this is very unlikely, since he was one of seven children each of whom inherited a million dollars from their father, James H. Lucas, at his death in 1873. However, it is true that he eventually did lose his money as a result of baseball and other ventures. He later could be found working for the Vandalia Railroad, where he eventually became head of the ticket office.

By late August it was already apparent that the Unions were on the downgrade, and they went from bad to worse. Their Washington Club sought membership in the Association, and Cincinnati indicated it wanted to do the same. Some Union players were trying to get back their former jobs in Organized Baseball—another unmistakable sign. Only five clubs were represented, one of them by proxy, at the December 18 meeting of the Unions in St. Louis. At a second meeting January 15 just two clubs registered, and Lucas himself was among the missing, whereupon the Milwaukee and Kansas City delegates voted to disband the Union Association.

Actually, the fate of the Unions had already been determined by Lucas's defection to the National League. Before the second Union meeting he began arranging with League representatives for the admission of his club. It became known that he was reconciled to the reserve clause as a necessary evil and was willing to give up Sunday ball and liquor selling to get League membership. He went so far as to pay $2500 to the Cleveland owners, $500 in cash with the balance on account, for their franchise. Unfortunately for him, he thought—or at least claimed—that the deal included the Cleveland players, who would strengthen his club if and when he entered the League. But to his chagrin, Brooklyn signed them first, in a transaction that was anything but above board. The Cleveland owners may have known about the transaction, but at any rate they denied that the players were part of their bargain with Lucas. When Lucas angrily refused to pay the balance, Cleveland sued him and recovered.

League men were very interested in having Lucas join them. They would be getting a strong replacement for their shattered Cleveland Club and in the process destroying whatever remaining life that might be left in the Unions. It did not matter to them if they received their chief opponent, the man whom Mills wanted to ban "forever," the one who had vowed to "break up the League and the American Association." Lucas finally did become part of the National League, but it took some doing before it was finally accomplished.

Behind him was the wreckage of the Union Association, which represented the first overt challenge to Organized Baseball's reserve clause. The fact that Henry V. Lucas of St. Louis, the first staunch opponent of the reserve clause, ended by accepting it is strong testimony to its practical appeal.

15

THE REJUVENATED ALLIANCE

VICTORY over the Unions created problems which nearly led to a falling-out among the victors. The League's determination to establish a club in St. Louis headed by Lucas, even if it meant breaking the National Agreement, began a baseball cold war which lasted through the season of 1885 and several times threatened to bring open conflict between the League and Association. Outright war was avoided mainly because the Association was unwilling to take a strong stand against the League during this year of strain.

The League admitted Lucas and Newton Crane, his attorney, to its special meeting January 10, 1885, furnished them with contracts, and to all intents and purposes accepted them as members. A wire was sent to Von der Ahe requesting his consent for Lucas to share the St. Louis territory, and League owners pledged themselves to admit formally Lucas's club as soon as the Browns' owner gave his approval. Lucas was also supposed to see Von der Ahe personally.

"Der Boss President" was well aware of the money to be made from exhibition games between the two St. Louis teams, for it was only with the greatest reluctance that he had withstood heavy pressure from St. Louis business and professional men to play Lucas's club during the Union War. He also realized he had the advantage of Sunday games, liquor selling, and quarter ball, which Lucas, under National League rules, could not enjoy. So at first he indicated he would not oppose a settlement. But Lucas delayed seeing him until the last minute, and then was "so exact in his manner" that he annoyed Von der Ahe greatly. Besides, Von der Ahe saw a chance to extract a price for his consent. He demanded that Lucas pay him for losses suffered in the Union War and for giving the Union chief a "valuable business privilege." This Lucas "positively declined" to do.

To undercut Von der Ahe, the League, at a second special meeting in New York on January 21, called for a change in the National Agreement making St. Louis an exception to the rule covering territorial rights. At the same time more telegrams were sent pressing Von der Ahe to modify his demands. Relations between the two groups became tenser. The Association men were so concerned that a full complement of them were present in the city and were earnestly discussing the crisis in the bar and corridors while the National League was meeting. While the Association was willing to compromise, it wanted to go slow on changing the National Agreement. But the League was determined to have its way. When Von der Ahe still refused to yield, Denny McKnight, president of the Association, was called into the League meeting and told that the Association had already violated the National Agreement by breaking the ten-day rule in the Brooklyn-Cleveland player deal. The League demanded that the Association either expel Brooklyn or let Lucas move into St. Louis.

The New York *Times* had called the Brooklyn-Cleveland deal "the biggest sensation that was ever made in baseball." It happened just as the Cleveland League team collapsed. Knowing the club was about to leave the League because of its rocky financial condition, Cleveland Manager Hackett went on a twenty-day "pilgrimage" to the players' homes, handing out advance money in return for pledges to join him in Brooklyn, where he had made a deal to manage in 1885. The moment Cleveland officially released them, the players were brought together and kept under surveillance in a Cleveland hotel * so that other clubs could not approach them during the ten-day waiting period. They were signed to Brooklyn contracts a few minutes after midnight of the tenth day.

By reviving this episode and confronting McKnight with it, the League was plainly preparing to break the National Agreement by pleading that the Association had already done so. McKnight's answer was to call a special Association meeting at Pittsburgh later in the month. The League agreed to take no action until that time.

The situation was saved by a chance meeting of Lucas with Von der Ahe's representative, Congressman John J. O'Neill, on the train returning to St. Louis. O'Neill, who was also vice president of the Browns, had been looking after Von der Ahe's interests at the baseball sessions in New York. He arranged for the two men to have dinner at the popular St. Louis restaurant, Tony Faust's place, where they made a secret agreement which resolved their differences.† Commenting on O'Neill's strenuous peace-making, a local paper remarked, "It is denied that this . . . was due to any anxiety over the result of the next Congressional campaign in his district."

---

* Not in a small town on the Canadian border, as originally reported.
† One guess was that Lucas paid $2500 to cover damages.

Von der Ahe then wired Association leaders, who by then were convened at Pittsburgh, that matters had been amicably adjusted, clearing the way for the Association and the League to come together again. Committees from the two majors then met jointly. The Association gave the League permission to locate a club in St. Louis, and in exchange the League pledged to let the Association place a club in a League city if an "emergency" required it. The Brooklyn-Cleveland issue was dropped, because the joint committee decided there had been "so much of evasion of the actual letter of the law" by both major leagues.

Disposing of Lucas was not the last of the war's after-effects. There was still the question of the blacklisted players. Lucas was extremely anxious for them to be restored to good standing, because most of them were slated to go to his club if they were reinstated. They had either been with Lucas during the war or were needed there to create a strong team. Knowing this, Lucas and his attorney, Newton Crane, pleaded the players' cause "by every art known to them," including threats to withdraw the club from the League just as the season was to begin. Several trade unions protested that the blacklisted players were "workingmen kept out of employment by a body of capitalists" simply because they had left one employer to get higher wages from another. One member of a typographical union even called for a boycott against the major leagues if the players were not taken back.

Spalding threw his powerful support behind Lucas, telling his colleagues that unless the players were taken back, attendance in St. Louis would suffer, and the League would be placed in the "absurd position of punishing players for whose misconduct [Lucas] was largely responsible." Spalding said that it was "no longer a question of sentiment, but of simple business," and he proposed that the players be let off with fines instead. The influential Chicago magnate was praised in the newspapers as a shrewd businessman who had sense enough to see that St. Louis would show its gratitude at the box office when his White Sox played there: "Many shekels! Happy Spalding!" John B. Day, Giants' owner, agreed that it was a matter of dollars and cents to have a good ball club in St. Louis.

As a result, at its April meeting, without consulting the Association, the League removed nine of its players from the blacklist. Four of them —Daly, Gross, Dunlap, and Schaffer—were fined $500 apiece for ignoring the reserve clause, and the others—Briody, Glasscock, McCormick, Sweeney, and Shaw—were docked $1000 each for jumping their contracts. This solution elicited the uncharitable remark that the more the "virtuous League" looked into this plan for swelling its treasury, the more favorable it became. And Lucas was hailed as "the St. Louis Napoleon" because of his "master stroke of diplomacy."

The League's unilateral action angered the Association. Only a month before, the Association had instructed its members on the Arbitration Committee to vote against any effort at reinstatement of the blacklisted men, and it was the Association's understanding that any move in this direction must be taken by mutual decision. McKnight was indignant at the League's "cold-blooded treachery," and O. P. Caylor sneered at the League owners who, to suit Lucas, got "right down on their seven bellies" and asked "the late Union wrecker chief to walk over their carcasses."

Association Secretary Wheeler C. Wikoff wrote Nick Young demanding an explanation. Young's lengthy reply mixed hurt surprise with rationalization. It defended the right of each league to dispose of the blacklisted as it saw fit, on the ground that the Arbitration Committee's declaration banning them during the war was nothing more than a statement of policy and was not a part of baseball law. Young's justification did not mollify Association men. Asked to comment for *Sporting Life* readers, Denny McKnight said he was not going to quibble over Young's hair-splitting, because everyone knew perfectly well the real intent of the Arbitration Committee's statement during the war. Charles H. Byrne accused Young of taking the attitude of a "retained attorney." Then sarcastically referring to Young's government job, the Brooklyn owner added, "one who for years lives in and breathes the political atmosphere of the national capital must naturally become expert in turning sharp corners and exceedingly facile in framing opinions to meet all emergencies."

Association resentment was deepened by the loss of two of its most valuable players to the League in a brazen deal made by its own New York Metropolitan Club. The Mets had long been an Association problem child because their owner, John B. Day, also owned the National League's New York Club. He controlled both New York teams through his Metropolitan Exhibition Company—a situation which professional baseball no longer allows.

The Association had long accused Day of discriminating against the Mets—compelling them to start their games earlier when both his teams played on the same day, and relegating the Mets to the less desirable diamond on the old Polo Grounds, with only a canvas fence separating the two clubs. Worse yet, the Association found out that Jim Mutrie, manager of the Metropolitans, was also under contract to the Giants. Mutrie's dual role as manager of the Mets and under-cover man for the League probably commenced at the time of the Association's formation; he was seen at its first meetings talking with members and then was known to have left for Chicago to report to Hulbert.

The Association now openly charged Mutrie with being a spy for the League, and *Sporting Life,* commenting on his duplicity, called him "the sweet singer of Manhattan," and with pun intended, suggested he render a *"Baritone solo, with lyre accompaniment,"* entitled "New Yorks vs. Mets; or how happy could I be with either, were t'other dear charmer away." And there was evidence against Mutrie. For example, he had tipped off Day in advance about the Mets' playing schedule before it was published, giving his boss an opportunity to force the schedule committee to make changes in favor of Day's League club.

In the midst of the trouble over the blacklisted men, Day suddenly decided to shift two of the Mets' outstanding stars, Tom "Dude" Esterbrook and Tim Keefe, to his National League club. Esterbrook had hit a phenomenal .408 for the pennant-winning Mets in 1884, and Keefe had won 35 games on the pitching mound. Although they won the flag, the Mets lost $8000, so Day decided to switch his two stars to the Giants, where he could collect fifty cents from fans who wanted to see them instead of the Association's twenty-five.

This was not the first time Day had tried to juggle his players from one club to the other. The year before, he attempted to transfer James "Tip" O'Neill, then a pitcher-outfielder on his League club, to his Association team. But he missed, because he overlooked the ten-day rule. As a result the Browns were able to sign O'Neill by convincing him that his new contract with the Mets was worthless, since he had signed without waiting for the required ten days to elapse. To make sure there would be no hitch this time, Day hustled Esterbrook and Keefe out of the city and put them aboard a ship bound for the West Indies, to keep any "stray manager" from reaching them within the allotted time period.

No wonder Association owners talked freely of war when they met in Pittsburgh in April 1885. They were incensed by the League's reinstatement of the blacklisted players and were convinced that the Esterbrook-Keefe deal was nothing less than a League conspiracy to weaken the Association. Nevertheless, the Association backed down again. A motion to expel the Mets was voted down, and they escaped with only a fine. Mutrie was also fined, and a motion was passed barring him from employment in the Association—but the ban was removed at the end of the season. The Association also announced that it would no longer abide by the National Agreement in so far as the reserve was concerned, although existing contracts would be respected. Finally, the Association showed it was still interested in peace by calling for the Arbitration Committee to meet within thirty days.

Affairs between the two leagues drifted for several months. Speculation over the possibility of open war continued, but statements by spokesmen of both sides showed that they had little desire for it. "Truthful James" Mutrie put his finger on the reason. Only a "rattle-brained idiot" talked of war, he said, for it was "mere shallow nonsense" that the owners would imperil all the capital they had invested in baseball just because "a few half-crazy soreheads want to hurt somebody. Base ball is a business as much as anything else," he declared, "and all this talk of serious rupture is mere bosh."

It was new administrative machinery that brought a solution to the quarrel. Remembering the good work of the joint committee in solving the difficulties of admitting Lucas, the two leagues had set up at their spring meetings a standing conference committee to handle problems between them as they arose instead of postponing them until differences widened. This permanent committee arranged to meet at Saratoga, New York, on August 24. Preparations for Saratoga were made easier by the announced intention of Association leaders to recognize the reserve once more. When the Association met secretly at Atlantic City a few days before the Saratoga conference to decide upon the approach its delegates should take, it took the precaution of excluding the Metropolitans, because it did not want "its private business to be prematurely known to the League."

Decisions reached at Saratoga were not fully revealed at the time. The story of what really happened emerged later. It seems that the conference was chiefly concerned with changing the rule providing for a ten-day waiting period before clubs could sign players who had become free agents through either outright release or the disbandment of their clubs. Its original purpose was to give each team a chance to hire such men. However, in their eagerness to sign good men, impatient owners sometimes winked at the rules and began negotiations ahead of time. Owners were also finding it desirable to sell players' contracts to particular clubs. This was especially true in the case of clubs on the verge of collapse or disbandment. They naturally wanted to dispose of their players beforehand for the highest price they could obtain. The difficulty was that because such sales of players had not at first been contemplated, the rules made no provision for them. So owners at times resorted to subterfuge while trying to preserve the fiction that players were not sold. In the Cleveland-Brooklyn and Esterbrook-Keefe deals, players were taken out of town and kept hidden during the ten-day waiting period to keep other clubs from bargaining with them. Another dodge was to have a club officer sign a player to a personal contract. Then, after the period of grace had expired, the player was signed to a regular club contract, and his acquisition was officially announced. Another favorite trick was to reach a gentleman's agreement with the other owners to keep "hands off," a method which at least had the virtue of making everyone aware of what was happening by securing their consent to it. This was the device used in shipping Tony Mullane to Toledo during the Union War.

The co-operation of the players was necessary to put over these deals. The owners applied pressure on them in various ways. *Sporting Life* reported that in one instance "wine and women" were used. If the players refused to co-operate, as they sometimes did, they could cause much trouble to the clubs involved. For instance, the irrepressible Tony Mullane caused an uproar at the end of the Union War by not going along with plans of the owners. On the verge of collapse, the Toledo Club had sought to recoup some of its losses by selling Mullane and four others to some other Association club at the highest price possible. Von der Ahe was given the first chance and thought he had the players secured for his Browns, since he had reached salary agreements with them and had distributed advance money. Mullane himself was to receive $3500, $500 of it in advance. Von der Ahe even had all the players sign a notarized statement promising they would endorse a St. Louis contract ten days after they were released from Toledo. Toledo was to collect $2500 from St. Louis, half of it in advance, the balance when signatures were safely affixed to Brown contracts. Von der Ahe carefully included a provision for refunds, should any of the players have a last-minute change of heart.

A few hours before the deadline set for signing, Mullane feigned illness and sneaked out of the hotel where he and the others had been billeted for safekeeping. He met officials of the Cincinnati Club, who had become aware of what was happening, and signed with them for $5000, $2000 of it in advance. Later, President Colburn of Toledo admitted he had offered Cincinnati the players, but when he did not hear from the Reds, he had decided to do business with the Browns. Cincinnati's tactic was to deal directly with Mullane and avoid paying Toledo anything for the privilege.

Von der Ahe, complaining, "I paid my money for this man and he has been stolen from me," charged that Mullane had broken baseball law and should be blacklisted. Some other owners agreed. But Mills, who had once before charted the way around the rules in getting Mullane to Toledo and away from Lucas, now candidly stated he could see no excuse for condemning him, because nine out of ten times "the fault is directly traceable to the club managers."

Charges brought against Mullane by the Browns were heard in a courtroom-like setting before the Association's Board of Directors. Mullane was found guilty of "conduct tending to bring discredit on the base-ball profession, causing discontent and insubordination among all professional players, and setting an example of sharp practice almost equivalent to dishonesty." He was suspended for the season of 1885 and ordered to return $1000 of Cincinnati's advance money. Meanwhile, he was to remain the property of that club. No formal charges were made against St. Louis or Cincinnati, because their losses in the shabby affair were considered sufficient punishment.

O. P. Caylor of Cincinnati was "dumfounded," and talked loudly of pulling Cincinnati out of the Association. But he quickly regained his composure. Von der Ahe was still not in the clear. Toledo sued him for the balance of the money due them, and won a judgment of $659.30, which included interest and costs.

The New York *Clipper* observed that the very same men who had applauded Mullane for breaking his contract with Lucas were now "cursing him" for not allowing himself to be "trapped" and sold by a disbanded club. But the New York *Times* thought that the Association's decision met with "the approval of nearly every person who is interested in baseball."

With this parade of examples before them, the joint committee, meeting at Saratoga, secretly prepared a new National Agreement incorporating a provision which marked the beginning of the modern waiver rule. To prevent recurrence of deals like the Esterbrook-Keefe transaction, which had caused so much friction between them, each league would agree that for a period of ten days after a player was released, only clubs of the same league could negotiate with him. After the ten-day period, clubs in the other league were free to go after him. Neither league was to negotiate with players for 1886 before October 20. Post-season inter-league exhibition games would be resumed.

The other cause of tension between the majors—reinstatement of the men blacklisted during the Union War—resolved itself when the Association relented and restored them to good standing just before the end of the season. Even McKnight softened, deciding there was no point in punishing Association players after the League had shown "clemency," and Von der Ahe exerted his influence in support of the players after Davy Rowe, one of the blacklisted, agreed to call off legal action against him in exchange for Von der Ahe's efforts.

The details of the Saratoga recommendations were revealed in October when they were formally ratified by the two big leagues. Before the end of the year, each league specified how released players were to be handled within its own organization during the ten-day period. A player released by an Association club was permitted to state what other Association club he desired to join. If he did not express a preference, he was assigned to whichever club wrote the Association secretary asking for him. Should more than one club want him, the remaining clubs not interested in his services decided by vote which club should have him. Then, should he fail to report, he was to be blacklisted.

The National League's plan was identical except that when more than one club sought the services of the released man, the secretary determined by lot which would receive him. Thus the ten-day period, which used to be a time of waiting, was now to be one of activity in which the player's disposition must be settled. But these changes were only partial solutions; the sale of player contracts directly from one club to another was still not provided for.

Nevertheless, the practice continued. In fact, before the Saratoga peace was even ratified, another sensational deal rocked baseball. Detroit bought the entire Buffalo Club, a fellow League member, for $7000, primarily to acquire the so-called Big Four—star infielders Dan Brouthers, Hardy Richardson, Jack Rowe, and Deacon White. Buffalo was in critical financial straits, and to salvage what it could, it sold the franchise and players to Detroit but continued technically to be a League member, finishing out the schedule with a makeshift team. Practically every other League and Association club as well coveted one or more of the Big Four, and Detroit was confronted with protests and threats of expulsion.

League president Nick Young ruled that the Big Four were still members of the Buffalo Club, so without having played an inning for Detroit they returned to Buffalo. Later in the fall, one of the Detroit directors invited them to his Michigan hunting lodge, and in that atmosphere of good fellowship persuaded them to come back to Detroit for 1886. The quartet refused to return to Buffalo, saying they had their releases and could sign where they pleased. They won their point and remained with their new club.

Boston worked the same ruse later that year. When Providence began collapsing it suspended some of its players, including its pitching star, Radbourne, without pay for the balance of the season, but kept them on reserve. Then in December it sold out to Boston for $6600. Out of this package, the Bostons retained Radbourne and Con Daily as their star battery for 1886 and disposed of the others to their own advantage.

A number of unpublished letters found in the business records of the old Cincinnati Club reveal that Spalding and the Cincinnati management were actually conniving at shipping Chicago's pitcher Jim McCormick out of the National League to the Association club, by carefully arranged gentlemen's agreements with the other clubs in both leagues. But the contemplated sale fell through. And the old device of signing men to personal contracts to evade the regulations were certainly not dead. In 1886 the New York Giants cornered "a whole bunch" of minor leaguers by this tactic.

Before long, all pretense was dropped and players were sold openly from one club to the other. The subsequent sale of John Clarkson and Mike Kelly, already mentioned, was electrifying evidence of the practice. By 1889 the Association's constitution sanctioned such transactions, and of course modern major league rules make definite provision for the assignment of player contracts from one club to another. This selling of reserve rights in players was the last part fitted into the reserve structure, and its adoption meant that players became virtually complete chattels of the teams which controlled their contracts.

At least at the time, though, the Saratoga settlement was successful in closing the rift in Organized Baseball by restoring working relations between the two major leagues after the unpleasantness between them growing out of the Union War; and thus rejuvenated, the alliance between them endured, without trade wars, through four more prosperous years.

16

THE GAME ON THE FIELD IN THE 'EIGHTIES

MAJOR LEAGUE baseball, like any other business, ultimately depends upon its customers. It matters little to these fans what steps the club owners take to organize the game off the field. In the 1880's the people who were thronging the ball parks in ever-increasing numbers were not greatly interested in the owners' squabbles over territorial rights or over players' contracts. What interested them was what they paid to see—the game before them on the diamond. It is now time to take a look at the game of baseball as the fans saw it performed in the 'eighties, and to speak about the teams and players who captured their attention during that decade.

The two outstanding clubs were the Chicago White Sox in the National League and the St. Louis Browns in the American Association. Winner of the League's first pennant in 1876 was Hulbert's Chicago Club, which completed a modest schedule in which each club played the others ten championship games, five at home and five away. The White Sox had been strengthened by the acquisition of the notorious contract-jumpers from Boston—Spalding, McVey, Barnes, and White—and the addition of Adrian C. "Cap" Anson, destined for many years of stardom in Chicago.

Spalding, doubling as field manager and pitching star, led League hurlers with 47 victories against only 13 losses for a winning percentage of .783. Spalding's catcher was James "Deacon" White, one of the outstanding players of the era. White lasted twenty years in the major leagues (1871-90). Although he could and did play every position, in his early career he was best known as a catcher. Later he starred at third base. White was an excellent left-handed hitter who batted over .300 at least eleven times (records for his first two years are missing) and once led the National League with a .385 average.

Ross Barnes was a good-fielding second baseman for the White Sox and in addition had the distinction of being the National League's first batting champion and first .400 hitter, finishing the 1876 season with .403. The fourth member of baseball's first "Big Four," Cal McVey, covered first base and was the second best hitter on the club that year, finishing next to Barnes with a .345 average.

But after their auspicious start the White Sox fell all the way to fifth place in the six-club League of 1877. The main reason was the loss of Spalding from the pitcher's box. He had been the outstanding pitcher of his day but his arm was no longer strong, and besides, he was turning his attention more and more to his sporting goods business. After his last big year in 1876 he stayed on for two more seasons as playing manager, but in the few games he played it was as an infielder rather than as a pitcher.

Meanwhile, the Wright brothers took care of the pennants. Harry's Boston Red Sox won the next two, but their first one in 1877 was slightly tarnished because that was the year Devlin and his Louisville cronies were caught throwing games. Since Louisville finished second, only three games behind the Red Sox, it is interesting to speculate on what might have happened if the three players had remained honest. Providence won in 1879, aided by John M. Ward's superb pitching and the heavy batting of Jim "Orator" O'Rourke, who hit .351. Ward, a handsome, intelligent Irishman, was quite a pitcher before he hurt his arm and had to turn to shortstop. He won 44 games for Providence in its pennant-winning year and 40 more in 1880, including a perfect game (one in which no batter reaches first base), a feat achieved only six times in all major league history.* Curiously, the first year the Wright brothers were separated, George, as manager and shortstop at Providence, beat out brother Harry's Bostons, who finished second, six games behind.

In 1880 the Chicago White Sox came back strong. That year Cap Anson became manager and remained so for nineteen years. During that time his name became a household word—better known, it was said, than that of any statesman or soldier of his time. The fans in Chicago flocked to cheer him. On the road they came out in equally large numbers to jeer. Anson was a powerful, heavy-set six-footer, whose ramrod posture, clear blue eyes, and fearless, aggressive demeanor made him appear even more formidable. He was a professional ball player for twenty-seven years and ranks as one of the very best who ever played. When he first joined the White Sox he played third base, but soon moved over

* In 1959 Harvey Haddix of Pittsburgh pitched the record number of 12 perfect innings against Milwaukee, only to lose 1-0 in the 13th inning; so from one point of view this may be considered a seventh perfect game.

to first base, the position he is generally remembered for. But it was as a batter that Anson excelled. One of the most feared hitters of the nineteenth century, he finished the season with a batting average of better than .300 no less than twenty-one times, and four times he led National League hitters. During his lifetime he was one of a handful of men to make 3,000 hits.

Under Anson's strong leadership—he ruled the players firmly— Chicago won five pennants in seven years. They took three in a row, 1880-82, gave way to Boston and Providence the following two years, and won two more in 1885 and 1886. Like most winning teams, Anson's White Sox had good pitching. Larry Corcoran and Fred Goldsmith carried the load in the early part of the decade. In 1880 Corcoran pitched a no-hit game and then two more in 1882 and 1884—the first one to pitch three no-hitters. When Corcoran and Goldsmith faded, Jim McCormick and John Clarkson came along to replace them. Mc-Cormick was with the club only two years but he won sixteen straight games in 1886. Clarkson, in Anson's estimation, was the best pitcher Chicago ever had. The 1884 rules removing restrictions on pitchers' deliveries came just in time for him. He was a fast-ball pitcher who could now make the most of his speed. Clarkson won 52 games for the 1885 pennant-winners and followed with 35 and 38, after which he was sold to Boston for $10,000, the same phenomenal figure that Spalding received for King Kelly the year before.

The White Sox had numerous other fine players in the 'eighties. Ross Barnes's successor, Fred Pfeffer—"Unzer Fritz," as he was often called by the sports writers—was one, a star second baseman for many years who later wrote a book on baseball. At shortstop was Ed Williamson, one of the hardest hitters of the period. His 27 home runs, made in 1884, held the record until 1919 when a young man named Babe Ruth broke it. Even one of the White Sox part-time players was famous. Outfielder Billy Sunday, who won greater fame as an evangelist, was too weak at bat to play regularly. But Billy's great speed and base-stealing ability made him an exciting player to watch.

The greatest of all the White Sox, though, was the mighty Mike "King" Kelly. The flamboyant King was without doubt a star player on the field and one of the most colorful and notorious off it. He could play any position, but ordinarily played the outfield or caught. He was a fine hitter and a clever, daring base runner whose exploits on the bases inspired the well-known cry, "Slide, Kelly, Slide!" which later became the title of a popular song. Added to his great natural ability was Kelly's alert mind. In the days of one umpire he never hesitated to take short cuts on the bases when he could get away with it. One famous story tells how once in a crucial situation he leaped from the bench, announced "Kelly now substituting!" and caught a foul pop fly, retiring the side and saving the game for Chicago.

Kelly's love for baseball was equaled by his liking for the horses and for liquor. As Anson said, Kelly had "one enemy, that one being himself." Off the field the King lived life to the hilt. He was a free spender, a fancy dresser, and an avid pursuer of night life. Once Kelly reported a month late and out of condition. Told to get in shape, he sent word to his manager one day that he was in a Turkish bath and would not be at the ball park. Later it was learned he had spent the day at the race track. Following his sale to Boston, Kelly had several more fine seasons. After that he went downhill, going to Cincinnati, and back to Boston, and finishing with the Giants in 1893. He died of "typhoid-pneumonia" the following year at the early age of 36.

The 1886 pennant was the last that Anson ever won. Detroit, aided by baseball's second Big Four, won in 1887, and Jim Mutrie's New York Giants took the last two of the decade.

In the American Association, Chris Von der Ahe's St. Louis Browns were, if anything, even better than Chicago. They won four consecutive Association pennants, 1885-88, duplicating the feat of Harry Wright's Boston Club of the old Professional Association. The record of these two clubs stood unequaled until repeated by John McGraw's New York Giants of 1921-24 and again by Joe McCarthy's New York Yankees of 1936-39. The Yankees, led by Casey Stengel, later broke these records with five straight flags, 1949-53. The Browns not only took four straight but narrowly missed two more in 1883 and 1889, when they were nosed out by the Athletics and Brooklyn. The only others to win Association pennants during the decade were Cincinnati, which took the first one in 1883, and the New York Metropolitans, who won in 1884.

Von der Ahe himself could have played in vaudeville. He was a heavy-set man whose face featured a great bulbous nose and a full moustache. He wore loud clothes, spent money liberally, and liked to exclaim, "Nothing is too goot for my poys!" There are enough anecdotes about his ignorance of baseball itself and about his colorful and uninhibited life to fill a small book. Von der Ahe's naïveté in baseball matters as well as his craving for recognition are illustrated by the story of how he supposedly boasted to a delegation of visitors that he had the biggest baseball diamond in the world. When Charles Comiskey, his field captain, hastily took him aside and whispered that all diamonds were the same size, Chris retreated and simply claimed that he owned the biggest infield!

Chris was fortunate in having Charles Comiskey to run the team.

Like Anson, Comiskey was a first baseman. He was an intelligent player and leader who later became a key figure in the founding of the present American League as owner of the Chicago Club, which was still held by his descendants until 1959 when Bill Veeck re-entered baseball by purchasing a majority interest in the club.

The Browns's star pitchers were Robert Lee Carruthers and Dave Foutz. Their catcher was Doc Bushong, who later became a practicing dentist. Carruthers won 99 games for the Browns in their first three pennant-winning years, and Foutz 98. Von der Ahe, who saw a chance to convert these stars into hard cash, sold them to Brooklyn after the 1887 season. Silver Flint then filled the pitching gap with 45 victories as the Browns took their fourth straight in 1888. Despite the loss of their stars the Browns came close to taking five in a row in 1889, but lost out to Brooklyn, with the three former Browns—Carruthers, Foutz, and Bushong—playing important roles in their triumph.

In the outfield the Browns had Tip O'Neill, who registered the greatly inflated batting average of .492 in 1887—partly resulting because under the rules that year a base on balls counted as a hit. The best outfielder on the club was Curt Welch. He had the knack of judging where the ball was going by the sound of the bat, and turning and running to the right spot. He was also adept at reaching base by allowing himself to be hit by a pitched ball. The Browns' third baseman was the inimitable Arlie Latham, whose clowning made him a kind of opposite number to the National League's King Kelly as a colorful figure. Arlie played in the majors for seventeen years and managed the Browns for one of them. In later years he became a press box attendant at Yankee Stadium.

These big league clubs of the 'eighties were playing a faster, more exciting game created by further improvement and refinement in the rules. Much of the experimentation with the rules was directed toward striking the nicest possible balance between attack and defense. When the National League started in 1876, pitching stars like Al Spalding and Tommy Bond worked in a six-foot-square box only 45 feet from home plate, and had to deliver the ball with the throwing arm swinging nearly perpendicular to the side of the body, in order to make certain that the hand passed below the hip. Before the pitch, the umpire asked the batter whether he wanted a high or low ball, and then relayed his preference to the pitcher. Every third pitch that was not where the batter wanted it was called an "unfair ball," and after three of these the batter was given his base on balls. In other words, nine balls were required for a walk!

Three strikes were out, but until 1881 the umpire did not count every good ball. Before that, if the batter did not swing at the next good one after the second strike, the umpire simply warned him, "Good ball!"—meaning that he should start swinging. This amounted to giving the batter an extra strike.

For the next fifteen years or so, tinkering with pitching and batting rules continued—first to the pitcher's advantage, then to the batter's. In the late 'seventies, swift, underhand curve pitching and improved fielding seemed to many to stifle the attack. Fans complained of dull, low-score games and demanded less science and more scoring.

Soon the pendulum was swinging back to the hitters. In 1879 the pitcher's box was cut to six feet by four, and the pitcher had to face the batter as he started his motion. The catcher was also required to move up close and take the third strike on the fly in order to make the strikeout official; and the number of balls for a base on balls was reduced to eight. Thereafter, the number varied from seven, then to six, back again to seven, then dropped to five, and finally settled on four in 1889. Additional help was given the batter in 1881 when the pitching distance was lengthened to fifty feet.

Pitchers received an important concession in 1884, though, when they were allowed to throw with any motion. The main effect of this ruling was to allow them to throw overhand, thus making it possible for them to pitch with far more speed and to put "stuff" on the ball. This advantage was offset somewhat in 1885 by permitting bats with one flat side to be used, until 1893 when the orthodox round bat was made compulsory once more. Pitchers were again helped in 1886 when their box was enlarged to seven by four. The following year batters no longer had the privilege of calling for a high or low ball. From then on, pitchers were really free to perfect their art, because they could pitch where they wanted with any motion that suited them.

These concessions to pitchers aroused much debate. Some argued the futility of trying to enforce rules restricting the pitcher's motion, and welcomed the opportunity for pitchers to use more strategy. Others denounced overhand pitching as injurious to pitching arms, dangerous for catchers, detrimental to batting and fielding, and the cause of slowing down action on the field. They looked upon the pitcher as a "usurper." To these critics, he was not even a ball player; nevertheless, he dominated the game merely because he could curve a ball.

To compensate for helping the pitchers, the rulemakers took some steps in favor of the batters in 1887. Fat batting averages were practically guaranteed, not only by allowing hitters four strikes but also by counting a walk as a hit. No wonder Tip O'Neill could hit .492, an ample 150 points over his best previous mark! That year batters hit by a pitched ball were given first base. As if these favors were not enough, pitchers were forbidden to lift a foot until they actually delivered the ball, thus losing the speed they gained by taking a run and a jump before delivering the pitch. The three-strike rule was restored the following year. Then, with the base on balls set at four balls in 1889, as already mentioned, the familiar balls-and-strikes count was established for good and all.

Other new rules smoothed out some of the crudities in the game and speeded up the action. The changing rules on use of substitutes show how baseball men, by trial-and-error methods, tried to reach a fair solution to a practical problem. If a player became sick or injured during a game, he could be replaced; but since the decision was up to the umpire, there was a good deal of argument and delay. One pitcher who was doing poorly feigned illness to escape from the game, but at the insistence of the opposing manager, a physician examined him on the spot and reported that he was only "discouraged" and could continue!

The rules covering substitutions for reasons other than illness were changed repeatedly. It took time to grow accustomed to the idea that it was legitimate to take one man out of the game and send in another as a matter of strategy rather than because of injury. In the League's first year, such changes could not be made after the fourth inning, except that a pinch runner could be used if he were chosen by the captain of the opposing team—a precaution against pretending a substitute runner was needed in order to send in a faster man. Up until 1878 the pinch runner did not have to wait until the batter reached first. He stood behind the batter's box and started for first base as soon as the ball was hit—the way youngsters used to play on the sandlots as recently as the 'twenties. In 1880 no substitutes were allowed after the eighth inning, and by 1888 they were banned altogether. The following year one replacement was allowed at any time in the game, and in 1890 two could be used at any time. Not until 1891 were all restrictions removed and substitutes allowed any time for any reason. The one rule which has remained constant through the years is that a player who leaves a game, for whatever reason, may not re-enter it.

An obvious timesaver was an 1886 rule requiring the umpire to call for another ball immediately, instead of allowing five minutes to search for a lost one. Added safety factors were the introduction in 1876 of fifteen-foot-square white canvas bases "filled with some soft material" and, in 1887, a home plate of whitened rubber. Locating home plate within the diamond to fit the intersection of the two foul lines exactly (1877) and placing the first and third base bags entirely inside the foul lines, so that batted balls passing over them were in fair territory (1887), made it easier for the umpires and cut down on disputes.

The wiles and antics of ingenious players continued to keep the rulemakers on their mettle. Up to 1887 the umpire was to decide if a baserunner had intentionally let a batted ball hit him or had purposely kicked it, and if so declare him out. As a result, clever runners might interfere with fielders in this way and get away with it. So the rule was changed so that any runner struck by a batted ball was automatically out.

Beginning in 1881 each team's batting order had to be drawn up before the game. This was to keep team captains like Anson from improvising the lineup as they went along, to take advantage of developments as the game unfolded. The heavy-hitting Anson used to wait and see if the first two men hit safely, in which case he would bat next. If not, he would send someone else up, saving himself for a possible later chance to swing when runners were on base and a hit would drive them in.

In the summer of 1886 a rule was passed restricting coachers to boxes near first and third base, in order to prevent them from moving in near the opposing catcher and pouring all kinds of invective into his ears to disconcert him. The Browns, whose coachers, especially Comiskey and Bill Gleason, were particularly effective at abusing the opposition, accused the other clubs of trying to keep them from winning the pennant by passing this rule. But the Browns won it anyway.

Up until 1887 there was no single code of playing rules. National League rules dominated professional ball, but the American Association had its own code which varied somewhat from that of the older circuit. For example, three years before the League adopted the rule permitting a hit batter to take his base, the Association was already using it. The want of uniformity caused difficulty when League and Association clubs met in exhibition games. So in November 1886, the two majors appointed a joint committee which, after consulting three team captains from each league, took the important step of drafting a common code for all professional clubs party to the National Agreement.

Playing techniques were also being rapidly improved at this time. Experts urged "playing for the side" and "self-sacrifice." Fielders were beginning to back each other up in case of overthrows or muffed balls. Under Comiskey's direction, the Browns' infield learned to move in or back, depending on the situation and the stage of the game, thus making the inner defense more effective in cutting off runs. This shifting of the infield is now common strategy.

Pitchers were learning to rush over to first base on balls hit to the first baseman and take his throw whenever he was too far away to put the man out himself. Nowadays, it is mandatory for the pitcher to start immediately toward first base on *any* ground balls hit past

him on his left side. An unconscious tribute to the improved quality
of fielding as well as to the skill of Anson, Pfeffer, Burns, and Williamson was the name given the White Sox crack infield of the mid-
'eighties: Chicago's Stone Wall.

Even as specialization was progressing, there were still many examples of players who were adept at more than one position. Despite
the higher-grade requirements for each position, left-handers were
still used in ways unthinkable today. John Clements, a left-hander,
was a catcher. Even the noted Willie Keeler, another left-hander,
played short, second, and third in the 1890's when he first entered the
majors. Left-handers are no longer seen in these positions because it
takes them longer to get the ball away since they have to pivot before
throwing to first.

Batters of the 1880's were learning to "place hit," although some ob-
servers were disturbed that so few professionals knew how to do it.
Clubs were beginning to co-ordinate their attack. "Teamwork at bat,"
as it was called, was supplanting the "record batting" of old. One
writer commented that trying for home runs at all costs was "a very
stupid piece of play" when no one was on base to benefit. Besides, he
said quaintly, it subjected the batsman "to a violent sprinting for 120
yards," a "costly expenditure of physical strength."

Baseball tradition has long assigned credit for inventing the devastating hit-and-run play to the legendary Baltimore Orioles. But their
claim to this distinction is highly questionable. According to Cap
Anson, the White Sox were using it in the 'eighties, and John Montgomery Ward singled out the Boston Club of the early 'nineties as
experts at it—which would give them prior claim. The Giants were
also practicing the play before the Orioles. The hit-and-run play is
still one of the most effective methods of attack in baseball. It is most
commonly used with a runner on first base. When the batter gives his
hit-and-run sign, the runner breaks from base as the ball is pitched.
The hitter must try to drive the ball behind the runner, usually toward
right field, thus enabling him to go all the way to third base.* If the
batter grounds out to second or first, the chances are the runner will
at least make second, because his flying start usually makes either an
out at second or a double play on a ground ball impossible. The danger
in this play is that the catcher may anticipate it, prevent the batter
from hitting by calling for a pitch-out (throwing out of reach of the
batter), and throw out the runner at second. Or, if the batter should

* Modern clubs also use a run-and-hit play, a variation in which the runner
breaks for second and the batter has the option of swinging at the pitch or "taking
it"—that is, letting it go by.

hit a line drive at one of the infielders, the runner is easily doubled off first base.

It was this kind of higher strategy, now called "inside baseball," which was developing in the 'eighties and early 'nineties. But in those days, on a hit-and-run play, it was customary for the runner to first fake a start for second base, so that the hitter could see whether the shortstop or second baseman started over to cover the bag. On the next pitch the hitter would try to poke the ball through the spot vacated. Second base combinations have since learned not to tip off in advance which infielder will cover second, so that hit-and-run batters are now usually content to try to drive the ball behind the runner toward right field.

The bunt was becoming more common in the 'eighties, but it still was not fully accepted. Sometimes the fans booed players for bunting, and many players and baseball men wanted the bunt outlawed. But Harry Wright thought players should master it, and John M. Ward also favored the play. When Ward was running the Brooklyn team it was said that they had a bat made of soft willow, especially suited for bunting, and, to confuse the opposition, they also used a hardwood bat which appeared to be identical.

Daring base-running and hard sliding were common in the 'eighties. Most runners used the "Kelly spread," a contemporary version of the modern hook slide, in which the runner throws his body away from the base, extends his leg, and hooks the bag with his foot, giving the baseman as little as possible to tag. The most famous base-running exploit of the 'eighties was the so-called $15,000 Slide of Curt Welch, the Browns outfielder, whose steal of home settled the post-season championship series of 1886 in favor of St. Louis over Chicago.

New and improved equipment also raised the level of performance in the 'eighties. Introduction of the mask had already revolutionized the role of the catcher. Further improvement in his work was due largely to the new-style, heavily padded glove, with which "the swiftest balls can be readily stopped." The ability of the catcher to work up close under the bat was also facilitated by the introduction of the chest protector in the 'eighties. Sliding pads, brought in by Sam Morton of A. G. Spalding and Bros., were a boon to base runners, sufficient to protect them from bruises and burns ("strawberries," in baseball terminology), yet light enough not to impede them.

New machines and mass production methods were having an effect upon the manufacture of baseball equipment, which could now be standardized according to more precise specifications. In the early days, a bat was a bat, and players took them as they came. There was little room for personal choice. For example, Charley Fulmer of the Buffalo Club wrote a letter in 1878 mentioning that he had ordered "some long forty inch bats if the men do not like them they can easily be sawed." But in 1884 John Hillerich, son of a German immigrant who had established a wood-turning business in Louisville, made a special bat for the well-known hitter Pete Browning. Gradually other players insisted upon made-to-order bats, and the firm, later known as Hillerich & Bradsby, became famous as the manufacturer of Louisville Sluggers. No other piece of equipment is so subject to the individual requirements and vagaries of the players. And so long as they keep within the limits specified by the rules—2¾ inches in diameter and 42 inches maximum length—they can give full play to their own preference as to length, weight, and styling.

One great advance in the standardization of the game was the invention of a machine which made the baseball itself of uniform size and weight. By 1872 the dimensions and weight of the ball, which have applied ever since, were fixed: 9 to 9¼ inches in circumference and 5 to 5¼ ounces in weight. But even the machine failed to settle the recurrent argument over whether the ball was too lively. Henry Chadwick was charging back in the 1860's that the ball was "overelastic," and the debate has been going on ever since.

The umpire was also using a new gadget, a pocket-sized instrument for recording balls and strikes called The Umpire's Assistant—a forerunner of the present-day "indicator." It was made of black walnut with thumb screws operated by clockwork. One inventor created an electric base indicator, rigged up with underground wires, which was supposed to help the umpire make fair decisions. Whether he had the interest of the umpires at heart, or was merely reflecting on their eyesight, is not known, but he was unsuccessful in obtaining baseball's support for his invention. Still more fanciful was a baseball "curver," supposedly endorsed by professionals and advertised for many years with a picture and the legend, "With it any person can curve a ball in any desired direction"! One end of this twenty-five-cent gimmick fit over the index finger and the other was held in the palm of the hand.

The level of performance was also raised by a growing emphasis on spring training. To get their players in proper condition for the beginning of the season, club owners began sending their teams south. After a winter of loafing and, in some cases, dissipation, players might report overweight, "looking like aldermen." So, as one reporter said ironically, the owners laid out money to get players in shape to earn their salaries.

Sports writers still tell us every spring that the Chicago White Sox of the 1880's were the first team to go south for training. Research into the old records shows that this is only partly true. The White Sox

were first, but it was the 1870 club which did the pioneering, along
with Cincinnati. Both clubs made spring trips to New Orleans that
year. It may not come under the heading of spring training technically,
but even the year before that Boss Tweed sent his New York Mutuals
on a southern safari as far as New Orleans.

Judged by today's standards, early training programs were simple
indeed. Camps had no fancy facilities, scientific equipment, whirlpool
baths, vibrators, or left-handed pitching machines. But in the not-so-
good old days their program was considered very modern, because
before spring trips pre-season conditioning was done in local gyms,
rented halls, sheds, rinks, or any other shelter available. When it was
announced that the hard-bitten members of the Buffalo team had actually joined the Y.M.C.A. in 1878, amazed fans were immediately
assured that they were doing it because it was the only way to get
the use of the gym.

Following the example of the White Sox, Reds, and Mutuals, some
clubs began going south in the 1870's. New Orleans was a favorite
training base in those days, but it was not the only one. Some of the
teams did not get very far south. Cleveland tried Washington in 1883.
Louisville, Pittsburgh, and Detroit worked out in Savannah in 1886.
Another choice for a camp site was Charleston, South Carolina, where
the Phillies based that same year. Next spring they received an attractive offer from a Florida town, but Harry Wright decided the distance
was too great and settled for Savannah instead. Florida was invaded
in 1888 by the Washington Club, which numbered in its ranks a young
man named Connie Mack. That year Wright retreated somewhat and
settled for Cape May, a fashionable resort on the Jersey coast. His
men rose at 6:00 A.M., doused each other with bucketsful of briny surf,
and hiked over the clammy beach for an hour before breakfast, which
Harry said "they made look pretty sick." The rest of the day was
taken up with long work-outs with dumbbells and Indian clubs and
with more hiking. After supper the boys sat around "swapping lies"
until 10:30 bedtime.

The general custom for clubs who made the trip south was to have
only a short stay in camp and set out on long exhibition tours through
southern towns until the opening of the season. Minor league clubs
welcomed practice games with big leaguers because they were so
profitable. One year the Southern League even revamped its schedule,
postponing its own season until May 1 to make room for major league
visitors. The Detroits played in a great number of "whistle stops" in
1887. After breaking camp at Macon, Georgia, they covered over
4000 miles over a two-month period, journeying all over the South and
as far north as St. Paul, Minnesota.

Chicago introduced a new stunt in 1886 by stopping off at Hot Springs, Arkansas, to "boil out the alcoholic microbes," as a reporter put it, before heading south. That was the time that, before leaving Chicago, the team pledged themselves in Spalding's store not to drink until the end of the season. Soon after, the boiling-out process was considered essential for getting rid of the effects of winter "lushing," as drinking was called then, and Hot Springs became a center for big league clubs.

Gus Schmelz, manager of the Cincinnati Reds, wrote penny-pinching owner Aaron Stern trying to coax him into letting Cincinnati go south in 1888. Schmelz gave his boss a rough estimate of expenses and receipts, reminding him that "the boys" would have to be guaranteed half the profits to get them to go. He also spoke up for himself, telling Stern that he expected a cut, too, because of the extra work and because he would have to leave his family much sooner than under the old routine. The manager said he could not promise to make money, but he did not think they would lose any, either. Besides, he told Stern shrewdly, we will be "finding out what our new material is worth at a time when salaries would not be running and would be welding our team into working shape."

But even in the 'eighties the practice of going south was by no means universal. Before he joined in, Schmelz, in another letter, recommended hiring a gym in 1886, "if reasonable," otherwise he said to "scare up a hall, barn, or something," and impress on its owners the "big advertisement" the team would provide so that they will "let us have it for almost nothing." Gus planned to pay the players' board for a couple of weeks, and after that play one or two exhibition games to clear all training expenses. Running, throwing, catching, and (if space permitted) batting were featured in these gym programs, but handball and racquets were also included. Henry Chadwick recommended handball particularly and advised staying away from dumbbells. Another writer warned against the danger of taking sliding practice on gym mats. He advised sprinkling sand on the floor, or nailing a carpet to it!

The Metropolitans, Athletics, and Louisville were stay-at-homes in 1887. Some managers and players might swear by the benefits of southern sunshine for keeping away "muscular colds and rheumatism" and for putting the men in "the acme of perfect condition"; others were not convinced. Even Cap Anson, field leader of the much-traveled White Sox, thought that southern trips were "more harmful than beneficial." One objection was that players returning to the cold climate after being six or eight weeks in the South were subjected to sore muscles and colds. Players who did not like going south often stayed at home, working out on their own, and in those less organized days they were able to get away with doing so. Steve Libby of the Buffalo Club hunted, worked out with seven-pound Indian clubs, skated, and took daily walks of three to six miles during the off-season, according to a letter he wrote his club in 1878. Often players participated in informal scrub games wherever they were wintering before reporting to their clubs.

But even owners progressive enough to plan a southern trip thought of spring training only as a means of getting the team in shape without losing money. They did not at first appreciate the benefits of publicity and promotion. They did not understand how to arouse fan interest for Opening Day by providing them with colorful stories about how their heroes were preparing for the season. It took a newspaper reporter to show them these advantages.

A. M. Gillam, writing for the Philadelphia *Record,* offered three dollars a day for short bulletins on 1887 training camp activities, scores of games, merits of players, and so forth. He was imaginative enough to see the wonderful possibilities of spring training ballyhoo and what it would do for gate receipts. He said he understood that "the games you play in the South mean nothing, but the score of even a five-inning practice game will be greedily scanned by the enthusiasts here, and will boom your club for the coming season." Before long a springtime ritual began that has been observed ever since. Writers started sending highly optimistic stories from spring training camps touting rookie prospects as "worldbeaters" and hailing washed-up veterans as rejuvenated. By 1890 a newspaper announced that the South was overrun with Northern ball players, and in the course of the decade spring training in the South was adopted by all major league clubs.

Fans of the 'eighties enjoyed another attraction—the excitement of a post-season championship series. The taste for such fare was strong back in the days of the Fashion Race Course series. Its revival was assured after the League and Association made peace in 1883, for what could be more natural, after the two pennant races were settled, than for the winners to meet and decide who was the real "world's champion"? And what was more certain to bring in additional cash for the teams?

Chicago and Cincinnati, winners during the year of the Association War, 1882, made an abortive effort to play each other, as already mentioned. In 1883 the Association's Athletics were scheduled to play the Boston League champions, but they did so poorly against other League clubs in October exhibition games that they canceled the scheduled series. Then the following year the Providence Grays, led by their great pitcher Radbourne, defeated Jim Mutrie's Metropolitan Association winners on three successive days. This first "regularly arranged" series marks the birth of the World Series, an annual baseball event and an American institution. Each of the following six years, a post-season series was played, although the one in the strife-torn year of 1890 did not amount to much. Here is a summary of the first seven World Series:

Year	Association Entry	League Entry	Games Played	Winner
1884	New York Metropolitans	Providence	3	Providence
1885	St. Louis	Chicago	7	Undecided *
1886	St. Louis	Chicago	6	St. Louis
1887	St. Louis	Detroit	15	Detroit
1888	St. Louis	New York Giants	10	New York
1889	Brooklyn	New York Giants	9	New York
1890	Louisville	Brooklyn	7	Undecided †

* The Browns won three of the five games completed, one game ended in a tie, and the umpire declared another forfeited to Chicago when Comiskey took his team off the field because of an adverse decision by the umpire.

† Each team won three games and one ended in a tie.

There were no rules or set formulas for conducting these series in the 'eighties. One club challenged, the other accepted, and then details were worked out. The number of games varied, and all of them were not necessarily played in the cities represented by the contestants. In 1885, fans in Pittsburgh and Cincinnati as well as those of St. Louis and Chicago were given an opportunity to see some of the games; but when Von der Ahe challenged Chicago to a "World Championship Series" in 1886, he suggested that the entire series be played on the two home grounds as a way of ensuring gate receipts. Spalding replied, setting forth conditions to be agreed upon in advance because of "misunderstandings last year" and requesting that winner take all.

The series of 1887 was notable for length and itinerary. Detroit's challenge of the Browns called for fifteen games and a tour of various cities! Besides appearing in the parks of the principals, the show stopped at eight others—Pittsburgh, Brooklyn, New York, Philadelphia, Washington, Boston, Baltimore, and Chicago. In 1885 the two clubs split $1000 between them, but in 1886 players began to share in the receipts. On the eve of that series Spalding wrote Anson and the team congratulating them and urging victory in the series, promising a suit of clothes for each player and half the gate receipts to the team. When the Browns won, Von der Ahe handed over the proceeds, which totalled nearly $15,000—hence the name given Curt Welch's winning slide.

The long series of 1887 netted about $12,000 for each team, after about $24,000 was deducted for expenses. Brooklyn and New York divided $16,362.10 between them in 1889, after subtracting $8000 for traveling and advertising, and the eighteen New York players each received $200 out of the club's share. By 1886 the World Series games had become established as the finale of each season's campaign.

As much as any owner of his day, Chris Von der Ahe, then at the height of his fortune and influence, understood the publicity value of the World Series. He welcomed the post-season games as an opportunity to give full expression to his unquestioned flare for showmanship. In 1888 he reportedly spent $20,000 on lavish accommodations, including a special train for the trip to New York and suits of clothes for all his Browns and guests.

As for the games themselves—whether regular season or World Series—they resembled miniature wars more than athletic contests. The professionals were out to win, and were not overly scrupulous about their methods. In keeping with the attitude of American society, success counted more than the way it was achieved. Trickery and roughness which at times approached mayhem accompanied the vehement desire to win. The most observed rule seemed to be that everything is fair in baseball. As Umpire Billy McLean lamented, "Ball players are up to all sorts of tricks, and nothing but the closest watch will keep us from being beaten by them."

Cutting the ball "slyly" or hiding it in order to have a new one brought into play were among the tricks then in vogue. Switching from a "lively" ball to a "dead" one, or the other way around, was another. Balls were put in an ice box overnight to deaden them for use when the other team was at bat. Connie Mack, then one of the wiliest of catchers, reputedly did this frequently.

Years ago the author saw Frankie Frisch, the famous "Fordham Flash," limp to first base, pretending great pain after being hit by a pitched ball, and then on the very next pitch bring the fans to their feet by catching the Dodgers off guard with a clean steal of second base! This same stunt was executed by Sadie Houck of the Athletics back in 1884. The "injured" Houck, after swiping second "in fine style," raced home on a hit a moment later "midst the laughter of the crowd."

More dangerous tactics were throwing at batters, tripping and blocking runners, knocking down infielders, and other forms of what the papers called "dirty ball." Team coaches shouted to base runners on close plays, "Give them the spikes!" hoping to frighten the baseman into fumbling the ball. Things became so bad that for several years major league rules banned the use of spikes. The St. Louis Browns, by no means the only sinners, were said to be so given to such tactics that it was suggested the club might just as well hire "plug uglies." Possibly because they won so many pennants, Von der Ahe's Browns were singled out for their "rowdy play" and accused of "stopping at nothing" to win.

Mike Kelly was credited—if that is the word—with being the first catcher to throw his mask onto the base path to trip the runner trying to score. Buck Ewing once attempted this stunt with Paul Hines, but Hines, having plenty of time to reach home safely, ruined Buck's six-dollar mask by jumping on it like "a thousand bricks."

But in spite of all the rough tactics, baseball in the 1880's was much improved over what it had been. Contemplating the state of the game in 1889, Henry Chadwick exulted in the "remarkable exhibitions of skill in playing" and contrasted the improved playing rules and more advanced tactics with the fare offered at the Elysian Fields by the Knickerbocker, Eagle, Empire, and Gotham clubs of bygone days. Indeed, the game had come a long way since then!

17

OPERATING A CLUB

WHEN THE UMPIRE cries "Play Ball!" and the lead-off man steps into the batter's box, baseball's show begins. Like theatergoers and spectators at other entertainments, baseball fans are chiefly interested in the spectacle before them. Few stop to realize that it takes a good deal of planning and organizing behind the scenes to put on a performance.

Each individual ball club has primary responsibility for staging a good game in an appropriate setting. This was so right from the beginning. Under the constitutions of both the National League and the American Association, each club had the right to "regulate its own affairs." Club administrative machinery was not nearly so elaborate in the 'eighties and 'nineties as it is in modern baseball, but as the business grew the organizational end of it gradually became more complicated and specialized. Many of the owners were becoming conscious of the wisdom of improving their product and providing better facilities for its enjoyment. As *Spalding's Guide* observed in 1892, the business of catering to the pleasure of fans in the large cities required as much "energy, enterprise, judgment and tact" as that of "any of the large business establishments of the country."

Whatever may be said against the baseball magnates of the nineteenth century, the fact remains that they were confronted with many problems in trying to establish baseball as a new enterprise in the American economy. Some of the methods they used would not guarantee them honorary memberships in the Boy Scouts, but they were probably no worse than those used by many of the captains of industry in those days. Besides, the club owners were living much more in a goldfish bowl than their counterparts in other enterprises. Baseball was, and still is, a public spectacle in which the customers and the press not only see more of what is going on but feel that they are a part of it all. Even though they may not own a dollar's worth of stock in the club, they feel a certain proprietorship. They presume to share in running the team, and are not at all reluctant to give advice and criticism.

As a result, being a club owner has never been easy. Al Spalding once told how things looked from where he sat. He said that the owner must face the public and its "relentless demand for impossibilities." He must be a buffer between the press and his club, meeting the "impudent" questions of newspapermen with soft words. He has to provide accessible grounds and "fit them up," consider the complaints of jealous and ambitious players, do all he can to keep up the *esprit de corps,* attend as many games as possible, and see to it that order is preserved in the ball park.

In these personally owned clubs the operator was the boss. Stock in the clubs was closely held by a few individuals. These exclusive corporations, said *Sporting Life,* February 4, 1885, were like political machines; an "inside ring" enjoyed the increasing profits and barred outsiders who wanted to enter. In some clubs, several people held large blocks of stock, in which case they might share in the direction. Boston, for example, was run by the so-called triumvirs—A. H. Soden, J. B. Billings, and W. H. Conant—although Soden dominated. The triumvirs voted themselves $2500 salaries but did not even give the seventeen minority stockholders a financial report, although the club was becoming increasingly profitable in the middle 'eighties. When the small shareholders demanded an accounting, the triumvirs defeated them by insisting that a vote be taken on the basis of the number of shares held and by asserting that it was not good business policy to make public a financial statement.

It was the owner who decided who was to run the team on the field. He signed the players and determined what salaries they would receive. He hired the maintenance staff and other people needed to run the park. There were even instances when he left his box to argue with the umpire! Of course, like other companies, the ball clubs usually had a Board of Directors, made up of businessmen, which acted more or less as window dressing. The Giants and Pittsburgh, like so many other firms of the time, took advantage of the lenient New Jersey statutes to organize under the laws of that state.

To some of the magnates, who had made their money in other enterprises and were still deeply involved in them, baseball was secondary. A few, like Spalding and Reach, got their start in baseball and then branched out into larger undertakings. In cases like these they might delegate the task of running the club to somebody else. Davis Hawley, secretary of the Cleveland Club, held a good deal of responsibility and was on hand at League meetings with Frank Robison, who had other business interests. And Spalding made Jim Hart president of the club when the sporting goods business began absorbing much of his time.

The owner often received letters from men applying for the job of running the team, stressing experience, ability to fill in as a player, and perhaps their following among players whom they could secure for the team. At first the team was handled by a captain, usually a playing one. He had full charge on the field, selecting and placing the men and running the game. His authority was reflected in the rules, which provided for captain's "lines," a designated area closer to the diamond than the players' bench, where he and one "assistant" could direct the attack. Besides handling the game, he might also have to look after business matters, such as arranging for transportation and hotels, and keeping track of expenses and receipts. A good example of the jack-of-all-trades captain was Harry Wright, whose detailed account books and other records still survive.

As the business grew, all these duties became too much for one man to handle efficiently. Clubs began putting the business details in the hands of a separate man, called the manager, whose job really corresponded to that of a modern club secretary. This left the captain free to concentrate on directing the team on the field. The owners of the Philadelphia Athletics, for example, separated the two jobs, ordering that:

> The Captain shall have absolute control in directing, placing and playing the men during games and practice, without interference from anyone, the manager being as much under his control in these instances as any other men.

There was no set pattern, however. Club operation was in a transitional stage, and the lines of authority differed from team to team. Sometimes the game was directed by non-playing managers, who might or might not be responsible for the business affairs of the team as well. Mutrie of the Giants, for example, was such a "bench manager," although it was said that he was merely a figurehead who kept tab at the gate and collected New York's share, while the real leadership of the team on the field was in the hands of Buck Ewing, the captain. In the late 'nineties "Scrappy Bill" Joyce acted as manager, captain, and first baseman of the Giants. Then, when Anson was brought in as bench manager, Joyce simply continued as captain and first baseman. In fact by the 1890's bench managers, like Ned Hanlon of the Orioles and Frank Selee of Boston, were becoming more common. Teams still had captains, like Wilbert Robinson of the Orioles, who were important as kind of right-hand men to the manager.

Sometimes the owner himself would try to manage the team on the field. Perhaps the most ludicrous example was that of Von der Ahe, who took charge of the Browns in 1892 after Comiskey quit, inaugurating, as the *Sporting News* said, "a reign of terror." Another variable was the personalities of the captains and owners. A strong captain like Anson or a manager like Hanlon allowed no interference on the field. Comiskey was patient and diplomatic with Von der Ahe for years, but finally quit because of Der Boss's interference.

In baseball, more often than not, the front office either meddled with the running of the team or refused to follow the recommendations of the managers. In 1894 playing manager Connie Mack had a big row with President Temple of Pittsburgh, who signed a second baseman to take Louis Bierbauer's place without telling Mack about it until afterwards. In Boston Manager Selee's suggestions for signing players were known to be repeatedly ignored by owner Soden. Von der Ahe made the players nervous, watching their every move with field glasses, running around the stands blowing a whistle at them, or storming into the dressing room swearing at players whose errors lost the game.

Philadelphia owner John I. Rogers's suggestions were at least constructive. After the team lost two games in succession, he asked Manager Harry Wright to give the players a "very positive talk" every week and have a clubhouse meeting after each game to go over mistakes and discuss ways to improve. He wanted the players to rest or take short rides in the morning instead of playing billiards or going for long sight-seeing walks. He also urged Wright to stop them from taking a heavy meal in midday when there was a game scheduled for that afternoon.

Magnates did not maintain an expensive corps of scouts in those days. Recruiting new players was still rather haphazard. Young fellows wrote in for tryouts, as they did in Harry Wright's time, but as Charlie Mason, Athletics manager in 1884, pointed out, only a "very, very small" percentage made the grade. Jim Galvin, who became one of the standout pitchers of the day—his 560 complete games is still the record—offered to pitch for Buffalo in 1877 for $1200, adding "but I want to get some [of the money] in winter." A less illustrious candidate, signing himself "the twirler and puzzler," answered a Cincinnati Club advertisement with the assurance that he was a "reliable bater" and a "first class bass runner"! Both players and clubs also advertised in the newspapers, and the *Sporting News* opened its columns to them free of charge as a service to baseball. A. G. Spalding & Bros. established a baseball bureau, operating out of its Chicago, New York, and Denver stores, to assist young players to find jobs at no charge.

It was becoming apparent that ball clubs "remaining dormant" could no longer pick up good ball players. The White Sox and a few of the others had agents around the country who were watching for young players and advising the management on good prospects. Spalding was one who realized even in the 'eighties that the best way to get talent was to develop it from minor league clubs under his control. *Sporting News* pointed out that signing players sight unseen was useless, and suggested that it would be well worth it for the clubs to hire a couple of competent "judges" and send them on inspection tours of the minors to locate good players. Club managers themselves were beginning to take tours in search of players, and John Ward had the new idea of holding morning tryouts at the Polo Grounds for aspiring youngsters, who were invited to show their ability without any prior screening. Another forerunner of modern methods was a suggestion that a baseball training school be set up, with a man like Anson in charge, to develop young players who showed natural ability. And by the 'nineties the management was already realizing that in signing a rookie his habits, attitudes, and influence on his teammates should be considered as well as his playing skill.

Building and operating the park was almost entirely the responsibility of the individual club owner. He had to comply with certain league requirements, such as policing the park adequately, preventing pool-selling on the grounds, providing a players' bench, and the like. But otherwise he had free rein. Many of the magnates used some of the profits of the prosperous 'eighties for new parks or the renovation of old ones. The reserve clause helped make funds available which otherwise might have been used in bidding up prices for players. The cost of building these modest structures was relatively low. Baltimore's new Oriole Park in 1883 was built for only $5000. It boasted 1200 "elegant" chairs in the grandstand back of the catcher, and two large open stands on each side of the diamond, with a combined seating capacity of 5000. The entire plant was enclosed with 40,000 feet of fencing.

Buffalo built a new type of grandstand after making a $5000 profit in 1883. The stand was completely enclosed in the back, for protection against bad weather, and ventilated with louvers. Seating capacity was 5000, with standing room for another 1000; total cost $6000. The Philadelphia Athletics, Cleveland, and Cincinnati also constructed new parks in the 'eighties. In the 'nineties the Brooklyn Club, which had been paying $7500 annual rent for Eastern Park, moved to its new Washington Park at Fourth Avenue and Third Street when Charlie Ebbets took over the presidency of the club. In 1893 a new Sportsman's Park seating 10,000 was built in St. Louis. It featured "tall, majestic" iron columns placed back so as not to obstruct the view from the front seats.

Ball parks were being refurbished, too. A printed invitation addressed to Henry Chadwick in 1882 announced that the Philadelphia Club "at cost of many thousand dollars, fitted the above park in first-class order to cater to respectable audiences." Two years later, when it came back into the League, the club spent $2000 more on improvements. Baseball parks were also made more attractive by adding a players' bench and bat rack for each team, installing carpeted and numbered reserved seats, and making generous use of paint and flags.

The model park of the 1880's was Chicago's. An article in *Harper's Magazine* in 1883 called it "indisputably the finest in the world in respect of seating accommodations and conveniences." After a $10,000 remodeling job in 1883, $1800 for painting alone, it boasted space for 10,000 people—2000 grandstand seats, 6000 "uncovered seats," plus standing room—all without infringing on the playing field. A special accommodation was a row of eighteen private boxes which were "cozily draped with curtains to keep out wind and sun, and furnished with comfortable armchairs." Spalding's private box was equipped with a gong and the newly popular telephone, which allowed him to conduct all pre-game details without leaving his seat. This "palatial" park employed 41 uniformed attendants—7 ushers, 6 policemen, 4 ticket-sellers, 4 gatekeepers, 3 "field-men" (groundkeepers), 3 cushion renters, 6 refreshment boys, and 8 musicians.

The same trend toward improved and enlarged ball parks continued in the 'nineties. Besides the new construction in Brooklyn and St. Louis, there was a brand-new park built for the White Sox in 1893, timed with the World's Fair in mind. Philadelphia had an excellent park by 1896—it was called "the best athletic ground in the world"—after the club spent $40,000 on improvements. It had a seating capacity of 16,000 and standing room for four or five thousand more.

Most of the parks had groundkeepers. At Cleveland, one of the most attractive parks was maintained all year round by a groundkeeper, who kept the field looking "like a millionaire's lawn." Cincinnati's diamond was so smooth, it was said, that anybody who could not field well on it should look for some other job. In 1882 the Athletics soaked and rolled their field, and the next season hired "landscape gardeners" who made it "as level as a billiard table." According to the New York *Clipper*, the Browns' groundkeeper introduced "Tarpulins" in 1884 to protect home plate and the bases during wet weather. On the other hand, Soden's Boston park was reputedly the smallest and poorest, with the worst-kept grounds and a narrow, cramped grandstand. Soden even charged players' wives full admission, and ripped out the press box to make room for more seats. He was evidently trying to live up to his philosophy: "Common sense teaches me baseball is conducted primarily to make money."

The day of brick and steel stadia had not yet arrived. The parks of the nineteenth century were wooden structures, subject to fires. Philadelphia, Baltimore, Boston, and Chicago all had fires in 1894. The Phillies stand burned to the ground. St. Louis had no fewer than six fires in ten years. Pittsburgh had scarcely recovered from flood damages when a windstorm ripped off the grandstand roof in 1901.

There were other hazards in the life of a magnate. He had to face law suits from people injured when the crowd panicked in a fire, and was threatened with boycotts for using non-union labor. Once property owners in Louisville tried to enjoin a club from building a park in a residential neighborhood because it would be a nuisance, but the court ruled against them.

Even in those early days parking space was a problem to the owners. Most of the parks made provision for carriages. Buffalo, for example, had a covered shed where the "carriage trade" could park its equipages for fifteen cents or five dollars a season. Baltimore and Cleveland were others which had enclosed shelters for carriages.

Some of the old bills of the Cincinnati Club of the 1880's give an idea of the many details and expenses of maintaining ball parks: Sprinkling Western Avenue during the season, $52.50; repairing two lawn mowers, $2.50; fire insurance premium (on a $1000 policy), $12.50; building a 78-foot, 8-inch fence, 16 feet high, $64.00; water bill for a season, $25.00; one keg of nails, $2.60; attorney's retainer, $250.00; one gong bell, $10.00; plumbing, $55.27; carpenter work, $22.00; lumber for partitions, $24.34; sewer pipes, $2.76; rubber hose, $19.90; and even a demand for payment for a broken window:

> Dear Sir,
>
> I want to let you [know] that the Ball players brake [sic] a window for me the 19th of Oct. and would like to receive payment the amount of $2.50.
>
> Daniel Handrich.
> Mrs. [illegible]

Naturally club owners wanted to hold costs to a minimum, and some went to extreme lengths to do it. Cincinnati Owner Aaron Stern's credo was "to figure our own expenses as low as they can possibly be made and I shall spend as little money as possible in running the Cincinnati club." He ordered the "free list" to be "shut off," and instructed the gate man to be "just as strict at the door as possible [and] blame everything on me." Stern also cut the number of special police (they were paid $1.75 a day) from six to three on weekdays. The Philadelphia Club would not honor passes given out by players, and forbade the men to ask for them. Under their contract, players could be used to work at the gate, and it was not at all unusual for them to take tickets. Aaron Stern stationed them at the turnstiles in uniform, and Clark Griffith collected tickets when he started pitching in the big league for the Browns in 1891. Cy Seymour, as a rookie with the Giants, was assigned to gate duty but could not resist the temptation to "take a peep at the game." Owner Andrew Freedman caught him away from his post and fined him ten dollars.

To pull in the fans, the owners began turning to the esoteric arts of promotion and advertising. For direct advertising they relied on streetcar billing, sign boards at street corners, handbills, window hangers, posters, and boys parading the streets with banners. Washington sent up a large balloon after games, with the final score printed in great black letters. Von der Ahe displayed a golden ball inscribed "Game Today" or flew a flag reading "No Game Today" over (as one might expect of him) the Golden Lion saloon. John B. Sage, a Buffalo printer, advertised posters, window hangers, and colored scorecards in twenty-four designs for twenty-five cents a set in 1886. In 1880 clubs could place orders for posters drawn up by the League. There were even "baseball cards" in those days. They were not aimed at children, like the modern ones, but were used to advertise such products as cigars and patent medicine.

From these gimmicks the clubs turned to newspaper ads. Cincinnati advertised regularly in three local papers, and one bill from the *Enquirer* for thirteen ads cost the club $67.50. The Browns sometimes had a full-page spread loaded with superlatives: "THE BROWNS ARE HERE! The Hardest Hitters, The Finest Fielders, The Best Base-Runners, The Coming Champions." The club even ran large ads in the local German-language newspaper, *Anzeiger des Westens*. In 1884 Philadelphia spent $2,045.57 for printing and advertising, and Buffalo reported a $631.40 outlay for printing, bill-posting, and other advertising in 1878. Providence spent "much money" in 1879 for newspaper ads, circulating dodgers, and posting bills in town and for miles around.

Inside the park, brass bands often added color to the scene. Spalding had an eight-piece band blaring from a specially constructed pagoda. Cincinnati hired a three-piece regimental ensemble at five dollars a day, and occasionally the Cincinnati Grand Orchestra performed. In Buffalo on special occasions Poppenberg's band held forth. Opening days were always gala affairs, heralded by processions of ball players riding through town in decorated carriages to the accompaniment of music. Harry Wright started games with a real flourish, having his team march nine abreast to first base, and then run along the base lines, each man dropping off at his position en route. Then as now, critics objected that baseball did not need these extra trimmings. Just give us a good ball club, they said.

Other features used were Children's Days, when youngsters were admitted for 10¢; Ladies' Days, when they were admitted free; * and Amateur Days. In 1891 Chicago held a "Base Ball Day," when all amateur clubs in the area were admitted to the park if they appeared in uniform. There were an estimated 400 such teams around Chicago, and the result was the greatest turnout of "ball players" ever seen in one place.

Owners began staging doubleheaders in the 'eighties. Cleveland, for example, had its first "bargain bill" in 1884. Edison's incandescent bulb forecast night ball, first tried in 1880, although not in the major leagues. Two amateur teams played a game at Nantasket Beach, Massachusetts, but the performance was marred by "innumerable" errors because of imperfect light. Another night game, played at Fort Wayne, Indiana, in 1883, has generally but incorrectly been considered the first contest under lights. Some clubs also went on barnstorming tours after the regular season.

The most spectacular piece of showmanship was the six-month world tour of 1889, promoted by Al Spalding. Back in 1874 Harry Wright's Red Stockings and the Philadelphia Athletics went to England, playing ball against each other and cricket against English teams, astonishing the English with the speed and skill of baseball but converting few. Spalding's junket was far more ambitious. His White Stockings and a team of all-stars, captained by John M. Ward, started out for Australia and en route decided to continue on around the world. All told, they visited thirteen countries and every continent, playing in Honolulu, Sydney, Colombo, Rome, Paris, and Cairo. Before returning home the travelers repeated the visit to the British Isles made by Harry Wright fifteen years before. The Prince of Wales and other dignitaries attended one of the games, and afterwards, when a reporter asked him his opinion of the American game, Edward gave him a written statement:

> The Prince of Wales witnessed the game of Base Ball with great interest and though he considers it an excellent game he considers crickett [sic] as superior.

Games and festivities continued on the last lap of the tour from New York back to Chicago, but the real climax was the welcome-home banquet at Delmonico's restaurant. It was on that glittering occasion, graced by Theodore Roosevelt, Chauncey Depew, Mark Twain, and

* See below.

many other prominent figures that A. G. Mills avowed that baseball was an American game, undefiled by any strain of rounders. The long excursion was hardly a great financial success, but it was hugely successful in other ways. Baseball and Spalding's sporting goods business were well publicized, and the enthusiastic reception given the players everywhere on their triumphal tour was evidence of the growing stature of baseball.

Ticket sales of course was the backbone of the magnates' income, but there were numerous other ways to supplement it, many of them serving the double purpose of adding to the comfort and enjoyment of the fans while bringing in welcome dollars to the owners. The concession business was beginning. It was to become increasingly lucrative until it became a major source of income for big league clubs.

Most profitable was beer selling. Beer had always gone hand in hand with the American Association, and in the 'nineties, when the League and Association consolidated into one 12-club circuit, clubs were given the option of selling liquor. Critics attacked the League for deserting its early principles in allowing it, but old Association clubs like St. Louis and Cincinnati continued to do a thriving business. Waiters were kept busy on Sunday serving St. Louis fans of the 'nineties, who drank early and often to avoid the "rotten ball playing they frequently see." Von der Ahe ran into union trouble by hiring non-union bartenders and waiters at less than union rates. The New York *World* charged that Cincinnati, where beer was sold in the stands, had long had a reputation as a place to watch for flying mugs, and it told of the "cheap sports and toughs" who gathered behind home plate, drinking and insulting the umpire and visiting players.

The Giants had a bar in full view on the right field side of the field, with Dasher Troy, the old ball player, in charge. In 1893 the club directors closed the "unsightly" bar because it was a nuisance, particularly to ladies who had to pass by it. As the *World* said on July 9, 1894, "It was heartrending." The Giants were playing bad ball; it was the hottest part of June, "and not a drink in sight!" When the Giants returned from their western trip, the beer flowed freely once more.

Beer was not the only commodity sold. Youngsters moved through the stands hawking peanuts, sandwiches, pies, soda water, chewing gum, or "most any thing." Spalding, however, sold refreshments from a stand rather than allow peddlers in the aisles. And as far back as 1871, the Washington Olympics anticipated the modern Yankee Stadium by providing a first-class restaurant on the premises so that business people could leave work and go directly to the ball park without stopping elsewhere for lunch. Alert vendors wrote letters asking for sales concessions. One offered the Buffalo Club $225 in 1878 for "the exclusive privilege of selling fruits, nuts, confectionaries, refreshments, cigars, temperance drinks, score cards, etc." as well as the privilege of having five boys, admitted free, to help him.

By 1886 Cincinnati was offered $1000 for the scorecard concession alone. Aaron Stern was so delighted with a check for concession privileges—it was "just like finding $225"—that he wrote his business manager, "I will retire very early tonight and hope to study up some other new privileges perhaps you may think of one."

In the early 'eighties the future "King of scorecard sellers" was just beginning. Harry Stevens was an English immigrant who turned to selling books when a strike took place in an Ohio steel mill where he had been working. He stopped off at a ball game in Columbus and, finding his scorecard inadequate, persuaded the owners that he could make a better one. They told him to go ahead and gave him a five-year concession. Stevens peddled the cards in the stands and even announced the batteries and changes in the lineup. Before long stories were printed about this "remarkable" youth with the "jolly English accent," "original flow of wit," and "hustling methods." The congenial Stevens soon made the rounds of League cities and secured the scorecard privileges in many of them. He then branched out, getting entire control of selling concessions in many parks, and by the 1890's he was already foremost in the field, well on his way to establishing the giant company still a leader in the business today.

The clubs garnered other income from renting the parks for all kinds of sporting events, like archery, lacrosse, pedestrian exhibitions, balloon ascensions, and clay pigeon shoots. Once the Browns advertised a Buffalo Bill Show, complete with Sitting Bull, plus a regular game, all for fifty cents, children half-price. These side shows reached such proportions that in 1894 the League passed a rule against changing the regular time of the ball game by more than a half hour, to prevent magnates from squeezing in other attractions to the detriment of the game. The owners also tried to capitalize on the bicycle craze of the 'nineties, but without financial success. According to Al Reach, thousands of dollars were lost in laying out tracks for bike races in many of the ball parks. In the middle 'nineties the baseball owners also gave serious consideration to setting up a professional football league, to be organized along the same lines as professional baseball, but nothing came of it. Most of the players then were collegians, and, besides, the American Football Association nipped the idea in the bud by adopting rules preventing its players from performing with anybody else before its own season.

When Von der Ahe began to lose his grip in 1890, he tried everything to raise money, converting his park into a honky-tonk with shoot-the-chutes, a merry-go-round, and a wine room, and advertised it as "The Coney Island of the West." He even renovated the park to put in a race track, and rented it for two years for $10,000, including concession rights, to a local promoter named Fred Foster. Von der Ahe was constantly attacked by the *Sporting News,* which called his transaction "The Prostitution of a Ball Park." The St. Louis *Post-Dispatch* also criticized him for allowing the park to become a hangout for the "worst rogues" and gamblers. But the National League dodged the issue.

Another source of income for the clubs was the sale of game information to telegraph companies, which purchased the privilege of relaying reports of the game directly from the ball parks to other outlets, especially saloons and pool rooms, which in turn bought the information from them. Sometimes the clubs received 50 per cent off on the telegrams they sent. In 1886 Western Union offered the Cincinnati Club $100 and free telegraph service. In 1887 it secured sole rights to Cincinnati business. According to the terms of the contract, Cincinnati agreed to do business with Western Union exclusively, at its regular message rates, and refrain from patronizing the lines of any competing company; but the letter constituting the contract did not reveal the price paid in exchange. Before long the owners learned to combine in dealing with the telegraph company, in order to force better terms. In 1897 the League as a whole made a contract which gave each club $300 worth of free telegrams in return for the wire concession.

There were drawbacks to these deals, and they bring to mind the plight of modern baseball men who, worried about attendance, have been debating the wisdom of "giving away" their product by allowing games to be televised. The problem is not new; it has only been magnified. Nineteenth-century owners had the same fear. They complained that fans, instead of paying their way into the parks, were loitering around other places waiting for telegraphed reports of the games.

Another danger was that pool-sellers and gamblers, who moved in with the wire service, might reach the players and persuade them to throw games. Western Union was not supposed to wire game information into pool rooms, but *Sporting Life,* September 15, 1886, charged the monopoly with violating agreements with ball clubs by simply furnishing the information over another wire. It called for action on the part of the owners, who, while recognizing the danger, did little but remonstrate with the telegraph companies for installing private wires into pool rooms. Hulbert had Pinkerton detectives investigate rumors that several key players were "owned" by a large "triangular pool clique" operating out of Cincinnati, Chicago, and New York, but nothing was uncovered. Several years later the much-maligned Tony

Mullane was completely exonerated of similar game-throwing charges after a "full and exhaustive examination" by the American Association.

Certainly pool-selling flourished, especially in Chicago, Cincinnati, and Boston. And in almost any town one had only to turn to his newspaper for quotations on pool prices and the names of places where they were sold. In 1887 Western Union's Cincinnati manager mourned over the small revenue from the ticker service, but six years later, after the "hardest kind of missionary work," the company's "bureau of sporting information" was so active that it was hard work to supply the demand. Baseball owners today try to stop betting in parks just as the old-timers did, but they can do little about it outside, and although it is not as greatly publicized, there is at least as much, if not more, gambling on baseball, as on horse racing.

The fact that baseball was sold over the wire is one of the proofs that it was an interstate business. When Justice Holmes ruled in the famous Federal Baseball Case of 1920 that the baseball business was not engaged in interstate commerce, he either did not know about this aspect of it or chose to disregard it. Even in its earliest days baseball was by no means an enterprise confined to a particular locality within a single state. And of course in modern times, when the game is sold across states lines through radio and television, to say nothing of the use of wire services, travel across state lines for spring training, and the interstate buying and selling of players, professional baseball is obviously engaged in interstate commerce.

One of the biggest problems in operating a club was providing for the team on road trips, and even today the road secretary has probably the most nerve-wracking job on a big league club, although the use of airplanes has eased his task somewhat. As late as the 'nineties there were disputed games caused by teams failing to arrive on time, or by a team simply walking off the field in the late innings to catch trains for their next destination. In such cases the League Board of Directors decided the winner, even though the umpire may already have ruled differently.

Considering the mileage they covered, big league clubs did well to keep their schedules. Not counting spring training and exhibition games, they traveled 45,650 miles in 1882, an average of 5,706 miles each. In 1895 League clubs covered 113,637 miles, but this mileage was for twelve clubs playing a longer schedule, and apparently included spring training as well. A single club, Chicago, spent $4,866.09 for railroad, hotel, and carriage expenses in 1877. The Phillies paid $5,655.37 in 1884. On its first eastern trip in 1887 Cincinnati spent $1,174.50. A further idea of traveling costs is given by a breakdown on the Phillies' expenditures for a long road trip to Brooklyn and then west, May 6 to

29, 1891: railroads and sleeping cars, $767.74; hotels, $656.25; carfare and other local transportation, $84.45; extra meals, $65.00; miscellaneous, including crepe rosettes in mourning for Jim Fogarty, former playing manager, $32.20; a total of $1605.64.

Without the railroads, the idea of an intersectional league with an extended, regular schedule would have been impossible. Railroads had been vital adjuncts to those early tours of the Excelsiors, Washington Nationals, and Cincinnati Reds, which did so much to arouse interest in baseball. Like its relationship with the newspapers, baseball's dealings with railroads were mutually advantageous and became increasingly so as the railroad network was completed and the big leagues lengthened their playing schedules. In 1889 major league clubs played each other 20 games apiece, making 140 games a season, twice as many as in 1876. By 1892 the present 154-game schedule was adopted.

The magnates quickly saw the advantage of having their complete schedules drawn up in advance. It helped managers book exhibition games on off days, and made it easier and cheaper to arrange road trips. The carriers and hotels, knowing in advance what business they could count on, were better able to assure accommodations at lower rates. In 1892 the courts decided that it was not a violation of the Interstate Commerce Act for railroads to grant reduced rates to amusement companies, and the resulting savings were estimated at $120 a club per season.

It is not true, as popularly believed, that big league clubs in those days used so-called Sullivan sleepers—beds improvised by laying the cushions across the seats. Minor leagues traveled this way, and it is likely that poorer big league clubs did, too. But most of them went by Pullman. Cap Anson, for instance, always insisted on the best accommodations for the White Sox, and, as already mentioned, Harry Wright's Red Stockings set a precedent in the sports world by traveling Pullman on their 1869 tour. Itemized expense sheets of clubs often reflected Pullman charges. The Michigan Central Railroad made a point of advertising that one reason it got so much baseball trade was because of its first-class accommodations, including elegance in sleeping cars. In fact, the railroads went out of their way to serve the ball clubs. A report on the great Red Stockings' tour of 1869 said, "The boys have received every attention from the officers of the different roads." The Chicago, Milwaukee & St. Paul promised "Special attention to this class of patrons," and announced "this is the route to travel in order to reach MORE AND BETTER PLAYING POINTS." Southern Railway representatives checked in at the League meeting in 1895, soliciting business from teams going south for spring training. Because of the wreckage of the Civil War and lack of capital, it was many years before the South could offer good, fast service. That was doubtless one reason clubs like the Giants and Brooklyn went to Florida by boat even as late as the 'nineties.

As an inducement, railroads offered special or "professional" rates to ball clubs. They arranged special excursion trains at reduced rates to transport fans from outlying districts to ball games. Clergymen, physicians, and politicians were not the only ones who received free passes for public-relations purposes; baseball officials wangled them, too, and they were not bashful about requesting them or happy when refused:

> The B & O gave me a pass from here [Columbus, Ohio] to Chicago after the Pennsylvania had refused [wrote Schmelz]. Please remember that in making contracts next season. I would not give the Pennsylvania a single mile if I could avoid it. They want all the favors without returning any. I am through with them.

Streetcar lines had a very close connection with professional baseball. Owners of transportation facilities were among the first sports promoters. To increase traffic, streetcar lines established amusement parks and went into the entertainment business. The *Street Railway Journal* of May 1896 estimated that in the previous ten years at least a hundred companies had trolley parks of their own. Traction magnates also recognized that ball games were well patronized, and found it profitable to co-operate with the ball clubs. As one of them said, it was in their interests "to keep in with the baseball people."

The close tie-up between car lines and professional baseball is revealed in several ways. Baseball magnates like Al Johnson, Frank Robison, and Henry V. Lucas were also active in the traction business. Regular "baseball trains" ran from town to grounds in some cities, and, whenever possible, ball parks were located near the trolley car lines. The Providence park was adjacent to three horsecar lines, one of which built a spur right up to the gate, and Baltimore's new Oriole Park of the 'nineties was convenient to four car lines. When Von der Ahe built a new Sportmen's Park, he gave the Lindell Railway Company 200 feet of land next to the stands for a loop.

Car lines sold excursion tickets to the games. Cleveland fans could purchase tickets covering round-trip transportation and admission to the game for sixty cents right on the trolley cars, without the inconvenience of waiting at the box office. Traction companies constructed ball parks, leased playing grounds, and even subsidized clubs. Cincinnati received $1500 from the Consolidated Street Rail Road Company in 1880, and the local trolley line paid for grading the field of the Providence Club.

Hotels, too, advertised for baseball business and contracted to house ball clubs for the entire season at reduced rates. Here another favorite baseball myth should be discounted. Again and again we are told that ball players years ago were all ruffians, unwelcome in respectable circles, who stayed in "fleabag" hotels because the decent ones would not accept them. The fact of the matter is that first-class hotels solicited their business in the 'seventies, 'eighties, and 'nineties, through advertisements and letters to the clubs. And the record shows that the major leaguers in those days stopped at the best hotels of the circuit. Their dollars were as good as any, and if some of the poorer clubs did not go first class, it was by choice, not because they were unacceptable.

Much evidence could be cited, but a few examples should suffice. Big leaguers stayed at Tremont House and Clifton House in Chicago, Monongahela House in Pittsburgh, Galt House in Louisville, The Continental in Philadelphia, Lindell House and Southern Hotel in St. Louis, and the St. James in Cincinnati. The *U.S. (Official) Hotel Directory* shows that all these were ranked as first class. Other hotel guides listed Chicago's Tremont House as "elaborate and well-managed," long prominent as "one of the representative hostelries in the West," and for thirty-five years "one of the leading hotels in Chicago." Clifton House offered ball clubs special rates of two dollars a day in the 1880's and in its ads cited "all the League Clubs for the past three seasons, who have made their home with us."

Richwood House of Boston offered the Philadelphia Club "large, airy rooms" at $1.75 for a single and $1.50 for a double. The proprietor called attention to its elevator, electric bells, bathrooms on every floor, and its central location: "Horse Cars for the Ball Grounds pass the house, and we are ... the most convenient house in the city to the grounds." The Giants spent several spring training periods at the Lakewood Hotel, Lakewood, New Jersey, a fashionable resort hotel which the New York *World* claimed had only three classes of people during the Giants' stay: wealthy New Yorkers, invalids staying for their health, and the ball players. *Sporting News* and other papers of the early 'nineties substantiate the fact that the fortunate players were traveling on Pullman Palace cars and patronizing the first-class hotels.

Usually the hotels furnished carriages to transport the club to and from the railway station and back and forth from the ball park. In those days few clubs had dressing facilities for the visting team. The Athletics and Orioles had a clubhouse under the stand with room for visitors, and as early as the 'seventies the White Sox boasted a first-rate clubhouse of their own, where, on off days, the players were required to stay from 10:30 A.M. until noon and from 2:30 until 5 P.M., amusing themselves by throwing baseballs and playing billiards. The

These advertisements of the 1880's show the impact of professional baseball on hotels and railroads.

Boston Nationals also had "large and comfortable club-rooms" in town at that time.

By 1892 dressing rooms for visiting clubs had to be provided under League rules, although in some cases they were very poor—"would not have made good pig pens," said the Cleveland *Leader*. Dressing facilities gradually obviated the need for players to dress at the hotels, with the attending nuisances of riding on passenger elevators in dirty suits and cutting up carpets with spikes, the latter a chief complaint of the hotels. Dressing rooms also eliminated riding back and forth in uniform, a practice which sometimes inspired fans to bombard the players with fruits and vegetables and other missiles.

On top of these many responsibilities and worries, the magnate always had to remember that he belonged to a league. He had to take time to work with the other club owners for the common good while at the same time looking out for himself. His league responsibilities were as important as his club duties. As Spalding once explained it,

> The magnate must be a strong man among strong men, else other club owners in the league will combine in their own interests against him and his interests, and by collusion force him out of the game.

But this is a story in itself.

18

ADMINISTRATIVE PROBLEMS

MANY OF THE MATTERS which concern the individual club owner can be decided only through the joint effort and agreement of all the owners. Each owner has to co-operate with the others on business policies which affect them all. Not only must each club respect the others' player contracts and territorial rights, it must have an understanding with its partners on other important business matters like prices and division of gate receipts. As already seen, the League from the beginning fixed its admission price at fifty cents. But this charge did not always suit all League members. Some agitated for the right to charge less. The particular soft spot was Philadelphia, back in the League once more in 1883 for the first time since the expulsion of the old Athletics seven years before. The Phillies simply could not compete with the quarter ball of the Association's local Athletics, especially since they had what baseball people call a "humpty-dumpty" ball club—that is, a team of mediocre players—so in June of that year they were granted a special dispensation to charge twenty-five cents. When Hulbert was in office he had "inexorably opposed" making such exceptions because he thought it cheapened baseball, and the private correspondence of Mills shows that he opposed giving Philadelphia relief and tried to prevent it. The Phillies wound up a poor last anyway, but figures published later showed unmistakable improvement in attendance under the reduced tariff:

Home Games	Attendance	Average Attendance
14 @ 50¢	4,557	339
37 @ 25¢	51,233	1,385

After that, the League's price policy toward the Phillies seesawed. The special agreement was ended after 1884, only to be restored in 1886.

Once the precedent had been set, other clubs begged for preferential treatment. St. Louis was granted the same privilege in 1886 to give it a better chance against Von der Ahe's Browns. Kansas City and Washington were denied quarter ball, but the latter was permitted to sell three tickets for a dollar in 1886 and 1887. League price controls were further loosened in 1887 when its fifty-cent rule was abrogated in cities shared with Association clubs—Philadelphia and New York—and Pittsburgh was allowed to join Washington in selling tickets three for a dollar.

In 1888 all special concessions were revoked. The League was no longer represented in St. Louis, and, with the sale of the Metropolitans to Brooklyn, the Association dropped out of New York. But in mid-season Philadelphia began to gasp once more for the life-sustaining twenty-five-cent admission, and again the League gave way after a mail vote. The before-and-after figures were just as graphic as previously:

Home Games	Attendance	Average Attendance
28 @ 50¢	31,488	1,123
30 @ 25¢	120,316	4,010

The Association has always been identified with quarter ball, but it is not generally known that it once experimented with League prices. In 1888 the Association broke its traditional scale, over the protests of Baltimore and Philadelphia. The change was soon regretted. By early July the shoe was on the other foot when the rival Philadelphia Nationals cut admissions to twenty-five cents. To match their competitors the Athletics were given permission to return immediately to their old price. By the end of the month the entire Association reverted to its customary practice, re-establishing quarter ball effective August 25. *Sporting Life* told how Billie Barnie, the "thick-headed magnate from Baltimore," was so anxious that he announced the sale of twenty-five-cent tickets without waiting for the decision to be made officially.

The quarters and half-dollars of the fans had to be divided among the clubs in some equitable manner. The home club and the visitor shared the money in either of two ways, by percentage or by a flat guarantee. Under the first, visiting clubs generally received 30 per cent of the base admission price. The home club kept the rest, plus whatever it made through extra charges for grandstand and reserve seats. The percentage plan tended to favor the financially weak clubs. Even if they did not attract large crowds in their home parks, they could always count on sharing the big gates of clubs which were drawing well. The guarantee system of division was based on the philosophy of home support for each club. Visiting teams received only a fixed amount, regardless of the size of the gate, so that the larger the crowds, the more the home club benefited.

For years the National League stuck to the percentage plan, with visiting clubs receiving fifteen cents out of every fifty-cent admission. But after the season of 1886, Eastern owners, led by Soden of Boston, demanded a change-over to a $100 guarantee for visiting clubs. After a heated debate, the Eastern owners threatened to pull out of the League. Spalding, who had refrained from voting, warned Soden that his faction might secede, but the National League would go on, and Fred Stearns of Detroit told the Easterners it would be good riddance if they left. In the end, they compromised, putting through a guarantee plan giving visiting clubs $125 except on state and national holidays, when receipts were split fifty-fifty.

Detroit was still unsatisfied. Manager Watkins informed a group of reporters and baseball men in Spalding's Chicago store that "we should be nice suckers ... to go to Boston or to Washington and put big money in their treasuries for $125." Spalding replied that the guarantee was put through because other clubs were "tired of carrying along a club like Detroit," which took on expenses in salaries far beyond what its receipts justified.

What Spalding was saying was that poor gate attractions were living off the prosperous clubs. He was getting at something which would become increasingly important as baseball progressed. Organized Baseball's rules governing territorial rights set up a system of competition "with the brakes on," in which financially unsound clubs were able to continue in business with the money they made from playing in the parks of the more successful clubs in the league.

Arguments like Spalding's made little impression upon Detroit. President Stearns claimed that Hulbert himself once said that the percentage plan was the "bulwark of the League" because it protected weak clubs, which were always bound to exist in the League. Stearns then played his trump, making provisional application for admission to the American Association, which he knew was going to have a vacancy. His strategy worked. The League, reluctant to lose Detroit and its recently acquired "Big Four," allowed it to operate under the percentage system. The issue was closed the following year when the League reverted to a modified percentage plan, giving visitors twelve and one-half cents on admissions but guaranteeing them $150.

In the main, the Association kept to its original principle of home support for each club, but like the League, experimented with the other system. And like the League, the Association owners clashed over the matter. Zack Phelps of Louisville thought a percentage was "the only fair method of doing business." Von der Ahe, who was satisfied with a guarantee to visiting clubs when his Browns were winning their first pennant and drawing well at home, changed his point of view when they were less of a novelty in St. Louis but continued to be a big attraction on the road. He used the same tactics as Detroit in the National League—threatening to leave the Association and join the League.

At times the debate became quite personal. Charles Byrne of Brooklyn said Von der Ahe's effusions were "simply a case of abnormal enlargement of the cranium in a mentally small man, supplemented by an acute attack of disappointment." Byrne said he had invested $50,000 in his club and could see no justice in having teams from small towns leave his city "with a good fat pocketbook," while he received only "small change" when his club visited them. All these arguments only went to show that each owner favored whichever plan promised to give him an advantage at the moment.

Again compromise smoothed things over. When Association men came together for their meeting at New York's Fifth Avenue Hotel, Byrne ran into Von der Ahe at Westerman's Saloon a block away, where Chris was busy at one of his favorite pastimes. A reconciliation took place, other owners came along and joined them, and as *Sporting News* reported, soon the gathering turned into a "love feast." At the meeting Von der Ahe accepted Byrne's compromise giving visiting clubs 30 per cent—that is, seven and one-half cents—with a minimum of $130 guaranteed. After the Association's brief experiment with fifty-cent admissions and its return to twenty-five-cent ball, it readjusted its division of gate receipts once more, allotting 20 per cent to visiting clubs but guaranteeing at least $100.

It became easier to keep track of gate receipts when the self-registering turnstile, patented in 1876, came into use. Bright's turnstile, advertised for fifty dollars, could count to 10,000. The League made turnstiles mandatory in its parks, but the Association did not. Despite turnstiles, some magnates still tried to steal from each other. Before an exhibition game between the Chicago White Sox and St. Louis Browns at the Association's Cincinnati park, A. S. Stern, Cincinnati owner, ordered his business manager, Louis Hauck, not to use the turnstiles, and if questioned to say they were out of order. He also instructed Hauck not to say anything about other tickets sold in advance at Hawley's, a downtown store. By concealing the agency's ticket sales and cheating on the count at the gate, he could collect much more than his rightful 20 per cent share.

Some of the profits from gate receipts were put into a sinking fund established by the League in 1886 to cover current expenses and to guarantee against club violations of the Constitution. Every club was to put in $5000, payable in annual $1000 installments. If a club re-signed for business reasons, it could get a refund, but if expelled, it forfeited the money. A year later the Association adopted a similar plan to stabilize and solidify itself.

Another policy on which clubs acted in unison was playing Sunday ball and selling liquor on the grounds. The League held fast in its opposition to these practices, and the Association was equally zealous in allowing them. In the 'eighties Spalding was on record as "irrev-ocably" against Sunday ball for the National League. He thought the "better class," at least in Chicago, was averse to Sunday amusements. But as time passed, he was to liberalize his views considerably.

Pressure for Sunday games was growing. Advocates thought it was better for men, both young and old, to attend a ball game of a Sunday afternoon than to hang around "low saloons and questionable resorts" or go on "tough excursions . . . where fighting forms one of the principal amusements." They suspected that the "straight-laced" League really had no scruples about playing on Sundays and refrained simply because most of its games were played in towns where it was not allowed any-way. The least the League could do, they advised, was to forget its "Sunday piety" and leave the matter of Sunday games to local option. Actually, the League did make some small concessions in the 'eighties, allowing clubs to play exhibitions on Sunday. St. Louis continued to ask permission to schedule regular championship games on Sunday, and quit the League in 1887 when denied the privilege.

The younger major league won a good deal of praise for catering to the masses by playing Sunday ball, which was said to benefit "those people who are obliged to labor during the week days." Local authori-ties, however, often took a more orthodox view, and Association execu-tives and players were sometimes arrested and haled into court. Once, when Von der Ahe had to appear before the Court of Criminal Cor-rection, Congressman John J. O'Neill defended him, arguing that the best classes attended Sunday games. He said they were "a God-send" to the laboring man and, according to the Catholic clergy, the salvation of many a youth. Judge Noonan finally decided it was not unlawful to play Sunday ball in St. Louis.

There were other instances of the Association going ahead with Sunday games and paying fines afterwards as a matter of routine. Sometimes Cincinnati met the problem by shifting its Sunday games across the state line to near-by Covington, Kentucky. And in deference to some of its patrons an Association club might set aside a section of its grandstand for ladies and families, where smoking and drinking were prohibited.

The ins and outs of price fixing and division of gate receipts illustrate how difficult it was for clubs to work together and adhere to business policies even after they were once established. In this respect the National League was fortunate in having able presidents to give its club owners a strong lead during the important formative years. Like the United States' presidency, the office was to a considerable degree what the man made it. Hulbert was a strong executive who ran the League and, as one newspaper said, made it what it was. His decisive actions against recalcitrant clubs and dishonest players show his forceful personality. He steered the League safely through its first grim years.

Following his death and the brief presidency of Soden, another vigorous leader stepped in. A. G. Mills not only was an able president, he also had the advantage over his predecessors of being independent of any club. As a graduate of George Washington Law School, he brought his legal knowledge to bear in drawing up the first National Agreement. He led Organized Baseball to victory in the Union War. Mills believed that baseball was "beneficial alike to participants and spectators." His sole interest in it, he once wrote, was "to foster it, to keep out all contaminating influences, and to maintain it on a plane where it would command the support and respect of all good citizens." His correspondence shows that baseball men from all over sought his counsel and advice. The League suffered a heavy loss when he resigned at the end of the Union War.

It should be pointed out that Mills did not quit the presidency simply because he was disgusted when the League restored the players blacklisted in the war, as repeatedly claimed in numerous baseball books. His private papers reveal that months before the men were reinstated, he wrote to the club presidents in all leagues, telling how "onerous" were the duties of his office, and when he did quit in November 1884, he wrote Spalding and McKnight that he was merely taking the step which he had contemplated for some time. The controlling factor in his decision was the pressure of other business interests, which prevented him from giving his baseball job the requisite care and attention without serious inconvenience, to say nothing of financial loss; and it is worth noting that he was also forced to curtail his activities in amateur athletic circles, in which he was so much interested, for the same reason.

The Association never had the same caliber of leadership as the League, which is unquestionably one of the main reasons why, despite its considerable success, it never reached full potentiality during its ten-year existence. Although Denny McKnight had a college background and previous administrative experience both in private business and in baseball, he was at best only an adequate president, and his connection with the Pittsburgh Club, although nominally severed in 1884, was a handicap. He was followed by an undistinguished group— Wheeler Wikoff, Zack Phelps, Allan W. Thurman, and Louis Kramer, and of the four only Wikoff lasted any length of time.

It took a while for clubs to bring themselves to give up some of their autonomy and hand over real authority to a president and board of directors. The old National Association never learned the lesson and fell apart as a result. The National League and the American Association, of course, did far better. Even though their clubs saw the necessity for increasing the presidential power, there was still a great reluctance to do so.

In the middle 'eighties, National League presidents were given authority to appoint and remove umpires. They could also discipline a player, manager, or umpire who was guilty of being drunk or fighting in public, or who "in any manner brought disgrace upon the profession of base ball playing by his open conduct." These presidential prerogatives have long since been accepted without question in the major leagues. But when they were first conferred, back in the 'eighties, there was skepticism about transferring these club privileges to the president's office. Putting him in command of umpires was one thing, but allowing him to suspend club managers and players was "open to serious objection." Some baseball writers recognized that giving League presidents such "autocratic power" was a significant experiment, but they warned that it would take men of judgment and restraint to exercise the new authority. Their fears were unwarranted. Outside of selecting umpires, these powers were not to be exercised for a long time to come.

When a weak president held office, there was a good deal of backsliding on the part of the club owners. If they could get away with it, owners were quick to assert their own ideas and privileges, often at the expense of the general good. When this happened, the business ran into serious difficulty.

After Mills's resignation the National League elected Nick Young both president and secretary. Although Young lacked the stature and forcefulness of his predecessors, the League managed to function successfully throughout the rest of the 'eighties. Young had the advantage of serving his first years in a time of League financial prosperity. Besides, the massive figure of Spalding was still on hand to keep things running smoothly. When Spalding became more deeply involved in his other enterprises and spent less time on League affairs, trouble began. In fairness to Young, it must be admitted that in the 'nineties, when he was on his own, he had some very difficult problems to contend with, and there is no assurance that even a stronger man could have surmounted them.

The American Association ran into trouble well before the League did. McKnight's successors, Wheeler Wikoff and Zack Phelps, were too weak to hold things together, and in the late 'eighties, internal dissension started the Association's decline and led to its demise. The story of the Association's decay began with the humiliating loss of its two Metropolitan stars, Esterbrook and Keefe, to the National League in the spring of 1885. This blow had hardly been absorbed when the Mets produced more trouble. In December 1885, John B. Day, owner of both the League and Association New York clubs, sold the Mets to Erastus Wiman's Staten Island Amusement Company for $25,000—a deal which touched off a sensational fight.

Wiman, a millionaire promoter, controlled the Staten Island Rapid Transit Railway, a ferry running between Manhattan and Staten Island. Wiman also owned grounds on Staten Island, easily accessible from downtown New York, where he offered such entertainment as the Buffalo Bill Wild West Show, Forepaugh's Circus, summer evening concerts, and fountain displays to stimulate his ferryboat business. He advertised the Mets as a "Famous Baseball Club," one of the leading attractions presented by his Staten Island Amusement Company. His ad announced that the Mets would play a series of championship games with the other American Association clubs, and then reeled off some of the big figures which impressed Americans so much in those days:

> These eight clubs, include ... 128 Famous Professionals whose united Salaries for the Season of 1886 ... total over $150,000 while the aggregate cost of maintaining the clubs for the current year is estimated at fully one-quarter of a million dollars.

Wiman was also involved in another business deal. The Baltimore & Ohio Railroad was planning to make Staten Island its New York terminal, and, before taking possession, was going to pay Wiman a percentage for the use of his ferries and facilities, based on the volume of his business over a certain number of years. So Wiman had additional incentive for crowding as many people on his ferryboats as he could before the railroad moved in.

He ran into a snag immediately, though. The Association was convinced that Day's sale of the club to Wiman was fictitious. The owners regarded it as a National League scheme to get the Mets out of Manhattan, give the Giants "full swing" in New York City, and still leave the Mets a tool for Day and an instrument of espionage for the League. Coming on top of the Esterbrook-Keefe deal, this new development caused Association owners to decide they had had enough of the Mets,

A. Harry Wright, manager of the first professional baseball team, the Cincinnati Red Stockings of 1869. *New York Public Library*

B. Nicholas E. Young, fifth president of the National League. *New York Public Library*

C. Chris Von der Ahe, owner of the St. Louis Browns. *New York Public Library*

D. John Montgomery Ward, leader of the players in the Brotherhood revolt. *New York Public Library*

E. Henry Chadwick, first important sports writer. *New York Public Library*

A. William A. Hulbert, founder of the National League, and its second president. *New York Public Library*

B. Byron Bancroft Johnson, founder and first president of the American League. *New York Public Library*

C. Andrew Freedman, owner of the New York Giants. *New York Public Library*

D. Albert G. Spalding, Chicago Club owner and sporting goods manufacturer. *New York Public Library*

E. Abraham G. Mills, fourth president of the National League. *New York Public Library*

The amateur Brooklyn Excelsiors of 1860. *New York Public Library*

Union prisoners in the Civil War, playing baseball at Salisbury, North Carolina, in 1862. *New York Public Library*

Hurley, Sub.; G. Wright, S. S.; Allison, C.; McVey, R. F.; Leonard, L. F.

Sweasy, 2d B.; Waterman, 3d B.; H. Wright, C. F.; Brainard, P.; Gould 1st B.

RED STOCKING B. B. CLUB OF CINCINNAT

B

C

D

A. A Currier and Ives sketch of "The American National Game of Base Ball: Grand Match for the Championship at the Elysian Fields, Hoboken, N.J., 1865." *New York Public Library*

B. The Cincinnati Red Stockings of 1869, baseball's first professional team. *New York Public Library*

C. The champion Boston Red Stockings of the 1870's, the first team to win four consecutive pennants. *New York Public Library*

D. A view of the old Polo Grounds, New York City. *Culver*

A

B

PLAYER'S CONTRACT,

as adopted by the National League of Professional Base Ball Clubs.

1. Articles of Agreement, Between the Chicago

Ball Club of the City of Chicago,

in the State of Illinois party of the first part,

and A. C. Anson of the City of

Chicago in the State of Illinois,

party of the second part.

2. Witness, That the said A. C. Anson,

party of the second part, for the consideration hereinafter mentioned, covenants

and agrees to play base ball, practice, attend gates, and perform all other duties

pertaining to the exhibition of the game of base ball, at such times and places

as may be required of him by said party of the first part, for the period of

seven months, commencing on the first day of April,

A. D. 1884, and ending on the thirty-first day of October,

A. D. 1884, inclusive.

The Chicago Ball Club with A. C. Anson

A. The champion Chicago White Stockings of the 1880's. *New York Public Library*
B. Excerpts from "Cap" Anson's contract for the 1884 baseball season with the Chicago White Stockings.
C. The new grounds of Erastus Wiman's New York Metropolitans on Staten Island, 1886. *Culver*
D. Jim Mutrie's champion New York Giants of 1889. *New York Public Library*

C

D

The Boston champions of the 1890's.   *New York Public Library*

The champion Baltimore Orioles of the 1890's.   *New York Public Library*

so they gathered together a couple of days before their annual meeting and, without Wiman's knowledge, expelled his club and planned to parcel out his players among themselves. They had made the same arrangement only the year before, when Indianapolis was dropped, although it had broken no rules, after it had invested capital and engaged a team for the coming season. Indianapolis protested, but to no avail. The Mets were not to be handled so easily.

Wiman arrived at Philadelphia for the meeting full of great plans for his Mets and, still in the dark, munificently invited the other club presidents to dinner to tell them about his ideas—only to be handed a paper telling him that his club was expelled! Indignant at this shabby treatment, he immediately secured in the Philadelphia Court of Common Pleas a temporary injunction restraining the Association from ousting his club until the case was heard. He threatened that even if he lost in court he would start a league of his own stronger than the Association, whose sharp tactics, he said bitterly, reflected "very little credit on baseball ethics."

The plaintiff's affidavits claimed that the Association had already sanctioned both Wiman's purchase of the club and its move to Staten Island, and that players had been signed and heavy expenditures incurred. The plaintiff would suffer "irreparable injury" from loss of large sums anticipated from fifty-odd Association games, at which it was "not unusual" to have crowds of five to ten thousand people.

The Association's defense was simple but ingenious. It tried to prove that originally the Association had been formed for one year only, so each succeeding year the old combination had been dissolved and a "separate and distinct" one organized in its place. In the course of those years certain clubs were not admitted simply because the others did not want them. These one-year Associations had no capital and no assets. Their members were merely taxed to cover operational costs. The Mets were expelled because their unauthorized shift to Staten Island would mean financial loss to the other members. On this last point, the Association's own minutes partially contradict it. They show that permission had been given the Metropolitans to play some of their games on Staten Island.

Judge Thayer ruled that the Association, contrary to what it claimed, had all the organic parts of a permanent body, including a written constitution. It was not a "sort of fugitive association." Membership in it was property, and conferred the privilege of playing profitable ball games with the other clubs. These property rights, said the judge, deserved legal protection, and one could not be deprived of them without due notice and trial. The plaintiff had been denied both. Nor did the Association constitution mention anything about expulsion because of a change in the location of a club's playing field. Thayer granted continuation of the injunction until further orders from the court.

The Association's counsel then asked the judge whether he meant the Mets could be expelled if proper charges were preferred against them in another Association meeting. Thayer told him that was not the question before the court, but in any case the Association would have to state the grounds for expulsion and, if they were not according to its constitution, the court would still restrain the Association.

After this setback the Association reconvened to finish its business, with the Metropolitans on hand enjoying equal rights. Brooklyn dragged out the dispute by refusing to relinquish its claim on Metropolitan players awarded to it when Wiman's club was expelled, and the two New York clubs carried on a private feud for months. Brooklyn finally was allowed to keep Ernest Burch, the chief player involved.

But in the end the Association achieved what it had set out to do. Two years later, after Wiman reputedly lost $30,000, he sold out to the Association's Brooklyn Club, which kept the pick of the Met players for itself and handed over the franchise to the Association, leaving the National League's Giants as its only competitor in the metropolitan area.

The Metropolitan litigation inadvertently uncovered other discord in Association ranks. The original stenographic records of the case reveal that Jim Hart and Zack Phelps, owners of the Louisville Club, were playing both ends against the middle. They privately told J. H. Gifford, manager of the Mets, that they deplored the Association's action in expelling his club, claiming it had been done without their knowledge. The manuscript material also contains a letter of doubtful propriety in which McKnight assured John B. Day, the dual owner, that "I never thought that your double connection made any difference but some of our people are always suspicious." These records even reveal that Hart used undercover diplomacy in the hope of gaining advantage over a fellow owner. Dave Orr and James Roseman, two Metropolitan players, had been given the choice of going to either Brooklyn or Louisville in the Association's plan for parceling out Metropolitan players. Hart offered to bribe the Mets' manager if he would use his influence and persuade the two players to pick Louisville.

More grave than the Metropolitan incident was the factionalism involved in the movement to unseat McKnight. The letter he wrote to Day shows that he was aware that some of the owners were working to undermine him, and that he was willing to curry favor with the Metropolitans to get their support:

They are talking of putting Jimmy Williams in my place. I don't know why it is, and cannot get any explanation, except that Byrne is working it. Well, four of our clubs have volunteered me assurances of support, including Gordon [titular president of the Mets before Wiman]. You know ... that it was I that prevented the expulsion of the Mets last spring, so I think I ought to count on their support. I guess I will come out all right.

McKnight guessed wrong. Intrigue to depose him died out for the moment, but he was soon undone by the tangled Barkley case.

Sam Barkley, a dissatisfied infielder with the Browns, made no secret of his desire to be traded. Von der Ahe followed his wishes and let Baltimore and Pittsburgh know that he was available for $1000. Both clubs were interested. After Barkley had made a verbal commitment with Pittsburgh, Billie Barnie convinced him to sign a private agreement to join up with Baltimore as soon as St. Louis released him. Barnie also obtained his signature on an undated Baltimore contract, and sent the $1000 to Von der Ahe by registered mail. But he was too late. Von der Ahe, impatient at not receiving the money when he expected it, agreed to Pittsburgh's offer and released Barkley to that club. At that point Barkley reversed himself and signed a Pittsburgh contract, after wiring Barnie that the deal with Baltimore was off.

This was only the beginning. Barnie appealed, and the Association's Board of Directors "tried" the case. McKnight presided but did not vote, since his connection with Pittsburgh made him an interested party. In its report the Board found Barkley guilty of "duplicity" and "dishonorable conduct," recommending a fine of $100 and suspension for the entire season of 1886. After the penalty was satisfied, he was to be the Pittsburgh club's property, because it had "legally" purchased Barkley's release.

When the report was read before the Association, McKnight rejected it but was overruled five to two, St. Louis abstaining. Many people felt that Barkley was being made the scapegoat, although he was hardly the only responsible party. Some owners placed the blame on McKnight. They believed that he had tempted Barkley to ignore his agreement with Baltimore and go with Pittsburgh, promising him protection against any disciplinary action the Association might try to impose. As a result, the move to oust McKnight was revived.

Meanwhile, Barkley threatened to sue the Association. Recalling its unhappy experience with the Mets and not wanting to make the same mistake twice, the Association made certain to observe the proper procedure this time. Barnie drew up specific charges and sent them to McKnight, requesting him to give Barkley a copy and to ask the player to appear for a hearing at a special meeting of the Association in Cincinnati. McKnight failed to hand Barkley a copy of the charges and to invite him to the hearing. In fact, he did not attend the meeting himself. The Association wired him that it was "surprised and displeased" with his recent actions and that his resignation would be accepted by telegraph. McKnight pleaded illness and claimed that he had previously wired O. P. Caylor that he could not come for that reason. It made no difference.

The owners prepared a bill of particulars against McKnight. They charged him with failure to file bond for faithful service, conduct which created discord, lack of careful attention to details, showing partiality, absenting himself from a meeting he had called without notifying the owners to cancel it, and neglecting to send the books and minutes of the Association to the meeting. Then by a vote of seven to one they removed him from office, and they unanimously elected Wheeler Wikoff of Columbus, former secretary and treasurer, in McKnight's place. McKnight's reaction was published in the Cincinnati *Enquirer:* "Their intention is plain. They will give Barkley a hearing and withdraw his suspension, and they want to crawl out by getting rid of me."

Barkley carried out his threat in Common Pleas Court, Pittsburgh. The Pittsburgh Club was in the peculiar position of nominally being a defendant, yet standing to gain if Barkley won his case, since it would have the benefit of his services. At the first hearing Judge Stowe, on a technicality, refused a preliminary injunction to keep Association clubs from playing Pittsburgh unless Barkley played. He heard the case again a week later but put off a decision for another week so he could study the case further. According to *Sporting Life,* however, the judge gave the impression that Barkley had a good case with "fair prospects of winning."

Finally, the Association settled with Barkley out of court. He was fined $500 but his suspension was lifted. There is evidence, however, that Pittsburgh paid the fine for him. Baltimore was appeased by getting a substitute first baseman, Milton P. Scott, from Pittsburgh. Wikoff blamed everything on McKnight. *Outing Magazine* approved of punishing the player, but added, "A rebuke to such club officials as bribe players to break engagements would not have been out of place."

President Nimick of Pittsburgh, who had protested all along over the treatment given Barkley and his club, seized the opportunity the following November to move his club into the National League. He had a perfect right to do this, because under the National Agreement clubs could change from one league to the other. Nevertheless, the loss of Pittsburgh corroborated the Association's conviction that the League had been tampering with its clubs and was determined to ruin it. The exodus from the Association continued. Two years later, at the end of 1888, Cleveland left to join the League. The following year Cincinnati and Brooklyn also changed allegiance.

The story of how Brooklyn and Cincinnati came to leave exposed the growing disintegration of the Association. The direct cause was a disputed game between Brooklyn and St. Louis in September 1889: As the game dragged on, it began to get dark, and the Browns tried to hold onto a narrow lead by stalling in various ways, thus hoping to delay until the umpire would have to call the game on account of darkness. When Von der Ahe gave the umpire an unsubtle hint by putting lighted candles in front of the players' bench, the fans gleefully hurled beer mugs at this target. When a few of the candles were knocked over by this barrage, they set fire to some paper, which blazed up and came close to burning the grandstand. Finally Comiskey, already fined once for arguing with the umpire, ended the fiasco in the ninth inning by pulling the Browns off the field. The players were mobbed, their clubhouse windows smashed, and the game awarded to Brooklyn. Von der Ahe refused to play the next game of the series, and the umpire gave that one to Brooklyn on a forfeit, too.

The dispute was brought before the Board of Directors, which made a compromise decision. It ruled that the score of the first game was to revert to the eighth inning and the Browns given the victory, because the umpire should have called the game on account of darkness. The second forfeit to Brooklyn was sustained, and the Browns were punished with a $1500 fine as required under Association rules.

As usual the compromise pleased neither side. Brooklyn was reported "boiling over." Von der Ahe was enraged at the fine, and bitter feeling developed among other Association owners. The weak President Wikoff made a convenient scapegoat for the dissatisfied owners. He had been criticized for some time. During the fight over division of gate receipts, Von der Ahe had openly attacked him as a "catspaw for Byrne," so this latest incident rekindled Chris's ire. Cincinnati's president, Aaron Stern, did not think much of Wikoff, either. Once he told a Cincinnati newspaperman that the Association lacked a head, and that he favored paying A. G. Mills $10,000 to assume the leadership of the Association to give it "weight, wisdom and dignity." And now the newspapers joined in. Calling the unfortunate Wikoff a "figurehead" and "utterly incompetent," they said that this latest incident made "painfully apparent" the Association's need for a capable man at the top.

The dissension culminated when the Association gathered to elect a president. Wikoff was ignored, and two factions battled for control of the Association. The election was a test of which side would win.

Brooklyn, Cincinnati, Baltimore, and Kansas City backed L. C. Krauthoff of the Kansas City Club, and the other four supported Zack Phelps of Louisville. The issue was deadlocked on the first day. It was broken the following afternoon when Brooklyn and Cincinnati resigned to join the League, and Phelps was elected by the rump.

The loss of these strong clubs reduced the Association to a state of great insecurity. It had had fair warning though. Its owners had been scolded for washing their dirty linen in public and advised to emulate the League by talking less and thinking more. *Sporting Life* put its finger on the Association's weakness when it warned that its danger lay within itself. This paper diagnosed the Association as "lacking in business sense, in shrewdness, in knowledge, in foresight, in strategy, in unity of purpose, in faith in each other and, finally, in a positive head"—for its chief executive was constantly "intimidated by aggressive owners."

The difficulties which affected the Association—the trouble over gate receipts, the humiliation over having to restore the Metropolitans, the Barkley case leading to the ousting of McKnight, the weak leadership of Wikoff, the defection of its clubs to the League—all had their telling effect. As major league baseball approached one of its greatest crises, the American Association was weakened and torn, just when it most needed to be robust and united.

19

THE GREAT PLAYER REVOLT

THE REVOLT of the players in the Brotherhood War of 1890 was the climax of their long-festering resentment against the policies of the owners. The reserve clause and its abuses, limitations on salaries, arbitrary fines, the blacklist, and the absence of effective means of redress all played their part in provoking the revolt. As far back as 1880, the New York *Mercury* recommended that the players "rise up in their manhood and rebel," and the Cincinnati *Enquirer* predicted that one day they would. For that matter, from the very inception of the National League there were periodic rumors that the players were planning to organize. But the owners and their spokesmen always dismissed such reports as highly unlikely.

They were proved wrong. In 1885 William H. Voltz, then a Philadelphia sports writer, tried to form a protective association with the primary object of establishing a benefit fund for sick and needy players. But little came of this first effort. It lacked a militant program, and besides, Voltz, as an outsider, did not have the confidence of the players. They were suspicious of his motives.

Taking up where Voltz left off, nine members of the New York Giants formed a local chapter of the Brotherhood of Professional Base Ball Players on October 22, 1885. Their objectives were to protect and benefit themselves collectively and individually, to promote a high standard of professional conduct, and to foster and encourage the interests of baseball. Among the signatories were stars like Buck Ewing, Roger Connor, and Tim Keefe. They chose John Montgomery Ward for their president.

Ward, a man overlooked by labor historians, played a highly influential role in baseball's labor relations. He was a rarity among the players of his era: a college graduate. After playing ball at Penn State he turned professional in 1877 and became a first-class pitcher, helping Providence to the pennant in 1879 and leading the League with 44 won and 18 lost. After an arm injury forced him to quit pitching, he became a star shortstop. Later he managed Brooklyn and New York. While playing with the Giants Ward took a law degree at Columbia University and eventually became a successful attorney. Like Joe DiMaggio much later, he surprised his public by voluntarily quitting baseball while he was still a leading player.

His background, unquestioned leadership ability, and popularity made Ward a well-equipped spokesman for the players. Under his energetic direction, Brotherhood chapters were soon set up in various National League cities, and toward the end of the 1886 season the organization publicly announced its existence.

The news caused no great stir. A baseball paper welcomed the Brotherhood as "sorely needed" to offset the "simply shameful" abuses many managers forced upon the players. Even the National League took the announcement in stride, Nick Young going so far as to praise the Brotherhood as an organization of the most reputable players in the game and therefore worthy of respect and consideration. Up until a year before the trouble began, the Brotherhood was tolerated by the League, which only asked that it use its influence for the general good of its members and the game.

Yet there were signs the players were growing more bold, and some of the more articulate among them were beginning to speak out. The New York *Times* carried a statement by one of them at the time the salary limitation rule was passed:

> The time has arrived when the players must take some action in the matter. . . . legislation has been solely in the interests of the clubs. The players have been ignored at every meeting, and restrictions one after another have been placed upon them until now they can stand it no longer. The first piece of injustice was adopting the reserve rule. A club can engage a player, reduce his salary to $1,000 and compel him to play for that sum, although he may have a standing offer of five times that amount elsewhere. . . . Stockholders of clubs will find before long that they have placed the last straw on the camel's back. We make the money, and it is only just that we ought to get a fair share of the profits.

When Fred Dunlap was sold to Pittsburgh, he astonished Detroit President Stearns by having the temerity to ask for half the selling price. In 1889 a couple of player strikes occurred spontaneously, one over the incident of Yank Robinson and the dirty pants which has already been described.

Ward himself published a scathing attack on Organized Baseball in 1887. He bitterly criticized the buying and selling of players and the blacklisting of those who would not sign at club terms. He condemned the one-sided contract as a means of instituting serfdom in baseball, and denounced the reserve clause as an ex post facto law, a product of the owners' distrust of each other. While he did not call for its repeal in so many words, he did say that baseball should return to ordinary business practices and allow supply and demand to regulate salaries, and he predicted that improvement would come only "when the law of the land governs the game."

By 1887 the Brotherhood, with an estimated membership of some ninety players, felt strong enough to seek formal recognition by the League and to negotiate contract reform. Nick Young and the owners were willing to discuss the contract but, like other business leaders of their day, unwilling to accord the Brotherhood official recognition as a union. The League branded the players' group a secret organization, and said it preferred to bring about reform by the "old and usual means"—to which Ward replied, "What ones?"

Nevertheless, the League authorized Young to write Ward that it was willing to meet with him and some of the players to learn their objectives. Conceivably, Spalding influenced this step, because he was an exception among the owners in that he was willing to recognize the Brotherhood and sit down with their representatives to discuss the contract. At any rate, a players' committee of Ward, Ned Hanlon, and Dennis Brouthers * appeared at a League meeting and asked that players have full salary figures written into their contracts, and that none be reserved at a reduced salary.

The players succeeded in obtaining a new type of contract, which incorporated the terms of the reserve specifically, rather than by general reference to the National Agreement, as was the case up to then. But the League stalled over the question of writing in full salary figures, because it would necessitate repealing the Limitation Rule. This, of course, was an admission that many players were being paid more than the rule allowed. The League argued that to repeal the rule, it would have to get the consent of the American Association—which it promised to do at the spring meeting of the Board of Arbitration. Hailing Ward's work during negotiations, the *Sporting News* called him "the St. George of baseball, for he has slain the dragon of oppression."

But after the players had signed their contracts for the season of 1888, the League told them that nothing could be done about the Limitation Rule because the Association refused to surrender it. After the season, the League also ignored the request not to reserve men

* A fourth player, Arthur Irwin, was an alternate.

at lowered salaries, with the excuse that since the Limitation Rule could not be repealed, the rest of the bargain was also nullified.

This setback, while disappointing, made little real difference. The Limitation Rule was largely a dead letter anyway, and few players were actually reserved at reduced salaries. As for the reserve clause itself, the players were by no means dead set against it. During negotiations with the League they could offer no substitute for it. To the contrary, Ward allegedly supported it, and the player representatives conceded not only the League's right of reservation but its authority to reserve players of disbanded or expelled clubs in order to make it "easy" to replace them and "preserve the autonomy of the League."

Certainly Ward was no radical. He once said that the "gravest offense" a player could commit was to break his contract. A year before publishing his strong magazine article, he was reported in *Sporting Life* as saying that he believed the reserve would not be attacked, and that the majority of players felt it was necessary, although it had been abused. Then in his book, published the year after his article, he went so far as to accept the reserve as an evil necessary to stabilize the game and protect the capital of investors. Furthermore, during negotiations the players were willing to accept a system of graduated fines for "dissipation," ranging from twenty-five to one hundred dollars, and they even agreed to blacklisting after a player's fourth offense. So it is conceivable that had the owners been more willing to conciliate, or at least to let matters continue in the same manner for a while, the eruption of 1890 would have been avoided.

Instead, they crowded the players still more and brought to an end the rather joyless honeymoon with the Brotherhood. In the off-season of 1888, when the men were scattered in their homes or, like Ward and Hanlon, off on Spalding's world baseball tour, the owners put through the Brush Classification Plan described earlier, under which players were to be grouped according to skill and paid on that basis.

When Ward heard about classification, his first impulse was to leave the exhibition tour and return home at once. However, he completed the trip, possibly persuaded by Spalding. As soon as he returned, Brotherhood men held secret conferences, and predictions of a player strike were freely circulated. The players did consider striking, but decided against it, because many of them already had signed their contracts for the next season and were afraid that if they broke them they would lose public support. Instead, at a Brotherhood meeting on May 19 they appointed a grievance committee for the purpose of trying to negotiate with the League once more.

In June the committee petitioned President Young to repeal classification and to end the practice of selling players. The League assigned a three-man committee headed by Spalding to talk matters over, but on June 25 Spalding and Ward met alone. Spalding dismissed the issue as not important enough for immediate action, and maintained with some plausibility that it could wait until the regular League meeting in the fall. Ward disagreed, and cautioned that, while the Brotherhood was not threatening anything yet, the League would be unwise to put the players off. When Tim Keefe, secretary of the Brotherhood, heard of this setback he warned that the players' organization would take action, adding ominously, "The League will not classify as many as they think."

Strike talk revived, only to bring scoffs from the owners. Day of the Giants called it "nonsense," and Spalding discounted it as "a Little Blue-Beard story." Soden of Boston said the idea was "absurd," adding, however, a threat to use strikebreakers, because his club had made a business contract with the public to furnish them baseball and he was not going to "close up shop"! The owners did not know it, but the players were already planning something far more drastic than some isolated strikes. Two facts point this way. First, a general strike for the Fourth of July was actually considered, but voted down. Second, Ward succeeded in holding back Jack Rowe and Deacon White, who were threatening to test the reserve rule in the courts.

These two stars were sober, steady men who had saved their money and were prepared to invest in the Buffalo Club, an International League club at that time. The trouble was that they had been sold to Pittsburgh a short time before they bought into the Buffalo Club. Fred Stearns, Pittsburgh president, insisted on his property rights, and said the players would play in Pittsburgh or "get off the earth." The players avowed that they owned the Buffalo Club and they were going to play for it; White made the pungent remark, "No man can sell my carcass, unless I get at least half." But, after a letter from Ward, the players gave in and reported to Pittsburgh in mid-season. The contents of the letter have never been revealed, but in all likelihood Ward advised the men to lie low for the same reason that the strike was probably called off. Ward and the Brotherhood leaders did not want to disturb matters while they were preparing something far bigger—a league of their own.

When they received the final provocation of the Classification Plan, and saw that Spalding and the League were stalling negotiations, the players decided that matters had gone far enough. For some time they had been aware that a number of wealthy men were prepared to back them in forming a new organization. Foremost among those anxious to enter baseball was Albert L. Johnson, brother of Cleveland's renowned reform mayor, Tom L. Johnson. Al, like Tom, was very much involved in urban transportation. The two of them were operating a couple of streetcar lines in the Cleveland area. Streetcar companies were always interested in having ball parks or other amusement parks along their routes. In Johnson's case a ball park would give him two businesses, each enhancing the profits of the other. As he admitted later, he had "visions of millions of dollars of profit." He had "seen street cars on the opposition street road loaded down with people going to games and it occurred to me here was a chance for a good investment as I could get grounds on a street car line owned by my brother and myself." Like his brother, Al Johnson also had a strong streak of idealism. When he learned about the reserve clause and the so-called laws of baseball, he is said to have exclaimed, "If the League can hold a man on a contract for any or all time that it may desire, when it simply guarantees to him ten days' pay (for that is everything in the world it does for the players), why, then the laws of our land are worse than those of any other nation on earth, and instead of progressing, as we suppose that every civilized country is struggling to do, the sooner we turn back the better."

A genuine baseball enthusiast, Johnson knew many ball players and often met with them socially. It was natural that Ned Hanlon should sound out Johnson during the summer of 1889 on the Pittsburgh Club's second trip to Cleveland. The Brotherhood representative met with the Cleveland businessman at his hotel and told him how the League had "broken faith" with the players. Hanlon presented Ward's idea for getting backers for a new league in which they and the players would share the profits. The plan could be put through, said Hanlon, if Johnson would help.

Johnson was interested immediately, and asked to discuss the matter further with some of the other players. After this was done, he agreed to do everything in his power to put the scheme across. That summer, meetings were held with the players of other League clubs when they came to Cleveland to play. Johnson posted a man in the corridor of the Hollenden to keep anyone else from breaking in on the discussions, and he took the added precaution of paying off the policeman on the corner so that he would not report the comings and goings of all the ball players. In these meetings, players of the various clubs were apprised of plans and given a chance to express their views about them.

Next a contract was prepared and players were signed. To gauge their possible attendance, the Brotherhood got Cub Stricker, Cleveland second baseman, to watch the turnstiles at his park. Johnson followed up his Cleveland meetings with a trip to several League cities, including Boston, New York, and Philadelphia, to sign up more players and to make final arrangements with people who were willing to invest in the new venture. Thus by the end of the summer most of the organizational groundwork was finished.

That the owners remained in the dark while all this was going on was a tribute to the skill of the Brotherhood leaders in controlling the men. The first intimation that something more than a strike was afoot did not come until early September when A. G. Ovens, correspondent for *Sporting Life,* managed to get one of the players to talk, and learned enough to break a story about a "widespread plot." After the story broke, Johnson's brother Will verified it. Although he had been sworn to secrecy along with the others, Will felt justified in speaking now that the news had leaked.

The surprise of the League men was exaggerated somewhat by *Sporting News,* whose editor, Al Spink, was sympathetic toward the players' organization. He chortled in the columns of his paper that the magnates were "wild" and that Spalding was "in conniption fits." But the League owners made calm public statements. Nick Young said that the season had been full of scares and that the League would proceed as usual. Although Spalding was not prepared for such a "ponderous plot," he was not so disconcerted as to miss a chance for a propaganda blow at the players. He branded the Brotherhood "an oath-bound, secret organization of strikers," and questioned whether the public would have confidence in such an outfit. In a "confidential" letter to Mills, he said that, as far as he knew, the players had absolutely no grievance against the League, and he was rather amused at their great efforts to find some cause for complaint. Nevertheless, he agreed with Mills that there was room for improvement in the way baseball was run, although the game was safer in the hands of the League than it would be in those of the players collaborating with a lot of "sore heads and speculators." In later years, when he looked back on these events, Spalding placed chief blame on businessmen who, with the help of star players, wanted to break into baseball and exploit it for their own gain.

In his next move the able Chicago owner tried to force the issue with Ward. He wrote the Brotherhood leader asking when the players' grievance committee could resume talks with National League representatives. But Ward was also skilled at playing cat-and-mouse. He replied that since the League had failed to answer the players' proposals satisfactorily early in the season, the committee had been dismissed, and the issue would now have to be placed before the entire Brotherhood. Now the League knew it was definitely in trouble, and the teams began quietly signing some young players. As the Cincinnati *Enquirer* predicted, there were "piping times ahead" for baseball.

Early in October, Ward abandoned all secrecy and told his boss,

John B. Day, of the Brotherhood's intentions. That month Brotherhood players failed to follow baseball custom as they refused to sign contracts for the coming year. Spalding, who was highly indignant, threatened his reserved players with injunctions to prevent them from jumping to other teams. On November 4, 1889, thirty or forty players convened in New York City. Ward opened the meeting by reciting the failure of the previous summer's negotiations. The players received a good laugh from a telegram from Mr. Bright, the turnstile manufacturer, who was already bidding to supply Brotherhood parks. The following day the Brotherhood and their backers, in joint session, formed a Players' National League of Base Ball Clubs and spelled out the business relationship between them.

The venture was unique in the American business world. Farmers' and workers' co-operatives were an old story in America, but the Players' League went them one better. It was a democratic alliance of workers and capitalists in which both were to participate in the government and share in the profits of the enterprise. It was a startling contradiction of traditional communist dogma that capitalists always formed a united front against workers. Here was a group of capitalists, associated with employees, preparing to wage a bitter fight against other capitalists!

The Players' League planned to invade seven National League cities —Boston, New York, Brooklyn, and Philadelphia in the East, and Pittsburgh, Cleveland, and Chicago in the West. Jack Rowe and Deacon White, with additional local backing, brought in the Buffalo Club to complete an eight-club circuit.* Each club was controlled by its own local eight-man board, four elected by the players and four by the "contributors," as the backers were sometimes called. They chose officers and looked after the financial affairs of each club.

For the first time since the break-up of the old National Association in 1875, players were going to share in the administrative end of the game. The Players' League was to be governed by a "senate" of sixteen men, two from each club—one chosen by the players, the other by their backers. The senate was to select a president and vice president from its own ranks and bring in an "outsider" for secretary-treasurer at $4000 a year. It was to be tribunal in all matters of league welfare and was to have final decision on all appeals from local boards and players.

The economic blueprint of the Players' League at first called for all profits and losses to be pooled and shared by all clubs in common, but this idea, attributed to Ward, was soon rejected in favor of putting each club on its own financial feet. Gross receipts from each game were

---

* Washington and Indianapolis were originally included, but their franchises were transferred to Buffalo and Brooklyn.

to be shared fifty-fifty between home and visiting clubs, but the home club could keep profits from concessions.

Each club was to deposit its share of gate receipts in its own fund, out of which all obligations were to be met in a specified order of priority. First, all running expenses were to be paid. After that came players' salaries, because at first the backers refused to assume personal liability for them. They soon changed, agreeing to guarantee salaries and establishing a fund of $40,000 as insurance. Next, each club was to contribute $2500 to the league as its portion of a $20,000 prize fund, to be allotted on a descending scale to each club, depending on where it finished in the pennant race. First prize was $7000.

These commitments discharged, the backers and players could dip into additional profits, if any—the first $10,000 to the former, depending on the amount of stock held, and the second $10,000 to all league players, share and share alike. Any additional money was to be split equally between the clubs and the players. This meant that profits had to climb above $20,000 before one club began supporting another.

Both the reserve and classification rules were discarded, but players signed three-year contracts at the same salaries they received in 1889. In cases where classification had caused pay reductions, players were to receive their 1888 salaries. No player could be released until the end of the season, and then only by majority vote of his club's board of directors. Players could also purchase stock in their clubs, and many did so. The hated blacklist was abandoned, but those guilty of drunkenness or corrupt practices were liable to severe penalties.* This was a more liberal deal for the players. But although the reserve clause and classification rule were discarded, their restrictive effect remained— an admission that an arrangement akin to the reserve was necessary to stabilize the business. Players were still tied to their clubs, although for a limited time, and salaries were frozen at old classification levels.

A committee drew up a constitution for adoption at the next meeting on December 16. At that time Col. Edwin A. McAlpin, New York real-estate operator, was elected president of the Players' League; John Addison, Chicago contractor, vice president; and Frank H. Brunell, former sports writer, secretary-treasurer. The financial backers of the Players' League had an opportunity to get into a new business without having to start from scratch. Unlike Henry V. Lucas and his associates in the Union Association, the Brotherhood backers were acquiring the player assets of their competitors with relatively little initial outlay.

Securing sites and building ball parks was comparatively simple for the Players' League. There were plenty of open spaces available in

---

* Players also took a prescribed oath to promote the objectives of the Brotherhood and to assist each other in distress.

those days, and a fence and wooden stands could be put up inexpensively and almost overnight—quite a different situation from the problem that would confront anybody trying to establish a new league in these days of high real-estate prices and enormous construction costs for elaborate stadia.

National League spokesmen were quick to point out weaknesses in the Players' League set-up. They mentioned that players were binding themselves to go wherever assigned, relying on the uncertainties of gate receipts for their salaries. They even sneered at the $40,000 salary guarantee of the Players' League investors, A. G. Mills calling it a "fake substitute" for the "no-gate-receipts-no-salary clause." John T. Brush vouchsafed that he would be glad to sign players under such conditions.

At their first meeting the Brotherhood published a "manifesto" aimed at winning public support. In forceful phrases the Brotherhood declared its position, reviewed player relations with the National League, and recited the failure of arbitration efforts:

> There was a time when the League stood for integrity and fair dealing; today it stands for dollars and cents. . . . Players have been bought, sold or exchanged, as though they were sheep, instead of American citizens. Reservation . . . became another name for property-rights in the player. By a combination among themselves, stronger than the strongest trusts, they [the owners] were able to enforce the most arbitrary measures, and the player had either to submit or get out of the profession.

The formation of the Players' League was said to have brought "consternation and commotion" among National League owners, who could see their expensive "stock in trade, their teams," about to disappear. Knowing they must prepare themselves for an all-out fight against the "outlaw" league, they appointed a three-man war committee, John I. Rogers, Philadelphia owner, who was also an attorney; John B. Day of the New York Giants; and Al Spalding, the most influential figure in the League.

Spalding had to be on the committee. His name was synonymous with the National Game, since his career had spanned its growth from early professional days. As one of the founders of the National League, he had a hand in bringing an end to the old National Association. An excellent organizer, skilled diplomat, and first-rate promoter, he was known at home and abroad through his baseball interests and his sporting goods enterprises. As his wordly success grew, he took on the appearance, air, and even the girth of the successful businessman of his era. His penchant for pious remarks won for him such nicknames as "the Messiah." Yet, he always had an eye for the main chance and unfailingly acted to further his business interests, which he placed above "sentiment." Withal, his massive contribution to baseball in the formative years of the business cannot be denied. He was a formidable antagonist for John Ward and the Players' League.

Spalding's hand was at once apparent in the work of the War Committee. It immediately circulated an "Address to the Public" to counteract the Brotherhood Manifesto. The wordy document recalled the "untarnished record" of the National League and emphasized its role in eliminating corruption. It defended the reserve clause as the savior of the game in the League's early desperate struggle for solvency. By checking competition, the reserve had been instrumental in raising the incomes of clubs and players alike; however, the League denied making large profits. It was nonsense to speak of "bondage" and "slavery," because League players had never been sold without either their consent or their financial gain. The League rebuked the players for refusing to confer at the end of the season, and denounced the conduct of the Brotherhood as "false," "mendacious," and "evasive." Then, with a typical Spalding touch, the statement charged that the Brotherhood had "no moral foundation and must perish," and promised that the National League would "fight for supremacy."

The Brotherhood answered the League Address with a statement which went over the same ground as its Manifesto. The propaganda battle was going full tilt. The press joined the argument and kept at it throughout the strife-torn year of 1890. There was much newspaper criticism of the players. One paper predicted their defeat almost before the Players' League was under way, and ridiculed the appearance of the players at their first meeting. It reported them dressed in fur-lined overcoats, silk hats, and patent-leather shoes, carrying gold-headed canes, wearing five-thousand-dollar brilliants in their neck scarves, smoking Rosa Perfectos or Henry Clays at twenty-five cents apiece, but wearing no gloves because it was too much trouble to pull them on over the "flashlights" that encircled their crooked, broken fingers. The parting jibe was,

> Don't mistake them for the poor, miserable, overworked, under-paid, haggard, starving slaves of the League tyrants. Nor is it a meeting of the Vanderbilts, Goulds, etc.; it is but a gathering of the Brotherhood men.

An especially severe critic of the players was Henry Chadwick, the veteran sports writer. As editor of *Spalding's Guide,* a semi-official League organ, he accused the players of issuing a "revolutionary pronunciamento," and charged them with secrecy, ingratitude, and a desire for "self-aggrandisement." Chadwick asserted that two-thirds of the players would never have revolted had they not been forced into line by the "terrorism" characteristic of all revolutionary movements. We can be charitable toward Chadwick for making extravagant statements; he wrote them in the heat of conflict. It is more difficult to countenance the opinion expressed thirty years later by a sports writer who eventually became secretary of the New York Giants—that the Brotherhood was a "bolshevik movement which merely preceded the Russian Revolution"!

Naturally, Ward was singled out for a full measure of personal criticism. He was the "master-mind" behind the baseball "secessionists." The Cincinnati *Enquirer* changed his name to John Much-Advertised Ward and accused him of wanting a new league so he could take off on "oratorical flights." The players as a group were denounced for repaying a generous League by "snatching away" the business of their employers and giving it to others. "Now that you are on your own," they were warned, "your little sprees, escapades, until early hours in the mornings, and drunkenness on the ball field won't be excused as readily as it once was."

The St. Louis *Sporting News*, destined to become the "Bible of baseball," championed the cause of the players. It boldly proclaimed that it preferred their friendship to the paid advertising of Spalding. It took particular delight in needling the Chicago owner. Recalling that he had himself been a contract-jumper, it made fun of his "pomp and bluster," and charged that he had "skinned" the fans on his score card and cushion "racket." As for A. G. Mills, his initials stood for "Awful Gall." At the root of the trouble, said *Sporting News,* was the "mean, niggardly, close-fisted acts" of the League owners, who had treated the players in a "high-handed manner" and now "squealed to the public."

The popular weekly *Sporting Life* also joined the players' side, much to A. G. Mills's distress. Mills was "amazed" at the "tirades" of its editor, F. C. Richter, against the reserve clause, which he had once favored. Mills said that, although he disapproved of much that the League had done, the "indefensible" attack of Ward and others forced him to speak out. He entertained Richter at dinner a number of times, once remarking that "after [dinner], arming ourselves with cigars, I proposed to wipe up the floor with you on the base-ball question!" Always mindful of public relations, Mills suggested that the League owners could do themselves some good if they would follow his example and put on a "feed" for newspapermen.

Organized labor also supported the players. To Major Samuel L. Leffingwell, a trade unionist, the issue was whether capital would rule despotically over baseball as it would like to do in other industries, and he urged the players to join either the A.F. of L. or the Knights of Labor, where they would have a million skilled men behind them. But the players did not respond to the invitation.

As in all of Organized Baseball's trade wars, much of the struggle revolved around the effort of each side to gain control of as many players as possible. Right after the Brotherhood's first convention, Ward hastened to the Middle West to convince players to stay behind the Brotherhood. He must have done a good job, for a newspaper survey of fifty players showed that with the exception of "Judas" Glasscock, a "spy" and "informer," the men were standing by the Brotherhood "like rocks." Before the end of December, seventy-one League players, sixteen Association men, and four minor leaguers were reported to have signed with the Players' League. A couple of months later Secretary Brunell was claiming 188 men, whereas the National League, according to him, had only "about 20 deserters and a bunch of unknowns." The Pittsburgh Nationals, for example, were supposed to have signed "a crowd of stiffs," with only "four ball players in the lot."

Some players changed sides as often as three times, but the Players' League gained control of most of them. According to one estimate, the League succeeded in holding only thirty-eight of its players. Many of its best men deserted, among them Charles Comiskey and Connie Mack. John K. Tener, who later became governor of Pennsylvania, joined the new league. The outstanding exception was Cap Anson, whose ownership of stock in the White Sox may have influenced his decision. The League filled the gaps in its ranks by purchasing released players and taking on the best minor leaguers. It picked up a few more replacements from among the more than 300 ragtag and bobtail from various parts of the country who applied for jobs.

But the League never quit trying to win back its regulars. Hurried reforms and fat financial inducements were held out. To match the Brotherhood, the League offered three-year contracts, repealed classification, and modified the system of selling players to give them more voice in the assignment of their contracts. Players were also allowed to appeal fines and penalties to League directors. Clubs even agreed to pay expenses home for players released while on the road. And in spite of Nick Young's earlier statement that the League would not "place a premium on desertion and unfaithfulness" by "buying off" stars, owners were soon busy offering them bribes. On Spalding's own admission his colleagues assigned him the dirty work of tempting King Kelly with $10,000 to desert the Brotherhood. Doubtless in a dilemma, Kelly left the secret rendezvous, took a walk to think it over, and returned with a refusal.

During the war season Mills instigated a similar attempt to break the solidarity of the players and undermine their League. This time Buck Ewing was the target. Mills drafted a statement for Ewing to sign and sent it to J. Walter Spalding, Al's brother, cautioning him to keep the matter secret. In the document Ewing would declare that he intended to return to the Giants next season because the Players' League could not win, and that he did not like to see money poured into a losing cause. He would also say that he did not think continuing the war was in the best interests of baseball. Mills thoughtfully left space on the paper for the signatures of any others who could be persuaded to desert.

Ewing was the player chosen not only because he was a star but because he had expressed sympathy for his employer, John B. Day, on the eve of the players' revolt. Later on, there were stories about a carriage ride under cover of darkness, a clandestine meeting in the back room of a dimly lighted Westchester cigar store, and a proposal for another secret meeting at an obscure railroad stop—all arranged by Cap Anson. The scheme fell through because Ewing reneged when other players refused to join him. Ewing denied everything when confronted, claiming that he was merely spying for the Brotherhood and had told Al Johnson everything that was going on. However, the players were unconvinced and for some time they refused to have anything to do with him.

The struggle for players between the rival leagues hit the American Association hard. In a shrewd bid for Association neutrality, Ward promised at the outset that its players would remain untouched. In fact, he went to a special Association meeting December 4 to explore the possibility of amalgamating the Players' League and the Association. The rumor was that the two circuits would combine their teams in certain cities to form a single ten-club league. Von der Ahe did a little flirting with the Players' League on his own. At first his attitude toward the war was that capitalists should "stick together" against labor; but inside of a month he was quoted as favoring the Brotherhood and hoping for their success. Al Spink claimed afterward that he had convinced Von der Ahe to support the Players' League and that some dickering had taken place. However, Ward, in sizing up the Browns' owner, said they could "use his financial backing" but he "would injure our cause" because "he talks too much."

For a while the National League was very much worried that an "unnatural alliance" between the Association and the Players' League might materialize. Mills was convinced that the Association was negotiating with the "players' gang," and he strongly urged that "someone should do something to keep the American Association in line." But, fortunately for the National League, nothing came of all this. The result was that the Association was soundly buffeted by the other two parties to the baseball triangle. The Players' League raided it, and the war strategy of the National League weakened it. To strengthen its own circuit, the League dumped its Washington and Indianapolis clubs, replacing them with Cincinnati and Brooklyn of the Association. In the course of these shifts the Players' League was able to pick up many of the men involved. All told, the insurgents captured about thirty Association players. Mills complained that such "looting" was completely unjustified, even if the National League was wrong—and he thought it was right—in taking Cincinnati and Brooklyn.

Although the League opened the season of 1890 seriously weakened by the loss of so many players, it nevertheless boldly revamped its schedule so that its games would conflict with those of the Players' League in the cities where both leagues were represented. It also increased the visiting teams' share of the gate receipts from the usual 25 to 40 per cent in order to give a lift to its weaker clubs. Both sides strove to make their opening day games as attractive as possible, and the profusion of banners and flags made each opener look like a circus. Each side went to any lengths to hurt the other. As usual, truth was the first casualty, as Spalding later admitted:

> If either party . . . ever furnished to the press one solitary truthful statement as to the progress of war from his standpoint; if anyone at any time . . . made true representation of conditions in his own ranks, a monument should be erected to his memory.

The Players' League bid for the use of National League grounds, forcing the incumbent either to pay more rent, obligate itself to a longer lease, or both. On its part, the National League attempted to undermine the Players' League by trying to buy into its clubs.

The struggle spilled over into the courts. National League owners tried to get injunctions to prevent their employees from jumping to the Players' League. This move again placed the baseball contract, and therefore the long-debated reserve clause, in the spotlight of legal contention. League officials entered litigation with the assurance of their noted corporation lawyers—Evarts, Choate & Beman—that they would be victorious. Choate was the famous attorney who once disdained taking a labor case, saying that if a big strong Irish woman wanted to sweat in a bakery more than ten hours a day, that was a private affair between her and her employer. Mills had an equally confident legal opinion of the League's chances. But as it turned out, the courts were overwhelmingly on the side of the players.

The first test came in January 1890, when the New York Club was denied an injunction against Ward on the grounds that his 1889 contract did not fix the terms and conditions of his next contract contemplated by the reserve clause. Justice O'Brien ruled that when the terms of a contract are indefinite or uncertain, specific performance cannot be ordered. He decided that Ward's contract was wanting in fairness and mutuality because it bound the player not only for the current playing season but year after year, so that he always had to commit himself a year in advance under the same terms, as long as he played ball, whereas the club could terminate the contract on ten days' notice. O'Brien concluded: "We have the spectacle presented of a contract which binds one party for a series of years and the other party for ten days, and of the party who is itself bound for ten days coming into a court of equity to enforce its claims against the party bound for years."

While action against Ward was still pending, the Giants tried for an injunction against Buck Ewing and failed again. Judge Wallace ruled that the baseball contract was merely "a contract to make a contract if the parties agree," but as a basis for damages or enforcement of specific performance it was "wholly nugatory." Wallace differed with Judge O'Brien, however, in deciding that the terms of the reserve were definite; it was the lack of mutuality in the contract which led him to deny the injunction.

Again in March the League suffered another legal defeat, this time in Pennsylvania, when the Philadelphia Club tried to keep George Hallman from joining the Players' League. Judge Thayer decided against the plaintiff on essentially the same grounds as in the Ward and Ewing cases. It seemed to him that for $1400 a year Hallman had sold himself to the club for life; yet he had no claim on it for more than ten days. As Thayer saw it, Hallman was "absolutely at their mercy, and may be sent adrift at the beginning or in the middle of a season, at home or two thousand miles from it, sick or well, at the mere arbitrary discretion of the plaintiffs, provided only they give him ten days' notice."

In cases like these, where ball players have jumped their contracts to play for other teams, clubs seeking relief have often pleaded the English doctrine laid down in the case called *Lumley* v. *Wagner*, which involved not baseball players but instead a singer who was the daughter of the famous composer Richard Wagner. According to the precedent established in the classic case, the law cannot compel specific performance under a personal service contract, but it can keep the party guilty of a breach of contract from performing for another—if his services are of a special, unique, and extraordinary character. In the Ward, Ewing, and Hallman cases, the courts decided that the absence of mutuality in the baseball contract prevented them from restraining the players. But in another Brotherhood case, the doctrine of *Lumley* v. *Wagner* was upheld, and the owners were successful in securing an injunction. This case concerned John Pickett of the Association's Kansas City Club.

The club had bought Pickett from St. Paul in May 1889 for $3300. Pickett received $800 of the purchase price and $340 a month, even though he was out half the season because of sickness. He signed to play with Kansas City again in 1890, this time for $2200, but several months later notified the club that he intended to break the agreement, giving as his excuse Kansas City's transfer from the American Association to the Western Association, a minor league. He also argued that the club had released other players with whom he wanted to play and, mindful of the uncertainties of minor league ball in those days, said he was afraid his salary might not be forthcoming. What he was really after was a chance to play with the Players' League.

The court brushed aside Pickett's explanation with the observation that "his ingratitude was shown to be equal to his bad faith." Applying the *Lumley* v. *Wagner* principle, Judge Arnold decided that, while Pickett could not be forced to play for Kansas City, he could be enjoined from playing elsewhere. However, Pickett played second base for the Philadelphia Players' League Club, where the court had no jurisdiction.

Hoping to forestall future legal objections to the contract, the League experimented with a reworded agreement giving clubs the "option" of renewing player contracts for an agreed-upon number of years. But in practice the effect was the same as the reserve clause, since players were required to sign contracts with identical renewal features.

Court victories did not mean that the Players' League won the war. In the long run, the gate receipts would decide. Here competition was ruinous for both sides, and Nick Young frankly predicted that "someone had to go to the wall." Each league falsified attendance figures for propaganda purposes. Again the ingenious Spalding demonstrated his astuteness. He secretly stationed his own agents at Players' League gates to keep count, and then discredited his opponents by publishing their inflated figures alongside those of his checkers!

In view of the phony attendance figures compiled on both sides, it is highly unlikely that the published totals of 980,887 for the Players' League as against 813,678 for the National League are worth much.

Probably the combined attendance of both warring leagues was less than that enjoyed by the National League alone the year before. Interest in the game declined as the public became more and more disgusted with the chaotic state of baseball affairs. Fans grew increasingly tired of reading and hearing about the political and business problems of the game, and longed for a return to stability so that they could concentrate on the pennant race. And of course with another league in the field, the money that was taken in had to be divided three ways instead of two, leaving that much less for each.

The Players' League had the advantage of being something new to baseball, and it boasted most of the established players. But even though it doubtless outdrew the National League, by July it ran into trouble. Not one game out of six was drawing enough to cover the cost of playing it, and it was necessary to assess all member clubs an extra $2500 apiece. According to Secretary Brunell's estimate, the Players' League finished the season with a total deficit of $340,000, of which $215,000 was invested in plants, leaving an operational loss of $125,000.

The National League was in a bad way, too. Figures given out on losses varied all the way from $231,000 to $500,000. Pittsburgh was a particularly heavy drag on the League. It lost the staggering total of 114 games, winning only 23, for a miserable percentage of .168. New York was hardest hit. After finishing first in 1889, the club was stripped of its stars by the Players' League. Knowing the importance of having a strong entry in the metropolis, the National League engineered a deal transferring some players from its abandoned Indianapolis Club, among them stars such as Amos Rusie, Jack Glasscock, and Jesse Burkett. But even with these reinforcements the club was in such poor condition that John B. Day sent out a secret call for help to the other magnates in July, telling them that he must have $80,000 at once or he would be forced to sell out to the Players' League. Spalding and the other "dazed" owners realized that New York must be saved "at all hazards" or the war would be lost, so they bailed out Day. The Spalding brothers took $25,000 worth of stock, some of which they parceled out to others, including Anson; Soden of Boston put up the same amount; John T. Brush canceled $25,000 in notes which he held against the sale of his Indianapolis stars; and F. A. Abel of Brooklyn, a professional gambler, and Al Reach of Philadelphia contributed $6,250 apiece. Day insisted on retaining $20,000 worth of stock for his "sacrifice."

Worse yet, Cincinnati gave up the battle in October when Aaron Stern cut his losses and sold the club for $40,000 to a syndicate of Players' League owners. Stern indignantly replied to being branded

"League traitor" by saying there was nothing wrong in selling out for a good price. It was a choice between sacrificing baseball or giving up his more profitable clothing business.

As the 1890 season ended, all three majors were deeply drained by the losses they had suffered. As Spalding reported, "Not in the twenty years' history of professional club organizations was there recorded such an exceptional season of financial disaster and general demoralization as characterized the professional season of 1890." The somber prospects of baseball were cleverly described in a parody which put full blame on the players:

Who Killed Baseball?

Who killed baseball? "I," said John Ward: "of my own accord, I killed baseball."

Who saw it die? "We," said the slaves; "from our own made graves, we saw it die."

Who'll make its shroud? "I," said Buck Ewing, "I'll do it well, I'll do the sewing, I'll make its shroud."

Who'll dig its grave? "I," said Brunell, "I'll do it well, I'll dig its grave."

Who'll be the parson? "I," said Cub Stricker, "I'll let her flicker, I'll be the parson."

Who'll carry the link? "I," said Jay Faatz; * "I watched the gates, I'll carry the link."

Who'll be chief mourner? "I," said Tim Keefe; "I'm filled with grief, I'll be chief mourner."

Who'll sing a psalm? "I," said Comiskey; "though it's rather risky, I'll sing a psalm."

Who'll toll the bell? "I," said "King Kell."; "I'll toll it like _____, I'll toll the bell."

And now all the cranks have forgotten the game
And the ex-slave perceives that D. Mud is his name.

* Non-playing manager of the Cleveland Players' League team.

20

THE PEACE THAT BROUGHT WAR

THE FANS and the press were disgusted with baseball after the debacle of 1890. They were fed up with the "senseless wrangling" of the club owners and the "bickering" and "politics" that were smothering the game. The heavy losses of the campaign and the pressure of the public for a settlement put the owners in a mood to listen to the peace proposals of Allan W. Thurman, who was promptly called "The White-winged Angel of Peace." Thurman, who was a director of the Columbus American Association Club and had friends in both camps, presented his plan in an eloquent speech before the National League in early October. The core of his proposal was a consolidation of the three major leagues into two new eight-club circuits. He had arranged it so that certain cities would have two clubs and others just one.

Using this opening, three Players' League owners—Al Johnson, Wendell Goodwin of Brooklyn, and Edward Talcott of New York— who just "happened" to be at a hotel a block away, arranged to meet Spalding and John B. Day. This was the Players' League's first mistake. From this point on it was outgeneraled by Spalding. He had just returned from a European trip and learned of the staggering loss of Cincinnati to the Players' League, so he entered the conference room only too well aware that the National League was in bad shape. Nevertheless, he prepared to bluff. To his surprise, he wrote later, the Players' League men "greedily" accepted his demand for "unconditional surrender."

What really happened that day may never be fully revealed, but overcoming the Players' League probably was not as easy as Spalding claimed, because the end came only after long, tortuous negotiations. The fact that Goodwin and Talcott were among the first to merge their clubs with their opposite numbers in the National League leads to the suspicion that they were primarily interested in salvaging what they could for themselves.

It is also likely that the three Players' League men accepted talk of consolidation at face value and, assuming it would be a deal among three equals on a quid pro quo basis, were hoodwinked into showing their hand prematurely. We do know that after this initial conference the National League stiffened its attitude and became "non-committal" about what it could do for peace. It merely indicated that a committee would be appointed for further discussion. The League, which had concentrated its attack on the players during the war, with court actions and attempted bribes, now shrewdly seized the opportunity to center its fire on the capitalist flank of the Players' League. Some League owners still wanted to carry on the fight, but Spalding counseled against it.

The next day the League appointed Spalding, Day, and Charles Byrne of Brooklyn as its committee. Keeping Day and adding Byrne was hardly an accident. It meant that the rival New York and Brooklyn clubs would have representation on both committees, and reinforces the suspicion that Talcott and Goodwin must have revealed their willingness to make a deal when they first met with Spalding and Day.

It also "just happened" that some of the American Association magnates were in town. They now chose Billie Barnie of Baltimore and Von der Ahe to work on a committee with "White Wings" Thurman. The three committees met on October 9. Nothing was settled conclusively, and they decided to meet again on October 22, but they agreed that in the meantime there would be a truce, during which the three leagues would respect each other's player contracts. They also decided that the rival clubs would have to work out any consolidation plans among themselves, and promised to talk to their fellow club owners and see what could be done.

There is no doubt that the opposing groups understood each other's language. The papers were now quoting them about how it was necessary for "something to be done for the game and the capitalists." And by putting off their next meeting until later in the month they were giving the rival owners in each city time to see each other. The Players' League representatives agreed to the arrangement without consulting either the other owners or the Brotherhood. Instead of standing together as a unit on a common policy they were preparing the way for piecemeal surrender.

Rumors of double-dealing were soon becoming widespread. It was said that the truce over signing players was already broken. The Pittsburgh and New York magnates on both sides were reported to be reaching agreement. Mistrust spread within the Players' League. The Wagner brothers, Philadelphia butchers who held the Players' League franchise there, became alarmed and telegraphed Colonel McAlpin protesting the "deals" being made with National League men in New York.

Ward did not immediately grasp the significance of what was happening. He had a plan for compromise on an equal basis, and when he saw that some Players' League backers were planning to work out deals of their own, he fought a losing battle to keep the Brotherhood from being by-passed. The Brotherhood met in New York October 20, just before the triple committee of owners was scheduled to reconvene. Many of the players were bitterly outspoken against their backers for negotiating without consulting them. Ward was more diplomatic. He made a bid for unity by trying to pin on the League the onus for what was happening. As a result the growing breach between the backers and the players was temporarily repaired. The Brotherhood passed a resolution of confidence in the Players' League and met with the capitalists the following day. A letter from Colonel McAlpin was read, thanking the players for their confidence and promising to work still harder in their interests. The three-man conference committee reported, and then John Addison, backer of the Chicago Club, proposed that three player-stockholders be added to the committee when it sat down with the League and Association delegations.

McAlpin spoke at length against the idea, warning that the other two leagues would not stand for changing the committee and would break off negotiations. He made it plain that the backers had to safeguard their interests without regard for sentiment. But after much debate, Addison's motion carried, and Ward, Hanlon, and Irwin were appointed to join the three Players' League capitalists on the committee.

The showdown came the next day. The League and Association learned that three player representatives were to sit down with them, and they determined beforehand to have nothing to do with them. At the appointed hour the original nine capitalists trooped into the room followed by the three player delegates. Thurman, who took the chair, spotted the three players and refused to open the meeting because the membership of the Players' League committee was not the same.

A stormy session followed. Johnson presented credentials authorizing the presence of the players on his committee, and argued that the change only made representation equal—six against six. He warned that, unless the players were accepted, the Players' League would halt negotiations. The League and Association people answered that they had no authority to do business with anyone but the original Players' League committee, and Thurman disputed Johnson's interpretation of equality, maintaining that the three Associations already stood on the same level, with three delegates each.

After nearly everyone else had spoken, John Ward made a last appeal.

In a spirited speech he said that League and Association objections were "trivial" and "based on a technicality." The two older leagues were acting together, so that adding three players to the Players' League committee only made things even. As far as that went, Ward said, it should make no difference how many people were on a committee or who they were, because each committee was a unit representing its own circuit. He charged that the real objection was against the participation of the players, even though they were also stockholders. He personally, for example, had more to lose than anybody, since he had invested "every dollar he had" in the Players' League. It was a fundamental principle of the Players' League to have equal representation of players and capitalists, Ward went on.

He finished by reminding his listeners that each of the other subcommittees contained a former ball player. "Do these gentlemen," he asked, "wish to go on record as saying that the occupation of a ball player bars him from business association with respectable men?" Then turning directly to the National League's leader, he challenged, "Mr. Spalding, are you willing to place such a stamp of infamy upon the profession of which you were for years a member and to which you owe your start in life?"

Undismayed, Spalding moved skillfully to split the opposition by using his strongest weapon: "Before the National League consented to any negotiations whatever, it was mutually decided that the question of a compromise should be settled between the moneyed men of both organizations on a purely business basis." The capitalists were acting "in good faith," Spalding continued, but their hands were being tied by the Brotherhood. Ward and the other two players had no more right to a voice in the meeting than players from his own league. Then, driving the wedge deeper between the players and their backers, Spalding accused the players of lacking confidence in the men who had "lost $500,000 pushing their cause."

After more squabbling Johnson finally gave way, agreeing to let the original three committees decide whether the players would be admitted or not. When the players left the room, the nine magnates put the issue to a vote. The result was not entirely unexpected: six to three against admitting the players!

The Players' League capitalists tried to mollify the players in the hotel corridor but were unsuccessful, since the players insisted negotiations should end if they could not participate. That ended the formal conferences, and from there on it was every man for himself. Spalding clung to his strategy of divide and conquer, blaming the players for breaking off negotiations and reiterating the League's willingness to meet again with the Players' League capitalists but not with the

Brotherhood. He and Thurman were authorized to travel from city to city helping the local backers to reach settlements on a "home rule principle."

New York, meanwhile, was the scene of a continuing round of luncheons and informal conferences among owners on both sides and on the same side, in a dizzy variety of combinations, with "White Wings" Thurman reported "flitting to and fro." Spalding, Byrne, Talcott, and Goodwin lunched together. Several others "locked arms" and went to Spalding's office to confer. Sometimes liquor flowed freely and conferences lasted many hours.

Rumors were still flying about. National League men were accused of picking off Players' League capitalists one by one and dismembering the enemy league piece by piece. Players' League capitalists were reported promising the National League to keep the players out of negotiations. Ward announced that he did not like the way "certain capitalists of the Players' League" were acting, and Keefe suspected they were "doing something underhanded," even though all along they "professed to have our interests at heart."

The players' fears were amply justified. Their league was dead. All that remained was a few months of bewildering diplomacy. Each Players' League club scrambled to make peace on its own, with little or no concern for its fellow clubs. If the National League's purpose was "to break down a fair and open business rivalry," as Ward charged, and "continue [its] monopoly of all the professional baseball players in the country," then it had succeeded.

Annihilation of the Players' League began with the consolidation of the rival New York clubs. Talcott announced early in November that he had merged his club with the Giants, even though his club secretary had promised that nothing would be done until other Players' League clubs had a chance to make similar arrangements. J. Earl Wagner rushed to New York to urge against it, and the secretary of the Boston Players' League club demanded action against the "selfish" move. But Talcott went ahead on his own anyway. When Ward blasted him as a "weakener," he answered that he, McAlpin, and others had put up $3000 a month to keep the club on its feet and had received nothing in return "except high-priced ball playing."

The Pittsburgh Players' League Club quickly followed suit, combining with the old Allegheny Club, which formally resigned from the National League in favor of the newly formed Pittsburgh Athletic Company. The new organization included several former Players' League capitalists on its board of directors.

Then Addison agreed to sell his Chicago Club to Spalding for $25,000, but the transaction was held up because his players hired an attorney to protect their interests and Spalding was afraid he might be purchasing "a flock of law suits." Addison finally received $18,000, to be pro-rated among his non-playing shareholders, on the basis of 60 per cent of the stock held. The rest was to go to the players in cash settlement of unpaid salary balances, less 10 per cent, and to pay off six player-stockholders at 50 per cent of par.* McAlpin and Talcott handed over $15,000 worth of their new consolidated Giant stock to Addison "for peace all along the line." Spalding gave complimentary season passes to Addison and the other ousted stockholders when he formally took over the Players' League Club—grandstand, lease, chairs, books, and player contracts—on December 29.

Brooklyn's turn was next. A new organization was set up with estimated capitalization of $200,000 to $250,000, in which Byrne, Joseph Doyle, and Ferdinand Abel remained majority stockholders. Wendell Goodwin, John Wallace, and other Players' League men were to buy an interest in the club for $40,000. Byrne was to continue as president, with the other four chief stockholders on the board of directors. However, Edward Linton and some other "minnow magnates," as minority stockholders were called, did not like the settlement and blocked the transaction for the moment with a temporary court order. So the Brooklyn merger was left up in the air for a while.

With three of its clubs eliminated and a fourth on the verge, the remnant of the Players' League still maintained that it was "in better shape than at the close of the season." It appointed a new committee in a feeble effort to resume negotiations with the National League, but Nick Young stood firmly on technicalities and turned it down.

This first stage of consolidation was accomplished with relative ease, because it was chiefly a matter of capitalists in the same city reaching agreement on the terms for fusing their clubs. The liquidation of the rest of the Players' League was more complicated. Much of it involved revamping the American Association circuit. The Association had expelled the Philadelphia Athletics for not meeting certain financial obligations. Spalding and Thurman planned to have the Philadelphia Players' League Club take its place. The Association also wanted to drop its "little three"—Toledo, Rochester, and Syracuse—and replace them with more profitable cities. So Spalding and Thurman contemplated having the National League open its Boston territory to the Association by allowing it to admit the Boston Players' League Club. This plan would conveniently dispose of two more Players' League clubs and help the Association to complete a stronger circuit. Sharing Chicago with the Association was also put forward as a possibility,

* Fred Pfeffer waived his share because he made a "separate deal" with Addison.

and the other replacement would be Washington, which had been dropped by the National League the season before.

Numerous obstacles stood in the way of the Thurman-Spalding plan, however. Minority stockholders of the ousted Athletics wanted to keep the Wagner brothers, backers of the Players' League team there, out of Philadelphia and take over the new Association franchise themselves. Boston's "triumvirs"—Soden, Conant, and Billings—objected to the idea of anyone treading on their exclusive territorial rights. They insisted that if the Association needed another Eastern club it should try some city other than Boston. There was also the question of whether Toledo, Rochester, and Syracuse would agree to withdraw from the Association, and if they would, how much would it cost to get rid of them?

For mutual protection of their interests against the malcontents of the old Athletics and the obstinate League owners in Boston, the Wagner brothers joined forces with Charles A. Prince, owner of the Boston Players' League Club, each promising not to make a separate settlement. They were soon reinforced by Al Johnson, who still held onto his Cleveland and Cincinnati interests, and then by Edward Linton, spokesman for the "minnow magnates" of Brooklyn, who were blocking consolidation there. This belated united front stirred rumors that the American Association and the remains of the Players' League might combine into a new circuit and defy the National League if the latter did not suffer the Association to enter Boston and Chicago.

This confused situation prevailed as baseball men from all over the country gathered together at New York in mid-January 1891. Describing the hum and bustle at the Fifth Avenue Hotel, the New York *Tribune* said it was "the most animated scene" since the Great Revolt, with owners and players "all looking out for the mighty dollar which is so eagerly pursued."

Growling that the League had made their organization "its tool for ten years," Association men were determined that this time they would have their way. They dug up the old incident of admitting Lucas and the St. Louis Unions into their own territory in 1885, and said now it was the League's turn to do as much for them. A reporter said Von der Ahe arrived "loaded for bear," ready to stay a month if necessary to win his point. The belligerent attitude of the Association supposedly "non-plussed" the League, which until then "swung the parental rod" over the junior circuit. Not so the Boston triumvirs; they came "with their war paint on." A writer for the New York *Herald* predicted, however, that in any event, the League would "get the best of the bargain," because its "magnates are a shrewd lot, and will not allow a rival organization too much power if they can help it."

Three days spent discussing the Thurman-Spalding plan produced no results. The stubborn stand of the Boston triumvirs was the main stumbling block, and until the National League could remove it, nothing could be accomplished. While the League cajoled the Boston owners the Association men stood by and waited, meeting and adjourning in monotonous regularity, broken only by a court injunction restraining them from dropping their Toledo Club.

Finding that Syracuse and Rochester were inclined to retire quietly if they received a reasonable price, the Association commissioned Thurman, Barnie, and Von der Ahe to make a package deal with them and Toledo, and they finally succeeded in disposing of the lot for about $24,000. Meanwhile the League, after exerting heavy pressure, got grudging consent from the triumvirs for the Association to share their Boston stronghold, but only under "killing conditions," as the New York *Tribune* termed them. Prince's Players' League Club would be allowed to operate in Boston under the banner of the American Association only if it charged fifty cents for admission, returned all its former League players, and refrained from using the name "Boston."

This compromise settled the composition of the Association and seemed to assure peace. The Association admitted Washington, moved into Boston, and awarded the Wagner brothers the Philadelphia franchise, as well as the name "Athletics." It also expected to occupy Chicago. The Players' League was officially dissolved, and all players were assigned to the clubs by which they were originally reserved—an important decision which shortly led to a full measure of trouble.

The now-smiling owners did not include Linton, Johnson, or the Buffalo people. With no one to amalgamate with, Buffalo ceased to exist. Linton and his minority group finally succeeded in securing their price for their Brooklyn stock, and by the end of March, Byrne and Goodwin were able to sign papers fusing the League and Players' clubs legally. However, the amalgamated club's affairs were still kept "chaotic" by a few remaining dissatisfied stockholders, who badgered them for the next few years.

Al Johnson bore out the scriptural admonition, "The first shall be last," for although he had shown the way to the other Players' League capitalists, the "grandmother of the lost cause" was still unaccommodated. Repeated talks with Frank Robison, Cleveland National League owner, produced nothing but disagreement. In Cincinnati Johnson was equally frustrated. Prince and the Wagner brothers, who were part of the Players' League group which had helped Johnson purchase the Cincinnati franchise from Aaron Stern, turned over their portion of the Cincinnati stock to him as a kind of consolation prize when they made their own deals with the League. Johnson was told to work out the Cincinnati end of his problem with John T. Brush, who had been given the National League franchise there. He failed to reach any agreement with Brush, but before long Johnson was once more deeply involved in interleague politics.

Why did the Brotherhood collapse? John Ward said it was because of "stupidity, avarice, and treachery." J. Earl Wagner avowed that the National League was beaten until the betrayal by Ewing and the New York Club. He said that the Players' League's greatest mistake was to parley with the National League at all. The absence of a strong leader when the crisis came was the reason given by *Sporting News*. Spink's paper also blamed the Players' League for depending on anticipated profit without taking possible losses into account. The Pittsburgh *Dispatch* pointed to the impractical, Utopian structure of the Players' League. It was "organized on the most beautiful principles.... Its theories were captivating, but so were some of Sir Thomas More's, and so are some of Bellamy's," but "unfortunately they did not work."

After the Players' League was smashed, Frank Brunell, the Players' League secretary, attempted to analyze the causes. Claiming that the players had "stood adversity better than the capitalists," who proved staunch fighters only in Boston, Philadelphia, and Cleveland, Brunell thought that his league might have won through in spite of everything, except for the "treacherous eagerness" of its Brooklyn and New York Clubs to get in "out of the wet." Just at the time the National League was reeling from the loss of Cincinnati, the Players' League's "vapid" committee allowed itself to be outsmarted in conferences. Brunell also mentioned stories "industriously circulated" by the National League which "distributed distrust" and brought the Players' League to an "inglorious end." Finally, he listed "three vital business mistakes" made by his side: (1) its clubs should have raised $50,000 each in stock instead of $20,000 when they started; (2) eight of its best non-playing business managers should have been assigned one to a team; and (3) the National League should have been fought in its own way, by ruthlessly getting back players who returned to it.

F. C. Richter's pre-war estimate of the strength and weakness on both sides, and his prediction that the National League would win, were remarkably prescient. He foretold that although the League entered the fight handicapped by the loss of its players, it would have the advantage of longer experience, the prestige of age, abler management, and more money; whereas the Players' League, even with the best playing talent, would suffer from newness, inexperience, organizational weaknesses, extraordinary expenses, and high salaries. Richter's analysis comes closest to the truth, although the other factors played their part in the outcome.

To National League owners, the failure of the Players' League experiment proved that players were incapable of directing baseball affairs, and the club owners seldom tired of mentioning this point in later years. Perhaps they were right, but the collapse of the Players' League does not prove it. The players did not hold the reins in 1890. Administration of their league was at most a dual arrangement between the men and their backers, and not one of the league's officers was a player. For that matter, baseball's long history gives little evidence of the owners' ability to run the business themselves. That is one reason they finally had to appoint a Commissioner of Baseball in 1920, and why in the 1950's the United States Congress twice looked into the workings of professional baseball. Actually, the stigma of failure must be placed on both players and capitalists of the Players' League.

Before 1890 ended, a new instrument of government for Organized Baseball was written by Mills, Spalding, and Byrne, and adopted at a joint session of the National League, American Association, and Western Association, a minor league. This new National Agreement was broader in scope than previous ones. It placed control in the hands of a National Board of three members, one from each of the associations party to it. Board members were to elect a chairman, one of themselves or an outsider. They were to "approve" contracts of players and umpires and assign the latter to games. The Board also had authority to hear all disputes and complaints, and could mete out fines and suspensions to all associations, individual clubs, players, umpires, or scorers, and there was no appeal from its decisions.

The reserve system was continued, and players could still be sold if they gave their consent. The Board could release a man from reservation if his club became more than fifteen days in arrears on his salary, or failed to offer him a contract by March 15. Players could bring their complaints directly to the Board. These mild reforms, however, scarcely warranted premature declarations of newspapers that the sales system was destroyed, the blacklist abolished, and the abuses of the reserve corrected.

Members chosen for the National Board were Allan W. Thurman of the Association, John I. Rogers of the National League, and L. C. Krauthoff of the Western Association. An attempt was made to bring A. G. Mills back into baseball by electing him chairman of the National Board, but he declined because of the pressure of private business and recommended Spalding for the post, but he also rejected it. So the Board selected Thurman to act as chairman.

Adopting the National Agreement was the last step in ending the Players' League War. But unfortunately it was not a solution to baseball's troubles. For scarcely had the owners dispersed to their home cities before trouble arose once more, and the magnates and the public had to endure another hard year of war before a more lasting peace was achieved.

21

THE SECOND ASSOCIATION WAR

THE BROTHERHOOD peace set the stage for another war between the National League and the American Association. The direct cause of this fresh struggle was a quarrel over two star players, Louis Bierbauer and Harry Stovey. Bierbauer was an outstanding second baseman, and Stovey was a hard-hitting outfielder and fast base-runner. His record of 156 stolen bases in 1888 still stands as the all-time high for a single season. Both men had been with the old Athletics in 1889, and in 1890 they had jumped to the Brooklyn and Boston Players' League Clubs, respectively.

So many players had joined the Players' League that it would have been completely unrealistic for the leagues to use wholesale blacklisting for the 1891 season. Therefore the peace terms provided that all players were to return to their old clubs, the ones which had reserved them in 1889. Each club was to send to the National Board a list of its reserve players, plus the names of any surplus players, so that they could be distributed among the weaker clubs.

The Wagner brothers, who had been awarded the Association's Philadelphia franchise, failed to reserve Bierbauer and Stovey. The Pittsburgh Nationals seized this opening to sign Bierbauer. Pittsburgh's president, J. Palmer O'Neill, was immediately tagged J. Pirate O'Neill, and his club nicknamed the Pirates—as they have been known ever since. The Association planned to transfer Stovey from the Athletics to its new Boston Club. But Stovey, not satisfied with Prince's terms and knowing he was a free agent, walked over to Soden's office and signed with the Boston League Club instead.

The Athletics immediately appealed to the National Board, which met in secret session at Chicago early in February 1891. After an exhausting discussion lasting from 8:00 P.M. until 3:00 A.M., it took up the cases afresh the next morning and finally decided "reluctantly" that the two stars were to stay with the League clubs.

They were not the only players in dispute. Connie Mack, for instance, had signed a personal contract with President Prince. But according to the peace terms he was assigned to Pittsburgh. The cases of Mack and a couple of lesser lights were relatively clear cut, and the decisions were accepted with good grace. But Bierbauer and Stovey were a different matter.

The Association was infuriated over the loss of these two players. Maybe, under the letter of the law, the League clubs were technically within their rights, but, in the eyes of the Association, signing them was a clear violation of the spirit of the peace agreement so recently concluded. Association owners upbraided the League for its "deceit" and "cold selfishness." As *Sporting Life* said, the Wagner brothers, the Association, and the public took it for granted that players of the old Athletics—including Bierbauer and Stovey—were to go to the new Philadelphia Club, and the general decision allocating all players to their 1889 clubs should have been sufficient to protect the Athletics, even though the Wagners had neglected to observe the formalities of listing the players in question. After all, players had been kept on reserve continuously in the past, whether they played on the club or not. Even the old League champion, A. G. Mills, did not understand why the two League clubs had acted as they did. To him, it did not matter "how the record of reservation by the Athletics may stand, technically."

Association men were particularly incensed at their own president, Thurman, who, as chairman of the National Board, had voted with the League against his own organization. Since Krauthoff, a former Association man, had voted to return the players to the Athletics—even issuing a "minority report"—it was Thurman's vote which carried the decision for the League. Thurman was excoriated for his "duplicity" and "treachery." Al Johnson, still biding his time, said it was only what could be expected, because Thurman had always done Spalding's bidding. However, Krauthoff was generous enough to write Thurman telling him that although he disagreed with his decision, he admired the bold and courageous stand Thurman had taken and promised full co-operation in upholding the Board's decision.

It was also noted by the Association that the National League was keeping hold of surplus players thrown on the market by combining three leagues into two, rather than allowing them to be divided among the other members of the National Agreement. In fact, League owners were bickering among themselves because some of them were keeping up to twenty-seven men on reserve, each fearing to give them up until they saw what the others would do, instead of sharing them with the have-not clubs. Some League owners made a special trip to Chicago hoping to pick up a few through the National Board, but there were none available. Spalding defended keeping twenty-three players on his reserve list:

> It is all right to get the reputation of being a good fellow, but one cannot rob himself to acquire such a reputation. When I have gotten the team I want for Chicago I will let the rest of the players go to some of the clubs, but not before.

Actually, the League never had any intention of sharing its surplus with the other parties to the National Agreement on an equal basis. Spalding's brother explained that it planned to divide up any extras among League clubs first, before sending the leavings, if any, to the Board. To him, it was only "natural" for the League to take care of itself first.

The Association acted fast. Prince wired Thurman to call an Association meeting to dissolve the National Agreement. The unpopular president angrily refused, saying he would stick by the National Board in any revolt, so Vice President Barnie took over. At the meeting Thurman was expelled from the Association and Louis Kramer, a Cincinnati lawyer and one of the founders of the Association, was elected to the consolidated offices of president, secretary, and treasurer. A formal message was sent to Young, as Secretary of the National Board, withdrawing the Association from the National Agreement. The Association dropped its plans for going into Chicago, and instead brought in Al Johnson to establish a club in Cincinnati and sit on the Association's board of directors. "It was bad enough to have Spalding's fingers on our throats for nine long years," blustered Barnie. "Spalding says he wants war and we will give it to him."

The National Board stood by the National Agreement. It resolved that the Association by its own action had removed itself from protection, and all its players were therefore released from reservation and fair game for any National League or Western Association club that wanted to sign them. Thurman was still chairman of the Board but could no longer vote because he represented no one. About a month later he resigned altogether and returned to private life. In his place Nick Young assumed the chairmanship.

Can you imagine, asked the New York *Herald*, a war over two players when hundreds of thousands of dollars are involved? It was true. With the National Agreement broken, the fourth trade war in the League's fifteen years of existence was on. The same familiar tactics used in other wars were employed—raiding each other's players, boycotting games, running to the courts, and always the usual war of words in the press. The experience of previous wars had taught the magnates how to refine some of their methods, and the war itself produced some interesting ramifications of its own.

The League quickly muddied the issue by announcing that the real reason the Association had broken the National Agreement was because it, the Association, wanted to move into Cincinnati. Spalding called the Association's action "the work of a few irresponsible professional managers with anarchistic tendencies." Even if it had Bierbauer and Stovey, he charged, the Association would have found some other excuse for disrupting the National Agreement, because Cincinnati was the real "jam pot" it was after. The League even claimed to have evidence that the Association was conspiring all along to enter Cincinnati. How much truth there was in this is impossible to say. But the tale was played up in the newspapers and made effective propaganda for the League.

Nevertheless, Cincinnati did become a crucial factor in the war. Both the League and the Association were resolved to gain control of Cincinnati. In the process, the League bought something it already had, and Johnson sold something he did not have, and it took ten years of litigation to figure out who had what.

The Cincinnati maze goes back to the sale of the Club during the Players' League War, when a syndicate of Brotherhood backers purchased it from National League owner Aaron Stern. Consolidation of clubs after the war landed some of the Cincinnati investors, like Prince and Wagner, in the Association, and others, like Addison and Talcott, in the National League, so that, as the Second Association War broke out, both camps had stockholders in Johnson's Cincinnati Club.

The League, of course, was already in Cincinnati. John T. Brush had been given the franchise after the Players' League War, and Johnson, who had been excluded by the settlement, was shunted off to Cincinnati and told to work out some agreement with Brush, but the two failed to come to terms. No sooner was Johnson in the Association than the League bought him out for $30,000, each club contributing about $4000 apiece for the purpose. The League made the deal thinking that a minority stockholder named Weidenfeller had sold his shares to Johnson. Weidenfeller's shares were strategic; without them, neither side held control. It was true Weidenfeller had made Johnson an offer, but, getting no response and desiring to clear out of baseball, he gave the League power of attorney over his shares on condition it be kept quiet and his name not even mentioned. However, J. Walter Spalding could not keep from blurting out the news. Weidenfeller was so angry he wrote the League rescinding power of attorney. His letter was read at a League meeting, and the panic-stricken magnates jumped to the conclusion that he had sold his stock to Johnson. Later, after the League had shelled out its money, Al Spalding was shocked to have Weiden-feller walk into his office with the stock still in his pocket. "Well, we have been a crowd of chumps," Spalding exclaimed. "We have paid $30,000 for something we had already." Such are the small incidents upon which big events often turn.

When the Association owners learned that Johnson had double-crossed them and sold out to the League, it was their turn to be shocked. They immediately threw together another club, backed chiefly by Von der Ahe, and sent King Kelly from their Boston Club to captain it. At the same time they filed a petition in the Superior Court of Cincinnati to prevent the League from taking over Johnson's holdings and paying him for the stock. Prince and Wagner claimed that they had not given him their Cincinnati stock outright after the Players' League War, but had merely let him hold it in trust. Johnson replied that they had sur-rendered their interests to him "in atonement" for deserting him after the Players' League War. If the plaintiffs were right, it meant that Johnson had sold to the League something he did not possess. And the court decided they were right. It enjoined the League from paying over the money to Johnson. The money was held in escrow while he and the other claimants fought it out in the courts. The litigation was carried on until 1901—the year Johnson died—when the money was finally divided among the various parties.

In the meantime, both Brush's National League Club and the Associa-tion's makeshift team were losing money. Von der Ahe, who controlled 75 per cent of the Association Club, besides owning the Browns, got to-gether with Brush and sold out to the League in August for about $12,000, shifting the team to Milwaukee. Although it was a member of the Western Association, a party to the National Agreement, Milwaukee agreed to amalgamate the two clubs and join the Association.

Von der Ahe said he made the move to strike a blow at the Western Association, the League's ally, and he insisted that Cincinnati had not been surrendered. The franchise had merely been abandoned tem-porarily, and the Association would have a club there the following season. Actually, he was looking out for himself. He had made the deal on his own initiative, and was now evidently trying to square himself with the Association and the public.

The usual wartime player-raiding was carried on by both sides right from the beginning. *Sporting Life* knew what was coming when the war started and printed in a black-bordered box:

Recquiescat in Pace
THE RESERVE RULE
Died Feb. 19, 1891

Both leagues were about equally proficient in stealing one another's players. Once more jumpers were threatened with "no mercy" and blacklisting "forever." Yet counter-raiding went on, and jumpers who returned were accepted. *Sporting Life* sneered at the contradiction by suggesting that Nick Young hang out a shingle inscribed,

N. E. YOUNG

Base Ball Law To Suit Anybody Furnished upon Application

The courts again refused to uphold the baseball contract. Baltimore tried to keep "Fatty" Childs from jumping to the Cleveland League Club, and was denied an injunction on the ground that the Association's withdrawal from the National Agreement invalidated the contract. Another Association club, Columbus, tried unsuccessfully to restrain Charles Reilly from jumping to Pittsburgh. The judge said, "Professional base ball has become a business, and should be treated as any other business, with no greater consideration and no less." He applied the *Lumley* v. *Wagner* doctrine and decided that, since the player's services were not unique, relief could not be granted.

A third player case backfired on Von der Ahe. Mark Baldwin, nicknamed "Fido," was not satisfied to jump from the Columbus Club to Pittsburgh and let it go at that. He acted as League agent to get others to follow him. While Fido was traveling on this mission, Von der Ahe accused him of conspiracy to break up his business. Baldwin was picked up in a St. Louis poolroom and jailed, but the case was thrown out of court. As soon as Baldwin stepped out of the courtroom Von der Ahe had him re-arrested on new charges, and the process was repeated. Baldwin did not like being thrown into a jail infested with cockroaches and bedbugs, and retaliated against Von der Ahe's harassment with a suit for $20,000, charging false arrest and malicious prosecution. Four years later a jury awarded him $2500.

The League offered players a choice of signing two types of contracts, one for seven months containing a renewal clause (reserve) for one or more successive seasons, the other without a renewal clause but for a term of years with salaries to be paid in twelve monthly or twenty-four semi-monthly installments. Evidently the League made the change in the hope of strengthening the contract legally and gaining more control over the players in the off-season. The players liked it because they would receive money during the winter. However, the League stayed away from the courts. It had most of the players to start with, and its Philly owner, John I. Rogers, an attorney himself, advised keeping out of court because it was expensive and a doubtful remedy. John T. Brush was also skeptical. He warned that "base ball in court has always proved disastrous."

Neither side was overjoyed at having to fight another costly trade war on top of the disastrous Brotherhood season. Competition inflated player salaries, and buying out clubs in fights over territorial rights added to the drain on treasuries. League clubs were taxed 10 per cent each for a sinking fund. More money was lost by the League's cancellation of the spring exhibition games with the Association. To compensate for them the Association voted to extend the season a week.

After the season the Association challenged the League to pit the Nationals' pennant-winning Boston Club against its own Boston Reds for the world's championship. But Nick Young refused to "trample the National Agreement under foot" to accommodate one Association club. So the Association declared its own Boston winners World Champions, and another chance to make some money was missed.

Not more than four or five clubs in the two leagues cleared expenses, and some were thousands in the red. Even the minor leagues suffered from raids. The only ones that did not were those whose players were not worth taking. Cleveland's secretary, Davis Hawley, had the cheek to advise cutting the minors off from the protection of the National Agreement, and raiding their players without paying. He argued that the Association was doing it, so the League should have the "same privilege of feeding upon the small fry."

Of the two majors, the Association was less able to stand adversity. Racked by internal dissension, it lacked the cohesiveness of the National League. It had too many poor-paying cities in its circuit, like Columbus, Louisville, and Milwaukee, all of which were in serious financial difficulty by mid-season. It lost out in Cincinnati, and even before the season began it had to pay off its old Rochester, Toledo, and Syracuse clubs for dropping them after the Players' League War. The Association even tried special financial measures. Gate receipts were divided equally between home and visiting teams, and on holidays receipts were placed in a common pool for division among all. To prevent the "dinky-dink" (a term coming into frequent use on the sports page during the 'nineties, meaning betrayal or jilting), each club had to hand over a majority of its stock to the Association president. In August, Boston in desperation cut back to twenty-five-cent admission, breaking the agreement made with the triumvirs in the Players' League settlement. These measures did not offset the heavy expenses and losses.

Talk of peace started early. Columbus was for it in June, and the Association considered it at a meeting that month. A big step was taken when Brush and Von der Ahe met about Cincinnati in August. The evidence indicates that they also sounded each other out on the possibility of a general peace conference. Both sides appointed peace committees right after their meeting—Kramer, Phelps, and Von der Ahe for the Association, and Brush, Byrne, and Hart for the League. This time Spalding was not officially a member. Von der Ahe objected to his presence on the committee, so his "henchman and mouthpiece," Jim Hart, whom Spalding had installed as president of the Chicago Club, showed up in his place.

The committees met in Washington August 25 with many other magnates on hand as well. Negotiations had just begun when word came that King Kelly had jumped back to the National League, signing a fat contract which included a trip to Europe for him and his wife. This broke up the conference. The Association demanded Kelly's return before it would continue talks, and when the League hedged in its reply, the Association withdrew, taking time only to remove Kramer from the presidency and to re-elect Zack Phelps. Kramer was accused of deception in forcing a resolution pledging each side to respect the other's contracts when he already knew about Kelly. Ironically, when Kramer had taken over the presidency, he said that he did not know how long he would be associated with this "funny business," because, "There is much in baseball that they call diplomacy which I should say was trickery and intrigue."

Sporting News blasted the Boston triumvirs for grabbing Kelly while a truce was on, saying that common decency was foreign to them, and asking whether the other League clubs would agree to be "milked in order that the Boston glutton shall thrive." League men replied that taking Milwaukee from the Western Association was a more serious offense than their signing Kelly. After the dispute died down, it came out that the Boston Club had wired Kramer at the Washington conference that the subject of Kelly should not interfere with negotiations, since they did not want him anyway. But by then it was too late.

Both sides made a great show of continuing the fight into the next season. The League prepared for a price war by abandoning its long-standing policy of higher admissions to allow all clubs to charge twenty-five cents. It added a new technique to player-stealing by introducing division of labor. Instead of all its clubs competing with each other hit-or-miss for Association players, each club was assigned to go after certain ones. One of their best catches was Charles Comiskey, the future magnate, who was making his second jump, this time to Brush's Cincinnati Club.

The Association made a strong thrust by obtaining the backing of a group of Chicago businessmen and setting up a club in Spalding's territory with a capital stock of $50,000. It also decided to let the home clubs keep all gate receipts except on holidays. A renewed bid for players was made by President Phelps in a public statement. He claimed that the Association treated players like "gentlemen" rather than "slaves or brutes," and that those who joined its ranks would be liberally paid and "allowed to be and feel themselves men." Phelps told the press that there would be plenty of room for two leagues, and the Association was going to be one of them. It was "tired of eating cheese as a regular diet so long as there is plenty of sweet apple-pie lying around."

In passing these warlike measures the owners were behaving like young boys whistling in the woods when dark approaches. It was clear that if something was not done, the business would go bankrupt. In their hearts the owners knew they could not endure more losses and still bigger payrolls. The Cleveland *Leader* said that skyrocketing salaries had become "a business absurdity." It was becoming practically impossible to discipline and control players. An unpleasant word or cross look from an owner and they jumped to another club. The Chicago *Post* invented a typical interview with a Chicago player to illustrate the cavalier attitude players might take:

> Mr. Ryan, the eminent exponent of field practice, has not gone into winter quarters yet.
> "What association club will you captain next year?" he was asked.
> "I have not yet selected my club," James replied, as he toyed with one of his $500 diamonds.
> "You will not say officially, then, that you will captain any association team?"
> "No," he replied, as he gently rubbed a $750 emerald.
> "Then you will play with the Chicagos again?"
> "I will notify you when I sign my contract," said James. Then he critically scrutinized an $800 ruby and bowed low, indicating that the interview was at an end.

Many of the magnates were having second thoughts about the Washington conference. The League did not disband its peace committee till about a month afterward, and even then left the way open for the Association to rejoin the National Agreement, after which amendments to it could be worked out. President Robison of Cleveland thought it was ridiculous to break up the conference over Mike Kelly:

> Why, I would give up a hundred Kellys before I would let him stand in the way of my money interests. It was like breaking up a railroad conference because a brakeman went from one road to another.

If the Association would pick three representative men—"those with money interests at stake"—a new National Agreement could be drawn up inside of an hour on one sheet of paper, Robison declared. Then expressing the antipathy which professional baseball has felt ever since toward attorneys and outsiders, he added that the trouble with

the Washington conference was that the Association sent a couple of
hired lawyers "busy getting reputations" and without a dollar to lose.

In September and early November newspapers continued to quote
owners on the "folly" and "suicide" of going on the way they were.
Byrne of Brooklyn went to Columbus and talked peace. Prince of the
Boston Association Club wanted to leave baseball. Robison went east
to talk to executives on both sides. Vonderhorst of Baltimore was sending "confidential" telegrams to Von der Ahe (who promptly showed
them to reporters).

Soon the press made the sensational revelation that the owners were
making plans for consolidation into a single twelve-club league. To
conciliate newspaper critics, Brush, Byrne, and Robison invited five
newspapermen to dinner. For the first time the press was "recognized
semi-officially as a power in base ball." Robison, who was chiefly responsible for the peace plans, sounded out the newsmen on the twelve-
club idea. Some were unfavorable, fearing a "throw-down." Robison
asked them: If there were no throw-downs and everything was settled
honorably, did they think it would be a success? They agreed there
was a chance for it to work.

When the League held a regular meeting in New York in mid-
November, Prince and some other Association men were on hand for
further conferences, and so much progress was made that the League
appointed another peace committee. The next big step was to pull in
Von der Ahe, who was the most influential Association figure. League
men Brush, Byrne, and Robison journeyed to St. Louis with an Association delegation including Editor Frank Richter, who had been working
closely with Robison following the press dinner and had endorsed the
plan in *Sporting Life*. Der Boss President was at first skeptical of tying
up with the League, and he was especially worried about Sunday ball,
but when he saw that Boston and Milwaukee were "weak as dishwater"
and that he would have to dig deep into his own pocket to keep the
Association going, he decided to accept consolidation.

The delegates signed a preliminary agreement drawn up by Byrne,
and each was given certain other club owners to call on and convert
to the plan. A grand meeting of both leagues would then be held at
Indianapolis on December 15 to iron out any details and to adopt the
plan officially.

Under the terms of this momentous agreement, four Association
clubs—Baltimore, Washington, St. Louis, and Louisville—were joined
with the eight National League clubs to form a single major league,
the National League and American Association of Professional Base
Ball Clubs. To ensure that some of the clubs would not be dumped
by the wayside later on, they were bound together for ten years in

an "ironclad" agreement. The remaining Association clubs—Boston, Philadelphia, Columbus, Milwaukee, and the new Chicago Club—were bought out for varying amounts totaling about $130,000. All twelve clubs in the new circuit assumed this debt, planning to pay it off over a period of years by contributing 10 per cent of gate receipts to a common league fund. Sunday ball was permitted for those clubs wanting it, and the standard admission was fifty cents, although clubs were given wide leeway in providing twenty-five-cent seats, too. All player contracts were upheld as they presently stood, with each club retaining fifteen men. The rest were to be turned over for distribution throughout the entire circuit. To stimulate fan interest, a split season, such as the Association had tried back in 1884, was adopted for 1892.

The plan was realized without much trouble. Prince and Soden reached agreement in Boston. Wagner was willing to leave Philadelphia and was able to purchase the stock of the Washington Club so that he could stay in baseball. Columbus came to terms after protracted talks, but Von der Ahe neglected to provide for Milwaukee and the new Chicago Club, as he was supposed to, thus raising a problem for the owners at their Indianapolis meeting. Another difficulty arose because of the objections of Rogers to charging fifty cents in Philadelphia. But these problems were soon resolved. A new constitution was drawn up by Byrne and Brush, who arrived a couple of days in advance to prepare it. *Sporting Life* greeted it with appropriate hosannahs for incorporating "all the modern ideas awakened within the recent eventful years and developed at the ever-memorable St. Louis conference; and embodying the broad principles of base ball government for which the best friends of base ball have contended, lo, these many years, and which only the shock of rebellion and the fire of revolution could force into permanent practice." The two leagues then met in separate session. The Association dissolved the partnership, and the five outgoing clubs duly resigned. The four surviving clubs then joined the League in adopting the new constitution.

Robison thought $130,000 was a cheap price for peace, and, with "unhealthy competition" removed, the owners would save close to that on players' salaries in a few years. *Sporting News* welcomed the return of the "sentimental" side of baseball and the pushing of the financial end, so "nauseating" to the fans, into the background. *Spalding's Guide* foresaw the game being run in the future on "true business principles," something never "fully enjoyed before."

The disappearance of the Association was both the end of two years of dreary warfare and the culmination of a colorful ten-year era in professional baseball. The Association, with its quarter ball and Sunday games, had introduced big-league ball to cities that did not have it and contributed immensely to the popularization of the game. Its picturesque, lively people made the League look stodgy by comparison. The strait-laced League had never been wholly pleased with its more uninhibited rival. As *Sporting News* said in 1889:

> From time immemorial [all of eight years!] the League has been inimical to the American Association. It has made its clubs free warren and pounced upon them whenever the situation demanded anything of the sort. It treated the younger body with contempt until forced to recognize it for protectionary measures.

Unfortunately for the Association, it had opened a quarrel with the League when it was least able to see it through. The so-called consolidation which ended it was not a consolidation at all. It was absorption. Although the Association formally dissolved, the League never took that step. The destruction of its once-great rival gave the National League an undisputed monopoly of professional baseball for an entire decade, in which it would have full opportunity to run the game as it saw fit to do.

PART FOUR

MONOPOLY AT ITS APEX

22

MONOPOLY RIDES HIGH

Big League baseball was an undisguised monopoly in the 1890's. To be sure, the National League once before had the field to itself, but that was when it was too weak to exert a full sweep of authority. When two major leagues shared the business, as in the 'eighties, and in the modern era after 1903, the baseball monopoly was not quite so naked. But now all major league clubs belonged to a single circuit, and only by its sufferance did the minor leagues exist. As *Sporting News* commented in 1893, the failure of the Players' League and the absorption of the Association have "enabled the magnates to do about as they please without let or hindrance." A newspaper clipping dated 1894 put it stronger: "There is probably no business—unless it is the gas office—that is conducted more in the Vanderbilt-public-be-damned principle than base ball."

The new set-up had Spalding's imprimatur. In April 1892 he was quoted as saying that he had always wanted just one major league. By moving in this direction baseball once again was reflecting the American scene. This was the era of the trusts, when American business was wiping out competitors and forming giant monopolies. Professors Nevins and Commager have described the remarkable influence which these trusts exerted on the life of the average city-dweller:

> When he sat down to breakfast he ate bacon packed by the beef trust, seasoned his eggs with salt made by the Michigan salt trust, sweetened his coffee with sugar refined by the American Sugar trust, lit his American Tobacco Company cigar with a Diamond Match Company match. Then he rode to work on a bicycle built by the bicycle trust or on a trolley car operating under a monopolistic franchise and running on steel rails made by United States Steel.

They might have added that when he saw major league baseball, it was a production of the National League monopoly. In another important entertainment business the trend was the same. As vaudeville spread, theaters were organized in chains, and a nation-wide system of booking acts developed in the 'eighties. By 1896 a theatrical syndicate or trust was in operation.

The League lost no time in increasing its monopolistic trappings. The players were the first to feel the weight of the new regime. After two long years of war and losses the magnates were faced with the unrelished necessity of setting aside 10 per cent of their gate receipts to pay off the $130,000 debt for buying out the four Association clubs. Competition between warring leagues had pushed player salaries to new highs. Retrenchment was the order of the day.

According to the peace settlement, players who had signed contracts before December 5, 1891 (the date of the preliminary peace conference at St. Louis) would stay with whom they had signed. The rest were thrown into a pool and distributed arbitrarily by a two-man committee, Phelps and Young, wherever it decided they would do the most good. Each club was limited to fifteen men. This plan had the advantages of eliminating bidding for the surplus and helping to equalize playing strength among the clubs. Left-over players were generously allowed to "go where they pleased"—that is, to the minors or out of baseball.

As Nick Young said after the club rosters were set up, "certain prominent players have apparently been relegated to minor leagues," but he could not help it if they had not been chosen. Only 180 players could be signed, and he could do nothing "even if a seeming hardship has apparently been imposed upon some tried and trusty ball players." There were a few disputes among owners over the allotment of players (one manager was accused of pre-dating a contract so that he could claim the player had signed before December 5), but these were eventually settled.

Although Young promised that players would receive promptly "every penny" under the terms of their contracts, the owners soon reneged on this. As far back as the collapse of the Brotherhood the magnates made plain their intention to slash salaries, but they were foiled by the Second Association War. Now that they were back in command, they reiterated this goal. An official of the Baltimore Club was quoted as saying that salaries would be regulated in such a way "that it will be impossible for us to lose," and Soden of Boston predicted cuts of 20 to 30 per cent in 1893.

These prophecies were conservative. The season of 1892 was only half spent when the blow fell. In June the magnates decided to reduce all club rosters to thirteen men. Young estimated that about eighteen players would be thrown out of work, but said he hoped the savings would be enough to pay off the League's debt. The owners also decided to prune salaries right away. Each club could do as it saw fit, but it had the assurance that others would keep hands off any players who were fired for refusing to sign a new contract at reduced pay.

So without ceremony all clubs cut their payrolls 30 to 40 per cent, except Brooklyn and Philadelphia, and these two had already sliced them before the season started. Louisville reduced half the team. Boston reduced everybody, although it was leading the League in the pennant race. In St. Louis the players were called into the office one by one. When Jack Glasscock's turn came he cracked, "Excuse me, . . . I'm going into Von der Ahe's barber shop to get my salary shaved." And he got it—to the amount of $500. Others on the team underwent $400, $350, and $200 reductions.

Tony Mullane of Cincinnati refused to submit to being slashed from $4200 to $3500, and held out the second half of the season. He said he nearly "dropped dead" when Brush told him his contract was not "worth the paper it was written on" and yet had "the nerve" to ask him to sign a new one. He said he asked Brush what protection a player had, and was told, "None." Mullane did not capitulate until the following January, when he signed for only $2100 for 1893. A Philadelphia writer remarked, "The price of coal in Cincinnati is $6 a ton, and Tony has a wife, a baby and a base 'burner in his family."

Tony was not the only holdout. Thomas Lovett, a Brooklyn pitcher, turned down a reduction in his contract at the beginning of the season and stayed out all year, sacrificing $3000. But he too signed for 1893 at a reduction. George Haddock, another Brooklyn pitcher, who had won 34 games the year before, held out for a couple of months before he signed. Charles Buffinton of Baltimore was a third who objected to a mid-year cut. This ten-year veteran refused to report in 1893, and never played big-league ball again.

There were two other cases with a little different slant. Tom Burns, who had a three-year contract at $4500 a year to manage and play for Pittsburgh, was fired after only two months. He fought back through the courts and succeeded in getting a settlement of $1500. In the case of John Pickett, the court ruled against the right of the Baltimore Club to release him. He was dropped in mid-season, although his new contract did not contain the usual clause giving the club the right to release him on ten days' notice. Pickett sued for breach of contract. In its defense the club claimed he was lacking in skill and ability, and asserted that custom gave it the right to let him go on ten days' notice even though the clause was not in the contract. A jury awarded him $1285.72 on the ground that all a player was required to show was the ordinary skill of his profession, and other players had attested to

Pickett's ability. The club appealed, but the judgment was upheld. However, he did not play again, either.

President Jim Hart of Chicago said the salary slashes were "only the natural consequences of baseball history," pointing out that "the same thing is done every day in other lines of business, only no talk is made of it." However, he neglected to add that employees in other lines could get jobs in other companies, whereas the baseball owners, through collusion, had agreed to freeze out players who refused cuts. Nick Young admitted there was criticism, but he thought that from a business standpoint the magnates could hardly be blamed. "We are through with the hurrah business," he said, "and having achieved a share of the glory of the game, we propose now to get a share of the money." The League president went further, predicting additional cuts at the end of the season that would "raise a howl from the players, but it will not avail them anything." He was right.

In October nearly all clubs gave their players ten days' notice that they would be "released" at the end of the playing season. Since the contracts ran to November 1, the players would lose two weeks' pay. But the men were not really free agents, because the clubs again acted in collusion by agreeing not to hire each others' men. As the New York *World* said, these were "releases that did not release." The whole thing was simply an expedient to save on salaries. It also softened up the players for further salary cuts in 1893.

The patent disregard for agreements on the part of the owners was certainly in sharp contrast with their pious insistence on the sanctity of the contracts when the players were breaking them. O. P. Caylor denounced the maneuver as "nothing but a repudiation of contracts ... unjust and uncommercial transactions." The Boston, Cleveland, and Chicago clubs were exceptions to the fake release policy. The first two had to keep their teams intact so they could play each other for the post-season championship, since each club was a split-season winner. Chicago decided to wait and talk salary reduction "in a determined way," as Anson put it, for the next season. Besides, its contracts ran to February 1.

In New York, Shorty Fuller, Mike Tiernan, and Amos Rusie, the great pitcher, had refused to take mid-summer cuts, so Day caught up with them at the end of the season and "released" them as an object lesson to impress on the squad that it "must yield to discipline." All took cuts the next year. The club had a bad year financially and was about three months in arrears on salaries—an average of about $1000 a man. Day told them the best he could do was to give them twenty-five cents on the dollar and promissory notes for the rest. They accepted. The Philadelphia players objected strongly to having two weeks' income lopped off, so Rogers, the owner, made them work out their pay by playing exhibition games after the regular season.

The players were squeezed again at 1893 contract time. By March it was apparent that the owners were clinging close to a $2400 maximum on salaries, and holding total payrolls to around $30,000, as they had planned. The maximum was not established formally, as in the 'eighties, and there were exceptions, but $2400 was the unofficial limit through the 1890's.

An article in the *Yale Law Journal,* written by Peter S. Craig, contains a chart giving eloquent testimony to what was happening to player salaries in these changing times. It shows what the Philadelphia Philly players received in 1889, when the reserve clause held sway; how their salaries jumped by 1892, as a result of two years of free competition between warring leagues; and how they declined sharply when the owners once more held the whip hand in 1893:

Player	1889	1892	1893
Clements	$2450	$3000	$1800
Delehanty	1750	2100	1800
Hallman	1400	3500	1800
Thompson	2500	3000	1800
Allen	—	3000	1800
Hamilton	—	3400	1800
Cross	—	3250	1800
Keefe	—	3500	1800
Weyhing	—	3250	1800

The owners justified their wholesale salary cuts by pointing to the poor season and heavy expenses. They revived the hackneyed arguments of former years—that the players were now relegated to their "proper sphere," and that, compared with what they might earn otherwise, outside the profession, they were still being generously remunerated. *Sporting News* took issue, asking why ball players should not receive as much as possible, the same as actors. Their careers were short, and they could be injured at any time. Talking about what players could earn outside was "nonsensical," Spink's paper argued. "What would anyone earn outside his line? Sports writers, for instance?"

Salary cuts were no doubt in order. Even John Ward admitted as much. *Sporting News* estimated that, everything considered, eleven of the twelve clubs were in the red at the end of 1892. And it is true that the owners did not succeed in clearing out the debt. Despite raising the percentage of club contributions from 10 to 12½ and then 16, the treasury was short and promissory notes had to be given covering the balance.* Even so, the salary cuts seem unreasonable. Attendance figures for these early years are sketchy and unreliable, but on the basis of those estimates available, it appears that attendance during the season was good, although it was not one of baseball's best years. *Spalding's Guide* showed total League attendance of 1,097,049 for the first lap of the split season and a falling off to 715,190 during the second half. There was no question expenses were high, because of salaries and the Association War debt. But the magnates were overlooking the fact that they themselves had bid up salaries, and that, while the players certainly shared responsibility for the Brotherhood year, the Second Association War was an owners' quarrel, the costs of which they were now passing on to the players. *Sporting News* claimed the owners were giving out exaggerated figures of losses and were blaming the players for their own shortcomings.

There was little the players could do except take their cuts. Unionism had died among them as the result of the Brotherhood defeat. Now there was nothing for it but to take what was offered, or else, as Jim Hart said, "Retire from the business." The players' weakened bargaining power is demonstrated by a letter from the Brooklyn manager, the same John Ward who led the players' revolt, to Bill Joyce, one of his players, who had wired requesting $200 advance money. Ward's reply, while composed in a humorous vein, still brings out the change in the players' position:

> Either you are joking, William, or you are away behind the times. Haven't you heard yet of the consolidation of the League and Association into one big league[?] And, if so, don't you understand that the days of advance money are past? Why, my innocent William, hereafter it is the players who are to pay advance money to the magnates. ... Your inning is over, my boy. Wake up. ... Get a move on you, William.

Ad Gumbert was one player who resisted. He held out against a cut from $2700 to $1800 imposed by Chicago. In June 1893, he was traded to Pittsburgh, where he received $2400. However, he sued his former club for the salary differential and the loss entailed while he was unemployed. The case was in litigation until 1898, when the court decided against him. Another was the same Bill Joyce whom Ward had kidded. He was traded from Brooklyn to Washington, but his new club offered him only $1800, whereas he had been paid $2800 before. He held out all of 1893, but gave in and played for the Nationals in 1894.

Otherwise, labor relations fell into the old pattern. The reserve

---

* Newspaper estimates of the balance varied from $10,000 to $20,000.

clause continued, except that the former proviso that men could not be reserved at a lower salary was ignored. In 1892 players still had the choice of the seven-month or twelve-month contract, with some slight variations introduced by John I. Rogers. If they wanted to, they could take all their pay on a seven-month basis. Under the twelve-month agreement, they could either be paid in equal installments throughout the year or set aside whatever amount they wanted during the winter months. No club was to release a man while it was in arrears on his salary, and clubs promised not to control the player's actions during the off season "except as regards his physical condition and moral habits"!

There was still no obligation to pay men when they were ill or injured on the field. However, clubs sometimes did. Cleveland was praised for being "humane"—having "forgiven" men who fell sick and paid them money they did not earn. Baltimore did the same. When John McGraw returned after being out with typhoid, Manager Hanlon gave him a check for $1200 back pay, and McGraw was very grateful. Electric treatments, massage, and gentle exercise in warm weather were the remedies for sore arms. President Brush believed in hot water for sprains and bruises, and ordered a stove put in the clubhouse so water could be heated. Brooklyn even had a club physician.

The strength of the twelve-club monolith and its determination to monopolize control of baseball was just as clearly demonstrated toward outside competition as it was toward the players. On the one occasion during the decade when a competitor threatened, the League ruthlessly squelched it before it left the planning stage. In September 1894 a new American Association was in the offing. It planned to form an eight-club circuit, including many cities where the League was established, play twenty-five-cent ball, and set up a schedule that would not conflict with League games. Like the old Unions, the new organization intended to respect contracts but not the reserve clause. In supreme violation of the amenities, the Association disdained using the Spalding baseball in favor of adopting the Kiffe, a cheaper product, which was still popular among sandlot players well into this century. W. H. Becannon, who was backing the new circuit's New York entry, summarized its philosophy:

> There is room for two organizations.... We are convinced ... that 25-cent ball will find plenty of patrons in all the chief cities. It is not our design to fight anybody. We only want our share of patronage, and we think we can get it.

Sporting News was sympathetic. The New York *Clipper* thought the newcomer's aims worthy, and volunteered that contrary to what the

League monopoly might think, it did not "own the earth." *Sporting Life* was not only for it; its editor, Frank Richter, was deeply involved in the scheme.

When League owners heard of it, they had the usual disparaging comments, the most bellicose being John T. Brush:

> If these Association people think they can get protection from us and at the same time invade our territory they are mistaken. No one denies them the right to organize but the moment they infringe on our rights (and they will) there will be war. If any one tries to put another club in Cincinnati I will fight it dollar for dollar.

The League also threatened to blacklist "for all time to come" any players who deserted.

The chief difficulty was caused by the fact that three National Leaguers were identified with the organization of the new circuit. Billie Barnie and Al Buckenberger, who had managed Louisville and Pittsburgh, respectively, in 1894, and Fred Pfeffer, who had played second base for Louisville, were active participants in organizing the new league that fall. "Blue-eyed Billie, the bald-headed Eagle of the Chesapeake," as *Sporting News* dubbed him, also owned stock in two League clubs.

As soon as the League got wind of what they were doing, it moved quickly and inexorably against the three would-be magnates. At its November meeting it issued another one of its public "manifestos," which made clear its assumed role of self-appointed guardian of baseball, past, present, and future. It reiterated the dogma of territorial rights and the sanctity of the reserve clause. It condemned the "treachery" of men who, by disloyalty to the organization from which they had earned a good living over the years, would destroy "the splendid fabric of our national game." Then, proclaiming that there was no room for an "anarchistic element," it announced that the three were "suspended" and "ineligible to be employed" until they proved their innocence to the satisfaction of the League. They were given until December 31 to recant. To *Sporting Life*, the manifesto was a "tremendous bluff" that proved the League was "arrogantly determined to maintain its monopoly and crush out opposition by any means, yet [was] in mortal dread of business opposition." *Sporting News*, however, thought the League had a right to expect its employees to be loyal.

All three accused made public response. Barnie's line was that he had not dabbled in the new Association until after his League contract for the season had expired, and so he had not been disloyal to any League club, though he suggested a committee to which he would be willing to present his case. Buckenberger was also willing to appear before the League Board, if requested in "the proper manner." Both were carefully leaving a way open to get back in good standing if their frail new project did not survive. Pfeffer was much more self-assertive, declaring that the League magnates had no more right to question his intentions and business than he did theirs. He saw a chance to make money, he said, and why should the League refuse him the opportunity?

Buckenberger surrendered first, signing an affidavit, which Young had requested of all three, denying that he had furthered the interests of the proposed Association while employed by the League. He had his eye on a franchise in the Eastern League, a National Agreement minor league, and managed to get a clean bill of health just in time to attend the Eastern's deliberations. Although he did not gain the minor league spot he was after, he was hired to manage St. Louis in 1895.

As the deadline approached, Barnie and Pfeffer were invited to appear before the League Board. Barnie went, but Pfeffer sent a letter instead, explaining that when he was injured toward the end of the season, he secured his release from Louisville by forfeiting the balance of his salary, and it was only then that he decided to connect with the Association. He knew of no law, he said, which restrained a man from bettering his position, and the charge that he tried to get other players to go with him was false. This alibi did not convince the League, and it turned him down because his letter was "extremely indefinite and unsatisfactory."

Barnie was questioned by Soden, Byrne, and Young, and a five- or six-thousand word stenographic report of the hearing was released to the press. The League committee handed Barnie a loyalty oath to sign, which included a promise of future allegiance. Although Barnie indignantly refused, in the end the Board reluctantly reinstated him for lack of positive evidence, but served notice that he had declined to "put himself on record as owing allegiance," and warned all parties to the National Agreement to "take due notice ... and govern themselves accordingly." Barnie served as manager of Scranton in the Eastern League for 1895, and by 1897 he was back in the big league as manager of Brooklyn.

In the meantime, the abortive effort to form a new Association was to all intents and purposes defeated. Pfeffer signed as baseball coach at Princeton University but let it be known that he would rather play big-league ball. Fans went to his aid. No fewer than 10,000 of them signed a petition asking for his reinstatement and promising to boycott League parks if he did not get it. Louisville's president defied the League and mailed the controversial second baseman a contract.

These pressures put the League in a quandary. The December 31 deadline was already past, but after long deliberation it decided to let him off with a $500 fine, provided he play with Louisville and sign the loyalty pledge. He agreed, and within an hour his friends raised the money for his fine. The League also adopted a resolution that in the future any club official, manager, or player suspended for complicity in organizing a rival league would be barred "forever."

With the players once more brought to heel and no worries about competition from outside, prospects looked bright indeed for the twelve-club National League, as it was now commonly called, the Association part of its title being long since dropped by the press. The 1893 season was so successful that the League not only paid off the last of the Association debt but accumulated a $25,000 surplus to boot. The season of 1894 showed profits not known since 1889. All but one of the clubs finished in the black. One or two of the successful eleven came out even; the rest made profits of from $5000 to $40,000, with New York and Baltimore leading the list. The next season was the apex of the consolidated league's prosperity. These gains were registered despite the fact that the country was in the grip of a depression— indication that it takes a while for hard times to catch up with commercialized amusements. In fact, they may even benefit for a time because they provide an outlet and distraction for unemployed city workers.

So by the middle of the decade the new regime was solidly entrenched with bright prospects for the future. However, beneath the surface all was not well, and soon the expanded League was to run into new and more serious dangers.

23

THE GAME ON THE FIELD IN THE 'NINETIES

DETERMINING the beginning of modern baseball is as difficult as deciding when modern history began; it all depends on what is meant by modern. One might well choose 1920, the inauguration of the so-called "Ruthian Era," when Babe Ruth's towering drives gave the home run new popularity and revolutionized the style of play. But if one is judging by the rules, then the modern era dates from the 1890's. The last major rules changes of that decade ended half a century of experimentation and delineated the basic structure of the game on the field as it has existed down to the present day.

The long jockeying between batter and pitcher ended in 1893 when the pitcher was moved back to the present 60-foot 6-inch pitching distance and required to work from a 12-by-4-inch rubber slab. In 1899 the balk rule as we know it was established. Pitchers were now required to complete the throw, whether they were trying to pick a runner off first base or delivering the pitch. Until 1901, skillful batters like John McGraw could stand at the plate and foul off pitch after pitch. This was a means of wearing down the pitcher until he gave them a pitch they liked or until they had wangled a base on balls. Such tactics delayed games interminably, so in 1901 the first two fouls were called strikes. In the same year catchers were required to remain close up under the bat continuously.

In 1893 the infield fly rule was adopted, requiring that the batter was automatically out on a pop fly to the infield in fair territory when there were fewer than two out and runners on first and second base (or with the bases full). Before that, infielders could convert a pop fly into a double play by trickery. No matter what the runners did, a double play could be made. If they clung to the bases, the infielder could drop the ball intentionally, forcing them off their bases to make room for the batter, in which case they could be put out. If they took a chance and ran, the fielder could make a simple catch and double them off base.

The rule still was not foolproof. Teams got around it by having outfielders come in fast and handle the pop fly. So later the wording was changed, requiring the umpire to declare the batter automatically out if in his judgment the pop fly in such a situation could be handled by an infielder, even though an outfielder might actually make the play. It might be pointed out here that, contrary to what many fans think, the infield fly rule does not apply with a runner on first only, because a double play on such a hit is not possible if the batter runs it out, as he should. Nor is a pop fly bunt considered an infield fly. The whole idea is to prevent the defense from making a double play by subterfuge, at a time when the offense is helpless to prevent it, rather than by skill and speed.

To ensure exact measurement, big league clubs were required to have an "engineer" lay out the actual diamond according to geometrical principles, but this did not prevent magnates from rearranging the distance to or height of their outfield fence so as to give an advantage to certain hitters on their teams. Modern clubs have often done this. A notorious example was "Greenberg Gardens," the short left field fence erected by Pittsburgh in the late 1940's to give its right-hand hitting slugger, Hank Greenberg, an advantage in hitting home runs. But the stunt was nothing new. Back in 1895 Charles Comiskey rearranged the position of the diamond so that the right field fence would be located a short distance beyond first base, to give the seven left-handed hitters in his St. Paul line-up an inviting target.

In 1900 a new-style home plate was introduced. Instead of the old square one, with a corner facing the pitcher, the new type had five sides so that the pitcher had a straight line to aim at. This also made it easier for the umpire to judge balls and strikes.

Another innovation of the 'nineties was the idea of painting the center field fence black to help batters by giving them a dark background against which to hit. This experiment was tried by Cincinnati in 1895, after Bug Holliday complained that he could not see the pitched ball against the big white advertising sign covering the outfield fence.

The new pitching distance was hard on the pitchers until they learned to adjust their sights to it. The new rule may not have been entirely responsible, but batting averages rose sharply after it was passed, and it was not until near the end of the decade that pitchers showed signs of regaining mastery. The 'nineties produced a new group of hard hitters, including an unusual number who hit .400 for the season. No other decade boasts so many of them, except for the

1880's, but eleven of thirteen made in that decade occurred in 1887, the abnormal year when a base on balls counted as a hit and Tip O'Neill made his fantastic .492 average. Ten .400 averages were made in the 'nineties by seven men. Topping the list was Jesse Burkett of Cleveland, who reached the heights three times, a feat accomplished by only two other men in baseball history, Ty Cobb and Rogers Hornsby. The highest batting average ever made was Hugh Duffy's phenomenal .438 of 1894 (discounting, of course, Tip O'Neill's inflated 1887 mark). Willie Keeler, whose famous formula, "Keep your eye clear and hit 'em where they ain't," became a part of baseball lore, hit .432 in 1897, and Ed Delehanty, Philadelphia's powerful hitter, broke the .400 barrier twice during the decade.

Clark Griffith, just then coming into his own as a first-rate pitcher, told how the hurlers had to readjust to the new rule, pointing out that, more than ever before, they needed to have endurance. Griffith, a small man himself, advised that size did not matter, and emphasized good control and a "nervy heart" among the attributes a pitcher should have. He was one who practiced what he preached. He was not able to overpower the batters, so he relied on craft and artistry to fool them, and won for himself the nickname "the Old Fox."

Tim Keefe, now at the end of his major league career, was another who had pitching advice for youngsters which still holds good. He told them to learn control first and worry about speed and curves later. He explained how every pitch should be delivered with the same motion so as not to tip off the batter to what was coming. Keefe could back up what he had to say with a brilliant pitching record from 1880 to 1893, winning the tremendous total of 345 games during those years. His fine record included 19 straight victories in 1888, a mark unequaled until Rube Marquard, the Giant left-hander, matched it in 1912.

In modern times pitches are classified under a relatively few head-ings—fast ball, curve ball, change of pace ("change-up"), screwball (a curve which breaks in the opposite direction from a normal curve), and, in more recent years, slider, sometimes called a nickel curve. But in the 'nineties, pitchers supposedly had a bewildering assortment of deliveries—incurve, outcurve, reversing curve, drop, inshoot, jump ball, rising ball, downshoot, and a "disguised change of pace" which must be "a surprise party to the batter."

The custom of having the catcher signal what pitch to throw became routine in the 'nineties, and certain catchers teamed up with certain pitchers to form famous "batteries"—such as Cy Young and Lou Criger, and Ted Breitenstein and Heinie Peitz (known as the Pretzel Battery). Pitchers were learning to pace themselves, "pitching for catches," as it was then called—that is, trying to get the batters to hit to fielders, instead of attempting to retire them all on strike-outs.

That everlasting subject of controversy, the "beanball" or "duster," was even then an important part of the pitcher's repertoire. Jouett Meekin, Giant pitcher, told the *World* how to shake the batter's confidence in a tight spot by throwing the first two pitches "within an inch of his head or body," and then, when he stepped back, fooling him with a curve on the outside. "Driving the batsman away from the plate," he said, "is an essential part of baseball."

By the 'nineties many famous pitchers like Jim Galvin, Tim Keefe, Kid Baldwin, John Clarkson, Tony Mullane, and Hoss Radbourne were reaching the end of their big-league careers. Of the new names crowding them off the sporting page, several are worth mentioning. A young right-hander, Kid Nichols, beginning in 1891, won 30 or more games a season seven times, and was the bellwether of the five-time Boston pennant-winners during the decade. It was nothing for him to pitch over 400 innings a season, whereas even 300 is practically unheard of for present-day pitchers. Although he was not a big man, Nichols depended on sheer speed and good control. According to Ned Hanlon, Nichols, unlike most fast ball pitchers, never developed a slow ball to break up the batter's timing. However, he was an overhand pitcher, which is generally considered easier on the arm, but even at that he must have had a very smooth delivery and a very durable arm to win over 300 ball games while depending exclusively on speed.

Another standout was Cy Young, a big Ohio farm boy, whose "cyclone" pitching (as fast-ball pitching used to be called) set the all-time record by far, for number of games won, a staggering total of 511. Young was a gentleman, a man of exemplary habits, who spent the off-season back on the farm instead of loafing in the city. Amos Rusie was another big fast-baller who starred with the Giants. One of the best left-handers was Ted Breitenstein, who had the disadvantage of being mostly with the lowly Browns, perennial eleventh-place finishers. Around the turn of the century box scores listed names like Rube Waddell and Eddie Plank, pitchers whose great years were still ahead of them. On July 18, 1900, the New York *Sun* had an interesting news item:

> Manager Davis of the New York exercised his authority in the fifth inning when, with the score tied, he yanked Pitcher Doheny out of the box and substituted an untried semi-professional named Mathewson.

The story went on to say that "young Mathewson possessed great speed and plenty of confidence in himself, but he could not control his curves." This report, which marked Christy Mathewson's big league debut, may have been true that particular day, but Mathewson evidently corrected the fault, because he became one of the most famous pitchers in the early twentieth century, and his name, along with that of John McGraw, was indelibly associated with the New York Giants.

Pitchers worked much more often in those days than they do now, so it was possible for the good ones to win 25, 30, or more games a season, whereas 20 victories is considered outstanding for a modern. Because of this, some argue that the old-timers were more durable and had more stamina.

Such a claim is questionable. Comparisons are difficult because conditions were so different then. Pitchers of the earlier era were working with a less lively ball. A new ball was seldom brought into the game. An old, scuffed-up ball with the cover loosened ever so slightly is easier to grip and put "stuff" on, and consequently harder to hit for distance. Besides, most hitters did not hold the bat on the end and "swing for the fences." They "choked up" and tried simply to meet the ball and drive it safely past the fielders, so home runs were very rare. Pitchers could afford to put the ball over the plate without the constant dread of having even the weakest batters knock it out of the park, as is the case today. To the contrary, they could ease the strain on their arms by letting up a little against the poor hitters on the other team.

Today, pitchers not only have to put a lot on every pitch, they must pitch very carefully to each man, because one slip can cost them the game. They cannot make a pitch "too good," but must constantly aim at the corners of the plate. Also the strike zone is smaller now. As a result many more pitches miss the plate, more bases on balls are issued, and therefore the modern pitcher throws much more often in a game and takes much more out of his arm. He needs more rest between games, and, because he does not pitch as often, he has less chance of winning than the old-timers.

In former days a team might have only four or five pitchers, so they worked more often and were expected to finish a game they started. The larger number of pitching turns gave them greater opportunity to pile up victories. Modern managerial philosophy is different. Most clubs now carry nine or ten pitchers, including "relief" pitchers, who are expert in finishing up games. Therefore a modern manager like Casey Stengel can see no virtue in having the starting pitcher finish the game if he is doing poorly or the situation calls for using a pinch-hitter for him. Why let him stay in the game when there are others who can take over?

Some modern critics claim that pitchers nowadays are more susceptible to sore arms. If true, it is because pitching under modern conditions probably takes more out of a pitcher's arm than in the past. Besides, the old-timer generally worked only in the warm sunshine and could follow a regular routine of life, whereas the modern pitcher must perform both on warm days and cool nights, and has his eating and sleeping habits constantly upset. It should also be remembered that old-timers had sore arms, too. But we do not hear about them. Those we know about and remember are the great ones. No, it just does not seem to make sense to say that the modern player, who has benefited from our greater knowledge of diet, conditioning, and improved coaching methods, has less stamina than the stars of the past.

In 1958 there was considerable debate over a suggestion that substitutes be used more than once in a single game, and some sports writers, in showing the proposal was not new, mentioned a similar one put forth about thirty years before, providing for a tenth man, who would always bat in place of the pitcher. The suggestion was actually made as early as the 1890's. The argument given in 1892 was that batting in the latter part of the game tired the pitcher and made him an easy out. On the other hand, if he did happen to hit for extra bases, he was "fit for the ambulance" from running out his hit.

Aside from hard hitting, the decade was memorable for the high level of perfection achieved in co-ordinating the attack. The Bostons and the Baltimore Orioles developed the hit-and-run play into a fine art. Billy Nash, Hugh Duffy, and Tom McCarthy were Boston's hit-and-run experts. The Orioles had an especially deadly combination for this play, with McGraw, a first-rate hitter and fast runner, leading off, followed by Willie Keeler, possibly the greatest all-time "place-hitter." They also developed what became known as the "Baltimore chop," a kind of swinging bunt in which the batter swung down on the pitch, topping the ball and beating the throw to first base.

People continued the same arguments over batting which were familiar in the 'eighties. Henry Chadwick was still complaining about sluggers who waited for one kind of pitch and tried to "knock it out of sight." He had to admit that the majority of the crowd enjoyed the "splurgy long hit ball which yields a home run," but claimed it was only the "intelligent minority" who knew enough to appreciate scientific hitting. Chadwick and others also wanted more sacrifice hitting, which in those days did not mean a hitter advancing a man with a bunt at the cost of being put out himself; that was considered "veritable stupidity." When they said "sacrifice" they meant that the batter should try to hit safely but, in doing so, hit the ball in such a way that even if he were put out the runner would advance.

Bunting was still not a fully accepted tactic. Some still wanted it abolished because it was a "baby play" requiring no skill. Sam Crane, a well-known sports writer, ridiculed it, saying, "Who wants to see big Roger Connor—who . . . can hit the ball a mile . . . make a puny, little feminine bunt?" But the Orioles, reputedly the best of all clubs in bunting, helped make the art stick as a part of baseball. In fact, the other clubs paid more and more attention to it. For example, Buck Ewing, as manager of the Reds, gave his boys morning bunting practice.

George Davis, Giant shortstop who later managed the club for a while, gave some good pointers on how to bat in 1894. He recommended a free and easy swing, standing up at the plate as though you meant business, and striding forward to meet the pitch. He said that batting required plenty of nerve. One could not afford to be afraid, and must avoid stepping away from the pitch ("stepping in the bucket," as it is now called, reminiscent of the days before water coolers when teams simply had a bucket of water on the bench).

Davis also anticipated the modern practice of taking motion pictures of a batter's stance and swing so he can study them and detect flaws: he suggested standing in front of a big mirror to study one's swing. And speaking of water buckets, Comiskey was praised for the "sensible" move of having a drinking pail containing oatmeal water, "cool but not iced," with lemon juice in it, for his men. The lemon was to quench the thirst and the oatmeal supposedly furnished nutriment.

Another aid to hitting was the growing custom of having modern batting practice—letting the hitters swing against a practice pitcher instead of just knocking out fungoes, as they had been doing. George Wright reputedly inaugurated this innovation years before, but it was adopted only slowly.

In the 'nineties baseball games were beginning to look much more like the highly skilled performances of today. Newspapers carried how-to articles by various players, like the one by Davis, which show that the fine points of playing ball were well understood. Many of the tips they offered about batting, base-running, and playing the different positions are still sound advice today.

Catchers could no longer be content merely to receive the pitch and return it; they were expected to steady the pitcher and give him the benefit of their experience and knowledge of the batter's weakness. Most of them used the finger signs still in vogue, but Parke Wilson of the Giants said he gave the signs by rapidly winking his eyes or looking intently in one direction. He also cautioned that catchers must always take the pitch in front of them instead of on the side, so if they missed it they could still block it, and that they should call for a pitch-out if they thought the runner was going to try to steal. But Wilson did not advise youngsters to become catchers, because the job was too dangerous. In support of this, *Sporting News* had a story about Silver Flint in a train wreck. A physician attending the injured, seeing his gnarled fingers, started to put splints on them, until Flint told him he was not hurt; his fingers got that way from catching for the White Sox!

Connie Mack was one of the wiliest catchers and was not above tipping the bat as the batter swung. Another trick Mack used was taking off his mask pretending to fix it, when a batter had two strikes on him, and then having the pitcher deliver a sneak pitch while the batter was off guard.

The old-timers knew a lot about base-running, too, and the art was becoming increasingly admired. As one commentator said, "Any soft-brained heavy weight" could hit a home run, but skill on the bases required shrewdness and intelligence. The leading base-stealer was Billy Hamilton. Another who was an expert in this art was John M. Ward, who led the League three times. He knew much about base-stealing and was articulate enough to tell what he knew. Ward stressed getting a quick start and sliding away from the baseman's tag. He also gave tips on when and when not to try stealing. Another fine point he made was not to leap for first base on the last step in running out a hit, because it lost time and made the decision easier for the umpire.

Like the pitching records made in those days, Hamilton's amazing stolen base totals cannot be fairly compared with those of later stars because they were made under different conditions. Catchers were not consistently playing up under the bat until after 1900, and pitchers probably were not as highly skilled at holding the base-runners close to the bases. As Fred Pfeffer pointed out, when runners did come up against a good throwing catcher and a pitcher who held them close, their chances of stealing were greatly reduced.

Furthermore, there was more reason to try to steal in those days of low-score games, when one run meant a great deal and by stealing a base a man could put himself in position to score it. Now, with a lively ball, plenty of home runs, and big scores, a single run does not mean so much. Modern teams generally try to score runs in clusters. They know that under present conditions the possibility that the batter will drive home men on base with a long hit or home run is so great that it is not worth the risk of having the runner put out trying to steal, when he has such a good chance of scoring anyway.

Team play reached new heights of refinement in the 'nineties. *Sporting News* observed in 1895 that a faster, hustling style of play

was superseding the "slow, steady, matter-of-fact" methods of old.
McGraw, the Orioles' third baseman, was credited with speeding up
the defense with his fast handling and throwing of the ball. Jimmy
Collins, Boston third baseman, still considered by some to be the greatest, was another who was exceedingly fast, especially coming in on
bunts. He still holds the all-time record for third basemen of 601 total
chances accepted, made in 1899.

The champion Boston Club was known to take advantage of every
opportunity, and, besides being adept with the hit-and-run play, excelled in working the double steal with men on first and third. The
runner on first started for second and when the catcher threw down to
get him, the man on third broke for the plate and usually scored.

Another play requiring great skill and teamwork was the cut-off
play, said to be introduced by Brooklyn in the mid-'nineties. On this
play an outfielder's throw home, to catch a runner trying to score, is
intercepted by an infielder. The batter, thinking the throw is going all
the way to the plate, tries to reach second but is thrown out by the
cut-off man.

Squads were getting larger in the 'nineties. Clubs no longer depended
on one or two pitchers. They usually had an extra catcher and one or
two substitute fielders. The so-called platooning system, made famous
by Casey Stengel with the Yankees in the 1950's, was an old story in
the 'nineties. One of the things Cap Anson liked about his team was
the ability of several of his men to play more than one position. Having
these interchangeable parts was good insurance against injuries. Baltimore manager Ned Hanlon was another who recognized the importance of having a "strong bench."

It will be interesting to modern fans and baseball men, who are so
concerned with the problem of speeding up games, to know that there
were complaints in the old days, too, about long, drawn-out contests.
Players walked on and off the field, batters stalled by pausing to tie
their shoelaces, pitchers took a long time to warm up, and catchers
slowly put on their equipment. All this, said a sports writer, caused
games to take over two hours, whereas "a good, smart nine-inning
game ought to be played in about ninety minutes"! (A "modern"
game is "fast" if it is finished in two-and-one-half hours.)

No drastic changes were introduced in equipment. By 1895 only
catchers and first basemen were unrestricted in the size or weight of
their gloves. All other fielders were limited to 10 ounces and a 14-inch
circumference. Before that, some infielders used catchers' mitts! And
some were still arguing that no one except the catcher should be permitted to wear any gloves at all. Uniforms were not as brightly colored
as in the 'eighties—such as the "clown costumes" of 1882, when players

wore suits colored according to position (catchers—scarlet, pitchers—light blue, etc.) and each team was distinguished from the others by the color of its stockings. Owners tried to save money on laundry bills, and there were criticisms that road suits were all drab and monotonous, and teams looked dirty and sloppy. When numbers were put on the back of uniforms in the 1930's so fans could identify the players it was considered a radical measure by many people, but Jim Hart, Chicago owner, had advocated doing this as far back as 1894.

Prindle's twenty-five-cent Base Ball Curver was still heavily advertised and buyers were warned to beware of "worthless imitations"! One new device of more permanent value was the mechanical pitcher introduced in the 'nineties by Professor Charles H. Hinton of Princeton, who hoped it would reduce the number of sore-armed pitchers. His contrivance fired a ball to the plate through a tube by exploding a cartridge. One of his models had to be held like a gun and shot off by a player. Another was set up on its own carriage, like a cannon.

Remembering the pennant winners of the 1890's is simple: Omitting the Brotherhood year, Boston and Baltimore won them all, except for 1899, which was taken by Brooklyn—and even that was accomplished under Baltimore's former winning manager, Ned Hanlon, with several old Oriole players. The onetime great Chicago White Sox and St. Louis Browns fell on evil days in the 'nineties, and, as the saying went then, they "weren't in it." The White Sox never recovered their winning form of the 'eighties, although Anson frantically scoured the country and tried out practically anybody who had a baseball mitt. In St. Louis Von der Ahe's wheel of fortune turned, and the Browns went from bad to worse with him.

Boston's five flags in the 'nineties gave her the lead in number of championships—eight—during the nineteenth-century history of the National League. Chicago was second with six, and Baltimore third with three. Providence, Brooklyn, and New York picked up two apiece, and Detroit won once, in 1887, with the help of the Big Four. Of the twenty-two cities which were represented in the League at one time or another up to 1900, only two had clubs in the field every single year, Boston and Chicago, and of the lot, only seven won pennants. Of those cities which did win, three finished first seventeen times out of the twenty-four pennant races. Thus the reserve clause and the system of territorial rights established, we are told, to "preserve and stimulate competition for the League pennants," evidently did not succeed in doing so in the nineteenth century, and in the twentieth, the imbalance between winning clubs and perennial tail-enders was to prove even greater.

Boston's string of victories began in 1891. Soden was fortunate in getting Frank Selee to manage his club during the Brotherhood year. Selee, who remained at the helm throughout the decade, was regarded as one of the "brainiest, cleverest and best" leaders in the business. He was an excellent judge of talent and knew where to station the men to best advantage. He came to Boston with wide managerial experience in the minor leagues. Under his management Boston won three straight, 1891 through 1893, fell off the pace the next three years, and then came back in 1897 and 1898 to win two more. The cry "break up the Yankees!" heard so often in the 1950's had its parallel in the 1890's, directed against Boston.

Besides its ace pitcher, Kid Nichols, Boston had Herman Long at short stop. Long was one of the real stars of baseball, a natural player who covered a tremendous amount of ground, cutting off hits with what seemed to be "the greatest ease." He was also a good hitter and a fine base runner. The Boston outfield boasted two men who made the Hall of Fame—Hugh Duffy of the .438 batting average, and Tom McCarthy, who was a fleet baserunner and an outstanding fielder. He set a record of fifty-three assists in 1893. Bobby Lowe, Boston's third outfielder for a while, will always be remembered, along with Ed Delehanty, for hitting four home runs in a single game. Several others have since accomplished the feat, but Lowe and Delehanty stand out as something special, since they hit theirs in the era of the dead ball, and it took many years with the lively ball for someone to duplicate their sensational performance.

Boston's catcher was Charles Bennett, one of the outstanding receivers of the time, whose career was cut short when he was run over by a train and had to have both legs amputated. As time passed, Manager Selee "added some new cogs to his machine," as baseball writers would say, and shifted some old ones. Bobby Lowe was moved to second base, and Fred Tenney, a former catcher-outfielder, was converted into a first baseman. Tenney was an excellent fielder—what ball players would call a "Fancy Dan" around first base—and a pretty fair hitter. The legendary Jimmy Collins was brought in to cover third base. He, too, is in the Hall of Fame. With Dutch Long remaining at shortstop, the Boston infield of Tenney, Lowe, Long, and Collins was probably the best of any in the nineteenth century.

In Baltimore, Ned Hanlon, the "Napoleon of base ball managers," started getting rid of the "old lushers"—the heavy drinkers and bad actors—and replacing them with young players like John J. McGraw and Henry Reitz, who played second base. McGraw was described as a "jewel," who reminded one of "a bantam full of fire and determination." Hughie Jennings played an excellent shortstop, but at first he was not much of a hitter. The story is that he learned to overcome his habit of stepping away from the pitch by standing with his back to a wall so that he could not pull away, and having McGraw throw close to him until he overcame the fault.

The Orioles' captain and catcher was Wilbert Robinson, who still holds the record of seven hits in seven times at bat in a nine-inning game. He was the same jovial "Uncle Robbie" who later managed the Brooklyn Dodgers, the original "Daffiness Boys" of the 1920's. By then he had put on a tremendous amount of weight, and it was difficult to believe that he was once a famous catcher and hard hitter.

One of the best Oriole players and one of the most interesting was little Willie Keeler. He was only about five feet four inches tall but was one of the best proofs that baseball skill does not depend on size. Despite his stature Keeler was one of the great hitters of the era. He won two batting championships, and his record for hitting safely in forty-four consecutive games stood for many years. Keeler substituted science for power. He used a short bat and was possibly the most skillful of all players at placing his hits just out of the reach of fielders. As ball players say, he could drive the ball into a peach basket if one were put in the infield. He was also a first-class outfielder, and many stories have come down telling of how he climbed fences and stuck his hand through barbed wire to make sensational catches.

The Orioles had no standout pitcher, but Sadie McMahon was the best of the lot. The team won three straight pennants, 1894 through 1896, by skillful teamwork and strategy, hard hitting, speed, and extremely aggressive play.

The Orioles are one of the legendary teams of baseball, whereas the Boston Club of the 1890's has received comparatively little recognition, although they won five pennants against the Orioles' three. The Orioles supposedly invented inside baseball, including the hit-and-run play, and were reputed to be so rugged and tough that they stuck in the game despite injuries, merely rubbing broken fingers in the dirt and continuing to play. Unquestionably, the Orioles were a fine ball club, but they have been overrated. As already pointed out, they did not invent all the new plays, and the record shows that they were not as durable as we have been told. McGraw, for example, was sidelined once for a mere attack of tonsillitis, and Robbie was out for four weeks because of a sprained ankle—hardly consistent with the big reputation for endurance.

Six of the Orioles later became managers—McGraw, Robinson, and Jennings famous ones. McGraw, who managed the Giants for over thirty years and won ten pennants, was possibly the greatest manager in baseball history. These men had ample opportunity to enlarge upon the exploits of their playing days to receptive sports writers, and McGraw had a ghost-written book which also strengthened the legend. Robbie at least was candid enough to admit that the 1927 Yankees, which many think the greatest ball club ever put together, would have "knocked the Orioles' brains out." This sacrilege brought indignant outcries from his former teammates, but there is little doubt that he was correct.

The pennant-winning clubs, of course, did not sport all the new good players. As old-timers like George Gore, Harry Stovey, Jim O'Rourke, Tim Keefe, John Clarkson, King Kelly, Pete Browning, Buck Ewing, and Jim Galvin began to fade, new stars took their places—the inevitable cycle of baseball. Anson came up with a good young shortstop, Wild Bill Dahlen. Ed Delehanty and Sam Thompson, hard-hitting Philly outfielders, were two of the most feared batters in the 'nineties. In 1896 a young infielder, reported to be "rattling good," began with Philadelphia. After a few games, *Sporting News* said he was living up to his reputation as a hitter and "should prove a regular terror." His name was Napoleon Lajoie, and he became one of the outstanding hitters of baseball and one of its most graceful second basemen.

Picking all-time all-star teams always produces great controversy among fans and sports writers, except for one position—shortstop—which automatically is assigned to Honus Wagner. This great player began in 1897 with Louisville but played most of his career with Pittsburgh. If there was anything this bowlegged ex-coal miner with hands like meat-hooks could not do on the diamond, no one knew what it was. He could play any position, was deceptively fast, covered the short field like a rug, had a rifle-like throwing arm, and was not only a great hitter who led the National League eight times—still a record—but was a crack baserunner as well, leading in stolen bases no fewer than five seasons. Both Lajoie and Wagner starred in the big leagues for over twenty years.

One of the interesting players of the 'nineties was Dummy Hoy, who was totally deaf. Hoy was a good all-around outfielder, hitter, and baserunner, who, because of his handicap, arranged a special set of signals with his teammates to prevent collisions on fly balls.

With only one major league, the pennant winners of the 'nineties were left without an opposing league champion to meet in a World Series. The so-called World Series between the League and Association teams were ended by the Second Association War of 1891. In fact, even the legitimacy of the Boston victory in the National League that year was questioned. Chicago had the pennant practically assured until New York lost five games in three days to Boston, enabling Boston to beat out Anson's club for the championship. A great hullabaloo was raised, especially since a number of New York's best men were not used in the controversial series. Amos Rusie, New York's star pitcher, for example, did not start against Boston. It was thought by many that New York threw the series to Boston to keep Chicago from winning, to spite Anson for not joining the Brotherhood. The White Sox president, Jim Hart, angrily demanded an investigation; the League complied but found no evidence of dishonesty.

In 1892 the owners tried a substitute for the old inter-league series by having each split-season winner play the other. Boston won the first half and the Cleveland Spiders the second. Soden was against accepting Cleveland's challenge, fearing the fans might think his club had allowed Cleveland to win in the second half of the season so they could make money by having a play-off. The other owners disagreed, and Soden finally consented. The opener in Cleveland was one of those once-in-a-lifetime classics which fans tell their grandchildren about. The two best pitchers of the decade, Nichols and Young, opposed each other in a scoreless pitching duel which was finally called by the umpire in the eleventh inning. Boston took the next five straight for the championship.

The synthetic double pennant race did not go over well with the fans, so the next year the split season was abandoned. The champion Bostons had nobody to play, and all they won at the end of the season was the Dauvray Cup, which may have given Helen Dauvray, John Ward's actress wife, some publicity, but did not bring any additional money to the owners or players, and left the fans without the thrills of a post-season series.

William C. Temple of Pittsburgh came to the rescue the following year by offering an ornate $800 cup, thirty inches high, not counting its twelve-inch onyx pedestal, to the winner of a seven-game series between the first- and second-place teams. Baltimore finished first, but was beaten by John M. Ward's second-place New York Giants.

There was a little odor to the pennant race that year, too. The Baltimore players were accused of offering Red Ehret, Pittsburgh pitcher, $500 to lose a crucial game to them near the end of the season. Captain Robinson admitted the Orioles had offered $100 to Ehret if he beat the Giants, and pointed out, truthfully, that this business of one club's offering an inducement, of money or cigars or whatnot, to another team's players for beating a competing team was common practice. The danger was that this custom could easily degenerate into offering inducements to lose, and, as a matter of fact, later, there were serious incidents involving some of the game's biggest stars. Players are now forbidden to make such offers.

The first Temple Cup series was blighted by disagreements over division of gate receipts. Before the games even started, Baltimore objected to the 65-35 per cent split between winner and loser specified by Temple. The two managers agreed on their own division, 50-50, and it was only when Temple threatened to withhold the cup and the League cracked down that the series was played on the basis of Temple's specifications, but some were still suspicious that the players had agreed privately to divide their shares equally.

The post-season series for the Temple Cup continued for the next three years. In 1895 Baltimore lost again, this time to the second-place Cleveland Spiders, and again a wrangle preceded the series. Since it held the cup from the previous year, New York asserted that it had the right to play the Baltimore pennant winner, even though it did not finish one-two in the pennant race. But League clubs voted against this curious claim of the Giants.

Baltimore turned the tables on Cleveland in 1896 with four straight. In 1897 the Orioles finished second but again won the play-off, this time against Boston. This was the last of the Temple Cup. It was no real substitute for an inter-league series, and failed to create the interest which the World Series of the 1880's had stirred. One of the biggest handicaps was that the pennant-winner had everything to lose and nothing to gain by risking its laurels against the second-place club. And the constant squabbling each year over how the receipts were to be divided added nothing to the popularity of the games. Fans were dubious about the genuineness of the contests, anyway, feeling that the players were probably secretly dividing the receipts 50-50 so that neither club stood to lose on the financial end of it.

The 'nineties may have been gay in some respects, but big league baseball was anything but. Hoodlumism and dirty playing if anything were worse than ever. There was scarcely an issue of the *Sporting News* that did not tell of kicking and wrangling with umpires, fights among players, indecent language, and incidents of rowdyism in general. Coachers were so noisy and abusive toward opposing players that the idea of abolishing coaching from the sidelines altogether was seriously considered and argued.

The Phillies raised the art of coaching to new heights. They stationed Morgan Murphy in the centerfield clubhouse with a pair of field glasses so that he could steal the signs from the opposing catcher. He then tipped off the third-base coach by means of a buzzer system rigged up with underground wires. The coach was then able to signal the batter as to what kind of pitch was coming. John I. Rogers, Philly owner, thought this was perfectly fair and legitimate, but Hanlon denounced Shetzline, the Philly manager, as a "crook."

The Baltimore Orioles had the worst reputation for rowdyism and umpire-baiting. *Sporting News* minced no words in saying that, under Ned Hanlon's orders, they were "playing the dirtiest ball ever seen in this country," and that in their desire for the pennant, even maiming an opposing player seemed perfectly legitimate to them. It described how the Orioles would dive into a first baseman to knock the ball out of his hands, throw masks in the path of a runner trying for home, grab runners by the clothes to retard their movements, and crowd around home plate to interfere with the opposing catcher.

John A. Heydler, later president of the National League, who was an umpire in the 1890's, was even more blunt than contemporary newspapers in his condemnation of the Baltimore Club:

> We hear much of the glories and durability of the old Orioles, but the truth about this team seldom has been told. They were mean, vicious, ready at any time to maim a rival player or an umpire, if it helped their cause. The things they would say to an umpire were unbelievably vile, and they broke the spirits of some fine men. I've seen umpires bathe their feet by the hour after McGraw and others spiked them through their shoes. The club never was a constructive force in the game. The worst of it was they got by with much of their brow beating and hooliganism. Other clubs patterned after them, and I feel the lot of the umpire never was worse than in the years when the Orioles were flying high.

The fiery McGraw, "that toughest of toughs and abomination of the diamond," as one newspaper called him, was the ringleader of the Orioles. It was said he was known in every city, wherever he played, as a "rough, unruly man, who is constantly playing dirty ball. He has the vilest tongue of any ball player." The paper went on to say that he was known to be a fine player, but "he uses every low and contemptible method that his erratic brain can conceive to win a play by a dirty trick." Jennings was called "another of the same stripe."

McGraw defended questioning umpires' decisions. In an interview he was reported as saying that a certain amount of aggressiveness was necessary for lively baseball, and that the only clubs who won were those who had good coachers and good kickers—not rowdies, but fellows who knew when to protest. He pointed out rightly that every winning team is unpopular in rival towns, and maintained that "this parlor ball playing doesn't go worth a cent."

The Orioles were not alone in using aggressive methods. Before the 1894 season a newspaper writer advised Connie Mack to play clean ball that year and quit trying to hurt players with his "blocking off" trick. Even Cap Anson, who was well known for baiting umpires but not given to brawling on the field, hit Heinie Peitz, who had been riding him from the coacher's box. About the only manager who did not go after the umpires was old Harry Wright.

One of the most notorious teams for rough stuff was Patsy Tebeau's

Cleveland Spiders. President Byrne made the Spiders pay four dollars for repairs when they tore up the clubhouse after losing three straight to Brooklyn, and he charged them $1.25 for a ball Jesse Burkett threw over the fence. In a midseason game at Louisville in 1896 "Tebeauism" was at its worst. The Spiders were in rare form, ragging the umpire all day and mobbing him for calling the game on account of darkness. The fans then attacked the Spiders, who ended the day in jail. The League Board fined Tebeau $200, but President Robison, angrily denouncing the League, got an injunction to prevent both the collection of the fine and the boycotting of Cleveland by other League clubs if Tebeau played—which they had planned to do.

The incident was symbolic of the owners' tendency to wink at rowdyism and attacks on the umpire. They were constantly criticized for not maintaining better decorum on the field. Henry Chadwick's observation was typical. He asked whether fans paid to see a ball game or "a lot of toughs tripping each other, giving the shoulder and like action," supplemented by "as choice a selection of billingsgate as a natural born thug can command." The New York *World* warned that ladies and gentlemen would stay away from the games if something was not done. It did not want "milk-and-water, namby-pamby ball players," but it drew the line at ruffianism. And the veteran George Wright, in a *Sporting Life* interview, struck the same note: "It is impossible for a respectable woman to go to the games in the National League without running the risk of hearing language which is disgraceful."

Umpires levied fines, but often as not they meant nothing, because the clubs paid them for the players. Later in the decade, to penalize clubs more effectively, umpires were authorized to remove players from the game as well. Then, in 1898, President Brush's so-called Purification Plan was adopted to suppress "obscene, indecent, or vulgar language" in order to maintain the support of the "refined and cultured classes." Anyone, including fans, could report such incidents to a Board of Discipline, specially appointed, and after a hearing a player could be suspended for days, months, and even life. This was met with much protest, and the players on some teams refused to sign a paper indicating they had read the resolution and understood what was involved.

The Purification Plan seems to have brought some improvement, but it was not sufficient. Instead of waiting for reports of misdemeanors to be handed in, umpires and League authorities needed to have enough initiative and firmness to report breaches of discipline themselves. Many of the umpires were capable officials, but to function properly they had to have support from the League, and that support would not be forthcoming without a strong president to enforce discipline.

Unfortunately, President Young was not this type of leader, and the disorder on the diamond was part and parcel of the general inability of the twelve-club monopoly to operate its affairs efficiently and smoothly. In fact, as the decade advanced, it was to bog down in a morass of internal difficulties which required nothing short of a stiff jolt from outside to inaugurate a housecleaning and a new deal.

24

MONOPOLISTIC MORASS

THE EARLY SUCCESS of the twelve-club monopoly covered up its latent weaknesses. With control over the players restored, no outside competitor worthy of the name, and gate receipts good, inherent weaknesses may have been concealed, but they were still there. The League had a figurehead president, Nick Young, dominated by the owners, who ran things fairly much to suit themselves—and bungled the job. In addition, the twelve-club circuit simply increased the number of tail-enders.

These faults became increasingly apparent when matters turned sour in the second half of the decade. The business depression gradually caught up with baseball. The bicycle craze of the 'nineties, the growing interest in horse racing, and the distractions of the Spanish-American War hurt attendance. As gate receipts began to slip, the magnates made matters worse with their short-sighted, opportunistic policies, and further alienated public confidence by feuding among themselves.

The readiness of the owners to pre-empt authority in the absence of firm leadership was exhibited early in the decade. The Philadelphia Club was never really cured of its twenty-five-cent ball fixation, a carry-over from the 1880's when the League and Association had competing clubs in Philadelphia. At first John I. Rogers grudgingly submitted to the compromise plan of the new League—fifty cents general admission but permission to have some quarter seats, visiting clubs to get half, but home clubs to keep additional charges, usually a quarter, for grandstand or reserved seats. But in 1893 he reverted to quarter ball, claiming that the understanding at the Indianapolis peace agreement covered him. He even made a secret deal with the four former Association clubs, agreeing that the Phillies would accept a visitors' share based on a quarter, in exchange for their support on quarter ball in Philadelphia. Meanwhile, the other clubs had been innocently paying Rogers off on a fifty-cent basis at home while accepting a twenty-five cent one in Philadelphia. When they discovered that they were being tricked, they combined against the Phillies, and some of them carried out a threat to pay only on the basis of a quarter when the Phillies visited them. Rogers then retaliated by estimating the difference between what he should have received, had he been paid on a fifty-cent basis, and what he actually received, and then withholding it from the other club's share when it visited Philadelphia.

By the end of the season, the finances were in a fine muddle, and the League meeting degenerated into personal recriminations and threats of court action. The issue was finally compromised by letting each club keep what it had, and allowing Rogers to keep twenty-five cents of each grandstand admission (50¢) to go toward rebuilding his burned-down grandstand. But the gate receipt problem was never really solved. Near the end of the decade several other clubs were playing quarter ball, and others who did not like it were threatening to let everyone in for a quarter, then charge whatever they wanted for various types of seats after the fans entered the park, and pocket the extra revenue. It reached the point where Philadelphia made separate arrangements on its own with other clubs of the League for division of receipts. In 1899, when Brooklyn refused to make a suitable agreement, the Phillies spited them by raising admission prices when Brooklyn came to town.

The owners had the same cat-and-dog attitude toward the League sinking fund. Some of them constantly complained that they were contributing more than their share, and after a good deal of argument contributions were changed from a percentage to a flat sum.

The old Sunday ball issue did not create dissension among the owners in the way gate receipts did, because with the acquisition of Association clubs, the League retreated still further from its no-Sunday-ball position, leaving the question to local option. Big Sunday receipts broke down the traditional opposition of the old National League clubs. Even the Chicago Club, onetime citadel of Sunday piety, no longer could resist the temptation, and Spalding himself did a turnabout on the issue, now discovering that it was simply a matter of legality: play where it was lawful, otherwise abstain, was his revised verdict.

Cleveland was another. It could not play at home on Sunday, but by 1895 the Spiders were traveling on hot, stuffy trains for Sunday games elsewhere and then back home again the same night for Monday games in Cleveland. Eastern clubs succumbed as well, most of them clamoring for Sunday dates when they went West. Nick Young had a difficult time in making out schedules that satisfied everybody:

the few who played no Sunday ball at all, some who played it only away from home, and others who wanted it both at home and abroad.

Purists and many of the Protestant clergy still objected to Sunday ball, and there continued to be instances where teams were arrested for breaking the law. In Cleveland, where an unholy alliance between the Ministers' Association and the Liquor League forced the issue, the entire Cleveland and Washington ball teams were arrested one Sunday in May 1897. The Rev. George E. Hawes of Braddock, Pennsylvania, told the United Presbyterian Ministers' Association conclave in 1900 that the Lord had assumed management of the Pittsburgh Club and had crippled several of the players to punish the team for playing on Sunday. But, as *Sporting Life* remarked, he failed to explain why the Lord did not let Boston and Philadelphia, which played no Sunday ball, come anywhere near the pennant.

On the other hand, the Rt. Rev. John J. Keane, Catholic priest, in an address given at Buffalo in 1895, stated that, while opposed to the Continental Sabbath, the Church did not object to "popular enjoyments consistent with the pleasure of the day," provided Catholics did not frequent places where liquor was sold. He cited as his authority the official position of the Church set forth in 1884 at the Third Plenary Council of the bishops of the Catholic Church. From a different point of view, a Baltimore attorney attacked laws against Sunday ball as a violation of the United States Constitution because they represented a union of Church and State.

Breaking the Sabbath no doubt turned some people against baseball, but probably not nearly to the extent that the rampant rowdyism of the period did. Ball clubs were in tune with the times on the matter of Sunday ball. Like theaters, which were beginning to open on Sundays, the ball clubs were responding to the growing desire for Sunday amusements on the part of the urbanized laboring classes, most of whom had little other opportunity to see a ball game.

Gambling was something else again. Its increasing openness in the ball parks and its prevalence among managers, players, and owners were perhaps as sure a sign as any of the League's deteriorating standards. Knots of bettors congregated in the grandstands. In Boston, where betting was said to be especially strong, they gathered around third base, and betting right inside the Chicago park was portrayed in *The Runaway Colt*, a baseball play written by Charles H. Hoyt, which had a short run in 1895.

Even worse was the popularity of betting among the owners and managers themselves. In 1892 John Ward won twenty shares of New York stock from Edward Talcott, a director of the club, as the result of a bet on where the Giants would finish in the standings. Magnates made numerous bets with each other, as high as $500, on the pennant races. They also made wagers with players. According to Henry Chadwick, the players themselves purchased pools openly before games, usually on their own club but sometimes, he claimed, on the rival team.

But if the League owners had gone out of their way to create dissension and undermine public confidence they could not have done better than to allow Andrew Freedman to purchase control of the Giants, in January 1895, for an estimated $50,000. Freedman was a so-called self-made man who gained his fortune in real estate and transit deals by "devious" means "no longer traceable," as the *Dictionary of American Biography* describes them. He was closely involved in municipal politics through Tammany Hall, and was an intimate friend and associate of the notorious Boss Croker, whom he accompanied on lengthy trips as "secretary." He was another of the numerous baseball magnates with blemished reputations, like Boss Tweed, Honest John Morrissey, Erastus Wiman, Ferdinand Abel, Chris Von der Ahe, and more recently, Fred Saigh, former St. Louis Cardinals' owner, who served a jail sentence for income tax evasion.

Freedman's irascible personality, quick temper, and aggressiveness had him in constant trouble. He could be very amiable when not crossed; the trouble was that he was constantly crossed. His turbulent years as Giant owner (many charged that he was only a front man for others) kept the League in constant turmoil, and made the New York *World's* observation that he had "an astonishing faculty for making enemies" seem like a gross understatement.

He antagonized old fans and "freeloaders" at the outset by cutting off their complimentary passes, and, as a newcomer, rubbed the other magnates the wrong way by tactlessly pushing his own ideas about the way the League should be run. He suggested, among other things, that Byrne should take his Brooklyn Club into some minor league so the Giants could have the metropolitan area to themselves!

Freedman's seeming inability to stand criticism precipitated some venomous exchanges with the press. Sam Crane, then writing for the New York *Commercial Advertiser,* was refused admittance to the park for criticizing the Giants' management. He was not even allowed to buy a ticket after his press pass was confiscated. Another time Freedman barred two other New York reporters and three Cincinnati writers, including the well-known Ren Mulford and Harry Weldon. Freedman also punched a young New York *Times* reporter in the jaw when he followed up his written criticisms by blaming Freedman to his face for the poor showing of the Giants. When the venerable but needy Henry Chadwick, another of Freedman's critics, was voted a $600 pension as a member of the Rules Committee by the League, Freedman wrote him a nasty letter, accusing him of biting the hand that fed him. Chadwick boycotted the Giants' park. By 1900 Freedman had twenty-two libel suits pending against the New York *Sun.*

Whatever else could be said of the tempestuous Giants' owner, he did not discriminate in making enemies. He took on players, managers, umpires, and actors as well as newspaper reporters and fellow-owners. Within his eight-year regime the Giants had no fewer than a dozen different managers. In 1901 Freedman told Young he would not accept Billy Nash as an umpire. Young sent him anyway, and Freedman refused to let him in the park, using players instead, despite the Pittsburgh Club's protest. It may have been a coincidence, but Pittsburgh lost both games that day. After that, the weak League president ducked the issue by placing Nash alternately on the sick list or the substitute list. Tom Lynch, another courageous umpire who was fired for a time for criticizing the League's treatment of umpires, was barred from the Polo Grounds (and Cincinnati as well) even after he was reinstated.

Two long, drawn-out Freedman disputes with players not only piled up more enemies for him but were again eloquent evidence of the sad state of affairs into which the League monopoly was descending. The first collision was with Amos Rusie. After winning twenty-four games for the ninth-place Giants in 1895, the popular pitching star found $200 in "fines" deducted from his salary at the end of the season, supposedly for breaking training and for indifferent work in the last game. Rusie, who had had a number of salary disputes with the management in previous years, considered the $200 fine as nothing but a pretext for cutting his salary, and he refused to report to the New York Club until the money was refunded. Freedman was equally stubborn, with the result that Rusie became one of the few players in baseball history ever to hold out for an entire season.

The case aroused a great deal of public interest, much of it sympathetic toward the player. *Sporting News* asserted, "Every independent fair-thinking man is with Rusie in his stand against the New York Club. Every ball player of standing is with him." Fans wrote in to the New York newspapers urging Freedman to compromise. Some Wall Street businessmen were indignant. Several brokers hung a huge sign in a cigar store window on Broad Street urging a boycott of the Giants until Rusie was restored to the team, and the police had to break up a crowd yelling its approval outside the store.

With John M. Ward acting as his counsel, Rusie presented his case before the League Board, which upheld the club. He then turned to the courts. The case dragged into 1897. By this time the owners were increasingly uneasy because of the public clamor and their own wish to avoid a legal test of the contract. They held a meeting early in 1897 and strongly urged Freedman to negotiate a settlement, even indicating willingness to put up some money to recompense Rusie for his 1896 salary loss, but still Freedman refused anything less than unconditional surrender. However, Rusie signed shortly afterwards and dropped legal action, the other owners ending the dispute by reimbursing him a reported $3000 to compensate for his lost salary. Nick Young took little part in settling the affair.

Freedman's other quarrel was with one of his former players, Ducky Holmes, who insulted the owner by calling him a name reflecting on his Jewish religion during a game at the Polo Grounds with Baltimore, Holmes's new club. Freedman demanded that the player be removed from the game in accordance with the rule permitting the umpire to eject a player for using vulgar language. When umpire Lynch refused, claiming he had not heard the remark, Freedman pulled his team off the field, forfeited the game, and refunded the fans' money. He was fined $1000 by the League, whose Board also suspended Holmes for the rest of the season.

Some of the owners—Soden, Robison, and Brush—protested the Board's "illegal suspension of Holmes." The more callous attitude of those days toward the feelings of minority groups, as compared with the present—when such a newspaper comment would be unthinkable—was reflected by *Sporting Life*'s statement that punishing the player for the "trifling offense" of "insulting the Hebrew race" was a "perversion of justice." The Board yielded to the pressure from the press and reinstated Holmes after only ten days. Freedman protested every game Holmes played in thereafter, and continued to nurse his wrath.

It should not be supposed that Freedman's remarks and actions and Rogers's disputes over gate receipts were the only discordant elements in baseball's not-so-gay 'nineties. Far from it. The increased number of magnates in the bulky twelve-club league multiplied the opportunities for disagreements and favored the formation of factions. The club owners lined up in opposing groups on one issue after another. By 1896 newspapers habitually referred to the seven-club "Brush clique" and the five-club "Rogers faction" to designate the owners in each camp.

One of the biggest battles was over how many members the Board of Directors should have and what its powers should be. This particular issue was resolved by an amendment giving the League as a whole, rather than the Board, authority to amend the National Agreement in the future. The hard feelings engendered by this drawn-out wrangle were assuaged, one newspaper reported, with "cold bottles and small hot birds." But in reality the dissension remained. Later on, when Chicago switched sides and joined the Brush group, the papers acknowledged the realignment with the labels "the Big Eight" and "the Little Four."

Petty bickering and stories of unethical practices spiced up the sports pages. Magnates accused one another of secretly tampering with players on rival teams to give them swelled heads and create dissatisfaction. They charged each other with cheating on gate receipts. Pittsburgh, for instance, claimed that Cleveland cheated on the count by turning one of the stiles backwards. One of the Wagner brothers, owner of Washington, admitted getting the official scorer to add 40 base hits to infielder Gene DeMontreville's record, to bring his batting average above .300 so he could sell him to Baltimore for a higher price. Wagner said he thought "that kind of work is perfectly legitimate. I am not the only manager that ever had a player's average boosted." Every one of the magnates, said Harry Pulliam, later a National League president, wanted "a slight hunch over the other fellows, with the result that they are not quite on the level" with each other. Ferdinand Abel, Brooklyn stockholder, told a reporter that he never failed to check his money and valuables at the hotel office before entering a League meeting.

The owners were constantly chided by the press for their secrecy and skittishness about giving out news—keeping things to themselves "as though the fate of the nation depended on it," as reporter Sam Crane wrote. Nick Young was repeatedly criticized as a "catspaw" for the owners, and urged to quit trying to hold his Washington clerk's job and be president of the League at the same time. Although he finally gave up the government post in 1897, the benefit to the League was not readily apparent.

As the decade moved along, it became increasingly evident that the twelve-club league was unsound. Year after year the record showed a third of the clubs disproportionately weak. In the eight-year duration of the consolidated league, the combined average of the pennant winners was .684, that of the eighth-place finishers, .475, and twelfth-place tail-enders, a miserable .258, leaving a gap of 426 points between the pennant winners and the cellar dwellers. To put it another way, the average gap over the period between eighth place and last—217 points—was greater than that between first place and eighth place—209 points.

Also, usually it was the same clubs that brought up the rear. Louisville and St. Louis were never able to climb out of the lower third slough, and between them they occupied last place five out of the eight years. Washington escaped from the lower regions but once, and although Cleveland finished last only a single time it accomplished the feat in bang-up fashion, setting an all-time low record by losing 134 games and winning only 20, for a dismal average of .129.

All through these years, criticism of the lopsidedness of the circuit dominated conversation in big league circles. The 1894 special Christmas issue of *Sporting News* conducted an opinion poll on the twelve-club league among individuals connected with baseball, mostly sports writers but including some owners, managers, and players. It showed them to be overwhelmingly against it. The magnates themselves began to see that it was not working, but seemed unable to bring themselves to do anything about it. For one thing, they were harnessed by the ten-year consolidation agreement which stipulated no circuit change during that period. For another, they could not agree on a solution. Some realized that an eight-club league would be better, but they could not concur on what clubs should be lopped off. Others advocated adding four more clubs and splitting into two big leagues. One wanted to divide the twelve-club league into Eastern and Western circuits.

Before taking any of these actions, though, the owners made a series of moves within the framework of the twelve-club circuit which merely increased the damage. One of these involved St. Louis, and in some ways was rather pathetic, because it ended with Chris Von der Ahe's departure from the baseball scene, where he had been so prominent for so long. His once-proud Browns had become one of the "doormats" of the League, and Der Boss President, once king of the American Association, had become practically a pariah. He had dissipated his profits of the 'eighties in lavish spending and profligate living.

By 1896 the real estate in which he had invested much of his earnings was heavily mortgaged by the Northwestern Savings Bank of St. Louis. Having sold off his former stars, he was unable to replace them with another winning combination. Converting his ball park into a honky-tonk, instead of retrieving his fortune, simply brought heavier criticism on him. Numerous creditors harassed him. His private life, said *Sporting News*, was "an affront to the community." Della, his favorite mistress, made inviting copy for sports writers. In 1895 his wife finally sued him for divorce and alimony on charges of adultery, and his son sued him for property.

The old Mark Baldwin case continued to plague him. W. A. Nimick, then president of Pittsburgh, fearful of losing the money he had posted as bond for Von der Ahe at the time, had his attorneys and a detective kidnap the unfortunate Browns' owner in order to bring him into a Pennsylvania court. By a ruse, Nimick's agents lured Von der Ahe into a carriage, spirited him out of Missouri, and had him thrown into an Allegheny County jail, where, disheveled and disgraced, he reposed for several days before his attorneys could bail him out.

From one who had "hobnobbed with nabobs," wrote a local paper, the unfortunate Von der Ahe had changed to a "sour, crabid [sic], disappointed being." By 1898 he was trying to sell the Browns, but bidders could not get a clean bill of sale because of his many debts. Finally the court stepped in and appointed a receiver, who was then elected president by the club. Von der Ahe fought against this and even succeeded in getting himself reappointed president. As far as the League was concerned, it was just as glad to be rid of him, and not only did nothing to support him in his trouble but ignored Von der Ahe and recognized the receiver instead. Then, when the club was put up for auction, the League passed a resolution to protect itself against a possible undesirable purchaser, declaring that buying the assets of a club did not necessarily entitle the buyer to membership in the League. In the meantime, the club was suspended for not paying for a minor leaguer it had acquired.

The Browns passed through a rapid succession of owners in the spring of 1899, finally landing in the control of Frank Robison, who still owned the Cleveland Club—but not before a lively National League meeting in which Jim Hart thought Rogers was calling him a liar and made a rush to hit him, but was held back by the other owners. Robison had long wanted to dispose of his Cleveland franchise, provided he could get his price. He had had an opportunity to sell out to Detroit interests, but the League, not wanting the franchise to go to a smaller city, had not permitted him to accept the offer. Since no one in Cleveland would give him as much as he wanted, he had to stay put until the St. Louis opportunity came along.

Now, with two clubs under his control, he switched his best Cleveland men including Jesse Burkett and Cy Young, to the Browns to concentrate his efforts there. Actually, he was robbing Peter to pay Paul, and alienating what Cleveland fans were left; for while the Browns did jump to fifth place in 1899, the denuded Clevelands sank to the lowest depths in major league history with a record number of losses. In fact, they were so bad that they transferred nearly all their games from Cleveland to other cities that year.

This practice of transferring games from the home town to other League cities where the attendance gave promise of being greater was nothing new in the 1890's. Chicago, perturbed by what the World's Fair might do to attendance, got permission to switch some of its games, but when the great spectacle turned out to be a bonanza instead, other clubs rushed to have some of their White Sox games played in Chicago, rather than the other way around.

A bare-faced example of game-transferring was Washington's desire for more of a good thing. The club had received an unusually large visitor's share from a three-game series in Philadelphia, which drew exceptionally big crowds because the fans wanted to see the Phillies on their return home from a remarkable winning streak in the west. Greedy for more of the same, Washington then transferred all of its own home games with the Phillies to Philadelphia. Washington fans and newspapers denounced this selfish scheme, and *Sporting Life* headlined its story about it "An Outrage on the Washington Public."

The fans found some consolation when the move backfired. The transferred games did not draw as well as expected, and for once the League took action, fining the owners, the Wagner brothers, $1000. Yet this penalty did not stop other transfers and attempts at them. Transferring became a common expedient—additional evidence of the weak-kneed administration of the monopoly, which could countenance such laxity and cynical disregard for the home-town fans. The only difference with Cleveland in 1899 was the extreme to which it went, playing only twenty-four games in its home city and winning for itself the sobriquet "The Exiles."

While the St. Louis tangle was being unraveled, a similar deal was consummated between Brooklyn and Baltimore, combining the ownership of those two clubs. Harry Vonderhorst, the old Association's Baltimore man, who still owned the club, and Ned Hanlon together took 50 per cent of the Baltimore and Brooklyn clubs. Ferdinand Abel, Brooklyn's principal owner, took a 40 per cent interest in both teams, and Charlie Ebbets, the rising young Brooklyn executive, secured the remaining stock in each organization.

This deal made a travesty of genuine competition between major league clubs. Hanlon was made both president of Baltimore and field manager of Brooklyn for 1899. Openly announcing his intention to concentrate the playing strength of both clubs in Brooklyn, Hanlon took along with him enough of his Baltimore stars, including Hughie Jennings, Willie Keeler, and Joe Kelley, to win two successive pennants in Brooklyn. The managerial opening in Baltimore was filled by John J. McGraw, who at the age of twenty-six was started on his great career as a major league leader. A "perfect storm of press denunciation" arose over the syndicate's attempt to shift the fading Jennings back to Baltimore after he had played ten games for Brooklyn. So, after appearing in only two Baltimore games, Hughie was sent to Brooklyn once more.

Brooklyn's former manager, Mike Griffin, was informed that he was sold to Cleveland, but he declined to go until he was paid the balance of some salary due him. He received about $300 from Brooklyn, only to find that his Cleveland pay would be reduced from the $3500 he had anticipated. Then, without actually having accepted the transfer of his contract from Brooklyn, Cleveland suddenly told him it had traded him to St. Louis. Griffin refused to go and sued Brooklyn for his salary, winning a judgment of around $2400 when the court ruled that there was no legal acceptance of the assignment of his contract to Cleveland.

Neither the St. Louis-Cleveland nor the Brooklyn-Baltimore interlocking ownership was unprecedented. There was an example in the case of New York, where numerous owners of other major league clubs became involved during the Brotherhood War, when they secured blocks of Giant stock in bailing out the desperate John B. Day. It seemed that virtually everybody in the National League had a share in the Giants, and it would be almost easier to tell who did not own some of its stock than to list those who did. Players were "loaned" to New York to buttress the club, since the other owners realized it was so much to their interest to have a winner in the metropolis. Soden, for instance, loaned King Kelly to the Giants in 1893, at the end of his career, and, even after Freedman came into control, there were still other big league stockholders "donating players" to him.

Ward's transfer from Brooklyn to manage the Giants in 1893 was engineered by the group of club owners who had stock in the Giants. They felt that if they had a big-name player-manager in New York they could revive interest in the club. Brooklyn agreed to take a percentage of the Giants' gate receipts in payment, because New York did not have ready cash to buy him outright. Ward himself had stock in both clubs—another carry-over from Brotherhood days.

The whole New York situation aroused frequent comment and suspicion during the decade, and fans wondered about the genuineness of competition. Yet, in the face of this, the owners calmly intensified interlocking control of clubs not only by sanctioning Robison's coup and the Brooklyn-Baltimore union but by allowing the Louisville-Pittsburgh deal in the following year.

Louisville, just about the weakest member of the twelve-club circuit, was constantly in straitened circumstances. The club did so poorly that it was made fun of on the stage. In a scene from *The Runaway Colt*, in which Cap Anson was trying to avoid a gushing woman, he said to one of his players, "Don't leave me alone with her, or I'll expel you from the league. Worse, I'll sell you to Louisville!"

With his club going from bad to worse, Barney Dreyfuss found a way out by taking over the Pittsburgh Club for a reported $25,000 and assuming its presidency, Dreyfuss followed the usual pattern of taking the pick of the Louisville players with him—notably Honus Wagner and Fred Clarke, who later managed the club to several pennants. Louisville was left with a skeleton team for 1900, but other developments quickly intervened, and the city was not represented in the major leagues thereafter.

At the end of the decade it was difficult to keep track of who owned what in the majors, but by March 1900, as near as can be found, the syndication of the League looked like this:

Brush—Owned Cincinnati; held stock in New York. (He also owned Indianapolis of the still-minor American League.)

Soden—Owned one-third of Boston; principal minority stockholder in New York.

Abel—Owned 40 per cent of Brooklyn and 40 per cent of Baltimore; minority stockholder in New York.

Robison—Owned both St. Louis and Cleveland.

Vonderhorst—Owned 40 per cent of stock in Brooklyn and 40 per cent of Baltimore.

Hanlon—Owned 10 per cent of Brooklyn and 10 per cent of Baltimore.

Ebbets—Owned 10 per cent of Brooklyn and 10 per cent of Baltimore.

Spalding—Owned large block of Chicago stock, with Hart as his front man; owned a few shares in New York.

Thus, instead of doing something constructive about the unwieldy twelve-club League, the owners simply strengthened its monopolistic character with a complicated maze of interlocking ownership which made competition among them a farce. Newspaper criticism grew hotter and fan confidence ebbed. A typical polemic was this one from *Sporting News* of April 8, 1899:

What's the matter with these National League magnates? What a shame it is that the greatest of sports ... should be in the hands of such a mal-odorous gang as these magnates have proven themselves to be on more than one occasion, but never so conspicuously as within the past few weeks ... [League meetings were characterized by] mud slinging, brawling, corruption, breaches of confidence, dishonorable conspiracies, [and] threats of personal violence.

Meanwhile, Andrew Freedman was still brooding over the fine levied on him in the Ducky Holmes affair. Freedman, one of those who advocated reverting to an eight-club league, now loudly proclaimed, "I will not attempt to improve the New York Club until the circuit is reduced." He also criticized the new interlocking ownerships, conveniently forgetting that his club was the oldest and most flagrant example of the practice. He avowed that he would not strengthen the Giants just to "increase the chance of money-making for any base ball syndicate." This vindictive threat to let the Giants go to seed, if carried out, would sabotage the League, which depended so much on a good drawing card in New York. Freedman's subversion was not the sole reason for the great circuit reduction of the spring of 1900, but it probably helped prod the magnates into taking the step they had been considering for some time.

The subject was brought up officially for the first time by Frank Robison at the League's December 1899 meeting. When a committee, appointed to make recommendations, named Louisville, Cleveland, Washington, and Baltimore as the clubs to be eliminated, owners of the four unwanted teams met and placed a price of $150,000 on their withdrawal. The figure would include about eighty players and the four franchises. The departing owners even showed how their severance money could be raised: all their players could be lumped together and auctioned off among the eight survivors, and their evacuated territories could be sold to minor league clubs. This would leave an approximated $50,000 to be obtained, over the two-year period left of the ten-year consolidation agreement, by the old method of a tax on League gate receipts.

The Brooklyn-Baltimore syndicate stalled the proceedings for a while by making a long series of demands, among them the right to dispose of their own players as they saw fit, and a twenty-five-year agreement to keep the new eight-club National League intact! But in March the four clubs were duly cut adrift. Louisville was paid only $10,000 for its franchise, since Pittsburgh already had the cream of its players. Robison received $25,000 for Cleveland. Baltimore obtained $30,000 and the right to dispose of its own players, and Washington $46,500, minus $7500 already received for three men sold to Boston. Left-over players were put at the disposal of whoever bid for them through a committee. This left a league consisting of Boston, Brooklyn, New York, and Philadelphia in the East, and Pittsburgh, Chicago, Cincinnati, and St. Louis in the West—the circuit which was to remain intact as the National League until 1953, when Boston transferred its franchise to Milwaukee.

The new streamlined League agreed to set aside 5 per cent of its gross receipts in the next two years toward a fund to pay off the $104,000 indebtedness. The four dismissed clubs would technically remain members of the League for these two years, to prevent them from joining a rival organization (there were two threatening at the time), and their votes were vested in the League's Circuit Committee. Each of the four clubs consented to appoint a groundkeeper to maintain their idle parks, salaries to be paid by the League. By thus claiming control of cities without even operating teams in them, the League brought territorial rights to the pinnacle of arrogance.

Circuit reduction did not pacify Freedman. He kept adding to his demands and imposing new conditions under which he would consent to build up the Giants. He wanted Young to quit the presidency; he insisted that his $1000 fine be returned; and he refused to pay his share of the circuit reduction debt unless he was given certain players for the Giants. His colleagues kept appeasing him, instead of having a showdown. He was given back his $1000 with 6 per cent interest; he was offered first choice of the Washington players left jobless by the diminished circuit, as well as a chance to purchase surplus players on the remaining League clubs at a nominal cost. The League also rescinded a rule preventing the Giants from playing Sunday exhibitions in Weehawken.

Behind the "long controversy with and abject submission to the Dictator," *Sporting Life* reproved, there was no question of "honor or principle," but only "a mercenary fear of diminished profits, and a base hope of financial gain." And this paper's observation that there was no guarantee these concessions would make Freedman behave proved correct. He continued his refusal to pay the 5 per cent of his gross receipts toward the cost of circuit reduction, and pursued a private war with Brooklyn, claiming the entire metropolitan area to himself, now that the borough was a part of Greater New York.

At the end of the century the steady, dismal decline of the National League left it in the poorest condition of its twenty-four-year history, not discounting the early grim years, when at least it had strong leadership. Editor Frank Richter, writing in 1900, remarked quite correctly that the League's government was characterized by the magnates' "gross individual and collective mismanagement, their fierce factional fights, their cynical disregard of decency and honor, their open spoliation of each other, their deliberate alienation of press and public, their flagrant disloyalty to friends and supporters and their tyrannical treatment of the players."

Ironically, the League, which deep down had always desired a monopoly of baseball, did not know how to handle it once it had achieved it. Now, with its affairs in a mess, it was wide open for another attack from a rival organization, and there was one ready and equipped to make the challenge—the toughest competitor it ever had to face.

25

THE NATIONAL LEAGUE MEETS ITS MATCH

SOME PEOPLE believe that the man makes history. Others argue that history makes the man. More likely, history is made when the times are ripe and the right man is on hand to seize the opportunity. Byron Bancroft Johnson's successful challenge to the National League at the beginning of the new century is a story of such a fortuitous combination. The decline of the National League provided the opportunity, and Ban Johnson proved to be the one capable of seizing it.

Johnson was a big, impressive-looking man with a square jaw and a strong face who was just as imperious and impressive as he looked. He was born the son of a college professor in 1864, and attended both Marietta College and Oberlin. He played college baseball and had some brief experience as a semi-pro before turning to sports writing for the Cincinnati *Commercial-Gazette*. When he bowed out of baseball in 1927 Johnson closed a long career as one of the greatest organizers, and executives in the history of the game, another example— O. P. Caylor was an earlier one—of a sports writer who rose to baseball prominence.

Johnson got his real start in baseball administration when he became president of the revived Western League. The Western, a descendant of the old Northwestern League of the early 'eighties, had been organized in 1892 and had already gone through a couple of failures and reorganizations when Johnson assumed command in 1894. He took over a circuit made up of Indianapolis, Kansas City, Milwaukee, Minneapolis, Toledo, Grand Rapids, Detroit, and Sioux City.

After a year Sioux City was replaced by St. Paul, whose franchise was secured by Charles Comiskey. He was to become Johnson's closest confederate in bringing about a new era in baseball. The friendship between the two had begun in Cincinnati while Ban was writing sports and "Commy" was managing John T. Brush's Reds after the Brotherhood War. Johnson had been highly critical of the way Brush ran his club, and there is reason to believe that the Reds' owner, anxious to be rid of him, was instrumental in securing the presidency of the Western for Ban.

Johnson's departure from Cincinnati did not end his differences with Brush. Through his ownership of the Western's Indianapolis Club Brush was able to meddle in the minor league's affairs. Johnson was particularly incensed over his method of drafting Western League players ostensibly for his Cincinnati team but actually for shipment to Indianapolis. He fought back vigorously, and with the help of some National League magnates won Brush's lasting enmity by forcing him to dispose of his Indianapolis stock.

Under Johnson's strong administration the Western proved astonishingly successful. Inside of two years it was looked upon as the "strongest minor ever," second only to the National League. But this accomplishment was not enough to satisfy a man of Johnson's talent and ambition; he very soon had visions of making the Western a major league. By 1896 he was declaring that the Western could go on its own. Soon it was no secret that he wanted to place a club in Chicago and was eyeing other League cities like Cleveland and St. Louis as possibilities for expansion should the League reduce its twelve-club circuit.

Johnson and his Western League associates were not the only ones who had the idea of establishing another major league. The decline of the National League monopoly during these years was also the signal for another attempt to revive the American Association, despite the abortive effort in 1894. Involved in the movement were Al Spink, Cap Anson, Chris Von der Ahe, and, for a time at least, John McGraw. Spink claimed credit for conceiving the idea in 1898 while he was editor of the St. Louis *Post-Dispatch*.

After the preliminaries had quietly been prepared, an informal meeting was held at Chicago in September 1899. Ban Johnson was offered a chance to consolidate with the new American Association but would have none of it. Instead, he took his first big step toward making the Western a major league.

At an October meeting the Western changed its name to the American League, to give itself a more national character. Johnson then proceeded to expand into Cleveland and Chicago. In Cleveland, where he had the important backing of Charles Somers, a very wealthy coal dealer, matters were simple because the territory had been lopped off by the League's circuit reduction plan. In Chicago, League owner Hart's long opposition to a local competitor was overcome when he and Johnson were brought together. In exchange for Hart's permission to put a club in Chicago, headed by Comiskey, Johnson reputedly promised to abide by the National Agreement and to pay a sum of money for improvements made by the National League club in Cleveland. He also reportedly gave Hart the right to select a couple of American League players.

The transaction averted war, for Johnson and his men had made plain their determination to enter Chicago with or without permission. In fact, according to Hart's story, Johnson and Comiskey had already moved in before the deal was made, and the Chicago owner had little choice if war was to be avoided. The League gave its blessing to the invasion, because at this point it was more worried about the attempt to form the new American Association, and doubtless sought to block it by using the American League as a buffer.

With Chicago and Cleveland to go with Detroit, Minneapolis, Milwaukee, Kansas City, and Indianapolis, Johnson had a strong circuit for the 1900 season, although it was not yet a major league one, and the year turned out fairly well financially for the American League. According to *Sporting News* the quality of its ball playing was not as high as the National League's, but the fans came out because they liked the American's absence of rowdyism. In addition, the *Sporting News* said, the American lacked "the cowardly truckling, alien ownership, syndicatism, hyppodroming [*sic*], selfish jealousies, arrogance of club owners, mercenary spirit, and disregard of public demands" of the National League. Unquestionably, Johnson's firm hand was chiefly responsible for American League success. Even though the owners paid his salary, pointed out the New York *Sun*, Johnson's rule was "absolute." He appointed the umpires and gave them his full backing in following his orders to eject promptly players who protested.

In contrast, the National League continued to alienate the public by doing business in the same old way. In fact, another major problem arose to plague it. That season (1900) the players again took heart and organized—just ten years after the Brotherhood debacle. Behind the move lay a decade of abuses, dramatized by cases of injustice like the celebrated holdout of Amos Rusie in his dispute with Freedman. For some time feeling had been growing among the players that they should take action to protect themselves, and they had been discussing the matter in letters and on railway cars as they traveled about the circuit.

Finally, on June 10, 1900, three delegates from each League team met at the Sturtevant House, New York, to form the Protective Association of Professional Baseball Players. At first, names of officers were not revealed for fear they would become "shining marks" for the owners, but soon the news leaked. Charley "Chief" Zimmer, Cy Young's old battery mate who was then catching for Pittsburgh, was president; Bill Clarke, another catcher then with Boston, was treasurer; and Hughie Jennings was secretary.

Samuel Gompers, who had expressed sympathy for the players and offered them moral support even if they decided not to affiliate with the American Federation of Labor, sent Dan Harris to represent him at the meeting. Harris addressed the players, explaining the workings of unions to them, but they decided not to affiliate with the A.F. of L., out of fear, it was said, of antagonizing the owners.

At a second meeting, attended by nearly a hundred players at the end of July, Harry Taylor, a Buffalo attorney and ex-ball player, presented a constitution which was duly adopted. This document gave the broad purposes of the organization, and then stated in the by-laws that every effort would be made to "prevent any member from being lent (or 'farmed'), traded or sold to any baseball club without his consent, and unless said lending, trading or selling be arranged on terms and conditions entirely satisfactory to said member; to prevent any member from being unjustly deprived of any portion of his salary by fine or otherwise, or from being in any manner unjustly treated professionally or financially by any club owner." The players also wanted further changes in the contract, including some limitation on the reserve clause. There was a five-dollar initiation fee and monthly dues of two dollars. A grievance committee was set up, and players agreed not to sign their next contracts unless approved by their attorney. As one newspaper twitted, it looked as though the familiar "game called on account of rain" would soon be changed to "game called on account of strike."

The players were at pains to put to rest any ideas the owners might have that the Protective Association had radical intentions. Their leaders reassured the owners on this score, and Attorney Taylor's letter to the owners requesting a meeting to discuss grievances was a model of courtesy and tact. On their side, the owners were far from pleased at the prospect of dealing with a players' union again. John I. Rogers remarked that baseball was a sport and therefore had no place in a federation of labor. A. H. Soden was quoted as saying, "I do not believe in labor organizations or unions" and "when a player ceases to be useful to me I will release him." Yet the owners could not very well afford to slough off the request for a hearing. With the threat of new leagues hanging over them—new leagues to which the players might turn—the magnates believed they should go in for "diplomacy and handshaking," as the New York *Sun* expressed it.

Accordingly, at the December League meetings a committee of owners met with Taylor, Zimmer, Jennings, and Clark Griffith, who was then pitching for Chicago. Taylor brought up the main points at issue, and the players' representatives promised to assist in stamping out rowdyism.

The owners asked the players to put their demands in writing. Taylor complied, but included such additional items as a limitation on suspensions, payment of medical bills by the clubs, and provision for a Board of Arbitration, to consist of one member chosen by the owners, one by the players, and a third by the first two members. Taylor also produced a new form of contract which, in addition to the safeguards already asked for, contained a clause guaranteeing a player the right to his release upon giving ten days' notice if the owner violated its terms. This was too much for the League. It not only flatly rejected the whole package but turned down a request to reconsider.

With this, the players issued a public statement. They had no desire for a baseball war, they said, and had ordered all National Agreement players not to negotiate with the American League—at least for the present—to give National League owners ample time to think over their demands, "so that when the real trouble comes we will not be to blame."

"They're only bluffing," said Charlie Ebbets, Brooklyn's young owner, "and when the time comes around for advance money they will all weaken. The demands of these fellows are simply preposterous."

Perhaps the players were bluffing, but Ban Johnson and his able lieutenants were not. With a successful season behind them, they were ready for another leap forward, one which would end the American's sectional character and make it a real major circuit. In September a decision to expand into the East was taken. Plans were made to move into Washington, Baltimore, and Philadelphia. The first two gave promise of being relatively easy, for when the League reduced its circuit it ceased to operate clubs in those cities, although it still claimed control of the franchises. In Philadelphia, where the League was still entrenched, getting its consent would be far more difficult. Nevertheless, Johnson hoped to enter these cities peacefully, as he had been able to do in Cleveland and Chicago. To avoid overt antagonism of the League, Johnson did not broach the subject of invading Boston, which would have made an excellent fourth Eastern city for his circuit. He signified that he would be content with Buffalo instead, to go with Chicago, Cleveland, Detroit, and Milwaukee, the Western wing of his reorganized league.

To show his insistence upon being considered on an equal basis with the National, Johnson deliberately neglected to renew his application to the League for protection under the National Agreement. Although the American League's claim to major status and equality was no secret, Nick Young forced the issue with a telegram to Johnson which pointed out his failure to pay the usual protection fee required of all minor leagues. Johnson replied that the American League's intention to occupy Eastern territories had been made known to the National League, and that for two years the American League had been "menaced" by the formation of a league (the American Association) "hostile to our interests" and detrimental to Organized Baseball. He said the American League was shaping plans to "checkmate" this threat, and therefore it was "unreasonable to assume" that it could continue along the "old lines" of the National Agreement.

He expressed his willingness to go along with the suggestion he claimed President Hart of the League's Chicago Club had offered— that committees from the two leagues confer on the question of the American's occupation of Eastern cities. However, Johnson made clear that his league would no longer tolerate having its players drafted by the National. In conclusion, he said that "should complications arise" they would be of the National League's making, but added that if fairness and common sense were used, there would be no friction between the two organizations.

But the National League, meeting in New York that winter, ignored Johnson, who was waiting with Charles Somers in near-by Philadelphia, hoping for a call to come before the League and explain his position. The League, sensing that the American League now constituted the larger threat, was changing its strategy. It was shortly given out that the League was sympathetic to the American Association's ambitions to establish clubs in the East. The League also awarded Johnson's Kansas City and Minneapolis territories to a new Western League.

With this double stroke the League hoped to stop Johnson by preventing him from expanding eastward and by burning some of his bridges behind him in the West. The apparent effort to keep the American League a minor, along with the snub given to Johnson, made him decide to go forward with his plans to invade the East. The American League not only moved into Washington, Baltimore, and Philadelphia, in the process abandoning Minneapolis, Kansas City, and Indianapolis, it also changed its plans for going into Buffalo and instead placed a club in Boston, stronghold of the League's triumvirs.

A key man in the expansion was Charles Somers. He had already backed the Cleveland Club and financed Comiskey's move into Chicago. Now he put up more money to help start teams in Boston and Philadelphia. Connie Mack, who had been managing the American League's Milwaukee Club, was awarded part of the Philadelphia ownership and management of the team, and, before long, others, notably Ben Shibe, partner of Al Reach in the sporting goods business, bought into the club. This made Reach and Shibe partners in business but competitors in baseball, since Reach was running the National League's club in Philadelphia.

In Baltimore John J. McGraw, who had been enticed away from the still tentative American Association, was Johnson's choice to head the club. Mack and McGraw were to become two of the most famous and successful managers of the twentieth century. Mack stayed on with the American League, managing the Athletics for nearly half a century, but McGraw left after two years to manage the National League New York Giants.

In February 1901 President Johnson made a statement announcing his league's intentions:

> The National League has taken it for granted that no one had a right to expand without first getting its permission. We did not think that this was necessary, and have expanded without even asking for permission. . . . If we had waited for the National League to do something for us, we would have remained a minor league forever. The American League will be the principal organization of the country within a very short time. Mark my prediction.

The baseball business was thus plunged into still another trade war. Again much of the action revolved around player-grabbing, and, as usual, the players were the chief beneficiaries as salaries were bid up and other concessions were won. The Protective Association was in the happy position of being able to play off one league against the other. Right after its demands were turned down by the National League, Zimmer went to see Ban Johnson. Ban formally recognized the Association and acceded to its demands.

Zimmer then went back to the National League with a modification of the players' original requests. The League agreed to abolish farming and selling without the players' consent, and was willing to put a limit on the reserve. But it would grant these concessions only on condition that the Protective Association suspend any of its members who jumped to the American League. Zimmer was in a quandary. If he accepted this condition, he would in effect be asking the players to blacklist themselves.

However, he agreed to the proposal, but shrewdly left the Protective Association a loophole. When the players heard about the Zimmer Agreement, they decided they had been "bunkoed"—until their attorney reassured them by pointing out that Zimmer had merely agreed that players who jumped would be suspended "pending final action by the Protective Association as a body." As it turned out, players ignored the Agreement and transferred in droves to the American League. The

Protective Association, of course, took advantage of Zimmer's loophole and reinstated them to membership.

The American League respected the National League's contracts but paid no attention to its reserve clause. Even at that, it was extremely successful in raiding National League stars. Players were eager to go after the salary increases offered them by the American League. Besides, they liked the way Johnson ran his league, and were glad of an opportunity to escape to it from the National, which had repressed them ever since smashing the Brotherhood and the American Association.

A check of club rosters made by Lee Allen, historian for the Hall of Fame, showed that of 182 players appearing on American League teams in 1901, 111 were former National Leaguers. However, as Allen pointed out, this does not mean that every one of them was a reserve jumper. Some had merely played for a National League club at one time during their careers. The *Spalding Guide for 1902* reported that 74 players went over to the American League in the first two years of the war. American League attendance increased from a reported 1,683,584 in 1901 to 2,206,457 in 1902, with six of its clubs showing profits that year. Meanwhile, National League attendance fell off from an estimated 1,920,031 in 1901 to 1,683,012 in 1902.

In the fight for players the American League received a serious setback in the courts which momentarily threatened to strip it of its newly acquired corps of National Leaguers. In March 1901 the Philadelphia League Club brought suit to prevent Napoleon Lajoie, its star second baseman, and pitchers William Bernhard and Chick Fraser from jumping the reserve and playing with their local American League rival. The Common Pleas Court of Philadelphia refused to grant an injunction on the ground that the baseball contract was lacking in mutuality. The Phillies then appealed to the Supreme Court of Pennsylvania, and succeeded in getting the lower court's decision reversed on Lajoie, who was the key player.

Lajoie pleaded that the old doctrine of *Lumley* v. *Wagner* did not apply to him, because his services were not of a unique or extraordinary character, and the Phillies could hire an adequate substitute. However, the judge denied his contention, saying that Lajoie "might not be the sun in the baseball firmament, but he is certainly a bright, particular star," hence his loss would result in irreparable injury to the plaintiff.

Furthermore, the higher court was not persuaded that Lajoie's contract lacked mutuality, for it differed from most baseball contracts in that its reserve clause was limited to three years, and Lajoie's salary, if the club's option to renew the contract was exercised, was fixed at $2400. Besides, his contract included paragraphs giving the club the right to enforce specific performance and to enjoin him from playing with another. So what may have appeared to be a reversal of previous baseball law, as handed down notably in the Brotherhood cases, was not, because of the special features in Lajoie's contract.

Although disturbed by the decision, the American League quickly found means to circumvent its effects. Lajoie and Bernhard were transferred to the Cleveland Club (Fraser voluntarily returned to the Phillies). When Cleveland came to play the Athletics in Philadelphia, Lajoie and Bernhard spent the time relaxing at Atlantic City. The Phillies appealed to the Common Pleas Court in Cleveland to hold the players in contempt for ignoring the Pennsylvania court's injunction, but their suit was dismissed on the ground that the Ohio court lacked geographical jurisdiction.

The National League tried unsuccessfully to restrain reserve jumpers in other states, notably Missouri. There a St. Louis court denied injunctions to the local League club to restrain Bobby Wallace, John Heidrick, and Charles Harper from playing in the American League, because their contracts lacked mutuality, were "elements of a combination in violation of the Sherman Act," and abrogated the players' Constitutional rights to follow their chosen occupation.

The chief victims of player-snatching were the minor leagues, which were raided by both the American and the National Leagues. The American League, as an "outlaw" league which had abrogated the National Agreement, could be expected to pirate minor leaguers. But the National League, as the reputed defender of the National Agreement and stability in baseball, might have been expected to continue to follow "baseball law." Instead, thinking only of its own interests, it renounced the National Agreement, leaving the minors without protection at a time when they badly needed it.

This blow culminated years of minor league dissatisfaction with the way the majors treated them. The minors had been members of the National Agreement ever since the early 1880's, when they were permitted to join under the "Articles of Qualified Admission." Under this arrangement they got some slight benefits from membership, but were not given the protection of the reserve clause. Therefore their players could be taken by major league clubs at the end of each season, when their contracts expired. With their property rights in players unprotected, the minors led a precarious existence, and each year many leagues were forced to cease operation.

Not until the end of 1887 did the minors succeed in winning the right to reserve their players by paying a $250 protection fee per club. Although this reform helped the minors, casualties among them were still high. Big payrolls were chiefly blamed, but, when minor league owners tried to cut expenses by establishing salary limits, these same owners broke their agreements just about as fast as they made them. Major league club owners, too, were left dissatisfied. They complained that giving the reserve right to the minors compelled them to pay "exorbitant" prices for players.

Compromise was reached in 1892 in the new National Agreement at the end of the Second Association War. The minors retained the right to reserve their men, but at the end of each season the majors could draft promising players at fixed prices. The minors were divided into two classes, A and B. Class A leagues and the National League could draft players from class B clubs for $500. The National League could requisition men from class A clubs for $1000. Any minor leaguer could be drafted, but selections could be made only between October 1 and February 1.

Classification of minors and the draft were not new ideas. They had been proposed in the late 'eighties as part of the much-publicized "Millennium Plan," a grandiose scheme conceived by Frank Richter, editor of *Sporting Life*, for combining all professional clubs as equal partners in "one grand confederation." And in 1889 A. G. Spalding also drew up an elaborate reorganization plan to solve the difficulties of the minors, but under Spalding's plan the majors would control the whole system. Both Richter's and Spalding's plans contained provisions for classification of minor leagues, salary limitation, and the draft— ideas which were later adopted.

The compromise of 1892 helped stabilize the minors and at the same time allowed the majors to pick their best players at nominal cost. It also encouraged the minors to sell the contracts of outstanding players (who would have been drafted anyway) at a good price before the draft period set in. From the player's point of view, the compromise had the advantage of aiding him to advance in his profession.

Even so, there was still great dissatisfaction during the 'nineties, and year after year the newspapers were filled with complaints. Major league owners constantly objected that draft prices were too high, and the minors were indignant over the subterfuges employed by big league owners in bypassing the draft rule. Especially were they aroused over the increasingly prevalent farming system, by which the major league sent players to the minors for further seasoning and at the same time still held the players under contract.

Time and again minor league owners talked of banding together to resist, and a number of attempts to organize were made. At the end of 1895 they did unite, electing Ban Johnson as their head, and succeeded in gaining some relief, notably a reduction in their protection fees. However, abuses continued, and the minor leaguers became progressively more dissatisfied until the final insult came when the National League abrogated the National Agreement in 1901. This action threw the minors on their own and compelled them to form their own organization, the National Association of Professional Baseball Leagues.

With Pat Powers, head of the Eastern League, as their president, the minors drew up their own National Agreement, which provided for protection fees among themselves, draft rules, classification of their leagues, and salary limits. They appealed to the National League to respect their rights in players, but were refused. Nevertheless, forming their own organization opened a new era in minor league history, and in the future they would be in a stronger position at the conference tables of Organized Baseball.

If breaking relations with the minors was a blunder by the National League, it was dwarfed in importance by the internal rupture in the winter of 1901 that split the League into two warring factions. In previous baseball wars the League triumphed because it had been able to present a united front under able leadership and take advantage of the weakness or inept leadership of its opponents. This time the reverse was true.

The factional wrangling among the owners which had become so prevalent in the 'nineties reached a climax at the December 1901 League sessions. The result was to divert the League's attention from Ban Johnson's challenge and to split its owners into two opposing groups. The bitter fight stemmed from secret conferences held the previous summer at Andrew Freedman's estate in Red Bank, New Jersey. Although there were many rumors, the details of what took place there were not revealed until the winter meetings of the National League, probably the most sensational in its history.

The Red Bank conferees, besides Freedman, were Brush of Cincinnati, Robison of St. Louis, and Soden of Boston. Brush, the author of the old salary limitation plan as well as the purification rule, created a scheme which would bring the syndicate ball of the 'nineties to its ultimate expression. Under his plan, National League clubs would lose their individual identity and be merged into a single new holding company.

Brush has been blamed as the instigator of the plan, and doubtless it was he who prepared the version worked out at the Red Bank meetings. But it is also true that, prior to Red Bank, A. G. Spalding had his own plan for a combine. Spalding had met with Ban Johnson and sounded him out on the possibility of ending the war by uniting the National and American Leagues into one baseball organization. Spalding hoped to convince a majority of National League clubs to give him an option to purchase them. Then, with the clubs in his control, he would be in a position to work out his scheme with Johnson.

Spalding asked for and, Johnson granted him, a month in which to pick up the options. However, he failed to secure them, and the scheme fell through. In the meantime, other National League magnates, particularly Brush and Freedman, learned about Spalding's idea. Later they were to claim that their own plan for consolidating the National League into what amounted to a trust—although they denied that it was one—came from Spalding's idea.

The details of the Brush plan leaked out and were published in the New York *Sun* on December 11, as the League magnates were in the midst of their annual meeting. According to the *Sun*, the plan provided that preferred stock drawing a 7 per cent dividend would belong to the National League as a body. Common stock was to be issued approximately as follows: New York, 30 per cent; Cincinnati, 12 per cent; St. Louis, 12 per cent; Boston, 12 per cent; Philadelphia, 10 per cent; Chicago, 10 per cent; Pittsburgh, 8 per cent; and Brooklyn, 6 per cent. In other words, about 66 per cent of the stock would be in the hands of the Freedman-Brush group, giving them control of the new enterprise, to be called the National Baseball Trust.

The combine was to be managed by a Board of Regents consisting of not more than five men selected for a period of years by the stockholders. From this Board a president and treasurer were to be chosen, the president to receive not more than $25,000 and the treasurer not over $12,000. The Board would have complete control of the League, appointing club managers at $5000 a year, licensing all players in the way jockeys are licensed, and assigning them wherever it chose.

The news that a trust was being contemplated brought an outcry from the press and alienated public opinion. This was the time in American history when the so-called muckrakers were beginning to expose the practices and machinations of the great monopolies—trusts, as they were called—and their revelations had brought the very word "trust" into bad odor.

Exactly what happened in the melodramatic National League meetings was later revealed when *Sporting Life* printed the stenographic record of the proceedings in its February 8, 1902, issue. The fighting started as soon as the meeting opened. Barney Dreyfuss of Pittsburgh nominated A. G. Spalding for the League presidency. There had long been talk of calling Spalding out of retirement to assume leadership of the League. For one thing, nearly a year before, Frank Robison had promoted the idea in a round-robin letter to the owners. Many of them realized that they needed a single strong leader, such as Spalding, if they were going to stand up against the American League. They were equally sure that hard-working, conscientious Nick Young was not the man for such a crisis, and they were not at all bashful about saying so.

But now, with Spalding nominated, the Red Bank faction immediately prevented a vote by raising a point of order and arguing that they could not elect a president until they knew what organization he was going to head. They went on to insist that since the Indianapolis Agreement, binding the National League clubs together for ten years, was about to expire, the League in its present form was at an end and had to be replaced. They knew that if they succeeded in getting their interpretation of the situation accepted, the way would be open for the trust plan. They claimed that what was needed was a new, improved organization which would eliminate the weaknesses of the past, give greater business security to the member clubs, and place them in a stronger position to combat the American League.

On the second day Spalding himself walked into the meeting. Claiming the right to speak, as an honorary member of the League, he delivered a long, impassioned address, pleading with the magnates not to kill the League. He dredged up and romanticized the League's early history and his part in it, and condemned the owners for abrogating the National Agreement. He inferred that they had soiled the glorious history of the League by not measuring up to their responsibilities. Spalding hoped they would not let the League die, but if it must happen, he wanted to be in on the last rites. He said he had not authorized placing his name in nomination for the presidency. Although he was not seeking the office, he wanted them to hurry up and decide one way or the other, because as things stood he was placed in a peculiar position before the public.

Spalding soon left the meeting so as not to embarrass anyone during the voting. Rogers then moved for Spalding's election by acclamation, but the result was a four to four deadlock, with the four Red Bank magnates standing together in opposition. However, the other block did succeed in getting a five to one decision (two abstaining on the ground that it was a legal question) that the League was not terminated because of the ten-year agreement but was a perpetual organization.

The following day the Freedman-Brush faction attempted to put over their plan under the guise of amending the constitution. During the long wrangle which followed, they tried to show that their program had developed out of Spalding's option plan. They implied that Spalding was not coming to the table with clean hands, that what he really wanted was to form a baseball trust similar to his bicycle trust. When he heard about this charge, Spalding denied it, claiming that his object in obtaining the options was simply to end interlocking ownership of clubs by putting local money behind them, and, secondly, to force Freedman out of baseball.

The stenographic record of the meeting also showed that Ebbets and Rogers complained indignantly of being kept in the dark about the Freedman-Brush plan, and were told that Brush's illness had prevented him from apprising each club owner of it before the League meeting, as he had intended. They finally got a chance to read the plan, but decided it was impracticable. They were not going to hand over their property in exchange for stock.

Meanwhile, Spalding called a press conference. Telling the reporters that the issue was between him and Freedmanism, and that one or the other must go, he called on them for support in helping him gain the presidency.

The climax came on the fifth day of the meeting—Friday the thirteenth of December. With efforts to put over the Brush plan by amendment frustrated, the owners turned once more to the election of a president. The pro-Spalding faction nominated him again, and the other block put up Nick Young. Ballot after weary ballot was cast, on into the night, with the same monotonous result—a four to four dead-lock.

Finally, at a late hour, the New York, Boston, St. Louis, and Cin-cinnati owners left the room, leaving Nick Young, with their proxies, in the chair. Young announced that they could not proceed because there was now no quorum. John I. Rogers, the Philadelphia owner, insisted that "once a quorum, always a quorum." Young left the meet-ing, telling the secretary not to take any more minutes. This left an opening for some fancy maneuvering by the four owners who were left. They elected Rogers chairman pro tem and then proceeded to elect Spalding president by a four to nothing vote.

Notified of his "election" in the early hours of the morning, Spalding got out of bed and appropriated the League records from the protesting Nick Young. The next day he called a meeting. The roll call showed only the four pro-Spalding clubs represented, but Spalding, in the chair, noticing a Mr. Knowles, an official of Freedman's New York Club, standing in the doorway, counted him as a fifth representative, and announced that since there was a quorum they could proceed with business.

With members of the press present, the rump president announced his platform in general terms. He would promote and elevate the game, eliminate features tending to disgrace or demoralize it, sub-ordinate finances to sportsmanship, and establish a central governing body with all professional interests, including the players, represented. He concluded by declaring that, now that he was president of the League, Freedman was out of baseball. However, in a matter of hours Spalding was served with papers enjoining him from acting as president or taking possession of the League's records. He put himself beyond the jurisdiction of the court by leaving the state, and then continued his campaign by sending letters to the owners asking their views on his position. Three who elected him continued their support; Dreyfuss of Pittsburgh hedged; Soden of Boston expressed willingness to sell his interest in the club; Brush and Robison suggested he retire. In the meantime, League affairs came to a standstill, and the playing season was approaching.

The impasse was finally broken when Spalding resigned the following spring from the office he had never really held. A three-man executive committee, made up of Brush as chairman, Soden, and Hart, ran the League in 1902, and then, before the season was over, Freedman left baseball, possibly as part of a deal between the two factions. Brush sold his Cincinnati Club to a Cincinnati syndicate led by George Cox, the famous political boss, and his crony August "Garry" Herrmann, who became president of the Reds. Brush then purchased the Giants from Freedman. Finally, at the annual meeting of the League in December, Harry Pulliam, secretary of the Pittsburgh Club, was elected president as a compromise candidate.

Meanwhile, in the midst of all the turmoil in the National League, Ban Johnson continued to press his advantage. For the 1902 season he dropped Milwaukee, transferring its franchise to the League's St. Louis territory, which except for Chicago was the largest city permitting Sunday games at that time. However, the steady success of the American League received one interruption during the season. The near loss of Baltimore, like the Lajoie case, temporarily posed a serious threat.

The truculent John McGraw, player-manager of the Orioles, repeatedly ran afoul of Johnson, who would not tolerate his umpire-baiting tactics. After suspending McGraw a number of times for brief periods, Johnson finally suspended him indefinitely in July 1902. The angry McGraw turned to John T. Brush, and the two, as agents for Freedman, succeeded in securing control of a majority of the Baltimore stock, which they sold to Freedman. They also took half a dozen Baltimore stars, four of them going to the Giants and two to Brush's Cincinnati Club. McGraw became manager of the Giants, signing a four-year contract at a yearly salary of $11,000. Terms like "traitor" and "deserter" were freely used as Johnson and McGraw blasted each other in the press, and the two remained bitter enemies for the rest of their lives.

McGraw always denied that he jumped his contract, maintaining that the club owed him $7000, money which he had advanced out of pocket for players' salaries, and that he had obtained a legitimate release in lieu of payment. Sports writer Fred Lieb has recorded McGraw's real motivation in leaving, on the basis of a conversation he had with the famous manager years later. McGraw said that he knew that Ban Johnson planned to shift the Baltimore Club to New York, but intended to drop him, so he acted fast and beat Johnson to the punch.

Johnson moved quickly to save the Baltimore situation. Announcing that he was taking over the franchise, he rallied the minority stockholders and, with Wilbert Robinson in charge, put together a makeshift team made up of players donated by other American League clubs, some minor leaguers, and whatever else could be picked up. Baltimore finished last that year, but Johnson had staved off a severe setback. At the end of the year he made his final change in the circuit by switching Baltimore to New York. The American League had now rounded out a circuit which was to remain fixed for over half a century: Boston, New York, Philadelphia, and Washington in the East; Chicago, Cleveland, Detroit, and St. Louis in the West.

Up to this point the American League was able to secure playing sites either by purchasing former National League properties, as in the case of Cleveland, or putting up their own parks, the way Comiskey did on Chicago's South Side. But in New York Johnson was confronted with the possibility that Freedman, through his political connections with Tammany Hall, could get the city to cut a street through any location Johnson might select. However, this danger was overcome when Johnson was himself able to get important political backing from Tammany leaders, so he went ahead and established a small park at 168th Street and Broadway.

By now, the fall of 1902, most of the National League magnates had had enough. They had undergone the financial drain of two years of war and still had no prospect of winning. It was they who made the first move to bring about peace. While Johnson and some of his men were in New York completing arrangements for their club there, peace feelers were sent out to them by some of the League men who were gathering for their December meeting.

When Johnson expressed willingness to listen, representatives on both sides got together for further talks. At first the National Leaguers tried the old approach so successful with the American Association. They proposed consolidation into a single twelve-club league. But Johnson firmly rejected this, and insisted that the American League must be left intact. The League had no choice but to accept.

With the preliminary sparring out of the way, two committees—

Johnson, Somers, Comiskey, and Henry Killilea of Boston, for the American League, and Hart, Robison, Herrmann, and Pulliam for the National League—met in Cincinnati on January 9, and after two days of hard work reached agreement.

The main problem was to settle territorial rights and ownership of players. The League agreed to let the American League stay in New York in exchange for Johnson's promise not to invade Pittsburgh. After full discussion of all contract claims of the various clubs, two lists were drawn up, one for the National and one for the American, showing which players were "legally awarded" to each club. This of course gave the American League the advantage, because they were able to hold onto many of the stars who had jumped from the National League. Both sides agreed to recognize the reserve rights of each other's clubs, and a uniform contract for the use of each league was adopted. It was decided that neither circuit could be changed without the consent of a majority of the clubs of each league, and there was to be no consolidation in any city where two clubs existed. Both leagues agreed to co-operate on playing rules and scheduling of games. Finally, each league appointed a committee of one—the respective presidents—to draw up a National Agreement governing all of Organized Baseball, and they were to invite P. T. Powers, president of the minor league organization, to confer with them on formulating it.

A few of the National League magnates were still dissatisfied, mostly with the distribution of players. But with the exception of John T. Brush, they decided to accept the peace treaty. Brush, bitterly objecting to an American League Club competing with him in New York, fought against Johnson's circuit to the last ditch, securing an injunction to prevent his fellow National League owners from concluding the peace. However, he finally relented and went along with the others.

The new National Agreement incorporated the essence of the Cincinnati peace and provided for a three-man National Commission to govern the game. The commission was to be composed of the president of each major league, plus a third member, chosen by them, who would also act as chairman. This eliminated the old Board of Control and further concentrated the executive power. The new governmental structure prevailed until superseded by the appointment of a so-called Commissioner of Baseball in 1920.

The minor leagues, united under the National Association, came back into Organized Baseball as a third party to the agreement, and received certain rights and protections, including a system for drafting players, reserve rights in its men, protection of territorial rights, and a stipulation prohibiting farming. As for the other groups which were factors in the complex American League War, the Players' Protective

Association quietly died, and the abortive American Association, which really never got going as a major, was relegated to minor league status.

The bitter struggle between the American and National Leagues turned out to be beneficial to baseball. Certainly it was a blessing in disguise for the National League, which had been on a steady downgrade until defeat and a new regime restored it to public confidence and prosperity. The war proved the feasibility and healthiness of having two major leagues of equal status in competition. With the conclusion of peace and the drawing up of the new National Agreement, the long era of nineteenth-century baseball came to a close. The business end of the game reached a new maturity, and the foundation was laid down on which Organized Baseball has rested ever since.

26

PLAYERS, FANS, AND UMPIRES

BASEBALL'S evolution from a simple participant's game to a commercialized amusement made spectators of the many and folk heroes of a few. Shut off from the traditional rural sports, city dwellers turned for a substitute to the vicarious thrills of spectator amusements. Even though the baseball fan had no financial equity whatever in his local club, he identified with it, following its daily fortunes, rejoicing in its victories, and suffering in its defeats. Even though not a single player might come from the team's city, the fans looked upon them as representatives of their city, and they tended to glorify and make heroes of otherwise ordinary men who happened to be highly proficient in batting, catching, and throwing a ball. In the nineteenth century the professional ball player, therefore, was already emerging as one of the new-style American folk heroes.

Fans were beginning to lionize ball players. Mike Kelly was presented with a house (well mortgaged, to be sure) and a carriage in 1891, and was made the subject of a popular song, *Slide, Kelly, Slide!* The great personal concern of New York fans over Amos Rusie's holdout and the $500 raised by Fred Pfeffer's admirers to pay his fine dramatized the inflated importance of professionals in the minds of the faithful.

Baltimore's first pennant evoked a remarkable outburst of civic pride. Business establishments shut down and the city had the look of a carnival. In New York, enthusiasts jammed their way into a testimonial for the Giants after they won the Temple Cup in 1894. The $4000 paid by the fans to honor their heroes made the victory all the more enjoyable for the champions.

Journalists had started the practice, now so prevalent, of furnishing the public with details about the players' private habits and personal idiosyncrasies. Fans were informed of Cy Seymour's "phenomenal two-handed" eating and provided with a detailed list of thirty-six dishes he supposedly once consumed before a game. They were told of Cy Young's good humor, and of John Clarkson's irritable temper. They learned that Dummy Hoy was a well-read gentleman with polished manners, and that, while McGraw was tough on the field, off it he was gentlemanly and pleasant-mannered. Newspapers and guide books divulged the weight, height, and other vital statistics of players. Even though they may never have seen him pitch, thousands of fans knew that Will White wore glasses on the field—the first player ever to do so as far as can be determined. A sketch appeared in the New York *World* showing the Giants getting off the boat on their return from spring training dressed in top hats, spats, and boutonnieres, and carrying canes.

Players' private domestic problems became public information. Fans were given blow-by-blow accounts of divorce actions involving Ward, Rusie, and Mullane. They knew about Latham's wife trouble, and were supplied with the lurid details of Pete McNabb's murder of another man's wife and his own suicide.

Sports writers anticipated Ring Lardner's classic stories of rookie players coming to the city for the first time. Humorous anecdotes were gleefully told about their naïveté, such as the story about the player who blew out the gas before going to bed and nearly asphyxiated himself and his roommate. Then there was one reporting a literary discussion between two players:

> That man Finis must be a great writer. I read his name at the end of more than 300 books.
> You blockhead, Finis is the name of the publisher of those books.

It was also claimed that experience in the big league quickly rubbed off the rough edges on such yokels and that their poise and polish was readily seen in their changed behavior and the new cut of their clothes. And occasionally players' names appeared endorsing sporting equipment, but this form of testimonial advertising did not become widespread until well into the twentieth century, when ball players, like movie stars, made extra money lending their names to the sale of products, from cigarettes to razor blades.

Baseball devotees were a very good cross section of the American population. Newspapers remarked that at the ball game, workmen and clerks were brought together and placed on the same level as the well-to-do. While differentiation in the prices and location of seats prevented the classes from rubbing elbows as much as was sometimes boasted, it was true, nevertheless, that people from all walks of life went to the games. Sketches of fans in the newspapers showed people decked out in top hats, with canes and cigars, as well as those in shirtsleeves, wearing derbies and caps. Government officials, professional people, businessmen, and stage celebrities enjoyed the game just as much as those who sat in the bleachers or were content with standing room.

Even in the late 1870's advertisements of the Providence Club helped to attract physicians, preachers, lawyers, judges, and other well-known citizens. President Benjamin Harrison, "a great lover of baseball," frequently attended Washington games, sometimes accompanied by members of his cabinet. State and city officials also were to be seen at the ball parks. In 1892 a political convention adjourned to go to the ball game. Wall Street bulls and bears "bellowed and growled" in the grandstand when the Giants were at home. In the play, *The Runaway Colt,* one of the characters, a bishop, explained that clergymen went to games, as well as merchants, bankers, lawyers, and college professors. So nineteenth-century fans were not just lower-class people or those of limited intelligence. The image of the fan as an individual from most any walk of life drawn irresistibly to baseball is illustrated in a poem printed in the *Official Base Ball Record* in 1886:

> "In court," says the card on the lawyer's door,
> "Back in ten minutes," on many more;
> "Gone to the hospital," on the doctor's slate.
> On another, "Sit down and wait."
> "Gone to the bank," on the notary's sign;
> "Arbitration," that young clerk of mine.
> "Back soon," on the broker's book;
> "Collecting rents," on my agent's hook.
> They were all too busy, a matter quite new,
> Very sorry was I, I had nothing to do.
> Then I hied me hence to the baseball ground,
> And every man on the grand stand found.

However, it seems likely that middle-class and professional people and the sporting crowd formed the bulk of weekday attendance. It is hardly likely that ordinary workingmen could get away on weekdays, except for bricklayers, longshoremen, carpenters, and various part-time workers who might have some days off between jobs. But it was workingmen who swelled the Sunday crowds.

As one might expect, second-generation Irish and Germans were among the most ardent baseball followers. The children of those who came to this country in the great wave of German and Irish immigration of the 1840's showed at least that much evidence of their Americanization. Some of the most rabid New York fans were the sons of Irish immigrants, who inhabited "Burkeville," as the bleacher section of the Polo Grounds was sometimes called. In St. Louis the interest of

German-Americans was revealed by advertisements placed in German-language newspapers by the ball club. Although the color line barred Negroes from playing in the big leagues, their patronage was quite acceptable. New York newspapers, for example, quoted not only fans with Irish accents but those with what passed for Negro speech characteristics as well.

Baseball was also greatly helped by the changing status of women in the latter half of the nineteenth century. No longer did the genteel prudery of an earlier day confine them to the home. The so-called new women sought new goals—jobs and general emancipation. American women began openly participating in sporting activities like archery, lawn tennis, croquet, and cycling. *Godey's Lady's Book*, which regularly carried feature articles on outdoor athletics for American women, was an unmistakable barometer of the new interests and broadening outlets available to women.

Another barometer was their growing interest in baseball and the efforts of the clubs to attract their patronage. Ministers like Henry Ward Beecher might rail against these new trends, but they did not change them. The presence of women at games was thought desirable for at least two reasons. It was believed that they elevated the tone of the audience and that men would be drawn to any place where women were. As the *Ball Players Chronicle* observed way back in 1867, women's attendance "purifies the moral atmosphere of a base ball gathering, repressing . . . all outbursts of intemperate language which the excitement of a contest so frequently induces." The words of a popular song of that era, *The Base Ball Fever*, connected the terminology of the game with the elaborate hairdos then in fashion.

It has been assumed that the first Ladies' Day was established in the 1880's, but actually it was introduced much earlier. The Knickerbockers set aside the last Thursday of each month as Ladies' Day in 1867, at which time members were requested to invite their wives, daughters, and girl friends, and appointed a committee to see that "suitable seats or settees" were available for them. When the professionals took over the game, the owners soon adopted the practice. On such days they usually admitted ladies free if accompanied by gentlemen. The Athletics and the Orioles designated each Thursday as Ladies' Day in 1883, and other clubs held special days for ladies that year, too. The success of the plan caused more clubs to fall into line, and the following year the leading parks had regular Ladies' Days.

The big league clubs also provided special facilities for women. Cincinnati had a set of enclosed steps from the field to the grandstand so that ladies who arrived in carriages could reach their special section without walking through the crowd. Parks also had ladies' rest rooms with a woman in attendance. Clubs frequently advertised their accommodations for women and promised protection from the annoyance of "distasteful expressions and spectacles." In some parks men were not admitted to the ladies' section unless accompanied by a woman, and they were not permitted to smoke there.

Once the complaint was made that the "charming deadheads," as the New York *World* called the women admitted free, swarmed into the Pittsburgh park and grabbed all the best seats, thus forcing the paying males to take what was left. On the other hand there was an occasion when the ladies were swindled. In his desperate days of the middle 'nineties Von der Ahe once advertised a Ladies' Day, but when the women arrived, they found to their dismay that they had the choice of sitting on the hard boards of the bleachers or paying twenty-five cents if they wanted a seat in the stands. The ignorance, real or feigned, of women about baseball was already a standard joke in newspapers, and it was said that some women came only because their boy friends were fans. Yet there were many cases of women who knew baseball well enough and were sufficiently versed in its mysteries to keep score.

A few of the more brazen—or more emancipated—women performed with women's teams. One of them from Pennsylvania, the Dolly Vardens, played in red-and-white calico dresses "of remarkable shortness," as one male observer noticed. Another "female team" played on a smaller-than-regulation diamond using a ball made entirely of yarn. Sometimes they played against male teams of only five men, who were also given handicaps, like fielding and throwing left-handed or using one hand to bat. One of these outfits, managed by a man, was reputed to be nothing but a traveling harem.

The baseball *aficionado* was already becoming a stereotype in American folk lore. The "krank," as he was called before the terms "fan" and "rooter" were used, was said to have achieved a high degree of cultivation, whereas the female of the species, the "kranklet," was only partially developed. Supposedly, the krank had a shell into which he crawled in November to hibernate until April. During his hibernation he subsisted on stray newspaper articles about baseball. His chief characteristics were "knowing it all" and "telling it all." He cheered his favorites, and sometimes booed them, and abused the opposition. The shouted comments of the more uninhibited were reported in the newspapers. Sometimes fans came equipped with noisemakers. In Brooklyn two young men were in the habit of shouting advice to the home team through megaphones and trying to rattle opposing pitchers. Such "grandstand managers," as they are known today, frequently gave gratuitous advice and assistance to the management. A letter from

one of them, still preserved, congratulated Owner Stern of Cincinnati
in 1886:

> We are very glad to see you signing young players, and hope you
> will continue the good work, and get rid of the old stiffs and played
> out players. . . . Let the Bums and Lushers go.

Some of the more persistent exhibitionists in the audience had the
satisfaction of getting publicized in the newspapers and becoming a
colorful part of the baseball scene. One of these, a Giant fan whose
real name was Frank H. Wood, became known far and wide simply as
"Well! Well! Well!" because of his habit of jumping to his feet after
every good or bad play and shouting this cry. Once he tried to sing his
pet expression instead, and was nearly buried under a deluge of hats,
umbrellas, cigar stumps, beer glasses, and a miscellaneous assortment of
projectiles. Zane Grey made him the hero of a boys' baseball book, *The
Redheaded Outfield.* "General" Hi Hi Dixwell, whose title was dubious,
was another famous fan. He attended all the Boston home games,
traveled with the club, and frequently presented the players with
boxes of cigars. "He lives," said *Sporting News,* "for the national game."
Other cities also had their representative cranks (the word was spelled
both ways). Miss Maggie Cline, "a buxom young lady" from New
York, won renown as a "thirty-third degree crank." Theater people
were also faithful fans. Two of the best-known in New York were the
famous actors De Wolf Hopper, who gained lasting fame for his rendition of "Casey at the Bat," and Digby Bell.

Even in those days Brooklyn fans were considered offensive by the
opposition. After one fracas with them, in which the team's safety
was endangered, a St. Louis player, Home Run Duffee, a native of
Mobile, declared he would rather hoe cotton down in Alabama for
ten dollars a month than "run the gauntlet" of Brooklyn fans the next
years. His teammate, Iceberg Chamberlain, agreed that the "Brooklyn
thug is the toughest of the tough. Oystertown can turn out several
tough 'uns but the City of Churches certainly walks off with the cake."
The fans could be fickle as well as loyal. Even the popular and respected
Cap Anson complained of the taunts of Chicago fans, whom he called
the worst in the world. He grew tired of the chaffing about his age:
"I'm 'Papa' and 'Pappy' and 'Uncle' and 'Unk' and 'Anse' and 'the old
man' and I must be roasted. . . . Why I would rather face Cleveland
hoodlums than play here at home."

Like the fan, the player was being stereotyped. Distorted impressions of him were already being formed. Newspapers thought it amusing to satirize his "hard life." One of them depicted him as a gentleman
of leisure six months of the year, who arose at 10:00 A.M. during the

season, had a "snug" breakfast, read the papers, smoked a Reina
Victoria, napped before his 2 o'clock dinner, strolled to the ball park
at about 3, where he took a little exercise for a couple of hours, and
then returned for supper, smoked, went with girls to the theater, and
of course drew his salary. Fans who were reading about sweatshop
conditions and the hard lot of miners were advised not to overlook the
suffering of baseball stars, who, ruthlessly roused from sleep at ten in
the morning, were compelled to change to their uniforms without the
aid of valets. Then they stood on their feet for a few hours, occasionally
catching a ball or beating the air with their bats, and later returned to
their hotels, where they spent the evening shooting dice or sitting
around the lobby. When the Phillies grumbled over having to report
for morning practice, O. P. Caylor, that expert of sarcasm, wrote that
they had that "tired feeling" brought on by the "hard hearted overseer,"
Harry Wright, who compelled them to work five hours a day instead of
the customary two.

Ruffianism and drunken brawling tended to be overemphasized in the
papers because such escapades made news. Writers liked to tell how
Indianapolis lost a game 24 to 0 because most of the team was drunk the
night before. Whenever teams did not play up to expectation, often as
not their failure was attributed to drinking. Occasionally players would
appear on the field under the influence of alcohol. *Sporting News* told
of King Kelly holding up an exhibition game while he quaffed beer with
disreputable characters in the grandstand. Attention was called to the
close relationship between the bench and the bar: players relegated to
the bench were generally practitioners at the bar! Once the New York
World, in reporting that the Browns were working hard on new signals,
suggested that one they would not need to learn was the "comprehensive wave of the hand which says eloquently, 'Set 'em up again!'"

Off-the-field capers, frequently enlivened by the consumption of
alcohol, made vivid reading. *Spalding's Guide* in 1889 asserted that
the saloon and the brothel were the prime evils of baseball. Some
notorious escapades have already been described in the discussion of
baseball's labor problems. These were only a sampling of the stories
about saloon brawls, hotel and sleeping-car disturbances, occasional
assaults on women, and even thefts which enlivened the sports pages.
Rules which some owners felt it necessary to impose are a clue to the
kind of conduct they expected to cope with. The Athletics were ordered
not to "flirt with or 'mash' any female or lady" while in uniform, and
Indianapolis players were "particularly requested" not to associate with
prostitutes.

From all this, many people gained a highly unfavorable impression
of the professional player. One Annie Burns's mother blocked her

daughter's elopement because she did not want a ball player for a son-in-law. And President Eliot of Harvard shared her opinion. He wrote other college heads to see whether they thought forbidding games between college teams and professionals advisable. A newspaper took this up, sneering that maybe he was on the right track, for if the professionals associated with the "rat-killing, cock-fighting" college men they would rapidly sink to the "lowest level of depravity." And again in *The Runaway Colt* the respectable family in the play was portrayed as very reluctant to entertain a big leaguer in its home. In 1889 a minister was quoted as saying that ball players were "men without character" who "would engage in no legitimate occupation."

Yet this view of the player was one-sided. Contrary to what some still believe, all players were not uncouth ruffians fit only for playing ball and driving beer trucks or tending bar in the off-season. Taken as a whole, they were not much different from any other men of comparable background and education. Some of them were even superior to men of similar background. Billy Sunday of the White Sox, for instance, "a very moral young man," already taught Sunday School in the off-season. Jim White was nicknamed "Deacon" because he did not drink, smoke, swear, or play stud poker, and went regularly to church. John Ward became an attorney after studying law at night. Harry Taylor, who played college ball before turning professional, was another who became an attorney and eventually served as a judge in Erie County, New York. John Reilly was an artist. Others, notably Christy Mathewson and the Indian, Chief Sockalexis, had college backgrounds, and a few, like Dr. Arlie Pond, a Baltimore pitcher, studied medicine. Doc Bushong and Dick Allen were dentists. Allen was good enough to become an instructor at the University of Buffalo Dental School. John McGraw and Hughie Jennings attended college in the off-season. Many old letters written by players showed excellent handwriting and a good choice of words, thus demonstrating that they were not all illiterates.

A study of ball players' activities in the off-season reveals a wide variety of talent and capabilities. Some players ran pool rooms and bowling alleys. One worked in a railroad freight office. Mike Kelly was a race track starter, and Nig Cuppy clerked in a bridge-builder's office. Yale Murphy and Huyler Westervelt were also clerks, in a stockbroker's office. One Buffalo player was an artist for a local newspaper; another was in the upholstery trade; and a third ran a dancing school and kept books for his father's brewery. Joe Kelley was superintendent of a draying business. Cy Young worked in a real-estate office. William Hassamaer helped with his father's coal business, and Joe Quinn lent a hand in his father-in-law's undertaking concern. Some went hunting, or played winter ball for nominal salaries and the chance to spend the cold months in a warm climate. Others, as one newspaper said, were experts at doing nothing.

A few of the stars like King Kelly, Arlie Latham, Tony Mullane, and Cap Anson exploited their fame with stage appearances, where they tried, with indifferent success, to sing or to remember their lines. It was true that many were connected with the saloon business. In fact, there was talk of passing a rule against hiring players who had an interest in a saloon, because some thought players should not use their names and fame to advertise such a business. Yet, as *Sporting News* pointed out, such talk belied the abilities of many players and created the impression that none of them could do anything else.

People who looked down upon ball players, as many did, did not realize that ball players were gaining increasing social acceptance. Dr. A. H. P. Leuf, director of physical education at the University of Pennsylvania, recognized this. In a book on hygiene for ball players published in 1888 he observed that "one of the most encouraging and significant features of the game is the steady improvement in the intellectual and social grade of the players." Newspapers corroborated him. *Sporting News* particularly was at pains to point out that players in general were not the "low-lives" that some seemed to think. Even Henry Chadwick once remarked that the professional athlete was able to gain greater social acceptance than in England, and suffered loss of caste mostly among what he called "a shoddy class of anglomaniacs" in American society.

There was plenty of evidence to support this view. President Chester Arthur received the Cleveland ball club in the spring of 1883, shaking hands with the men, complimenting them on their appearance, and making the rather debatable statement that athletes and ball players always made good citizens. And the White Sox were given audience by President Grover Cleveland, who favored each with "a cheerful word and a hearty grip" before they set out on their world tour in 1889.

Reports from their spring training camp at Macon, Georgia, in 1894 told how the Orioles were making many friends by their "gentlemanly deportment." Similarly, the Giants were said to be the "most orderly, dignified set of men that could have been selected," so well did they comport themselves at the fashionable Lakewood, New Jersey, resort where they trained in 1897. Ladies in hotel dining rooms remarked that they never would have taken the people eating there for ball players. As a rule, ball players dressed well and their table etiquette was quite acceptable. If a "sword-swallower" (one who ate with his knife) turned up, he was soon put straight by his teammates. On the 1889 World Tour the English were surprised at the fine behavior of the players, who appeared at social functions in full dress, and they were astonished

to learn that professionals included men who were pursuing other avo-
cations requiring special talent outside of baseball.

Unquestionably, second-generation Irish and Germans dominated
the professional ranks. In fact, so many Irish were in the game that
some thought they had a special talent for ball playing. Fans liked to
argue the relative merits of players of Irish as against those of German
extraction. Since the Irish immigrants who swarmed into the growing
urban centers were largely relegated to unskilled jobs like hod-carrying
in the building trades, and other construction jobs, their sons who were
fortunate enough to become professional ball players had advanced
considerably on the social and economic ladder.

Ball players came from practically every state in the Union, but a
check made in 1896 showed a majority of them originating in the heavily populated Northeast, with Pennsylvania, Massachusetts, Ohio, and
New York leading. Jewish players were acceptable, and Lipman Pike,
who had a big-league career of seventeen years, playing and managing
for several clubs, is generally regarded as the first of approximately
fifty Jewish players who have worn major league uniforms.

With the Negro it was a different matter, though. It will be remembered that the old amateur association banned colored players, but in
the 'eighties two managed to get a "cup of coffee in the big league,"
as the expression goes for those who spent only a brief time in the
majors. Moses Fleetwood Walker, not Jackie Robinson, as many think,
was the first colored major leaguer. Walker, who had attended Oberlin
College, was regarded as one of the most intelligent professionals. He
caught for the American Association's Toledo Club in 1884, and, when
teamed up with Tony Mullane, made a battery with great drawing
power that year. Another colored player who played a few games at
that time with Toledo was Weldy W. Walker, an outfielder. More
than fifty, like George Stovey, Bud Fowler, and James R. Jackson,
got as far as the minors. Frank Grant was such a fine second baseman
for the Buffalo International League Club that he was dubbed the
"Black Dunlap," after the famous big league star Fred Dunlap.

But their careers were blemished by racial prejudice, often of the
most virulent kind. Once in Louisville Fleet Walker had to sit in the
stands and watch his team play because an opposing player refused to
take part if he did. Another time the Toledo manager was afraid to put
Walker in the line-up for an exhibition game in Richmond, Virginia,
because of a letter from six local whites warning that seventy-five
"determined men" had sworn to mob the catcher if he showed up in
uniform.

It is a well-known historical paradox that, as the Civil War receded,

Jim Crowism in America became more pronounced. Southern caste attitudes spread increasingly to the North and West, much to the alarm of liberals and reformers. This blight included professional baseball in its contagious advance. White players objected to the "colored element." Even the redoubtable Anson refused to go through with an exhibition game against Newark if Fleet Walker and George Stovey played. So by the late 1880's the major leagues erected a solid, though unofficial, dam against Negroes, shutting off completely the tiny trickle which had previously flowed through. This color line, so damaging to baseball's vaunted claims to being democratic, held until 1947 when Jackie Robinson became the first modern player to be admitted to the majors. Of course, some big league clubs thought it was lucky and amusing to have a colored man or boy for a mascot, but, as far as playing was concerned, Negroes had to perform with their own professional clubs, although they sometimes had a chance to play against white teams.

One of the chief concerns of ball players was keeping in condition. Indeed, physical fitness was practically a fetish with them. In letter after letter written in the off-season to their managers, players revealed an almost compulsive need to assure the boss that they were keeping in trim by walking, hunting, joining gymnasiums, exercising, or tossing a ball. Those who became overweight during the winter were ridiculed in the newspapers and compelled to reduce in preparation for the season. The constant admonitions against touching strong liquor and the preoccupation of many of the men with diet were other manifestations of the cult. Cap Anson made a virtue of the bowl of bread and milk to which he limited himself before games, and some clubs had rules against eating a heavy dinner or even indulging in a cigar before donning uniforms for the day's game. One physician cautioned managers against relying on the "dangerous and useless shower," urging them to provide bathtubs and to insist that every man take a bath at least once a week under their own eyes at the hotel or on the club grounds.

Players, like other athletes, notably boxers, buttressed their confidence through a great variety of superstitions. The Boston Club looked for a white pigeon when losing. Chicago practically deified a black cat named Champion. Some clubs objected to having thirteen men on the team. Cross-eyed people were considered ill omens, but a wagonload of empty barrels supposedly meant good luck. One infielder kept a small sack of resin under the bag. Another did somersaults before going on the field. And some were convinced that any team selected by Henry Chadwick to win the pennant was doomed to failure.

In order to get his club to do well on a forthcoming Western trip, John Ward had the men play their last home game in their traveling uniforms, urging them to show extra "ginger," and be particularly on their mettle, in the hope that "the uniform might become accustomed to it." Fans did what they could to ensure luck for their team by sending in rabbit's feet wrapped in silk, lucky playing cards to be worn in their caps, and other fetishes. The players accepted these tokens for what they were worth and used them as directed.

After his active playing career was over, the player had a considerable degree of social mobility if he wanted to take advantage of it. Quite a few did. Some, like Al Spalding, Charles Comiskey, Connie Mack, Ned Hanlon, and John McGraw climbed all the way from player to magnate. Others became team managers, coaches, and umpires, although of course these jobs were limited. Most of them took work outside of baseball, engaging in a wide range of occupations open to men on a comparable level of skill and intelligence.

A reasonably comprehensive survey of ex-big leaguers made by the Buffalo *Times* in 1896 showed them engaged in a wide variety of jobs, including the professions, secret service, fireman, policeman, contracting, restaurant business, cigar dealer, evangelist, hotelkeeper, delivery man, farmer, politics, bookmaker, sports writer, dry goods, brick mason, engraver, boilermaker, artist, glassblower, orange grower, theatrical agent, motorman, and tramp. A few became criminals. One served a term at San Quentin, and another was hanged, but these were great exceptions.

Those who entered the saloon business were often, as one newspaper said, their own best customers. Some, like Billy Hamilton, Hugh Duffy, and Dummy Hoy, accumulated substantial nest eggs and acquired considerable property. Others, because of improvidence or ill fortune, suffered hardship and even destitution. Mike Kelly, for instance, died in poverty, and so did Ed Williamson. Friends of Jim Galvin had to hold a benefit to raise money for his funeral expenses. In those days there was no player's pension. In 1886 the League considered establishing one, but nothing came of it. Some of the needy players did receive aid through benefit games and voluntary collections from former teammates. The magnates raised a purse of about $1400 for King Kelly's widow, and Hub Collins's widow realized about $3000 from a benefit game and player contributions.

While a few great stars lived on in legends and were eventually canonized in the Hall of Fame, most of them returned to obscurity after their brief years in the limelight. As one newspaper explained, in his prime the player was a pet, cheered, patted on the back, and called by his first name. Girls pointed to him on the street, and he swelled with pride and importance, even putting paper in his stockings to make the calves of his legs stand out. But at last the day came when all his glory disappeared. The crowd was quick to turn on him. His popularity vanished, the dudes snubbed him, and newspapers advised him to go back to husking corn. This was the familiar cycle for many a baseball hero.

Even more than the fan and the player, the umpire has become a stereotype. He shares the same low esteem in our American culture as the mule and the mother-in-law, and, traditionally, he is believed to have no friends other than his colleagues. It has been said that, psychologically, he is the product of an unhappy childhood. He is the "heavy" of the baseball drama, the villain of the piece and the object of antagonism and abuse from fans and players both.

Why this should be so makes an interesting subject for the social psychologist. The umpire is a symbol of authority, and many people dislike authority or for one reason or another are frustrated in their daily lives. Much as they might like to attack their boss or fellow worker, they are compelled to suppress such feelings. A henpecked husband, for instance, may be helpless to do anything about his predicament. For these people the umpire supplies a convenient scapegoat. The average person can cut loose at a ball game and take out some of his hostility by directing it at the umpire.

Whatever may be said against the practice, it does provide a more socially acceptable way of letting off steam, and may even be a safety valve for people who might otherwise do something more damaging. Certainly it is preferable to have people boo the umpire, kick chairs, or perform some other relatively harmless act, than to take out their antagonisms by persecuting minority groups, as they have so frequently done throughout history. A contributing explanation of the umpire's position may lie in America's frontier tradition of violence and disrespect for law. For the baseball fan the umpire represents law, and thus for many is an object of dislike.

Aside from the crowd's motives, the umpire is affected by the nature of his job, which exposes him and his decisions for all to see. Close decisions in particular, coming at a crucial point in the game, are bound to foil the hopes of a large part of the audience and 50 per cent of the players. While there is much to boo him for, there is little or no reason to cheer him. If he calls a third strike at a decisive time, either he or the batter might be booed, but any cheering is directed toward the pitcher.

In the course of a game, a baseball umpire must make countless decisions, many of them extremely difficult. It is not easy to decide whether a speeding, curving pitch cuts the corner of the plate or misses it by a fraction of an inch. or whether a runner, hurtling into a base with a tricky slide in a cloud of dust, has been tagged in time or even touched at all. Yet each of these decisions can have an important bearing on the outcome of the game, and each can bring frustration and disappointment to players and fans. The umpire is also a convenient foil for players who sometimes cover up their own failures by blaming him and directing the anger of the fans away from themselves.

This image of the umpire as a character worthy only of abuse was already well formed by the 1880's, as this rhyme, printed in 1886, shows:

> Mother, may I slug the umpire,
> May I slug him right away?
> So he cannot be here, mother,
> When the clubs begin to play?
>
> Let me clasp his throat, dear mother,
> In a dear, delightful grip
> With one hand, and with the other
> Bat him several in the lip.
>
> Let me climb his frame, dear mother,
> While the happy people shout;
> I'll not kill him dearest mother,
> I will only knock him out.
>
> Let me mop the ground up, Mother,
> With his person, dearest, do;
> If the ground can stand it, mother
> I don't see why you can't too.
>
> Mother, may I slug the umpire,
> Slug him right between the eyes?
> If you let me do it, mother,
> You shall have the champion prize.

A similar conception was displayed by a sadistic picture in Thomas Lawson's little book *The Krank, His Language and What It Means*, showing an umpire stretched out in a coffin, with brickbats hurtling through the air upon him, and under it the caption:

The Umpire

> Only a murdered umpire,
> Only a bushel of bricks,
> A can, and a cat, and such things as that,
> And an umpire done with his tricks.

Yet the much-maligned umpire has had a vital role in the game, for the foundation of professional baseball rests largely on his skill and integrity.

At first almost anyone, including players, could umpire. Anybody who was familiar with the rules and had common powers of observation, said the New York *Clipper* in 1866, could handle the job. A handbook for umpires put out in 1875 recognized the necessity for special training, and pointed out that it was much more difficult to get a qualified man, fearless and impartial, for the post than it was to get good ball players, especially since there was no inducement beyond the position's "honorary character."

The old Professional Association's plan of having the home club choose an umpire from among five names submitted by the visiting club was carried over, with slight variations, into the National League. But in 1879 the League took a significant forward step by appointing a staff of twenty men from which clubs could choose their umpire. This reform was instituted to remove local influence over umpires. But it did not go far enough. What was needed, as critics pointed out, was higher salaries paid by the League if good men, independent of local pressures, were to be obtained.

However, it was the American Association which took the lead by hiring a permanent staff of umpires in 1882, paid and assigned by the Association itself. The following year the Association spelled out its regulations for umpires in more detail. The four regulars on the staff received $140 a month, about $1000 a season, and two assistants were paid $10 a game. The Association required double-breasted blue flannel coats, and caps trimmed with gold cord and buttons, which the arbiter had to pay for and keep clean and repaired. The Association also allowed its umpires three dollars a day expense money while on the road, and they did not have to travel with the team or stop at the same hotels. Neither were they allowed to officiate in a city where they resided, and each had to take an oath before a notary promising to do his duty faithfully, honestly, and impartially, and swearing he would have nothing to do with a pool, wager, reward, or any form of gambling. In addition, Association umpires were forbidden to borrow money or accept a present from anyone connected with a ball club. They could be removed if five Association clubs requested it, or if two testified that an umpire had been drunk on the field or had broken the rules. The National League quickly copied the system, and also gave its men a chance to brush up on the rules at an umpire's "school" in Washington under Nick Young's direction.

Selecting umpires was a fairly haphazard procedure. They might be recommended by magnates or through other connections, but there was no systematic method of training men for the job or selecting them on the basis of set qualifications. Near the end of the century a letter from a magnate or a friend of President Young was still the usual way of getting an appointment. The *Tammany Times* satirized the process in 1893:

> Magnate: Ever umpire before?
> Applicant: No.
> Magnate: Play ball?
> Applicant: Never.
> Magnate: Then what are your qualifications?
> Applicant: I've been leader of a church choir for ten years.
> Magnate: Name your salary.

Why anybody wanted the job in those days was a mystery. The well-known umpire Billy McLean was telling the truth when he said, "We get it from all sides." One of the oldest rules of professional baseball, which goes back to the first professional association, bars appeals in decisions involving the umpire's judgment. Only his interpretation of the rules may be questioned. In practice, however, this principle has always been a dead letter, for the main issue has been how far players and managers were able to go in protesting on judgment decisions. They went a great deal further in the nineteenth century than they would ever be permitted in modern baseball. Players and managers abused and insulted umpires as a matter of routine, and all too often assaulted them physically. Club owners and even League President Hulbert were not above going on the field to dispute a decision, or into the umpire's dressing room after the game to reprimand him. The fans were worse. "Mob him!" "Stone him!" "Rotten egg him!" were cries familiar to every umpire, and even the shout "Kill the umpire!" was not always just an idle threat. Many an arbiter probably would have been killed had he not been rescued in time by the police or the players. Newspaper stories of mob attacks on umpires were common.

A crowd of 2000, including well-dressed men and handsome women who "forgot themselves," became a "wild and uncontrollable rabble" as it attacked an umpire at the Polo Grounds in New York in 1884. The police had all they could do to save him as they beat off the crowd with their clubs. Once in Cincinnati, when a player got into a fight with the umpire, and his brother jumped from the stands to help him, the crowd began hurling beer glasses, forcing the umpire to take refuge in the dressing room. It took the entire police force to quell the disorder and rescue him. Hank O'Day, the former pitcher turned umpire, was given a severe beating by a crowd in St. Louis before players and police were able to get him off the field to safety. Especially in the late 'nineties matters got out of hand. Instances of assaults on umpires appeared with monotonous regularity in the press, as the League monopoly seemed utterly unable to control the players.

Psychological war was waged on umpires by means of threatening letters. One irate fan warned Billy McLean that he would set foot on the Bostons' grounds only at his peril. McLean replied:

> Sir, you are a coward. If you are not, write and inform me where you can be found, for in that case I shall certainly find you when I go to Boston again.
>
> Wm. McLean
> Gentleman, and not Monkey.

Sometimes the umpires turned the tables. The fiery Tim Hurst once picked up one of the beer mugs thrown at him and heaved it back into the stands, injuring a fireman badly. He was arrested, tried, and fined twenty dollars. Tom Lynch lost his temper once, too, and struck a player who was heckling him. He apologized to the crowd the next day and was applauded for his "manliness." Once Billy McLean flung a bat at jeering spectators, hitting one of them and getting himself arrested after the game. He too apologized publicly:

> Goaded by uncalled for, as well as unexpected taunts, I for a moment— and but for a moment—forgot my position as an umpire and did what any man's nature would prompt if placed in a similar position. For this I was and am sorry.

Another umpire attacked a reporter for criticizing his decisions, and one quit because he was tired of trying to fill "the most thankless position in the world."

In spite of all its handicaps and tribulations, strangely there were plenty of applicants for the job. In the 'nineties the large number was attributed to the depression: "Death on the diamond is preferable to dying of starvation."

Through all his travail the umpire stood alone, for it was not until the early twentieth century that more than one umpire was used in a game with any frequency. The difficulties confronting one man trying to umpire a game alone were obviously immense. It was not so bad when the bases were empty, for he could stand back of the catcher and call balls and strikes close up. But whenever a runner got on base, the umpire had to move out into the diamond behind the pitcher, where he tried to call balls and strikes long distance, so to speak, and at the same time be alert for possible plays on the bases.

A suggestion for a three-umpire system somewhat reminiscent of Knickerbocker days was made in the mid-'eighties by J. Walter Spalding and given a brief trial in the World Series that year, but the plan was discarded. The idea of having more than one umpire persisted, and the question of using two was debated constantly in the 1890's, for it was beginning to dawn on some that the game was getting too fast for one man to handle efficiently. Occasionally the clubs experimented with an extra man, but seemed unwilling to undergo the additional expense of providing two umpires regularly. It was not agreed until 1895 that, when two umpires worked, one man should go behind the catcher to call balls and strikes, with his assistant acting as umpire on the bases, and it was not until 1898 that a two-umpire system was formally sanctioned in the rules. Even then, the rule was rescinded in 1900, only to be re-adopted the following year.

Other attempts to aid the umpire in his plight were just as ineffective. A rule was passed requiring that he be addressed as "Mister" instead of "Bob" or "Sport," but of course it did not solve the problem. After 1895, disciplinary tactics shifted from mere fining to putting players out of the game. Too many clubs were paying fines for the men, so the authority of the umpire to eject players from the game as well was stressed, in the hope that loss of the player's services would lessen complaints, but the improvement was negligible.

Nick Young, when president of the National League, urged umpires to be firm and dignified, and to "stick to your decisions if it be the means of losing what little hair on your head you have left." He also advised them to avoid familiarity with the players, but there was no rule requiring them to travel separately. They did not even have their own dressing rooms until some clubs began providing them in 1895. But the clubs were not required to do so, and the abuse which umpires often underwent in such close quarters with the players was one of their chief trials.

In 1895 Harry Wright was made Chief of Umpires, but his appointment was primarily an excuse for pensioning him. Following his death soon after, the post was not filled until 1900, when the magnates gave it to John B. Day, again chiefly to pay him a small stipend after his days as a magnate were over. While Day was more active than Wright, his power was very limited and about all he could do was investigate and report to the League.

All kinds of reasons were given for the disorder and rowdyism at the ball games. Some thought it was due to the incompetence of the arbiters themselves and their unwillingness or inability to enforce the rules. It was even charged that umpires were instructed to give close decisions to the home team. Newspapers claimed that the staff was a haven for "bums," and was a means of pensioning old and "decrepit" players. The magnates came in for a large share of the blame for not standing behind the umpires, and it was true that they did reverse umpires' decisions.

President Nick Young especially was criticized for his weakness in not upholding his men, and giving in to the protests and pressures of owners. He admitted that he sent umpires where they were popular because it was "good business policy." The New York *World* reproved him for trying to conduct everything by mail from his Washington office instead of getting out and observing his men in action. "To be brutally frank," it said, "the task is too big for a man of President Young's advanced years."

In spite of everything, umpires have had an enviable record for honesty and integrity. However, it is not true, as one commissioner of baseball has claimed, that none has ever been guilty of crookedness. Richard Higham was expelled in 1882 for telling gamblers how to bet on games in which he was officiating. His guilt was established by proving, through handwriting experts, that he was the author of an incriminating letter.

The same year a former umpire, Herman Doscher (or Doescher), then managing Cleveland, was expelled for "embezzlement and obtaining money under false pretenses." After signing to manage Detroit the following season, he accepted a temporary job to scout some players for his old club. When the Cleveland directors found that they were paying a man who was working for Detroit, they brought charges against him and had him thrown out. However, he succeeded in gaining reinstatement in 1886 and later returned to umpiring. A few others have been discharged for reasons like incompetence and drunkenness, but the only case of dishonesty on record in the major leagues is that of Higham.

Seldom were umpires praised, but it did happen. Billy Stage was presented with an "elegant" bunch of flowers in Cleveland. Hugh Duffy, the Boston star, expressed public regret at learning that Tim Hurst had been released for using vile language, and sent a letter to sports writer Tim Murnane defending the colorful arbiter. *Sporting News* praised Jack McQuaid for his bravery and honesty in refusing to dodge assignments in crucial games by feigning illness or purposely missing trains, as some of his colleagues were accused of doing. When Tom Lynch was persuaded to retract his resignation, made because of bad treatment by players, the *Reach Guide* applauded him for his courage, honesty, and dignified manner.

But it was not until the American League was organized that the umpire at last received strong official support from league headquarters. President Ban Johnson had already won a reputation for backing his umpires as head of the Western League, and when he organized the American League he made it plain that his umpires would have to be respected. In tribute to Johnson's contribution a veteran umpire, manager, and baseball executive, Clarence "Pants" Rowland, once said, "All umpires ought to tip their hats whenever Ban Johnson's name is mentioned."

Johnson selected umpires personally and dealt firmly with players, particularly those who had come from the National League, where they were accustomed to umpire-baiting. He ordered his umpires to remove "kickers" and rowdies, and promised not only to stand by them but even to impose additional penalties if he thought it necessary. While the American League was no lily-white organization either, players who dared to spit at umpires or trample their feet with spikes found themselves suspended indefinitely. The Cleveland *Leader* voiced the general recognition of Johnson's strong leadership, asserting that it was "conceded on all sides that the American League games are better conducted than those in the [other] major organization."

27

THE AMERICAN NATIONAL GAME

BY THE TURN of the century, baseball had thrust itself sharply onto the American scene. It had become, as Mark Twain put it so well, "the very symbol, the outward and visible expression of the drive and push and rush and struggle of the raging, tearing, booming nineteenth century." "No game," asserted *Sporting News* in 1891, "has taken so strong a hold on Americans as base ball." Other sporting papers believed that it was "a part of our very existence as a people," and "an actual necessity." Unquestionably, it was the leading spectator sport.

Long since called the "national game," baseball was truly entitled to that designation during the post-Civil War years. *Harper's Magazine* reported in 1886 that "the fascination of the game has seized upon the American people, irrespective of age, sex or other condition." Vacant lots all over the country were converted into ball fields, and youngsters were so familiar with the rudiments of the game that *Spalding's Guide* announced in 1881 that directions for playing it no longer need be printed. The big league professionals became the exemplars for all others to follow. As Frederick L. Paxson observed, "Baseball succeeded as an organized spectators' sport, but it did also what neither racing nor boxing could do in turning the city lot into a playground and the small boy into an enthusiastic player."

It was typically American that many people could not be interested in baseball for the sheer pleasure of it; they had to discover moral and material purposes to justify indulging themselves. The game was found to meet the demands of the most "fastidious moralists." It was regarded as a commendable means of exercise and an admirable antidote to the "immoral associations" to which city youth was so subject. Men were advised that going to ball games would help them make money, because the "enlivening effect on your brains" of getting out into the fresh air would "open more widely your eyes to your business interests." Baseball enjoyed the sanction of Cardinal Gibbons, who said it was "a healthy sport, and since the people of the country generally demand some sporting event for their amusement, I would single this out as the best to be patronized and heartily approve of it as a popular pastime." Some Protestant ministers not only agreed with the Catholic Cardinal but even wove baseball into their sermons. The Rev. George F. Degen of Nashville drew an analogy between baseball and the game of life in a sermon delivered in 1894, using as his text, "And Abner said to Joab, let the young men now arise, and play before us."

Indeed, baseball's momentum was so great it had already burst beyond the boundaries of the United States, gaining at least a beachhead in Cuba, Puerto Rico, England, Mexico, Germany, and as far away as Australia. To Americans it almost seemed that all else was secondary. As the Boston *Globe* expressed it: "Emperors may be shot down by the dozen; gigantic political frauds may be exposed; steamships may collide and go down with all hands on board; Europe may be plunged in bloody and universal strife," but baseball news would continue to take up "two-thirds of the space in the paper." Even the United States Congress was facetiously advised to adjourn for the summer to free telegraph wires usually devoted to Washington news for accounts of baseball games. The President himself was involved:

> If nothing else can draw President Harrison to Louisville, our beautiful base ball pennant should do it. What kind of a national President is it who takes no interest in the national game?

During the Spanish-American War a sketch appeared in the New York *World* showing a newsboy outside a ball park, hawking papers headlined, WAR EXTRA, with a fan motioning him away, and a caption reading, "Your true 'fan' is not interested in such a trivial thing as war." A few might cavil that baseball was a game which preyed on human craving for excitement, and gave to the coming generation the idea that greatness grew out of muscular development, but their voices were drowned in the general acclaim.

Baseball achieved its pre-eminent position because many of the same factors which had enabled it to take hold in the pre-Civil War era were still working in its favor, some of them more actively than ever. The game itself steadily grew better. It was faster, more skillfully played, and more exciting. The public had been conditioned to watch regularly scheduled games for the championship played day in and day out over a long season. This system of competition, well publicized in the daily press, excited great interest and intensified all the partisanship growing out of civic pride and personal identification with the local club.

Baseball was also being presented in a more pleasing and comfortable setting. And although the average fan might not have been consciously aware of it, the pull of baseball's aesthetic qualities was very strong. It was a game of beauty and finesse. The rhythmic swing of the batter, the smooth delivery of the pitcher, the quick stop and acrobatic throw of an infielder, the grace and speed of an outfielder racing and then circling under a high fly ball completing its graceful arc in the sunshine—these could delight the eye of even the uninitiated.

The other senses were also satisfied by the crack of the bat, the smack of the horsehide against the leather glove, the cries of the hawkers in the stands, the roar of the crowd, and the smell of cigars, peanuts, and hot dogs. And then there was the emotional appeal stemming from the suspense of many small crises, the stirring of hope, sometimes fulfilled or suddenly dashed, and the excitement of rapid change from apparent defeat to unexpected victory, the security and thrill of being part of a large crowd, the chance to let loose at the umpire or at the opposing team—in short, all the vicarious, atavistic satisfactions of combat, even though it be in the form of a sham battle between two groups of paid performers.

Baseball interest even carried over in the off-season, when it could be discussed during long winters with the aid of data furnished by baseball's unique and comprehensive mass of playing records, the likes of which no other game can boast. Loaded with this statistical ammunition, dedicated fans could not only argue the relative merits of contemporary heroes but also compare current stars with old-timers.

Besides having the advantage of supplying all these pleasures at low cost, baseball was still in the enviable position of having no serious competition from other commercialized sports. Boxing was developing rapidly in the late nineteenth century but yet labored under legal bans and public disapproval. Football created considerable interest, but it was still a college sport more for the classes than the masses, and it too was severely criticized for its brutality. Golf and tennis had not yet escaped from the socially elite. The spectacular bicycling craze of the 1890's temporarily posed a threat to baseball's popularity, but it died out with the appearance of a new contraption, the horseless carriage.

On top of these direct advantages, baseball fortunately operated in a climate increasingly conducive to the growth of commercialized amusement. America's march toward industrialism and urbanization, which had started in earnest a decade or so before the Civil War, proceeded with an irresistible rush in the latter half of the century. By 1900 the amount of capital invested in manufactures was nineteen times greater than in 1850. Only twenty-five years after Appomattox, the United States was the number one industrial country of the world, and by 1890 her railroad mileage exceeded that of all Europe. A multitude of new inventions, many of them unknown or unimportant before 1880—like the telephone, bicycle, trolley car, camera, typewriter, phonograph, and linotype machine—poured forth in the next two decades in time to have a direct or indirect effect on the baseball business.

Industrialism created at one and the same time the need for commercialized amusement and also the increased leisure and higher living standard necessary for the success of such amusements. America's population leaped from 31 million in 1860 to 76 million in 1900, much of it because of the rise of the city. Whereas one-fifth of the country's population was urban in 1870, by 1900 the proportion was one-third. In 1870 only seven cities had 200,000 or more inhabitants; by 1900, there were nineteen such cities, sheltering 15.5 per cent of the country's people. The great urban centers of the Northeast, teeming with industrial workers and crowded slum-dwellers seeking outlet, diversion, and excitement, provided a natural market for the promoters of commercialized amusement. Little wonder that the major league clubs operated on an increasing scale in the metropolitan areas which dotted the industrial region of the country. By the turn of the century baseball's long shaking-down process had relegated lesser towns to minor league status, leaving the ever-growing large cities to the majors.

Baseball also benefited, no doubt, from the growing emphasis on health and outdoor exercise given so much stimulus by the United States Sanitary Commission, whose work in the Civil War helped to make people aware of the desirability of physical fitness. The game also reaped the benefit of anti-British feeling and strained relations with England which pervaded the period. This circumstance, plus a certain degree of inferiority felt by a young nation toward the long-time leading sporting nation, made Americans only too ready to embrace baseball and glory in it as their own National Game.

The impact of this national pastime on America could be discerned in a variety of ways. In its own right it represented a new and growing business enterprise of substantial proportions in the American economy. While it did not compare with the giant trusts being created in that era, it was no neighborhood cigar store or grocery business either. An economic appraisal published in *Harper's Magazine* in 1890 estimated that 100 National Agreement clubs were employing 1500 players at an average salary of $1000, or a total payroll of $1,500,000. These clubs were spending an additional million for travel, hotels, rent, and other operational costs, and in return were realizing about $250,000 in profits. Business on this scale meant that some eight million Americans were paying around $2,750,000 to watch the professionals perform.

Another estimate, made a few years later, placed the figures somewhat higher.

But any evaluation of Organized Baseball's economic significance must go beyond the limits of the industry itself and take into consideration its influence on numerous auxiliary or related enterprises like the press, sporting goods business, transportation, hotels, and other businesses.

Baseball's impact on the press was especially pronounced. The affinity between the newspaper and baseball games, noticeable before the Civil War, became increasingly important to both. Space allotted to sports, on the increase in the 'seventies, was stepped up appreciably in the 'eighties when, under the influence of Joseph Pulitzer, who organized the first separate sports department when he purchased the New York *World*, the leading penny newspapers began devoting an entire page or more to the subject. From 1878 to 1898 space assigned to sports jumped from 0.6 to 4.2—a sevenfold increase. An English visitor noticed that on September 7, 1892, one paper gave only a single column to James Greenleaf Whittier's death as against nearly twelve to the Jim Corbett-John L. Sullivan prize fight. Day in and day out, baseball got the lion's share of this increasing sports coverage. Its news value was more and more apparent to editors, particularly with the advent of the colorful American Association, and the best papers endorsed the game as morally uplifting if properly conducted.

The New York *Tribune* was "compelled" to assign 500 columns to baseball in the summer of 1886. Another paper asserted it had to spend a minimum of $5000 on baseball coverage alone. The Cincinnati *Enquirer* said it was forced by the demand of its readers to keep its "base ball department" operating during the winter. Editors freely lifted stories by reporters on other papers without crediting them. A leading German-language newspaper, the New York *Staats Zeitung*, supplemented baseball news with a glossary of terms: *Unparteiischer* (umpire), *Faenger* (catcher), *Kraftiges Schlagen* (hard hitting), etc. Sometimes the game invaded other sections of the newspaper in the form of political cartoons presented in the baseball idiom. To the few who objected to so much space given to baseball news, O. P. Caylor answered that Congress could talk about free wool and ministers could debate whether or not unchristened babies went to heaven, but fans wanted to know the results of ball games, and editors would continue to supply the kind of news the public wanted.

New weeklies appeared and competed with the old, well-established ones like the New York *Clipper* and the *Spirit of the Times*. An outstanding one was *Sporting Life,* published in Philadelphia and edited by Frank Richter. By the end of the 1880's this paper, which featured baseball news, claimed the largest circulation of any sporting or baseball paper. In 1886 *Sporting News,* another weekly, was founded in St. Louis by Al and Charles C. Spink, uncles of its present dynamic owner, J. G. Taylor Spink. This well-known weekly, destined to become the trade paper of professional baseball, the so-called "Bible of the game," began with a feeble circulation of 3000, but in two years claimed 60,000 subscribers. Its editors pointed out that baseball owed its success, and indeed its very existence, to newspapermen, whose criticisms helped remove abuses. The Spinks stoutly announced in 1892 that their paper was "the organ of no clique nor association. Its lance is free."

While the dailies were becoming more active, the weeklies continued to dominate sports reporting until dealt a crushing blow by William Randolph Hearst's introduction of the separate sports section toward the end of the century. The detailed coverage of the sporting weeklies, the introduction of the penny press, and the spread of literacy resulting from the growth of public schools added up to mass consumption of baseball news. The craving for baseball stories was fed by the growing use of the telegraph, which greatly speeded up printed accounts of the game, and the use of the camera, which enlivened them with visual impressions as well. Another factor was the evolution from the pedestrian style of earlier sports writers, like Henry Chadwick, to a more breezy, jaunty style full of colorful figures of speech, aimed at entertaining and amusing readers.

The tendency of American speech toward colorful metaphor is well reflected in the baseball writing of the day. Teams that failed to score a run were "whitewashed," "calcimined," "skunked," "shut out," or "Chicagoed." Balls were not caught; "flies" were "hauled in," or "throws" "pulled down." Batters "wielded the ash," "slapped out a dandy single," or "slashed out a peach." They were not put out, but "died an easy death," "smothered," or "expired in anguish." Runners "galloped," "romped," "cantered," and "scampered." They "pilfered second," "tobogganed into third," or "tried to embezzle home plate." Teams fought each other "like two cats hung by the tails over a family clothesline," and a player hit on the head by a pitched ball might "stagger around like an alligator with the mumps."

Gradually baseball terminology and vivid slang became a part of the American language. The argot of baseball supplied a common means of communication and strengthened the bond which the game helped to establish among those sorely in need of it—the mass of urban dwellers and immigrants living in the anonymity and impersonal vortex of large industrial cities. Like the public school, the settlement house, the YMCA, and other agencies, baseball was a cohesive factor for a diverse, polyglot population. With the loss of the traditional ties known in a rural society, baseball gave to many the feeling of belonging.

Personal journalism and derogatory comments bordering on the libelous added pungency to the sports page. Reporters thought nothing of calling players "thickheaded" and "lazy," and magnates "maggots." Even the eminent Spalding was not spared. *Sporting News* once wrote that of all the "boobies" in baseball, he was the biggest. Among sports writers the outstanding dispenser of vitriol was O. P. Caylor, whose satirical pen won for him such choice appellations as "monkey-faced cur," "mongrel skeleton," and "cucumber-headed."

These factors not only sold newspapers; they also spread the cult of baseball among the masses. Even those who could not witness the games were able to enjoy them vicariously. People could learn the language of baseball and follow its development through the sports page. All this helped to establish the business as a commercialized entertainment, giving it a quasi-community status and making it an integral part of the American social scene. The owners had the tremendous advantage of getting reams of free advertising such as no other business enjoyed, and there were signs that they were beginning to recognize the importance of sports writers. They provided press passes and press boxes with better working facilities, and the more public-relations-minded among them, like A. G. Mills, made special efforts to cultivate the press. Before long reporters were deliberately called in and asked for advice on difficult problems, as in the case of Frank Richter and Henry Chadwick, who stood high in league councils.

Writers themselves were developing more *esprit de corps*. In December 1887 they formed the Base Ball Reporters Association of America at Cincinnati, for the purpose of bringing about a standard method of scoring games and to advance the interests of baseball through the press. George Munson of St. Louis was elected president and Henry Chadwick vice president. Dues were one dollar a year. Significantly, a number of major league team managers helped the scribes organize, and the *Reach Guide for 1889* declared,

> The time has come when the National game and the scorers and the base ball reporters of America look to each other for support and assistance. All sides now recognize that their interests are identical. The reporters have found in the game a thing of beauty and a source of actual employment. The game has found in the reporters its best ally and most powerful supporter. Hence the good feeling all along the line.

Still, much remained to be done. Some club owners lagged in providing reporters with decent facilities and treatment. Boston was criticized for not supplying adequate quarters for them, and Cleveland for being stingy with press passes. A common complaint even then was the secrecy in which the owners tried to wrap their affairs, and the meaningless news handouts distributed after big-league meetings instead of real information. Sometimes the press box was invaded by friends of the management and other outsiders, and owners long continued to bar overly critical writers from their parks.

Baseball's expanding influence also directly affected the manufacture and sale of sporting goods. The growth of this business is a good example of how baseball helped turn the wheels in many a workshop. When the game was in its infancy, two or three makers sufficed to supply clubs with baseballs, and most of the demand for bats could be satisfied by one man. After the Civil War, bats and balls were purchased by the hundreds and thousands, whereas before they were bought by the dozen or singly. By the 1880's each major league city had a "regular bat and ball manufactory."

New York boasted half a dozen baseball "emporiums" that supplied equipment in quantity. Among the earliest were Horsman's Base Ball and Croquet Emporium, Andrew Peck (later Peck & Snyder), A. B. Swift and Company, and A. Bassler the Hatter, who made baseball caps to order in the 1860's. Outside New York, George B. Ellard of Cincinnati was said to have the most extensive stock. Another western firm was G. McManus & Company's Base Ball Emporium of St. Louis. Especially well known were Wright & Ditson of Boston, one of whose partners was George Wright, and the A. J. Reach Company of Philadelphia, headed by another famous player. By the 1890's mail-order houses and department stores began to feature sporting goods. Sears, Roebuck's 1895 catalogue, for example, devoted eighty pages to sports items, including baseball paraphernalia.

The sporting goods house destined to be the largest in the field, A. G. Spalding & Bros., was established in 1876. Al and J. Walter Spalding started the business with a capital of only $800. Its growth and success was attributed to the mass manufacture of baseballs and uniforms and to lavish advertisement. Spalding's close connection with major league baseball did not hurt any when it came to securing orders.

Before long the Spalding Company began absorbing its competitors, in keeping with the process of amalgamation so typical of industrial practice in the post-Civil War era and which has continued ever since. The New York *World* said that Spalding's presumable object was to control the sporting goods trade of the country. In 1892 the company reorganized as a New Jersey corporation, with a total capital stock of $4,000,000. Included in the new consolidation were Wright & Ditson and the A. J. Reach Company. Peck & Snyder was also absorbed.

These companies continued to operate under their own names, but each concentrated on what it did best. The Reach Company specialized in making baseballs. Its leadership was due to the intricate machines invented by Reach's partner, Ben Shibe. A check of Department of Commerce records made a few years ago by a reporter for *Sports Illustrated* revealed that at least sixty-five patents have been obtained by people trying to improve the baseball. But the most prolific innovator was Shibe, who contrived machines for winding the yarn and cutting out and punching holes in the covers to exact specifications.

Women picked up the materials in baskets, stitched on the covers by hand in their homes, and returned the finished baseballs to the factory under the "putting-out system" so common in the early days of the industrial revolution. And for all the miracles performed by machines, human hands are required to this day for sewing on baseball covers. Nor did standardization succeed in ending the everlasting debate as to whether the baseball has too much "jackrabbit" in it—that is, whether it is too lively and if it had purposely been made so to stimulate attendance by making home runs easier.

Compared with present-day costs of equipment, early price lists seem quaint indeed. Spalding could advertise a complete uniform—shirt, pants, shoes, toe plates, cap, belt, and stockings, all of first quality—for only $10. The company offered bats for $7.50 to $10.00 a dozen, or 75¢ to $1.00 apiece. Major league baseballs cost $1.50, or $15 a dozen, but boys could get a baseball for as little as 5¢ or 10¢. By sending a dollar to J. F. Hillerich & Sons (later Hillerich & Bradsby) ball players could get one of their already celebrated Louisville Sluggers made to order!

In similar fashion, the operation of professional baseball touched the economic interests of hotels, railroads, streetcar lines, printers, and the concession business. The relation of these enterprises to the game has already been shown in the discussion of the business operation of big league clubs. The importance of the baseball business to these other enterprises was plainly revealed by their eager solicitation of club patronage.

Sometimes baseball's impact on another business was one step removed, as it were. Take the telegraph. Not only did it make a direct profit from baseball, but it also was the means of adding to the take of the poolrooms, bars, and cigar stores which in turn purchased baseball information. H. L. Mencken recalled how the high-toned saloons of Baltimore catered to the fans by having telegraphers write the scores on blackboards, and how his father would slip away from the office to glimpse results at Kelly's Oyster House on Eutaw Street—"one eye on the blackboard and a beer before him." There were others besides Mencken Senior's favorite spot. Walsh's Cottage Saloon in St. Louis

included in its ad "Base Ball Score received by innings." A saloon opposite the Polo Grounds ran a contest in 1893 offering a gold watch and
chain to the most popular Giant player, to be selected by patrons—one
vote for every glass of lager.

Other businesses likewise capitalized on the purchase of telegraphed
baseball information. The Forest City House in Cleveland attracted
big crowds by posting scores out front. Eating-places put up baseball
scores on slate bulletin boards, and a New York City slate company in
turn advertised that its slates would draw "a crowd about your place
of business which you could not gather by any other means short of a
fire." A more novel use of the telegraph was made by the Opera House
in Atlanta, Georgia. As details came over a special wire, small boys,
labeled with the names of the players, re-enacted the distant game on
a diamond chalked out on the stage!

Baseball had a still different impact on other types of business which
found it worthwhile to identify with the game, even though they might
not derive any direct financial benefit. An imaginative Cleveland jew-
eler, for instance, headed his daily advertisement with a notice about
that day's game and blended baseball language into the rest of his ad.
A Chicago cigar store issued cards with the baseball schedule printed
on them—a clever idea for 1879. Newspapers also began printing schedules and suggested fans clip them out and carry them in their hats.

Many other businesses also tied in with baseball in some way. A collection of early score cards in the possession of Dr. Charles Upson
Clark, an old-time fan, showed a wide variety of ads, including those
of a clothier, shoe store, piano renter, bookstore, hat manufacturer,
restaurant, taxidermist, milliner, drugstore, undertaker, optician, and a
dry goods establishment. On one of the scorecards, dated October 2,
1890, the Schwalbach Cycle Company of Brooklyn printed an obviously solicited testimonial from the Brooklyn Club:

> The members of the Brooklyn Base Ball Team desire to express to
> you their satisfaction and appreciation of Bicycle Riding as an exer-
> cise, it tones up the muscles, strengthens the legs and helped us win
> the pennant last year. It is the most pleasant exercise and best mode
> of training we have ever tried.

Railroads did the same thing. Besides going after the business, they
subscribed for scorecard ads. An old Browns' scorecard found in the
St. Louis Historical Society contained advertisements of the Ohio and
Mississippi Railroad and the Missouri, Pacific & Wabash Line. The
mighty Pennsylvania was another whose name could be found in scorecard ads, evidence that railroads thought baseball important enough

for them to identify with it. Scorecard advertising was used at least as early as 1877.

The value of a professional ball club to a community, both as advertising and as a financial asset, had already dawned on some businessmen and promoters in the 'eighties and 'nineties. Cities and chambers of commerce had not yet begun to vie with each other for major league status, the way they have been doing in recent years, but the more mundane dollar-and-cents aspect of baseball was beginning to be appreciated.

In 1889 the *Clipper* warned that if the Giants were forced to leave New York for want of a playing field, the city would suffer financially. The *Clipper* pointed out that other cities were gladly offering grounds, knowing that if they got the Giants, real-estate values would rise and business would benefit. Yet, sixty-eight years later both the Giants and Dodgers were allowed to escape to the West Coast. New York civic and business interests woke up to their loss after it was too late. Perhaps if they had known more about the early history of the game, they would have been alerted sooner to the financial loss to the city, and might have acted in time to save the situation.

In Cleveland, baseball was significant enough for Mayor Tom Johnson, a fan himself, to set up a bulletin board on Public Square in the heart of downtown Cleveland, so that citizens could follow the team's progress before the evening "extras" hit the streets. And in the early 'nineties, when the possibility that Frank Robison would sell the Cleveland Club to Detroit capitalists was much discussed, a significant statement revealing the importance of baseball to the Forest City appeared in *Sporting News:* "It is worthy of note that the Cleveland base ball club of the past two or three years has been a standing advertisement for the city. In all sections of the United States there has been more talk concerning Cleveland, owing to its base ball club, than from any other one source."

The same was true of other big league cities. Baltimore businessmen acknowledged that nothing had ever advertised the city as much as its ball club. In Cincinnati, where people came from miles around to see the games, it was recognized that they spent money to the benefit of the city and its merchants. Even in minor league towns the value of a ball club in terms of its cash nexus was felt. The San Antonio *News* recommended having a club to the city's real estate owners and merchants:

Purely as a matter of advertising. . . . Whether one has any love for base ball or not, . . . a base ball team is the cheapest advertisement any city can have . . . reports of . . . games are telegraphed all over the country, and the constant keeping [of] a city's name before the people of a nation, as is done by a ball team, has an effect that can scarcely be estimated.

Neither is there anything new about the eagerness of southern resort towns to get big league clubs for spring training. Back in the 'nineties, invitations flowed in every year from towns in South Carolina, Georgia, Florida, and Texas. An Atlanta traction company invited the Giants for training in 1892. New Orleans promoters traveled to Cincinnati for the same purpose. Owners of a beach park and hotel in Galveston offered exclusive use of their facilities at nominal rates, and suggested that a good plan would be for two major league clubs to come to Texas, one to stay at near-by Houston so that each could play the other several times a week.

These offers, endorsements, and blessings of business attested to baseball's economic impact. Seldom is attention called to this aspect of professional baseball. Yet the evidence shows that even in the nineteenth century the general business community had a financial stake in the progress of baseball. To be sure, the baseball business was already being encased in a thick coating of ballyhoo, sentiment, and talk of "sport" and "loyalty to the team." But if one scraped underneath it, he was likely to find the dollar sign.

And, since baseball was an asset to the business interests of the community, business in turn helped to spread the cult of the game. The interaction between the two resembled a circle. It was difficult to detect where it began. It was unbroken, and it continued until in time it was to become so well grooved that for an American to criticize professional baseball, or even to admit disinterest in it or ignorance of it, was to risk being thought at best odd, or at worst unpatriotic. As a modern observer has said, "Most males who don't care about big-league baseball conceal their indifference as carefully as they would conceal a laughable physical deficiency."

Baseball's impact also touched artistic and literary vehicles of expression. The favorite recitation of the time was *Casey at the Bat*, composed by Ernest L. Thayer and immortalized by the histrionic rendition of DeWolf Hopper, whose resonant delivery was heard for the first time at Wallack's Theatre in New York on May 13, 1888. Fans could still enjoy this treat as recently as the 1930's, when Hopper's recitation was a part of the elaborate program at the opening of Radio City.

Baseball was also burlesqued in a skit considered hilariously funny by nineteenth-century theatergoers. The skit was done to a song called "One to Nothing," as part of a now-forgotten drama, *The Black Hussar*, starring Digby Bell and Hopper. Bell appeared with a birdcage on his head and boxing gloves on his hands, pretending to be a catcher, while a Mme. Cotrelli wielded a diminutive bat. Charles Hoyt, already mentioned as the author of the baseball play, *The Runaway Colt,* used the baseball hero and the umpire as stock characters in his farces of the 1890's. The song *Slide, Kelly, Slide!* rivaled *Casey at the Bat* in popularity, and phonograph records of it sold widely:

> Slide, Kelly, slide!
> Your running's a disgrace!
> Slide, Kelly, slide!
> Stay there, hold your base!
> If some one doesn't steal you,
> And your batting doesn't fail you,
> They'll take you to Australia!
> Slide, Kelly, slide!

Reach's 1893 *Guide* even contained a baseball parody on the famous soliloquy from *Hamlet.* In this case the issue was over whether to bunt or hit away.

Hamlet at the Bat

> To sacrifice, or not to sacrifice, that is the question.
> Whether 'tis better in the average to suffer
> The absence and lack of base hits,
> Or take chances against a lot of fielders
> And by slugging make them. To find—to fan
> No more, and by a drive, to say we end
> The strike outs, and the thousand natural slips
> This flesh is heir to; 'tis a consummation
> Devoutly to be wished. To find—to fan—
> To fan! perchance to touch—ay, there's the rub. . . .

And so on.

The literature of baseball increased greatly. Prominent magazines like *Outing, Harper's,* and *Frank Leslie's Illustrated Weekly* carried articles about the game. Numerous books explaining the fine points of play appeared, a series by Henry Chadwick foremost among them. Wright & Ditson's book on batting, pitching, fielding, and base running included chapters attributed to well-known stars. Other players (or their ghost writers) produced entire books on playing ball. John F. Morrill's *Batting and Pitching, with Fine Illustrations of Attitudes* in 1884 was the first of these. John M. Ward followed with a more ambitious volume in 1888, *Baseball, How To Become a Player,* and Fred Pfeffer added his *Scientific Baseball* the next year. A history of the game by Harry C. Palmer, a sports writer, was published in 1889 as part of his *Athletic Sports in America.* Baseball also broke into fiction with the printing of Noah Brooks's *The Fairport Nine* in 1880 and his *Our Baseball Club and How It Won the Championship* in 1884.

Of the many guide books, those of Spalding covering the National League and Reach on the American Association were leaders. Both were quasi-official publications of the respective major leagues; but Spalding, overzealous in his advertising, for a time clearly implied that his was an official league work. He was severely scolded by A. G. Mills, who said Spalding's misrepresentation was "contemptible," and made simply to sell the guide. Mills also pointed out that a footnote in the guide saying that the Spalding ball must be used in all games played under National League rules was "an unmitigated falsehood." To Mills, Spalding's tactics showed "a disposition to use the League in any way he pleases to aid his money getting schemes."

Thus baseball clearly had made a deep impression on American society. After a long, eventful evolution, baseball had developed from a simple boys' game into an amateur sport for gentlemen, and then became a commercialized amusement and the leading spectator sport of America. Through trial and error its rules were refined, a functioning business organization was established, a labor policy worked out, and the business survived internal dissension, corruption, and five trade wars, including a player uprising.

In the process baseball had reflected the methods and development of the American industrial society around it. The impact of its growth had both influenced the American society of which it was a part and had been an expression of it. As *Sporting Life* enthusiastically exclaimed in 1884, "Verily, the National Game is great!" And, as professional baseball moved into the twentieth century, it could not be denied that the game had won a permanent and significant place for itself on the American scene.

BIBLIOGRAPHICAL NOTE

THERE IS a great variety of widely scattered material for research on early baseball history. Most important is the New York Public Library's vast Albert G. Spalding Collection, containing thousands of items including manuscripts, pamphlets, books, periodicals, scrapbooks, guidebooks, correspondence, and photographs, as well as the library of Harry Wright (which includes seven volumes of manuscripts and 18 volumes of business records) and that of Henry Chadwick; the Leopold Morse Goulston Collection of early baseball books and pictures; and the Bradshaw Hall Swales Baseball Collection. The New York Public Library also has the original records of the Knickerbocker Base Ball Club in manuscript, which includes minutes of meetings, game books, rules and regulations, and correspondence.

The Cleveland Public Library has the Charles Willard Mears Collection, an outstanding accumulation of newspapers, clippings, manuscripts, scrapbooks, photographs, legal documents, constitutions, playing rules, telegrams, and an excellent collection of guidebooks.

The Historical and Philosophical Society of Ohio at the University of Cincinnati has a mass of business records of the Cincinnati Club of the 1880's, such as account books, ledgers, correspondence, bills, receipts, players' contracts, salary lists, and check stubs. A complete file of *Porter's Spirit of the Times* (New York), 1856-1860, essential for the early history of the game, is in the Cincinnati Public Library.

Valuable manuscript material, the Abraham G. Mills Papers and Correspondence and the Abner Doubleday Papers, is in the Library of the National Baseball Hall of Fame and Museum at Cooperstown, New York. The Missouri Historical Society in St. Louis has a small collection of clippings, legal documents, and manuscripts. Joseph M. Overfield of Buffalo, New York, has a small but valuable manuscript collection including numerous letters written by early baseball players. Indispensable is a complete microfilmed file of the *Sporting News*, baseball's trade paper, in the offices of the publishers in St. Louis. The New York Public Library has recently added this file to its collection.

Newspapers are essential for research on baseball; for some phases of the story there is practically no other source of information. As the game developed, newspapers improved their coverage, but they must always be used with caution and judgment. The files of more than three dozen newspapers were painstakingly read. The most important baseball weeklies and the files of them which I examined are the New York *Clipper,* practically complete from 1853 to 1904 in the New York Public Library; *Sporting Life* (Philadelphia), 1883 to 1903, Cleveland Public Library; and *Sporting News,* 1886 to 1903 and 1948 to the present. Other sports papers consulted for the early period were *The New England Base Ballist* (Boston), *The National Chronicle* (New York), *The Ball Players' Chronicle* (New York), *The American Chronicle of Sports and Pastimes* (New York), *The Base Ball Tribune* (New York), and *Official Base Ball Record* (New York).

For certain phases of the work, local newspapers that had particular application were used. For example, the files of the St. Louis *Globe-Democrat,* 1883 to 1885, and St. Louis *Republican,* 1883 and 1884, were consulted in connection with the Union War, which centered in St. Louis. Files of local papers in New York, Brooklyn, Chicago, Cleveland, Cincinnati, and Buffalo were also examined, many of them extensively; for example, the Cincinnati *Enquirer* covering the years 1876-89; Cleveland *Leader,* 1876-86 and 1889-1901; and Chicago *Tribune,* 1875-84, 1889, and 1896.

Additional newspaper material was also supplied by clippings in Henry Chadwick's twenty-six volumes of scrapbooks, covering the years from 1858 to 1902, and twelve volumes of Albert G. Spalding's, covering 1874 to 1911. Besides newspaper clippings, these scrapbooks contain a variety of items ranging from baseball dinner menus to press passes, and including some manuscript. Clippings in the Birchard A. Hayes scrapbook in the Hayes Memorial Library at Fremont, Ohio, also yielded some valuable information.

The annual baseball guidebooks are also storehouses of information. Most valuable are Beadle's (1860-62, 1864-69, and 1871), DeWitt's (1868-85), Reach (1883-1903), and Spalding's (1878-1903), all of which were thoroughly combed through. The latter two were quasi-official publications of the two major leagues. Valuable information was found in constitutions of amateur clubs like the Takewambait of Natick, Massachusetts, the Eagle of New York, the Excelsior of Brooklyn, the Social of New York, as well as the Knickerbocker Club; the constitutions of the National Association of Base Ball Players, the National Association of Amateur Base Ball Players, the National Association of Professional Base Ball Players, the Union Association of Base Ball Clubs, the Players' National League, the National League of Professional Base Ball Clubs, the American Association of Base-Ball Clubs, the Protective Association of Professional Baseball Players; and the constitutions of various minor leagues. These organizations published their constitutions, with revisions, each year, as long as they remained in existence.

Other official baseball documents used were the agreements between leagues issued annually 1883 to 1903, and the playing rules of the leagues, published annually. Especially important were the minutes of the various league meetings, published with the constitutions, in the guidebooks, or in the newspapers.

The periodical literature on baseball is vast and constantly growing. Magazines and journals, both contemporary and recent, popular and scholarly, had to be searched, and information obtained from a great many articles was indispensable. Of the contemporary journals, the most useful were *Harper's Weekly, Outing Magazine, Lippincott's Magazine, Cosmopolitan,* and *Godey's Lady's Book.*

Best for more recent articles were *Collier's, Baseball Magazine, Saturday Evening Post, The North American Review, Fortune, Sport, Sports Illustrated, American Speech, Life Magazine, American Mercury, Everybody's Magazine, The New Yorker, The Nation, Scientific American, The American City, Scribner's Magazine,* and *The Commercial and Financial Chronicle.*

Scholarly publications containing articles useful for my study are *Mississippi Valley Historical Review, Ohio Historical Quarterly, The New-York Historical Society Quarterly, Missouri Historical Review, Missouri Historical Society Bulletin, Kansas Historical Quarterly, Proceedings of the Association of History Teachers of the Middle States and Maryland, Maryland Historical Magazine, Minnesota History, Niagara Frontier, Journal of the Illinois State Historical Society, Annals of Iowa, The Journal of Political Economy,* and *New York Public Library Bulletin.*

The legal aspect of baseball is a subject in itself. More than twenty law cases, and, when available, the briefs filed in connection with them, were studied. Numerous articles dealing with the law of baseball were drawn upon. Of these, the most important are in the *Yale Law Journal, University of Chicago Law Review, New York Law Journal, Cleveland-Marshall Law Review,* and *United States Law Review.*

Literally hundreds of books were read. Everything available on baseball was checked—general accounts of the game's history, stories of major league clubs, biographies and autobiographies (mostly ghostwritten) of players and other important figures in the game, early children's game books, and baseball how-to books. In addition, it was necessary to search such sources as old diaries, reminiscences, Civil War regimental histories, county histories, college histories, histories of other sports, books on the history of American music, drama, and journalism, and studies of American speech and American leisure time activities.

There are no scholarly histories of baseball, but the most comprehensive account of the early game, although biased and dated, is Albert G. Spalding's *America's National Game* (New York, 1911). Other early histories worth mentioning are George L. Moreland, *Balldom* (New York, 1914); Harry Clay Palmer, et al., *Athletic Sports in America* (Philadelphia, 1889); Alfred H. Spink, *The National Game* (St. Louis, 1910); and Francis C. Richter, *Richter's History and Records of Baseball* (Philadelphia, 1914). Among recent journalistic accounts, that of Lee Allen, *100 Years of Baseball* (New York, 1950), is the best. Others are Arthur Bartlett, *Baseball and Mr. Spalding* (New York, 1951); Frederick G. Lieb, *The Baseball Story* (New York, 1950); and Robert Smith, *Baseball* (New York, 1947).

Space permits citing only the most pertinent of the scholarly works on American history which were helpful or suggestive in placing baseball in historical perspective. Excellent for social history were Carl R. Fish, *The Rise of the Common Man, 1830-1850,* Allan Nevins, *The Emergence of Modern America,* and Arthur M. Schlesinger, *The Rise of the City,* volumes

6, 8, and 10 of the History of American Life Series (New York, 1927). For the economic background of the period, Louis M. Hacker and Benjamin B. Kendrick, *The United States since 1865* (New York, 1934), was particularly helpful. Foster Rhea Dulles, *America Learns to Play* (New York, 1940), and Robert B. Weaver, *Amusements and Sports in American Life* (Chicago, 1939), were the best for background history on American sports and leisure time activities. Other useful scholarly works were Charles M. Andrews, *Colonial Folkways* (New Haven, 1921), John Krout, *Annals of American Sport* (New Haven, 1929); Henry S. Commager, *The American Mind* (New Haven, 1950); Arthur M. Schlesinger, *Paths to the Present* (New York, 1949); and Jennie Holliman, *American Sports, 1785-1835* (Durham, 1931).

Finally, a wide variety of miscellaneous sources were used, such as pamphlets; encyclopedias, especially Hy Turkin and S. C. Thompson, *The Official Encyclopedia of Baseball* (New York, 1951), and appropriate articles in the *Encyclopedia of the Social Sciences;* government reports; sheet music for early baseball songs; baseball recordings; city directories; hotel directories; trade publications, such as the *Street Railway Journal* and the *Sporting Goods Dealer;* biographical dictionaries; pictures; baseball exhibits; manuscripts of stage plays relating to baseball; radio programs; and baseball advertisements. I also drew on my own experience and familiarity with the game as college and semi-pro player, coach of amateur and semi-pro clubs, umpire, unofficial scout for major league clubs, and batboy at Ebbets Field both for visiting clubs and for the Brooklyn Dodgers.

MAJOR LEAGUE CIRCUITS, 1876-1902

(Bold dates are pennant-winning years)

NATIONAL LEAGUE, 1876-1902 *	AMERICAN ASSOCIATION, 1882-1891
Baltimore, 1892-99 **1894-96**	Baltimore, 1882-91
Boston, 1876-1902 **1877-78, 1883, 1891-93, 1897-98**	Boston, 1891 **1891**
Brooklyn, 1890-1902 **1890, 1899, 1900**	Brooklyn, 1884-90 **1889**
Buffalo, 1879-85	Cincinnati, 1882-89, 1891 **1882**
Chicago, 1876-1902 **1876, 1880-82, 1885-86**	Cleveland, 1887-88
Cincinnati, 1876-80, 1890-1902	Columbus, 1883-84, 1889-91
Cleveland, 1879-84, 1889-99	Indianapolis, 1884
Detroit, 1881-88 **1887**	Kansas City, 1888-89
Hartford, 1876-77	Louisville, 1882-91 **1890**
Indianapolis, 1878, 1887-89	Milwaukee, 1891
Kansas City, 1886	New York, 1883-87 **1884**
Louisville, 1876-77, 1892-99	Philadelphia, 1882-91 **1883**
Milwaukee, 1878	Pittsburgh, 1882-86
New York, 1876, 1883-1902 **1888-89**	Richmond, 1884
Philadelphia, 1876, 1883-1902	Rochester, 1890
Pittsburgh, 1887-1902 **1901-02**	St. Louis, 1882-91 **1885-88**
Providence, 1878-85 **1879, 1884**	Syracuse, 1890
St. Louis, 1876-77, 1885-86, 1892-1902	Toledo, 1884, 1890
Syracuse, 1879	Washington, 1884, 1891
Troy, 1879-82	
Washington, 1886-89, 1892-99	
Worcester, 1880-82	

* The Consolidated 12-Club League, 1892-99, is included in the National League column.

UNION ASSOCIATION 1884	PLAYERS' LEAGUE 1890	AMERICAN LEAGUE, 1901-03 *
Altoona	Boston	Baltimore, 1901-02
Baltimore	1890	Boston, 1901-03
Boston	Brooklyn	1903
Chicago	Buffalo	Chicago, 1901-03
Cincinnati	Chicago	1901
Kansas City	Cleveland	Cleveland, 1901-03
Milwaukee	New York	Detroit, 1901-03
Philadelphia	Philadelphia	Milwaukee, 1901
Pittsburgh	Pittsburgh	New York, 1903
St. Louis		Philadelphia, 1901-03
1884		1902
St. Paul		St. Louis, 1902-03
Washington		Washington, 1901-03
Wilmington		

* American League circuit has been shown through 1903 in order to indicate final composition of its circuit at the end of the American League War.